My 60 Years
as a
Labor
Activist

By Harry Kelber

Published by:
A.G. Publishing
75 Varick Street
New York, N.Y. 10013

Contents

Preface

Writing an autobiography, I realize, is an exercise in vanity. It carries the presumption, possibly unwarranted, that the story of my life as a labor activist is of interest to a sufficient audience to deserve being published as a book.

This genre of self-exposure has its traps. There is the insistent temptation to exaggerate and glorify one's successes and to minimize or obliterate one's failures. It provides a handy weapon to settle old scores: to lacerate enemies and speak kindly of friends. It offers uninhibited opportunities to state my views on a variety of subjects as though they were indisputable truths. And there is some satisfaction in justifying one's existence by leaving a literary tombstone for posterity, whether or not it will be read or have some influence on future generations.

I have had the good fortune to have my wife, Mim, my best friend and severe critic, as my editor. Mim is a feminist writer who spent 12 years as a reporter and editor of *Federated Press,* a labor news service, and kept well-informed about developments in the labor movement. She not only corrected typos and my lapses into bad grammar, but also brightened many a dull sentence by inserting a word or phrase and blue-penciling unnecessary verbiage. More importantly, she jogged my memory, warned me about the pitfalls of nostalgia, raised questions about events that required further explanation, reminded me of situations that I had long forgotten. She kept urging me, with limited success, to think and write more about women in the work force and labor movement. Throughout, what I wrote had to pass before the critical eye of a woman who has been my intimate companion for 42 years and who knew at close hand the work I did, what I thought and how I behaved in all sorts of stressful situations. It made quite a difference in how I wrote.

This book covers the span of six turbulent decades that saw tremendous changes in the national economy and the trade union movement. I go back to the 1930s, the years of the Great Depression, when as a 23-year-old editor of two weekly labor papers and an adviser to CIO regional director Allan Haywood, I was a front-line observer and active participant in the greatest and most successful organizing campaigns in American labor history. And I go forward to the 1990s when at age 81 and as a rank-and-file member of the Communications Workers, I ran for AFL-CIO vice-president, the first and only independent candidate in 30 years, as a tactic to force the federation to hold an election with a printed ballot at its 1995 convention.

In all these years, my belief in the importance of unions for working people, as imperfect as they may be, has never wavered. I have served the labor movement in many capacities: as organizer, shop chairman, union printer, labor editor, educational director, pamphleteer, professor of labor studies, international lecturer and labor commentator on the Internet. I've recorded what I did and felt in each of these phases of my labor career.

I am grateful to have been a witness to some of the great struggles of working people and to have shared in their hard-fought victories as well as their heartbreaking defeats. It has been a long, rewarding journey and I intend to continue on that road for the rest of my life.

Harry Kelber

June 20, 1996

1. A Childhood in the Tenements

I was born on June 20th, 1914 of Russian immigrants. My father, Zalman Kelber, came to the United States in 1911 to escape military service in the tsar's army, leaving behind my mother, Ita, and my four-year-old sister, Lena, in a *shtetl* in the vicinity of Kishinev. A skilled tailor of men's clothing, he earned and saved enough money in two years to bring them to a small apartment in a Manhattan tenement on the corner of 11th Street and Avenue C, where the following year I was born, escorted into life by a neighborhood midwife.

My earliest memory—I was about three—is of squirming and shrieking in a barber's chair because I didn't want to have my hair cut. The barber sought my cooperation by offering me a ride on the pony that was pacing up and down the block at a penny a ride. I calmed down and accepted his offer. Even then, I was a fair negotiator.

I also remember my mother taking me to Wanamaker's department store, giving me a paper bag containing two cans of evaporated milk for starving Belgian children at the end of World War I, my first act of international solidarity. I stood on a long line with other kids and their mothers until I reached a fat Santa Claus, who took my cans of milk and put them in a large carton containing other canned goods. He mumbled some words I could not understand and gave me a rubber stamp which, when I took home and tried it, failed to print. I got the worst of that deal.

Papa was an experienced tailor who earned a comfortable living until the Depression came and brought grim years to our family. Every week, Papa turned over his pay to Mama in a little brown envelope, and that largely ended his responsibilities as head of the family. Mama did everything: she cooked, baked, cleaned, sewed, shopped, paid bills, arranged the family's social life and, of course. took complete charge of her four children (two sons and two daughters), to whom she was fiercely devoted, especially to me, her older son. I never heard her complain about the drudgery of housework. In fact, she took pride in her reputation among her neighbors as a "berraya," a superb homemaker. Until we became teenagers, Mama made the family's pants, jackets, shirts, dresses, blouses, skirts and coats, with stylish patterns copied from magazines. I still have a photograph of myself, a round-faced boy of four, with a buster-brown haircut, wearing a little Lord Fauntleroy outfit:

green velvet short pants, a silk, ruffled white shirt, white socks and patent-leather shoes.

Mama was determined that I become a "somebody" in America, either as a doctor, lawyer or teacher. She contrived to enroll me in the first grade of elementary school by insisting that I was six years old when I was only five. Unfortunately, and to her great disapointment, her efforts came to naught. I was "left back." It was not until a few years ago that I learned that my mother, though without schooling herself, came from a well-off family of teachers in an area that later became part of Romania. Her family name was Soifer, the Hebrew word for book. Grandfather was a copyist of Torahs. I never learned anything about my father's parents, most likely because I never asked.

I remember my childhood as a happy and busy time. There were always kids around to play with, after school or on weekends and throughout the summer. We never went on vacation to a summer resort or even out of the city, and I can't recall ever seeing a mountain or a forest or farm animals until I was sixteen. I spent most of my afternoons in the streets, playing with marbles, checkers, picture postal cards, stamps, spinning tops and whatever else we could gamble with or trade, depending upon the season. On hot nights, the sanitation department would set up a sprinkler system so that we kids in knee-length bathing suits could prance around under the shower and splash water on each other. And the hot weather was a good excuse to spend the night on the fire escape, looking up at the stars.

As I grew older, I dropped those children's games for punchball, stickball, roller-skate hockey and basketball. I'd stop at whatever I was playing only when Mama would lean out of the window of our second floor front apartment and shout for me to come up for supper.

A lot of fist fighting took place in the streets, especially between gangs of Jewish and Irish kids, usually over some trivial issue that turned into a test of pride, courage and ethnic superiority. Occasionally, it reached the point where both sides would throw stones and bottles at each other, a couple of kids would get hurt, and then the parents would become involved. There'd be tension and bad blood on the block for maybe a week or two until things returned to normal.

* * * * *

When I was nearly seven years old, we moved to East New York in Brooklyn, then a Jewish working class neighborhood, which later became a blighted, crime-ridden ghetto . It was here that my brother Marty, was born and several years later, my sister Julia. I remember very little of the early 1920s when I was in elementary school, except that life was pleasant and I was never short of friends. Since I read nothing but the comic strips in the *Daily News,* I knew almost nothing of what was going on in the world and cared even less.

While we eventually amassed a substantial number of phonograph albums, we possessed no books, except for a handful of Yiddish volumes that no one ever looked at. Until many years later, my parents could read and speak only in Yiddish and some Russian, and the only newspaper in our house was the *Jewish Daily Forward.* My sister Lena, who became an avid reader, got her books from the local library. I was still more interested in sports, and barely managed to keep up with my school work. Until junior high school, I was a so-so student. I studied just enough to get passing grades on my report card so I could avoid Mama's wrath.

When I was nine years old, I was stricken with diphtheria, I had nothing to do but lie in bed until I recovered. To while away the time, I started to read "Foes," number 3 in the Frank Merriwell series, a paperback which a friend had lent me and I had put aside. I finished the book in a couple of days and had my sister buy me several more Merriwells. By the time I was eleven, I had read not only a couple of dozen books in the Merriwell series, but also those about Nick Carter, Jack Lightfoot, the Rover Boys and Tom Swift. These were my heroes. What young boy did not want to grow up to be Frank Merriwell! One good thing happened: I acquired the habit of reading.

Our family had a lively social life. There were frequent Saturday night gatherings, either at our house or a friend's. After a dinner, at which it was almost a point of honor to serve more food than the guests could eat, the men gathered in the dining room to play poker, the women in the kitchen to gossip, and the children in the bedroom where we'd be left to play, unchaperoned. It was during those Saturday evenings that I learned to play "doctor." Sometimes my father would let me sit on his lap or stand beside him at the poker table and when he'd win a pot, I would sort and stack the coins and dollar bills in front of him. I liked it when he patted me on the head appreciatively when luck was going his way.

Papa loved the Yiddish theater. Occasionally, our parents would take my sister and me to a Second Avenue theater to see a play. The ones I loved best—and so did Mama—were the passion-filled melodramas. Although I didn't understand much of what was going on, I could distinguish the heroes and heroines from the villains, and I knew whether to be pleased or sad when any character on the stage was ruined or shot. Mama was always ready to help me when I looked perplexed. Afterwards, we'd get something to eat at a nearby delicatessen.

Papa's pride and joy was the latest model victrola which Mama had bought for him on one of his birthdays from the savings she had accumulated. The player was housed in a large walnut cabinet, and it had a thick golden arm, a large speaker and several shelves underneath for storing records. Mama dusted and polished it so it shone, and it had a place of honor in our dining room, next to the china closet. Every week, usually on Fridays, Papa would bring home another record: a Caruso, a Galli-Curci, a John McCormack or maybe one of the Jewish cantors whom he loved. After supper, we'd gather around the victrola and sit in rapt silence to listen to the latest record.

It is now more than sixty years since my father died, but I prefer to remember him as he looked in the large sepia photograph that my parents took shortly after they had arrived in the United States and when they were still in their late twenties. Papa wore a dark suit with a light gray vest and a striped cravat with a pearled stickpin. His face was clean shaven and boyish, rather thin, with keen, wide-set eyes and luxurious wavy black hair, combed meticulously to one side. Mama, tall and regal looking, wore a satin gown that extended below her ankles. She had a full bosom and an hour-glass figure. Her face was fresh and lovely: fair skin, high cheekbones, a dimpled chin and piercing eyes. A handsome young couple! How different from the middle-aged, careworn parents they eventually became! I can still recall Papa before his death, hunched over from years at the sewing machine, pale and sickly with all sorts of ailments. Time dealt less harshly with Mama: she had shrunk and broadened out, but she never lost her sense of personal dignity, and her voice was clear and rich until the very end.

Although I was not quite eighteen when Papa died, I realize how little I knew about him. From random remarks I heard at the kitchen table, I knew he was one of the founders of a local union of the Amalgamated Clothing Workers and that at one point he was having trouble with a man named Schlossberg. I was not at all interested in unions, didn't even know much about them, and never bothered to ask him to talk about his union activity. It was years later that I learned that he had been on the executive board of his local union and that Joseph Schlossberg was then the long-time secretary-treasurer of the Amalgamated Clothing Workers who retired in 1940.

* * * * *

One of my strong recollections of my early adolescence was my Bar Mitzvah in 1927 when, according to the Jewish religion, I officially became a "man." For a couple of years prior to that, I had gone to a Hebrew school where I studied the Torah and other religious works under a despot of a rabbi who would rap the knuckles of any student who made an error. He was a huge hulk of a man with an unkempt beard, a rasping voice and a terrible case of halitosis. It was he who trained me intensively for several months prior to my confirmation so that I could read, or rather intone, the entire weekly passage from the Torah, considerably more than what was normally required of Bar Mitzvah boys. For some reason, he had selected me as his protegé; I was to be the example who would impress the synagogue elders with how marvelous he was as a teacher. Under his tutelage, I wrote a speech in Hebrew, which I subsequently translated into Yiddish and then into English, all three of which I dutifully memorized after endless, torturous practice.

As I vaguely recall the speech, it contained all of the high-toned, obligatory sentiments that the congregation expected from a Bar Mitzvah boy: expressions of gratitude to the parents; a few choice quotes from the Torah that illustrated the principles of Jewish values; a reference or two to the early history of the Jews, and a concluding vow to live a life of honor and devotion to the Jewish faith. Apparently my performance was a notable success; several of the congregation elders congratulated my parents and even encouraged me to consider a career as a rabbi.

My parents regarded the confirmation of their oldest son as a major event in their lives, and they spared no expense to celebrate it. For two days and nights, they held "open house," one day for their friends and neighbors and the next day for my friends and schoolmates, with food, drink and hired Yiddish entertainers who improvised, in rhymed couplets, witty comments about the guests.

I was bewildered by it all, Every few minutes, a guest would come over to me and hand me an envelope containing a five- or 10-dollar bill, a check or gold coin, which I stuffed into my jacket pocket. There were several slim, little boxes I quickly recognized as pen and pencil sets, and numerous other gifts of shirts, ties, a basketball and a dictionary. The gift I admired the most was a prayer book with gilt-edged pages, whose front and back covers were made of ivory and decorated with rhinestones.

A few days later, my parents were visited by the synagogue's resident cantor who said that he had listened to me at the Bar Mitzvah and I had the kind of boy-soprano voice he needed for his choir. He had also been impressed by how many prayers I knew by memory. Would my parents be willing to have their little *"Hershele"* sing in the choir for the Holy Days at a fee of $50? Mama was flattered by both the praise and the fee. Without consulting me, Mama quickly agreed.

With less than three months to Rosh Hashonah, the Jewish New Year, the choir had to practice two evenings a week and sometimes on Sunday. I disliked the cantor, a short, dapper man with a thin moustache and pince-nez spectacles, attached to a ribbon. The lilac-smelling hair tonic he used made me nauseous. He was a perfectionist and made us repeat short passages endlessly until he was satisfied and I was furious. I was the youngest in this choir of four, two of whom were men at least twice my age. We had very little to say to each other. I was angry with Mama and vowed never again to work as a choir boy.

Little did I realize that my choral career would be cut short even sooner than I expected. It happened after about a month of rehearsals. My team was playing punch ball against a rival neighborhood group. It was customary and convenient for us to play in the street rather than in a school playground that was blocks away and often closed.

As usual, I was playing center field when a batter hit a high fly ball that I judged would go over my head. I quickly ran back, while following the ball with my turned head. I did not see a large truck backing into the middle of the street, and I ran smack into its tailgate. I fell to the ground, while the truck continued to back up slowly. Fortunately, I had enough consciousness and strength to roll out of its path, while people who were witnessing the scene screamed from the sidelines.

I had a broken collar-bone and was in too great pain to continue the rehearsals. After a month, I felt sufficiently healed to go back to the choir. But at the first rehearsal, to my dismay and the cantor's exasperation, I was no longer able to sing the soprano part; my voice cracked when I tried to reach the high notes in the upper register. Could it have been caused by the accident or growing adolescence? The cantor felt I had betrayed him and fired me on the spot. Any question of payment for rehearsal time would have been regarded as a gross impertinence. An abrupt ending to a possible singing career.

As an adolescent, I was skinny and fairly tall, 5 ft. 10. My most distinguishing features were my bright red hair, which I combed in the then fashionable pompadour style, and a face peppered with freckles. The kids at school called me "Red Kelly." I had brown eyes, thick reddish eyebrows and a bulging, Adam's apple that bobbed up and down when I talked excitedly. I was a fair athlete, competent to play on pick-up teams in basketball, softball and soccer, but not good enough to make high school varsity in any sport. One year, I ran in the 60-yard dash at a P.S.A.L meet and came in a humiliating sixth of eight runners.

I was never at a loss for friends, either at school or in the neighborhood. My teenage pals founded a "cellar club," which met weekends in a furnished basement, made available to us by the parents of our club president. We invited local girls to attend our "socials." It was here that I learned to dance the fox trot, waltz, and charleston. And when the lights were turned out, I was initiated into petting parties with partners who, by our mutual agreement, stopped short of "going all the way." The club broke up when, predictably, one of the youngest teenage girls, the daughter of the local butcher, became pregnant.

One of my more memorable experiences as a teenager—I was 14—took place in the local poolroom. I had become a good poolplayer by spending time there after school. I guess I was too naive to realize that the place was also the hangout for big-time gamblers and mobsters, including thugs who would later be identified as members of Murder, Inc. One early afternoon, it happened to be Labor Day, the police raided the poolhall. Several of the gamblers were arrested, including me, as frightened, I ran into the arms of a policeman. Crowds gathered to watch us as we were herded into a paddy wagon. I hid my face in shame, hoping that none of my neighbors at the entrance would recognize me. As the paddy wagon turned the corner into a main thoroughfare, I looked out through the rear door to see that we were in the middle of a Labor Day parade, just in front of a contingent of marchers carrying union banners and flags, led by a brass band blaring out some tune I did not recognize. My first labor parade! A few hours after our arrest, we were all released on bail by the pool-house lawyer. At a trial two weeks later, for which I had to cut school, charges against us were dismissed in a matter of minutes. When my mother found out that I had been arrested as a "criminal," she wept with shame and gave me a fierce tongue lashing. I promised never again to enter that poolroom—and I kept my word.

* * * * *

My parents were disappointed when I soon abandoned my Bar Mitzvah vow to continue as an orthodox Jew within the synagogue. For a month after my confirmation, I had been getting up every day at 6 a.m. to go through the morning prayer with phylacteries tied to my left arm and forehead, the little leather boxes that contained scriptural passages. I soon tired of the ritual. It gave me no spiritual feeling. I hated giving up sleep for this daily, meaningless exercise. I stopped doing it. Papa accepted my decision. After all, he had not used his phylacteries since coming to America, so why should his son? I could still be an orthodox Jew, observing Jewish dietary laws and going to the synagogue on Holy Days, he said.

I did not believe in a supernatural Being, a grandfatherly, bearded character, who was involved in all the details of human life. My parents refused to discuss the question when I raised it. When I asked why God would allow wars, injustices and cruelties to exist in the world, they would say who are we to question God's ways. They quickly closed the discussion by saying firmly that God exists and all Jews must pray to him for he is our guardian. I found such responses unsatisfactory on several grounds, but it was pointless to continue the argument since it made my parents unhappy. My mother and older sister continued to light the prayer candles on Friday evenings and keep two sets of dishes in conformity with Jewish dietary laws. Religion ceased to be a topic of discussion in our household.

My renunciation of Jewish orthodoxy became complete as a result of two incidents that occurred during the Yom Kippur Holy Day, just three months after my Bar Mitzvah. The first was when I saw an elderly, poorly-dressed man refused entrance to the synagogue by a bully-built guard (a *goy*, no less!), because he did not have a ticket and apparently could not afford one. Somehow, I was not satisfied by the explanation given me, that tickets at all prices had been sold out and there was no room to accommodate non-payers. I was particularly shamed to see the guard pushing the old Jew so hard that he staggered and almost lost his balance.

The second incident was even more disturbing. It is customary for a synagogue to hold an auction for each of seven passages in the reading of the Torah during Yom Kippur. This is one of the ways in which the synagogue raises money for its maintenance. The winner of each auction has the honor to go up to the platform where the Torah is displayed, recite a short prayer and kiss the Torah at the point where the passage begins. The *maftir,* the seventh and final passage, is the most valued one and naturally evokes the highest bidding, especially on the Holy Day.

This time, the bidding for the *maftir* had finally settled down to a contest between the wealthy owner of a bakery, a synagogue benefactor, and a very old, dwarf-like Jew with a tobacco-stained beard and rheumy eyes. a regular at the morning and evening services. I don't remember the exact amount of the bidding at this stage—I think it was above $200—when the old man, tears running down his wrinkled face, gave up. He had wanted this *mitzvah* because he might not live out the year. No compassion from the winner as he strode to the platform to get God's blessing!

That did it for me. I vowed never to enter any synagogue for Holy Day services from that day on. I made one concession out of respect for Mama. Every year, after the Yom Kippur sundown, I would meet her at the entrance of the synagogue, after she had left the veiled section reserved for women, and I would escort her home. Weak from fasting, she would hold tightly to my arm.

While I rejected organized religion, I did not proclaim myself an atheist, as some of my friends did. I was in awe of the universe and the existence of the varied life within it, and I felt there must be some primal force beyond my comprehension, not a man-made deity, that had initiated the world. Nothing has significantly altered this adolescent belief.

In a few short years, I would become immersed in the moral issues of peace and justice here on earth, which expressed my spiritual feelings.

2. School Days: Joy and Heartbreak

More than sixty years have passed since I was a student at Thomas Jefferson High School, but I still vividly remember those remarkable teachers who instilled a love of learning in the eager and impressionable adolescent that I had become.

Jefferson was a new high school in the heart of East New York, built in 1927, the year before I enrolled as a 14-year-old sophomore from junior high school. It had everything that a young student could ask for in the way of physical facilities: two outdoor playgrounds, a large gym, swimming pool, lunchroom, modern classrooms, and an auditorium that was a beautifully-designed theater. A block away, the school had a stadium for football and baseball games and an outdoor track for track and field meets.

One of the many things that were unique about Jefferson was its principal, Dr. Elias Lieberman, who was a recognized poet. One of his poems, "I Am an American," celebrating the contributions of immigrants and the diversity of American life, was widely printed and recited for its upbeat, inspiring message.

But the teachers, the teachers! Especially those who invited us into their homes for what were combined socials and intellectual discussions. There was petite, gorgeous Mrs. Pargot, our English teacher, who could hold us spellbound when she discussed "Macbeth" or Ibsen's "Hedda Gabler" or Whitman's "Leaves of Grass." There was hardly a student who wasn't in love with her, even though she must have been in her late thirties and married. A really "hot ticket" was a treasured oral invitation to a select few—me, among them—to visit her well-appointed apartment for a literary "conversation." We eagerly prepared for the event, whether it was on particular poets like Edwin Arlington Robinson, Carl Sandburg or T. S. Eliot or a play by Molière or Pirandello. Over tea and cookies, we did our best to sound like intellectuals, but it was Pargot who fascinated us, not only with her cosmopolitan charm but her vast knowledge of world literature.

Then there was Rose Russell, our French teacher. I was among the favored few who was invited to her "salon for students" on Barrow Street in Greenwich Village. We usually met on Saturdays, when one of the recurring topics was artificial international languages. Our little group was convinced that the nations of the world had to adopt a common language, not only for commerce, but for the preservation of peace. All of us had easily mastered the grammar and basic vocabulary of Esperanto, and several in our group formed an Esperanto Club at the high school. We also examined other artificial international languages, including Idiom Neutral and Volapük, and were stimulated to read articles on the origins of language.

From time to time, Ms. Russell brought up provocative subjects involving politics. I remember her asking us, "Why does poverty exist in a world of plenty?" I was always quick with an answer. I can paraphrase what I said in response, and with the assurance of adolescence: "There will always be some people who are smarter and stronger than others. They are the winners and the others are the losers. The winners are always greedy for more, and they take whatever they can get from each other and the poor. The poor are in no position to defend themselves, and that's why they become poorer. It's always been that way. It's immoral, but that's how it is and that's how it will continue to be." Several of my schoolmates nodded in agreement.

Ms. Russell, trying not to rely on her authority to refute me, asked, "What if the poor joined forces to oppose and defeat the current winners? Then the losers could become the collective winners. Aren't there examples in history where a people's movement defeated a despotic monarchy? Shouldn't we ask ourselves what kind of winners do we want?" I was not equipped to reply to those questions, but they disturbed me, even years later.

At age 15, I was an assertive defender of capitalism against the few who thought the Russian Revolution was the wave of the future. "Our economic system is the best in the world," I can hear myself saying. "It gives people who have ability a chance to get ahead. If you're smart and also lucky, you can be successful and wealthy. Communists are people who are jealous of those who have made a success of their lives. Communists want everyone to be treated equally, and that's impossible. It discourages initiative. Why should people work hard if they can earn no more than the people who are lazy and incompetent. Thank God, we live in America!"

I don't think Ms. Russell liked what I said. I could see that she looked annoyed while I offered these opinions. She probably considered me a smart aleck. She'd ask other students to challenge me, but their arguments were unconvincing. While she clearly disagreed with my political views, she gave me an "A" for her third- year French course and kept inviting me to her apartment.

About a dozen years later, I saw her name in *The New York Times* in a list of teachers who had been expelled from the school system for being members of the Communist Party. When she became legislative representative and then president of the New York Teachers Union and I was a labor editor, we became friends, and we had a good laugh about my political views in those bygone years.

The strangest teacher I ever met at Jefferson High was Kurt Stengler, who taught first- and second-year Latin. He was over six feet tall, with close-cropped hair, a grim expression on his florid face, and eyes that were quick to flash in anger. He was unmistakably German, and as he stood in ramrod posture before his class, he looked more like a Prussian army officer than a highly knowledgeable scholar, not only of Latin but several other languages.

Mr. Stengler was a martinet. He gave grammar and vocabulary tests twice a week and anyone who received less than a grade of 90 on a test would receive a frown and a sharp reprimand like, "Kantor, that will be the ruin of you." He terrorized us into learning, but he could also charm us by telling us interesting stories about the derivation of certain Latin words and tracing their development in several Romance and Teutonic languages. He set what seemed impossible academic standards that made us groan, but we managed to achieve them. In our class of maybe thirty students, we had an average of well over 90 percent in our Latin Regents examinations, with at least a dozen, including me, getting 100 percent.

I went on to study Cicero, Virgil, Horace and some Ovid. I joined the Latin Club and became its president in my final year. We spent several months in an extra-curricular effort to transform Latin into a living language, to create a modern vocabulary out of ancient Roman speech. The school's Latin faculty, including Stengler, were amused, and privately ridiculed our youthful enthusiasm for what they knew would be a doomed project.

All of us had to take a course in music appreciation, the goal of which was to name the title and composer of 50 classical compositions, including symphonies, operatic arias, overtures, quartets and other works. Your grade was based on how many selections you could identify during an exam. If you recognized all of the pieces, you received a bronze pin.

Our music teacher, I forget his name, was a middle-aged, bald-headed man who believed that music was by far the most important subject in the curriculum. His voice was unmusical, even raspy, but he was an excellent choral conductor, and he assembled a school choir that used to make a respectable showing in the scholastic competitions. He was enthralled by the operettas of Gilbert and Sullivan, and every year he produced one of them with whatever singers he could find. I remember his comment when I underwent a 30-second audition for a part in *Pinafore*: "Not much of a voice, but a good ear. Chorus. Tenor." The following year I made the chorus in *Iolanthe*. He drilled us so thoroughly that to this day I can sing almost all the roles from both operettas.

My worst subject was biology. I resisted memorizing the parts of a grasshopper and I loathed going into the laboratory, which always smelled of formaldehyde. I was an obvious *klutz* when it came to handling a scalpel or a bunsen burner, and I could never see anything when I stared into a microscope, while other students were commenting with delight on the figures and colors they were seeing. I dreaded taking the Regents exam and seriously considered playing sick to avoid it, whatever the consequences. I did take the test and managed a 70, to my relief and my teacher's disappointment.

* * * * *

During my senior year at Jefferson High, my father, although a skilled tailor of men's clothing, had been unable to get employment in any of the Manhattan shops where he used to work. I have a suspicion that he was blacklisted for union activity, although I have no evidence to confirm it. To support the family, he managed to persuade a fur contractor to let him sew linings in fur jackets and other garments on a piece-work rate of pay. He opened a store-front across the street from where we lived, bought a new sewing machine and hoped to earn a living as a subcontractor.

The problem was to get the fur jackets, stoles and other pieces from 26th Street in Manhattan to Papa's store and to return the finished product to the contractor. Who would do it? Unavoidably, it had to be me. Every Monday, I would rush home from school to find a bulky bundle of fur pieces waiting for me to take to Manhattan. I would toss the bundle over my right shoulder and, with several stops to rest, carry it to the subway station five blocks away. I would ride in the front car of the train where it was less crowded and I could stare into the dark, winding tunnel and count the red, yellow and green light signals. At the factory I'd have to wait at least an hour, often more, while they checked my bundle and the shipping clerk prepared another for me to take home. The return trip always seemed more grueling, because I was already tired. I would arrive home thoroughly exhausted. After a hot bath and supper, I'd settle down to my homework.

There were weeks when I'd report to the factory and, after hanging around impatiently, I'd be told no work was available, come again next week. I didn't dare show the anger I felt, because they might stop giving Papa any work at all. I had to admit it felt good not to have to carry that heavy bundle of furs onto the train and back home, but I also knew that Papa would be very upset when I broke the bad news to him. He had become dependent on that work. By toiling long hours, including weekends, and with Mama helping him a couple of hours a day, he was able to eke out an existence that paid the rent and bought the groceries but very little else. He could ill afford to miss a paycheck.

* * * * *

Although I did not spend much time on homework, I had no difficulty in maintaining an "A" average and receiving a "Certificate of Excellence" every semester. I can recall being elected to *Arista,* the national honor society, and being given a handsome certificate and a pin with the blue and orange school colors. I felt superior when I wore the pin on my jacket lapel, the most visible honor I had thus far achieved.

The school's grade adviser recommended that I and other qualified students take the examination for the Pulitzer scholarships, offering four years of free tuition at Columbia University, and the New York State scholarships, worth four years of study at Cornell University. I took both exams, losing the Pulitzer by a small fraction of a percentage point, but scoring high enough to win the Cornell scholarship. I was elated when I received the announcement in the mail. I immediately began imagining my life as a student at an Ivy League college. I would be living away from home for the first time in my life! I quickly decided that my major would be the so called "dead" languages—Latin, Greek and Hebrew. And thanks to the influence of Mr. Stengler, I would strive for an academic career in philology.

The summer of 1931, I worked as a clerk in my brother-in-law's grocery store in Brooklyn. I had some savings, less than $100, from my Bar Mitzvah and other sources, but I would need more to carry me through the freshman year. I checked with the Cornell Admissions Office in Ithaca, and I was advised that they would probably be able to find me part-time work.

In the three months that remained before my matriculation at Cornell, I tried to "educate" myself. With the help of a librarian at the local library, I managed to get a copy of the freshman curriculum at Cornell's School of Arts and Sciences, and I immediately started working on differential calculus, the history of Western civilization, and an anthology of English literature. I also checked out several books on grammar and writing style to prepare for a first-year composition course. I was determined to be an outstanding student, and I thought my summer studies would help me get the jump on the other freshmen.

The summer passed all too quickly, and there I was, both eager and nervous, on a bus to Ithaca in upstate New York, one of the rare times I had been out of the city. As a scholarship student, it was understood that I could not afford residence at a fraternity house, and so I ended up in a rooming house a few blocks from the campus, sharing a fairly large room with a young man from Missouri who had come to Cornell's agricultural school to study hennery. We had at least something in common—our mutual bewilderment—and we managed to get friendlier as the weeks passed.

I remember how annoyed I was at the first convocation of freshmen when the young man sitting next to me kept staring at me. Finally, I asked him, "What's wrong?"

He said, "Do you mind telling me: are you a Jew?"

I replied, almost belligerently, "Yes, what of it?"

He said, "No offense. I've never met a Jew before."

He volunteered that his father was a Cornell graduate and was now a partner in a law firm in Wichita, and that he, too, hoped to become a lawyer. He would be living at the same fraternity house where his father had. He was put off when I said my father was an immigrant tailor who had never completed elementary school, and I hoped someday to be a professor of philology. He probably had never heard of the word, and I didn't bother to explain. Thereafter, when we passed each other on campus, we nodded politely but never stopped to talk.

The part-time job I was given was to wash dishes and clean up at the fraternity houses during the weekends when there was much partying after the football or base-ball games. I loathed the work, but it paid 25 cents an hour and I needed all the money I could earn to pay my expenses. I felt angry and bitter that I had to be houseboy to students, some of whom sat in the same class as I did and were obviously intellectu-ally inferior to me. While they were dancing with their girl friends, I was in the kitchen cleaning up their slop and hand-washing the dishes. Some of them made a special point to humiliate me by ordering me in a loud voice to hurry with their coffee or empty their ashtrays. I pleaded with the administration for work in the library, but those jobs were filled; I would be notified when there was a vacancy.

Otherwise, I loved college life. I felt free and independent. This is where I belonged, and how wonderful it would be if I could spend my life here as a professor on the Cornell faculty!

I corresponded at least once a week with Mama and Papa in Yiddish. The letters I received followed a pattern: they hoped I was in good health and doing well in my college work; they were proud of me; they were feeling fine and I should not worry; some news about my brother and two sisters; a concluding sentence about how much they loved me. My letters were hardly different in tone and content: I was doing well in my studies; I missed the family, and I sent all of them my love.

In early November, I received a letter from Mama which had me worried. Papa had become ill and had not worked for more than a month. The following week, in a letter literally stained with tears, Mama asked if it was possible for me to come home. Papa needed me. He had consumption; he had difficulty in breathing, and his condition had become worse.

I realized that if Mama asked me to come home, it was serious. I went to the administration office and explained that I could not finish the semester. Could I use my scholarship next year, when I hoped to return? They said yes.

I quickly arranged all the details for my departure, notifying my teachers, returning library books, paying my weekly rent and buying a bus ticket to New York, which left me with a few dollars and some small change. I still had one problem: how to sell my R.O.T.C. uniform. I would hardly need it in East New York. I went to the store where I had purchased it. They said they would take it back at a reduced price, but only if it were cleaned and pressed, and the boots properly shined. It was a miracle that I managed to get the uniform in good condition for the sale and to catch the bus to New York just as it was leaving the Ithaca depot. I was in tears on the trip home and frightened about the future.

3. Surviving the Depression

When I arrived home, I was shocked to find that my sister Lee, her husband, Morris, and their two-year-old daughter, Phyllis, had moved in with us. Mama had not told me that Morris had lost his grocery store, had sold his car and could no longer afford an apartment. So now there were seven of us living in four rooms— and no one at this point with a job. It was December 1931, and I didn't have to be reminded that the country was in an economic depression.

It was Papa that I was most concerned about. He seemed to have become quite frail and more sickly in the few months since I had last seen him. My coming home, he said, was like a tonic to him. He even talked about opening a tailor shop with a partner.

During that month, I spent a great deal of time with him, usually in the after- noons, after I returned from my futile job hunt. We would take short walks in the neighborhood, listen to his beloved records or play casino for a couple of hours. But what created an even closer bond between us was the daily English lessons I gave him. The day after I returned from Cornell, he told me he wanted to learn English so he could become an American citizen. Would I be his teacher?

I can still see him hunched over a notebook, painstakingly copying rows of each letter of the alphabet, then simple three-letter and four-letter words. He would ask me to check his work, and he was very pleased, almost like a child, when I would say "perfect." By the end of the month, he was able to write simple sen- tences in English. On New Year's Day, 1932, we opened a bottle of wine and I toasted his progress toward becoming a citizen. Eight days later, he was dead.

I vividly remember the last hour I saw him alive. It was two in the morning and I was reading a novel, I forget which, when Papa came into the kitchen and said in English, "It's late, sonny. Go to bed." He patted my head and went back to the bedroom. Early that morning, I was awakened by a bloodcurdling shriek, and saw Mama tearing her hair and scratching her face as she came out of the bed- room. "He's dead! Papa is dead!" she screamed, as she clutched at her frightened and bewildered children. Wild with grief, she opened the kitchen window and shouted into the street in Yiddish, "My husband is dead! Do you hear me, he's dead!"

In a moment, neighbors came into our apartment and tried to console her. She was sitting on a chair in the kitchen, tears streaming down her face and moaning, "Why has God punished us? Oh, Zalman, my beloved, why did you have to leave us? Why? Why?" The doctor came and announced that Papa had suffered a massive heart attack. He had died in his sleep at about five that morning.

The funeral was an excruciating experience for all of us. Mama, unconsolable, had to be restrained from throwing herself into the open grave. On the trip home from the cemetery, she sat in dazed silence. All emotion had been drained from her.

During the seven days of mourning for Papa, I had plenty of time to reflect on how his death was going to change my life. For one thing, I had to forget my dream about going back to Cornell. As the older son, a young man of eighteen, I would be expected to take Papa's place as chief breadwinner. I didn't want that responsibility. It frightened and depressed me. I had no job, not even the prospect of one. While I was strong and bright and had a high school education, I had no marketable skills. How was the family to survive if I couldn't find work that paid a decent wage? I vowed that as soon as the mourning period was over, I'd follow up leads in the "Help Wanted" newspaper ads and I'd canvass every employment agency in the city until I landed a job. It was disheartening to realize that I would be competing with countless thousands of jobless people, many of whom were undoubtedly better qualified than I was.

It turned out that Mama considered herself, not me, the "head of the house." and she, fortunately, was a great deal more resourceful than I was. She was also an intensely proud woman, and was determined not to rely on even one penny of charity, either public or private.

The worst year for our family during the Depression was 1932. A series of misfortunes, beginning with Papa's death befell us. Morris, who had once had a prosperous grocery store that provided us with canned goods and dairy products, was now unemployed, and the few dollars he infrequently earned as a grocery clerk were hardly enough to feed his wife and daughter, much less the rest of us. Despite Mama's efforts at survival, including making clothes for the children of the grocer and butcher in return for food, she saw her bank account shrinking, as every week or two she was compelled to make a withdrawal for living expenses. The death-benefit check she had received from Papa's union had been set aside to pay the rent and utilities. By the end of April, it was almost all gone.

Mama's hair turned gray and her face became haggard as she tried desperately to cope with each new crisis. Tearfully, she prayed to God and called on Papa in heaven to plead for divine help for her misery.

It worked! A neighbor told Mama about a new factory that had opened up on Schenectady Avenue, a few blocks from our apartment house. The owner was looking for local people to whom he could farm out several novelty items that needed to be assembled. Mama rushed over to the factory and came home triumphantly with two large bags of patterned pieces of imitation leather that had to be assembled into a bow-tie with thin strips of white tape. The pay was 60 cents for a gross of completed bow-ties.

With the entire family working at the kitchen table, sometimes late into the night, we were able to complete five gross and earn $3. The factory owner was pleased with our production and continued to give us all the work we could handle. By the end of the week, we had earned $18. It was boring work and, for Morris, demeaning, but we were glad to have it. At the end of a month, our fingers had become so nimble, we were able to produce better than seven gross a day. Mama was pleased with our accomplishment. Then one afternoon. after my brother Marty and I had brought our completed bow-ties to the factory, the owner told us that the rate had been changed from 60 cents a gross to 50. If we wanted the work, we could have it at the new rate. Burning with anger, we accepted the bundles of materials and returned to tell Mama what had happened.

Our family continued to work at the bow-ties but without the same intensity as formerly. Mama, seeing how disheartened we were, told us we were still better off than other families that had no work. Three weeks later, the factory closed. We were now like the other families Mama had pitied.

That summer, I finally found a job as a soda jerk in an ice cream parlor within walking distance from our house. I worked from noon to ten at night, six days a week, with one week-day off. The pay was $12 a week, and I could have all the ice cream I wanted. I liked the work and became adept at serving everything on the menu. Unfortunately, at the end of the summer, business dropped off and I was let go, with the promise that if they ever needed anyone, they'd call on me first. Small comfort.

About mid-September, Mama withdrew whatever was left of her bank account to pay the bills that had been piling up. She used most of the money to pay the grocer with whom she had had a barter arrangement. He presented her with figures to show that, over the past four months, she had received $50 more in groceries than the value of the party dresses, skirts and blouses she had designed and sewn for his wife and two daughters. He had threatened to stop giving her credit at his store unless she paid the money he claimed she owed him. I was convinced he was cheating us, since *he* kept the books and Mama was so grateful for receiving credit, she never questioned any of the figures he wrote down when we ordered groceries.

Morris found a temporary job delivering rolls and bagels on a route of Brooklyn restaurants. He was now contributing a large part of his pay for food and rent. Even so, the bank money ran out. Mama was forced to pawn several precious possessions that also had sentimental value: the gold locket and diamond ring Papa had given her in the years when he was making good money; the gold watch, a tribute from Papa's union executive board, and the set of fine silverware from their friends and *landsleit* on their tenth wedding anniversary. The one thing she could not bring herself to sell or pawn was Papa's victrola, although it was rarely played after his death.

I don't know whether Mama prayed again for Papa's help or maybe it was the election of Franklin Roosevelt as President, but our luck began to take a turn for the better. In late November, Mama learned that an old friend of Papa's had opened up a new dress factory and needed first-rate operators. He had asked if she would come to work for him. She said yes, although she was somewhat nervous about leaving her home to work in a factory in Manhattan. We encouraged her to take the job. Marty, my younger brother, was twelve and entering junior high school; Julia, at ten, was in the fourth grade and very handy around the house, and I, until I found a job, would be there to take care of them, if necessary.

Mama, an expert dressmaker, quickly began to earn a good salary and, as it turned out, remained on the same job for twelve years until illness forced her to retire. My brother-in-law Morris also hit a streak of good luck. He was able to raise the capital to open up a grocery store in an ideal location near Coney Island, paying off his debts and earning enough income to move his wife and child into a comfortable apartment not far from the store. We were happy for them and also for us: three fewer people to share our four-room dwelling.

4. *Working at Weinstein's*

The first week in December, it was my turn to get lucky. A neighbor told me he had heard from his cousin, who worked in a large grocery store in Brooklyn, that the owner was looking for experienced clerks because he expected a pickup in business during the holiday season. I quickly rushed out of the house and took the half-hour train ride and four-block walk to Weinstein's.

It turned out that Mr. Weinstein himself was on the floor when I asked to see the manager. He looked me over and asked, "Do you have any experience in selling groceries?"

"I worked in a dairy and grocery store on Clarkson Avenue for a year and a half," I replied, stretching the truth.

Weinstein looked me over. He seemed amused by my red hair and freckled face."I've never hired a school boy. Did you finish high school?"

Yes," I said. deciding not to tell him about my Cornell scholarship.

"We work hard here. The hours are long. Do you have any health problems?"

"None," I said. He could see I was in good physical shape and eager to work.

"Alright," he said. "Let's see what you can do." He picked up a brown paper bag and wrote down a column of figures. "Add these," he commanded. I did. He looked at my answer and nodded approvingly. He then took me to the rear of the store and pointed to some cans, jars and boxes of groceries that lay on the counter. "What size bag would you use to pack them?"

"I think a number 20 would do it," I said.

"Here's a number 20. Let's see how you pack them." He watched me carefully as I placed the items in the bag, but did not comment when I had finished.

"We sell tub butter, both fresh and salt. Can you cut a slab of butter from the tub within an ounce of a pound?"

"I think I can, but maybe not always."

"Well, let's see you do it. Take your coat off and put on this apron and get behind the counter. There's the butter, the knife and the scale. Let's see what you can do."

I made what I thought was a good try, but came up two ounces short. "Not bad, but not very good," he said. "I'll tell you what I'm gonna do. I'm gonna hire you as an extra for Saturdays, and we'll see how you work out. The hours are from 6:30 in the morning until 10 at night, and the pay is $4. You get a half hour for lunch and 15 minutes for supper, and you can eat anything you want, free of charge. There's a table in the warehouse at the back of the store. You can start this coming Saturday, and make sure you come on time." It never occurred to him that I might turn down the job. I thanked him as we shook hands, my face expressing gratitude.

I had an uncomfortable feeling about Mr. Weinstein. He seemed so tense and unsmiling, also shrewd and manipulative. He spoke with clenched jaws in a voice that was harsh and commanding. Even as he was speaking to me, his eyes were darting up and down the store, observing what his clerks were selling to the customers. He was of medium height, with thinning brown hair and a ruddy complexion. I guess he was in his mid-forties. He had stooped shoulders and walked with a slight limp. When he shook my hand, his felt soft and clammy. I had a strong impression that he lived for his store and cared for little else.

I was disappointed that Weinstein had not offered me a full-time job. Still, a day's work was better than nothing. I needed it for my self-esteem. It had been months since I had earned a dime. I felt terrible asking Mama for money. Four bucks would at least pay for a couple of movies, a few paperbacks and a can or two of pipe tobacco. Sure, the hours were too long, but if the middle-aged clerks I saw behind the counter could handle it, so could I. The important thing was that I had a foot in the door at Weinstein's. I was confident that I would end up with a steady job there.

I arose at five o'clock Saturday morning after a sleepless night, full of anxiety about how I would do on my new job. Mama heard me showering, so she rose and made me a breakfast of oatmeal, bread, cream cheese and jam, and a cup of tea. "It's going to be a long day, and you won't be able to work if you're hungry," she said. I had no appetite for breakfast, I was too tense and worried, but I managed a couple of spoonfuls of oatmeal and a slice of bread, mainly to satisfy her. As I left the house, Mama handed me a dollar. "For carfare and lunch."

When I arrived at Weinstein's, it was 6:15, but already four men were there, including the manager, Louie, a short, friendly man, with an attractive face and trim moustache. He reminded me of Ronald Colman. After we shook hands, he said: "I want you to look around and get the layout of the store. You'll be working next to Gus, who'll give you all the help you need."

Louie introduced me to Gus who was standing beside him. The first thing I noticed about Gus was his huge, balloon of a head with a shiny bald top. He was at least six feet tall, big-bellied, well past forty, and, as I soon found out, had been working for Weinstein for eighteen years and was considered his top clerk.

When the store opened, at 6:30 sharp, I followed Gus to the warehouse behind the rear of the store, where we hung up our coats and donned clean white aprons. While the other clerks were putting away the milk and displaying the cheeses and smoked fish, I walked around the store, making mental note of where the canned fruits and vegetables, cereals, soaps and powders, condiments and other products were shelved.

The store was about 100 feet long and about 60 feet wide, one of the largest in Brooklyn at that time. The right wall consisted of a long counter in three sections: one for smoked fish and other appetizing products; a second for dairy products, and a third, extending to the rear of the store, for general groceries. The left wall, running the length of the store, was where most of the merchandise was stacked, on shelves that reached up to the high ceiling. Aside from a few separate displays of canned goods near the shelves, the center of the store was clear, with ample space to accommodate as many as 80 or more customers who might line up in rows before the counters, waiting to be served. In those days, self-service in grocery and dairy stores was virtually unknown.

Gus summoned me back to the counter. "You're being assigned the 'U' key on the register. Be sure to hit it when you ring up your sales," he said, adding, "I think you ought to know that Mr. Weinstein checks the sales of all of his clerks on the register tape at the end of the day. If I were you, I'd try to make a good showing." I didn't need Gus's advice. I had already made up my mind that I could work as well and as fast as any of his clerks.

At about 8 a.m, the store began filling up with customers, lining up before each clerk. I quickly found out that I was at a distinct disadvantage. All the regulars knew the customers who were big spenders and those who bought little, and each had developed his own clientele. While one clerk might be selling cases of canned fruit and tuna fish and other expensive items, I'd find myself stuck with a cranky woman who wanted a quarter of a pound of swiss cheese, no more, no less.

Once when I tried to ring up a big sale that amounted to more than $30, another clerk, also a Saturday sub, pressed his key before I could press mine, so he got credit for the sale. He apologized, but did not offer to compensate me with one of his big sales. I didn't think it wise to complain, nor could I afford the time.

I did have one advantage, even over the regulars. I was younger and could run faster than any of them when it came to hustling around the store to gather items the customers wanted. Nevertheless, I was worried that I was losing out in the competition. I even shortened my half-hour lunch break so I could pick up a few extra sales.

Weinstein showed up twice during the day, generally from nine to noon and from five in the afternoon to closing time. The moment he walked into the store, you could immediately feel the tension. The kidding and horseplay behind the counter suddenly ceased. Every clerk did his best to impress him as he walked the length of the store, his piercing eyes taking mental inventory of what each of his employees was selling. He would look pleased when he saw a clerk persuading customers to buy groceries in larger quantities than they had intended. He took note of the clerks who were selling items whose rate of profit was high, and those whose sales included too many "loss leaders," items that were being sold below cost to attract customers. I don't think any of the clerks liked Weinstein or even had a good word to say about him, but they surely were scared of him. He controlled their livelihood.

At 10 p,m., my quitting time, there were a few customers still on line in front of me, waiting to be served. Something told me to keep on working, that if I walked away from the counter, I'd be finished with Weinstein. Twenty minutes later, the last customer was gone. The clerks were cleaning up; two delivery boys were sweeping the floor. Weinstein called me to the cashier's booth. He handed me a small envelope and a bag. "Here's your pay and I'm giving you a package with whitefish, lox and cheese. I'll expect you next Saturday, same time." That was all.

I didn't know what to say. I should have asked him what he thought of my work, or about the prospect for a steady job. All I could say was "good night." My feet felt like lead, my body ached all over, and I felt dead-tired.

I worked as an extra for four more Saturdays and kept improving my skills. I now could cut up a large wheel of swiss cheese so the rind would be equally distributed when the cheese was sliced for customers. I could pour sour cream cleanly into a container while lifting the metal ladle high into the air. I could cut a pound of tub butter almost to the ounce, and slice a slab of smoked salmon razor thin if that was how the customer wanted it. I could stand on a high ladder and stack boxes of cereals on the highest shelves as they were thrown up to me.

I don't know how much longer Weinstein would have limited me to Saturday work, except for a stroke of "luck," which came just as I had decided to look for a job elsewhere. One of the older clerks who had worked at the store for many years was hurt in an auto accident and had to be hospitalized. His wife reported he had a fractured leg and would be unable to work for at least two months. Weinstein offered me his job at fifteen dollars a week. (I later learned the man had been earning twenty-two.) I accepted the job and thanked Weinstein profusely.

I was thrilled to have a full-time job and be able to contribute financially to the family, but the thrill kept diminishing, and by the end of the second week, it had all but vanished. After finishing a workday of twelve and one-half hours, I wasn't fit for anyone or anything. I wanted to tumble into bed so I could rest up for the next day's work. And then there was that fifteen and one-half hours on Saturday to look forward to! What kind of a life was this for a young man like me? Or for anyone?

It wasn't only the long hours that exhausted me. It was *how* we worked. To Weinstein, we were like entries in a horse race. Every Saturday night, precisely at 10:30, after the store had been cleaned and the perishables put away, the store would close its doors and the ritual would begin. All the clerks would stand around, waiting nervously while Weinstein studied the cash register tapes that listed the weekly sales totals of each of us. After ten minutes, sometimes more, he would announce the name of the clerk with the lowest sales record. If that man was on the bottom of the list twice within a month, he was automatically fired. The condemned clerk's only chance of winning a reprieve was if the grand total of the store's sales was larger than that of the week before.

Because all of us dreaded the consequences of being low man on the totem pole, we worked like demons to get not only the most sales but the biggest ones. Whenever we spotted a "big spender" entering the store, a woman who we knew would buy canned goods by the case and large quantities of staples, each clerk would try to position himself so that when it was her turn to be served, he'd be in line to do so. On the other hand, we avoided like a plague those customers who would take up our time with various requests and complaints for a sale under a dollar. There were many times when I and other clerks held off going to the bathroom or cut our lunch period short for fear we would be missing out on a big sale from a special customer whom we had cultivated.

Working a 78-hour week just about destroyed my social life. The only "free" time I had was Sunday, when I was so tired from the week's work, all I wanted to do was rest. I was recovering from a love affair that had left me depressed and heartbroken. I needed to meet other women, but when? Where would I find someone as lovely as Ethel? And how long was I going to spend the best years of my life as a mere grocery clerk, working my ass off for Weinstein? How was I going to get out of that trap?

One night the thought occurred to me: why not go back to school? I could take a couple of evening courses and eventually get a degree, and maybe settle into a career where the hours would be shorter and the pay considerably greater. I prevailed on Weinstein to give me the early shift so I could get off at seven o'clock. That would give me enough time to get to classes at Brooklyn College's Borough Hall center. Weinstein was generous enough to give me time off to register and even promised to let me get off at 6:30 because, as he said, he respected my interest in education.

I registered for courses in English Literature and Calculus 1. Since I had done some reading in both subjects, I figured I would be able to handle my homework without too much difficulty. Indeed, the first month after classes started in February, I was doing fine, although I was having periodic headaches. It became tougher when I had to prepare for tests, determined as I was to maintain satisfactory grades.

One cold night in early March, I hurried from Weinstein's to class, utterly exhausted. We had received deliveries of several hundred cases of goods that were to be put on sale the following week, and meanwhile, we had to stack them in the warehouse. It was hard, physical labor, and I had seriously thought of cutting classes, but changed my mind. Coming in from the bitter cold to a warm, comfortable classroom made me drowsy. I struggled to stay awake and listen to the lecture on Chaucer's *Canterbury Tales*, but I fell fast asleep and, worse still, began to snore. The teacher came to my desk and shook me, and when I awoke, dazed, I heard the class laughing. "Which tale were you dreaming about? Not the Wife of Bath's, eh?", he smiled at me. Again, the class broke out in laughter. I slowly rose from my seat, picked up my books and silently walked out of the classroom. I did not go back to college until nearly thirty years later.

5. The Union Organizing Campaign

Even though Weinstein had given me a five-dollar raise, I was getting fed up with the daily grind. The hours were killing me. I was determined to get out of this dead-end job, but then what? What kind of career was I suited for, and how long would it take to be trained for it? Again and again, I thought of going back to Cornell and claiming my scholarship, but rejected the idea as impractical. Maybe I was doomed to be a grocery clerk and end up like Gus.

An old friend of my father's who was visiting us listened sympathetically as I described my dilemma. "Why don't you join a union?" he suggested. "I hear they work a nine-hour day, fifty-four-hour week in union stores. Wouldn't you be happier working those hours? You could then go to night school and study for a degree without killing yourself. Are you interested?"

"I sure would like a job like that. How do I get one?"

"Why don't you call them. It's the Food Workers Industrial Union. You can get their number in the Manhattan telephone directory. See what they can do for you."

A week later, I managed to phone the union during my lunch break. After asking me a few basic questions about my purpose in calling, I was transferred to the union organizer, a man who introduced himself as Norman Eselson. He asked whether I could meet him the following evening at 8 o'clock at a coffee shop on Flatbush Avenue, a few blocks from Weinstein's. I said I'd be there. He wanted to know how he would recognize me. "I have red hair. I'm nearly six feet tall, and I'll be wearing a red and blue plaid mackinaw. And how about you?"

"I'll be wearing a brown fedora and a tan raincoat. You'll recognize me." He did not mention that he had a scar on his forehead and walked with a decided limp, the result, I was later told, of a beating by hoodlums during a textile strike several years before.

Eselson was at a corner table in the rear of the coffee shop, waiting for me when I arrived. As I sat down at his table, he smiled and shook my hand with a strong, firm grip. "What'll you have?" His voice was harsh, but friendly.

"A cup of coffee," I said.

The waitress came to our table. "Give him a coffee and a cheese danish." Turning to me, he said, "Their cheese danish is the best there is." Then he came straight to the point. "Why do you want to join a union?"

"I hear that your people work only a fifty-four-hour week and that the pay and working conditions are better than at Weinstein's. I'd like to work in a union store."

"Sorry, son, we're not running an employment agency. A lot of blood, sweat and tears went into establishing union conditions. If that's what you want, you're going to have to fight for it."

"What do I have to do?" I asked.

"The first thing is you're gonna have to convince the workers in your store to join the union. That won't be easy. It'll take a lot of your time and effort and there's no guarantee you'll succeed. And there are risks. You can get fired. If you're interested in going ahead with it, I'm here to help you."

"I'm interested. What do I have to do?" I repeated.

Eselson finished his coffee and took out a pad from his briefcase. He began by asking questions about my background and about members of my family. He wanted to know as much as I could tell him about each of the twelve full-time clerks and six extras who worked on Saturdays: their names, approximate ages, whether they were married or single and how many dependents they had; how long they'd worked at Weinstein's and their wages; how they felt about Weinstein and Louie, the manager; their education, hobbies, their general health, and what complaints they had about their work. I was unable to provide much of what he wanted because I had been working there for only several months. But I had plenty to say about working conditions in the store. Eselson quickly noted the complaints.

He also questioned me about Weinstein's hiring policies, employee benefits, discipline penalties for absences and lateness, job classifications, shift schedules, washroom facilities, warehouse deliveries, and evidence of favoritism. The questioning continued for more than an hour. By then, he had learned just about everything I knew about the store's operations, and he had also formed some opinions about how to proceed. He put the pad back into his briefcase and leaned toward me, lowering his voice almost to a whisper. "Now listen carefully, Harry, because what I'm gonna tell you is very important. First, I don't want you to say a word about the union to *anyone*. Do you hear me, *not a soul!*

"Point two: I want you to keep your eyes and ears open and make an accurate report to me about everything that goes on at the store that might be helpful to us. Little things can be important, so don't overlook anything. And don't trust your memory. Get a pad and write it down when you go to the toilet or during the lunch break or immediately after you leave the store. You're a high school graduate and you look intelligent, so will you do it?"

I nodded. Eselson appeared satisfied. "I want you to phone me every Monday and Thursday at 8 p.m. and on any other night when you've got something important to tell me. Here's my phone number and a dollar to cover your phone expenses. I'm counting on you." He smiled. "Maybe some day you'll be a good organizer."

He paid the check and as we left the coffee shop, I noticed his limp. I liked the man. I had never met anyone like him. I began to feel confident that as difficult as it would be, he'd figure out a way to unionize Weinstein's.

Three days later, at about noon, two men entered the store and proceeded to hand out leaflets to everyone, clerks as well as customers. I was dumbfounded when I read the headline in big, black type: "How Weinstein Exploits His Workers." Just as several clerks and a knot of customers started to read the leaflet, Mr. W. himself arrived. When he saw what was going on, he became apoplectic. His eyes blazing, he yelled, "Get the hell out of here, you bastards, or I'll call the police!" The two men, obviously from the union, scattered the remainder of the leaflets around the store and ran out, as Weinstein, livid with rage, his fists clenched, screamed, "Louie, get me a cop! I want those men arrested!" By now, the men had fled with two others who had been distributing the leaflets at opposite corners.

Weinstein stormed into his office behind the store, still clutching one of the leaflets. Several minutes later, he emerged and glared at the clerks behind the counter. "Which one of you is responsible for this piece of communist shit?" he snarled, as he held up the leaflet. No one answered. We stood there, frightened and wondering what he would do next. "I'm going to get to the bottom of this," he said and stalked back to his office.

Nearly all of us had grabbed a copy of the leaflet and hid it in our pockets. We dared not read it in public or in each other's presence. Several clerks suspected I was responsible for the leaflet. After all, I was a high school graduate, and there had never been anything like this until I started working there. One clerk took me aside and told me approvingly, "My hat's off to you. You did a great job!" I angrily denied any connection with the leaflet. "Do you think I'm crazy?" I said.

The important question was whom did Weinstein suspect? And what did he intend to do about it? He probably did suspect me, but he had not a shred of evidence to prove it. How wise Eselson was to warn me not to mention the union to anyone.

I read the leaflet in the safety of a toilet booth, as I assumed the others did. I was delighted at how well it described the long hours and horrible working conditions, including the methods Mr. W. used to speed us up almost beyond endurance. It addressed just about every grievance I had discussed with Eselson. The leaflet explained that in union stores employees worked 54 hours a week, compared to the 78 at Weinstein's. It told the clerks that if they were tired of being treated like work horses, they should contact the union. Everything would be kept in strict confidence. The address and phone number of the union appeared at the bottom of the leaflet.

That same night, after the store was closed, Mr. W., his face still flushed with anger, delivered a warning to us as we stood at our assigned places. He began by saying, "There'll never be a union at Weinstein's as long as I'm alive. I'll sooner go out of business before I'll deal with those communist bastards. If that happens, you'll all be up shit creek.

"I've told Louie that if we catch any of you talking about the union or having anything to do with it. that man is to be fired on the spot, and I don't care who it is.

If customers ask you about the leaflet, you're to say that it's the work of a bunch of communists who want to destroy our store. Don't get into any discussion with anyone. If you're not happy working here, you can quit now. So, as far as I'm concerned, the union doesn't exist. It's dead. Have I made myself clear?"

There was no response.

"Does anyone have a question or comment?"

Silence.

"All right, you can go home."

During the next two weeks, nothing occurred at the store to indicate there was an organizing campaign in progress. Everybody had taken Mr.W.'s warning seriously. I had little to report to Eselson.

Just as I was beginning to get disheartened, Mr. W. unintentionally gave our unionizing effort the lift it badly needed. He had always offered his employees a benefit he was proud of. He'd brag to his customers, "I let my men eat anything in the store they want, anything!" He'd fail to mention that he allowed us only a half hour for lunch and fifteen minutes for Saturday supper. By eating in the store's back room, we could offer no excuse for not returning to work on time.

Eat anything, Mr. W. had said, and so we did. Eselson told me, chuckling at his new tactic, "An army travels on its stomach, so eat as much as you can, and only the best. Set an example. Hearty appetite!"

Several of us began eating sandwiches of thick slices of sturgeon and spoonfuls of beluga caviar, whether we liked it or not. We'd select the most expensive canned foods and imported cheeses, eat what we liked and throw the rest away. It was a good way, we thought, to get back at the man who was abusing us.

One day Mr. W. looked into the garbage can and picked out two large, fat pieces of smoked whitefish, one containing a head, the other a tail. Butting the two pieces together to make what appeared to be an entire fish, he ran to the front of the store, screaming as he held up his catch, "Look at this!"

Our punishment was immediate: no more free lunches or dinners. We had no choice but to gulp our food—and pay for it—at the greasy-spoon coffee shop down the block where the food was terrible and the service slow.

When I informed Eselson about Mr. W.'s action, he was not at all surprised. I think he knew it was going to happen, wanted it to happen. Anyhow, he showed up at the coffee shop the next day, sitting at a nearby table where he could listen in on what the men had to say about the cancellation of their eating privileges. Most of them were either openly angry or quietly bitter, regarding it as a pay cut.

Eselson came to the coffee shop around lunch time for the entire week, managing to observe the clerks on every shift. By the third day, he had several men listening to him. He was quite a salesman! He talked mostly about personal dignity, that they deserved to be treated as human beings instead of Weinstein's work horses. He compared life and work in a union shop with the situation at Weinstein's, and said he was ready to help them.

A week later, Eselson asked me to come to the union office. He had something important to tell me. I was so eager to be there on time, I arrived a half hour early. The receptionist said Mr. Eselson had a visitor, but she would let him know I was here. He came out of his office a few minutes later and greeted me with a smile and a warm handshake. "Come into my office. Would you like a cup of coffee?"

"No, thank you."

His office was small and cramped, even though it contained only a few pieces of furniture: a battered desk, two chairs, a metal file cabinet and a coat hanger. A framed copy of the union charter and several faded photographs of people I didn't know hung on one of the walls, whose green paint revealed ugly blotches of plaster where it had peeled. The dirt-caked window looked out on a brick-walled factory building across the street. How can he work in this chicken coop, I wondered.

Eselson lit his pipe, took a deep puff, and said, "Harry, you'll be glad to know we're ready to go public." He showed me a sheet of paper on which were written the names of all Weinstein employees, broken down into three groups. "We've got nine men who've signed application cards, five who are sitting on the fence, and four who are definitely against us. The time has come to show the face of the union in the store. If we wait much longer, we'll start losing the support we now have."

I studied the names on the sheet. There were two on the pro-union list that I had not counted on, but there were no surprises on the other two lists.

"I'm sending a registered letter to Weinstein and a copy to his lawyer, requesting a meeting to begin negotiations for a union contract to cover all present employees. The letter will go out tomorrow. We'll give him ten working days to comply. If he doesn't—and I don't think he will—we'll move to the next stage of our campaign.

"Now listen carefully, I'm appointing you as shop steward for the union. Here is your steward's button. I want you to wear the button on the job starting tomorrow."

Noting my hesitation, he said, "Don't worry. We're not putting you on the firing line, unprotected. If Weinstein tries to discharge you or anyone else, he'll have a strike on his hands. We have the muscle to close down the store if that becomes necessary."

On the subway ride home, I had second thoughts about becoming a shop steward. I dreaded the idea of facing Mr. W. when he saw me with the button. He'd surely fire me. And then what? There'd be a strike, but I'd still be out of a job. What had I gotten into? Why couldn't Eselson have picked one of the other eight men as steward?

The next morning, as I entered the store, Weinstein was there to greet me. He said he wanted to see me in his office right away. He seemed surprisingly cool. Surely he must know. When we were alone, he offered me a cigaret. "I don't smoke, Mr. Weinstein, but thank you," I said, politely.

He put his hand on his chin and stared at me. "So you're the union's ringleader." When I started to protest, he held up his hand to stop me. "Don't deny it. I know it and so does everybody. I'm not angry with you. I just don't like to see an intelligent young man like you making a mistake that will ruin his life.

"Look here, Harry, you've become a first-rate clerk in the short time you've been with me. You've got a future here." His voice was friendly and sincere. "I'm ready to make you assistant manager of the dairy department at thirty dollars a week. That's ten more than what you are now making. And in a few years, Louie will be retiring and you'll be in line to take over as manager. Forget about the union. Let everyone know you've decided not to get mixed up with a bunch of commies. You're not going to let them ruin your career. I'm offering you a good deal, Harry. Whaddya say?"

"Thank you very much," I said respectfully. "It's a very generous offer. I'd like to think about it."

"What's there to think about?" Weinstein asked impatiently, but observing my reaction, added, "but I'd like to get your answer by tomorrow."

"First thing tomorrow," I said. I tried to leave him with the impression that I was favorably disposed toward his proposition, but didn't want to appear too eager to accept it. "I'm glad we had our little talk," Weinstein said, "Now get to work."

I decided not to wear my steward's button until I had talked to Eselson. He reacted immediately, "I figured he'd try to sucker you in with that ploy, What he wants you to do is to rat on your co-workers and when you've helped him get rid of the union, he'll be able to fire you. I know you're not going to buy that shit, Harry." His remark struck me as more of an order rather than an appeal. He looked grim-faced, tough.

"All right, I'll turn down Weinstein's offer," I said, weakly.

"Good!" he said, smiling as he slapped me on the back "You won't regret it."

After I left him, I began to be less sure of my decision. I needed my job. What would happen to me if Weinstein fired me? If there was a strike, what would I have to live on? What was Eselson's motive? He had not promised me a job in a union store if I were fired. Should I take Weinstein's offer, even if it was a risky one? I could not sleep as I pondered the alterntives over and over again.

Toward noon the next day, Weinstein entered the store and motioned for me to leave the counter and come to his office. "So what's your answer?" he asked curtly when we were alone.

"I haven't any. I'm still thinking about it," I answered truthfully.

"Don't give me that crap! I want your answer right now!" he said angrily.

I stood there, saying nothing.

"Well?" he insisted.

"I'm sorry, Mr. Weinstein, I don't think I can accept your offer."

"Then I'm firing you, you ungrateful bastard! Go to the cashier's desk and get your pay. And don't you dare come around again begging for a job!"

It was Weinstein who convinced me that I had made the right decision. I walked out of the store with all the clerks staring after me. Several of those who had signed union cards were undoubtedly worried that they'd be next to be discharged.

I telephoned the union immediately. Eselson was not there, but when I explained my situation, I was given a number where I could reach him. Eselson was not shocked when I told him what had happened. He tried to console me. "Don't get upset, Harry. We're not gonna let you down. You're still my steward, and we're gonna give him the fight of his life. Here's what I want you to do, and please listen carefully. I want you to hang around the coffee shop and give every clerk at their lunch time this simple message: I want each of them to come to a meeting at the union hall at twelve noon tomorrow, Sunday. They know the address of the union, but give it to them anyway. Don't discuss your case with them. Don't get into any arguments. Tell them it's urgent for their protection and their future that they attend the meeting. Make sure you cover every one. I know it'll get back to Weinstein, but that's unavoidable. We'll have other ways to surprise him. Do you understand my instructions?" I said yes half-heartedly. I was just beginning to realize what Weinstein had done to me.

As if reading my mind, Eselson once again sought to console me. "Look at it this way: you no longer have to be a slave and prat boy to that sonofabitch. He may have done you a real favor by firing you. Why should a bright young boy like you want to give that greedy bastard the best years of your life? Be thankful you're not back in the store running your ass off for Weinstein. Go to a movie. Lots of good ones around. Do you like ice hockey? The Rangers are playing Montreal at the Garden. It should be an exciting game. And get a good night's sleep. We've got a lot of hard work ahead of us. See you tomorrow."

Only seven men, including me, came to the Sunday meeting. If Eselson was disappointed, he didn't show it. "Thanks for coming, fellas," he said. "Let's get down to business. It's Sunday, your day off, and I don't want to keep you here very long. You know that Weinstein fired Harry, and I'm telling you here and now that the union is not gonna permit him to fire *anyone*, especially all of you who signed application cards. Weinstein knows you're for the union, and if he can get away with firing Harry, what's to stop him from getting rid of each of you any time he feels like it?

"So here's our plan of action. Tomorrow morning, I want all of you to be in front of the store at 6 o'clock sharp. We're gonna stand there as long as it takes, and no one—I mean no one—will set foot in the store until Weinstein agrees to sit down with us and negotiate a contract that gives you decent wages, hours and working conditions."

He looked grimly at each of us. "You get the picture?"

"What if some of the men want to go in to work?" one man asked.

Eselson scowled. "We have ways of discouraging anyone who wants to scab. I'm not gonna spell out what I mean. You can figure it out for yourself."

"You mean the union is calling a strike?" another asked.

"That's what it will be. And we'll have picket signs ready to inform the public so they won't shop at Weinstein's."

"Do we get strike benefits?"

"We're not gonna pay you your salary while you're out, but we'll make sure no one starves or gets evicted from their homes. We'll arrange it so that each striker gets a day or two of work at one of our union stores."

"Is this gonna be a long strike?"

"It depends on Weinstein. If he wants to be reasonable, we can come to terms tomorrow morning, and there won't have to be a strike. We'll just have to wait and see. We don't intend to lose no matter how long it takes. Any more questions?"

There were none.

"Okay fellas. See you tomorrow morning. And it's very important to come on time." He shook hands with each of us.

When the men had left, Eselson turned to me and said, "Let's have some lunch and then we'll make our social calls."

"What calls?" I asked.

"We're gonna pay a visit to every man who didn't show up at the meeting. We have to explain the facts of life to them."

He took me to Larry's Steak House on Second Avenue, where we both had prime ribs of beef, french fries, and apple pie with our coffee. "You're eating pretty well for a man who's unemployed," he joked as he paid the bill.

Eselson had a typewritten sheet with the names and addresses of all of the Weinstein clerks. When we visited the men who were undecided or opposed to the union, he strongly suggested they call in sick. In the presence of family members, he explained he couldn't vouch for the safety of any man who intended to scab on his fellow workers.

It was not until eight o'clock that night, and after countless hours of driving, that Eselson was able to check off everyone on the list as having been informed about the strike and instructed about what to do.

"Are you tired, son?"

I nodded. "How about you?"

"I'm used to this. I'll drop you off at your house, Get some sleep. Tomorrow is gonna be a rough day. We've got a lot of hard work ahead of us."

6. The Strike

Weinstein, as we had anticipated, got wind of our strike preparations from one of his informers and made arrangements of his own to foil us. At six the next morning, as we gathered in front of the store (there were eleven of us), we found a squad of policemen ready to make arrests in the event there was "labor trouble." A police van was parked not far from the store.

Eselson was not the least bit ruffled. Smiling, he walked over to Weinstein and said, "Hello, Mr. Weinstein. I'm Norman Eselson, the organizer for the Food Workers Industrial Union, Local 104. I'm glad to meet you." He held out his hand.

Weinstein, face flushed and eyes ablaze, ignored the outstretched hand. "I don't want to have anything to do with you or your union. Get the hell out of here so my men can go to work."

"Now, Mr. Weinstein, there's no need to get excited. We're not interested in causing trouble. I'm here representing your employees, and what they want is a written contract that will give them some improvement in their working conditions. They're not asking for the moon, but only things they think they're entitled to. I think if we sit down and talk it over calmly, we can arrive at an agreement that is fair to both parties."

"I don't need a union to tell me what to pay my men or how to treat them. No one is forcing them to work for me. If they can find a better job elsewhere, they're free to leave. I'm not going to let a union run my business, and that's final! There's nothing more to talk about." Weinstein looked at the police sergeant. "Officer, will you order this man to leave?"

"Listen, mister," the sergeant said to Eselson, "if you're gonna hang around the entrance to the store, I'll have to arrest you and your men for loitering."

"Now, sarge, we're not loitering. I'm discussing an important business matter with the owner of this store, and we'll be through with our conversation in a moment." Turning to Weinstein, Eselson said, "There's no point in beating around the bush. None of these men is gonna work for you until they get a contract. That's plain enough. So are you ready to negotiate?"

"Fuck you, you commie bastard!" Weinstein shouted. Staring at his employees who were gathered about Eselson, he commanded, "All right, men, get into the store and put on your aprons. We've got to get ready for our customers. We'll find time later to talk about any problems you have. Meanwhile, let's get to work."

None of the clerks moved to enter the store. They stood there silently, with eyes averted.

"Listen, you guys, I'm giving you one more chance. If you don't get into the store this minute, you're finished. You'll be out on your ass the same as Harry." Weinstein glared at me. "I'll have a replacement for each of you by nine o'clock. The store will get along without you. I'm giving you your last chance to save your jobs," he repeated.

The men stood there, nervous and speechless. I was sure that many of them would have returned to work if Eselson hadn't been there and if they hadn't been frightened by his threats about what he'd do to anyone who scabbed. The same was true for those who had agreed to call in sick.

"You're all fired," Weinstein snarled. He turned his back on them and walked into the store.

Eselson motioned to me. "There are a dozen picket signs in the back of my car. Take a couple of men and bring them here. We'll set up the picketline."

And so the battle began.

* * * * *

Weinstein, true to his threat, had arranged to replace us with unemployed grocery clerks whom he had hired through an agency. At nine o'clock, just as he had said, Louie, the manager, brought a group of ten men into the store under police protection. We cursed them as scabs, strikebreakers, lousy bastards.

Eselson was not as upset as we were about the scabs. Even if the union could get them to quit, he explained, Weinstein could find dozens of others who would be willing to work for him. At the meeting that night, he emphasized that "this is not a strike but a *lockout!* Weinstein locked you men out of his store for no other reason than to prevent you from exercising your democratic right to join a union. Don't forget it: *it's a lockout, not a strike!*"

The way to win our jobs back, he told us, was to cut as deep as possible into the store's sales. If we could persuade our customers not to patronize Weinstein's for the duration of the conflict, the scabs would have little to do but stand around. It would drive Weinstein nutty. At some point, he'd realize that if he wanted his customers back, he'd have to rehire all of us and negotiate a contract with the union.

To carry out Eselson's strategy, we scheduled daily visits by each clerk to neighborhood apartment houses and the private homes where many of our best customers lived. We explained why Weinstein had fired us and pleaded for their sympathy and support. If only they'd shop elsewhere for a while, they'd be helping us to win our jobs back, and how grateful we'd be to them. And we hoped the day would not be too far off when we'd be giving them our best service once again.

For those customers who were indifferent or unfriendly to our plea, we concluded our visit with a few comments that had many of them worried. We advised them for their safety and health to avoid shopping at Weinstein's. One could never tell when violence would break out. There'd be trouble, for example, if Weinstein's hired goons tried to beat us up and smash our picketlines. And you could not predict what those so-called grocery clerks whom Weinstein had hired off the street might do to the sour cream, butter, smoked fish and other products. "You'd be wise, madam, if you stayed away from the store until this dispute is settled," we'd say as we left.

We were delighted at how many customers said they would support us. When we reported this to Eselson, he suggested we get a few of the more prominent ones to form a customers committee to support our fight. The committee, he said, could be useful in putting pressure on Weinstein to negotiate. It could also be used to raise money if the lockout lasted a long time.

We soon felt less embarrassed about being on the picketline (none of us had done this before), especially when passersby gave us smiles of approval and encouragement. There were far more of them than those who shouted insults at us, like "Go back to Russia, you commies!" Charlie, the owner of the coffee shop where we used to eat, said he'd have a bowl of soup and a cup of coffee for us whenever we came into his place.

We could tell that Weinstein's business had dropped by more than half. Mr. W. looked haggard and distraught, as we saw him pacing back and forth inside the store. Many of us figured we'd be back on the job before the week was out. We underestimated him.

That Friday evening, after the store had closed and we were about to end our picketing, we were surprised to see Louie and two clerks making displays of "specials" in the two wide windows on either side of the entrance. We couldn't believe our eyes when we saw the prices they had placed on the stacks of tuna fish, canned fruit, tomato juice, jars of green olives, breakfast cereal, face soap, canned soups and other goods. Every item was priced at least 20 percent below cost! Had Weinstein gone completely mad? Or was he selling out his inventory so he could shut down the store? There was nothing we could do about it except wait until tomorrow, the busiest shopping day, to see what would happen.

What we feared would happen did. Word about Weinstein's "blockbuster bargains" spread like wildfire through the community. By nine o'clock, the store was jammed with customers waiting eagerly to buy large quantities of groceries at sensational savings before they were sold out. Mr. W. had the foresight to hire ten "extras" from the employment agency to handle the enormous crowd. And he had arranged for a police detail to guard the store against a possible disturbance.

Pushing into the store were customers who only a few days ago had promised us they'd shop elsewhere to help us regain our jobs. Many walked by us, pretending not to see the picketline or hear us when we chanted, "Weinstein took our jobs away; help us win them back!" Others looked shame-faced or turned their heads away.

Mr. W. stood at the entrance, acting like a *maitre d'*. He greeted each customer with a smile, some with a handshake, as he ushered them into the store. A few times, he went behind the counter to help out.

As the day wore on, we agreed it was the biggest sale that Weinstein had ever run. It must have cost him thousands of dollars, a price he was apparently willing to pay to recover all of his customers. We speculated how long he could continue to lose money at that rate and, if he stopped, whether the customers would remain loyal to him. No one could say for sure.

What we realized was that Weinstein had regained the initiative. Only yesterday, we were very optimistic about victory; now, we felt unsure and dispirited. What made us even more depressed was the knowledge that there'd be no paycheck that night. How many more payless Saturdays would we have to endure? Our only consolation was that tomorrow was Sunday and, thank God, there'd be no picketing assignment.

Three days later, when I arrived at the picketline at six in the morning, I was surprised to find Eselson with two men who I assumed were his bodyguards. He handed me a mimeographed leaflet and said, "Read this. It's the union's answer to Weinstein."

The headline startled me. In large type, it read:
"SAVE 10% ON YOUR GROCERY BILL
BY SHOPPING AT ANY OF THESE STORES!"

Any person presenting the leaflet to the six stores listed below would receive a 10 percent reduction on his or her grocery purchases, no questions asked. This was in addition to the savings they would gain from buying the advertised "loss leaders" at these unionized stores. The leaflet also explained the inhuman conditions under which Weinstein employees had been working and the cruel way in which they had been fired when they asked to be represented by a union.

"This is great!" I said, admiringly. "Wait till Weinstein sees this!"

"Never mind, Weinstein," Eselson said. "I want you to get your men to distribute it to every household in the neighborhood for a mile around. We've got three boxes of leaflets here, and we'll have plenty more by the afternoon. I'm sending you a dozen people later in the day to help you on the picketline and in the distribution. Call me at the union at three o'clock."

When our men saw copies of the leaflet, they were elated. Eselson was one helluva smart guy, they agreed, but they had also learned he could be as tough as nails. They respected him. When he gave them an order, they obeyed, because they were sure he knew what he was doing.

As union steward, one of my responsibilities was to see that every man did his required four hours of picket duty a day in split shifts of two hours each. In between their picketing assignments, they were to be available at the store site for any other activity that might be required. Today and tomorrow, they'd be spending their four "free" hours on leaflet distribution.

The leaflet produced huge crowds at each of the six stores. Bargain hunters who had stormed Weinstein's for nearly a week were now flocking to one or other cut-rate stores with leaflets in their hands, buying large quantities of "specials" that were purposely different from those Weinstein had advertised. The union's organizing campaign had become a price war. Public greed was now tipping the scale to our side. By the end of the week, the price war appeared to have settled into a standoff. Purchases in all stores, including Weinstein's, tapered off as people ran out of money to spend on stocking up on groceries.

When the third week of the lockout passed without any sign that Weinstein was willing to negotiate, we realized. to our despair, that he intended to hold out until he had starved us into submission. We were not enthused when Eselson said firmly, as he looked us over, that the union would continue the struggle "until hell freezes over." We were in for a long, exhausting battle, and we had no idea of what the outcome would be. Many of the men had second thoughts about their joining the union, but they dared not say so publicly.

We walked the picketline grimly, feeling more hopeless with each passing day. To make matters worse, it was bitter cold and it rained almost every day. The papers said it was the worst December weather in a decade. Eselson agreed to limit picket duty to three hours a day instead of four, but our morale remained low.

A few days before Christmas, Weinstein sent a registered letter to all of the men except me, inviting them to return to work. He was making this offer in the holiday spirit of good will. "We must forget this tragic episode that made us hurt each other because of the instigation of outsiders who do not have your best interests at heart," the letter stated. "I want you to know that I've always appreciated your ability, and it is unfortunate that this communist union came between us." The letter closed by promising a five-dollar raise to each man who returned to work, and wishing each of them a "Happy and Prosperous New Year."

Two of our men accepted Weinstein's offer. They explained they had families to feed and couldn't afford to stay out any longer. I sensed that several others were also thinking of going back to work. It looked like it was only a matter of time before the union would be defeated.

Eselson, realizing what was happening, launched a counterattack, employing tougher tactics to discourage customers from patronizing Weinstein's. Several times a day he'd send women into the store to buy sizeable amounts of groceries. When the clerk who was waiting on them would weigh the cheese or smoked fish they'd ordered, they'd shout that he was cheating them, complaining in loud voices that could be heard throughout the store. Then they'd stalk out, leaving all their groceries on the counter. Weinstein's clerks found it hard to distinguish between these troublemakers and regular customers, nor were there clear-cut reasons to arrest them.

Eselson found other ways to get under Mr. W.'s skin. All sorts of innocent accidents would occur at any time of the day. "Customers" would stumble and overturn tall displays of canned goods. They'd drop jars of olives and tomato juice, messing up the floor, and apologize for their clumsiness. They'd exasperate the clerks by changing their minds about everything they ordered.

People became fearful of shopping at Weinstein's after they heard that several shoppers had been accosted a block away from the store by a group of hoodlums, who seized their groceries and scattered the contents into the gutter. The most damaging blow to Weinstein came on a Saturday morning when a stink bomb exploded in the store, sending panicky customers into the streets and forcing him to shut down for the rest of the day.

Still, Mr. W. doggedly held on with not the least hint that he was ready to deal with the union. Week after week went by, as we settled into a routine of four days of picketing and two days of work at a union store at seven dollars a day. Just when our morale reached its lowest point and we, if not the union, were ready to admit defeat, Eselson received a letter from Mr. W.'s attorney, suggesting a conference to consider whether there was a basis for reaching a settlement. Eselson said he had agreed to meet with the attorney, but we would have the final say on any tentative agreement. For the next two days, we didn't see Eselson or hear from him. Mr. W., as usual, spent the day in the store. If negotiations were taking place, he was not participating. Finally, on a snowy Tuesday that was to turn into a blizzard by nightfall, Eselson called us together at a nearby store that had served as our temporary headquarters. He announced he'd reached an agreement with Weinstein's representative and that it would go into effect if we ratified it.

"I'm going to read the main features of the contract," he said. "Listen carefully and please don't interrupt. When I'm finished, we'll go over it again, item by item. I want you to understand that the contract was negotiated as a package. If you reject any item, we have to start the negotiations all over again from scratch. Okay?" No one said anything. We weren't interested in technicalities. We were eager to hear the terms of the settlement.

Eselson put on his glasses and read from his notes. "We've proposed a three-year contract with the following provisions: I want to start with the most important one. Every employee who was on Weinstein's payroll on the day before the lockout will be rehired. All other current employees will be discharged but may be rehired if required because of an increase in business."

"We won! We won!" the men shouted, hugging each other happily, several with tears in their eyes, thankful the ordeal was over.

Eselson smiled and continued: "On wages, we gained a five-dollar increase, across the board, for the first year; three dollars for the second year and three dollars for the third year. On hours of work, we negotiated a ten-hour day, plus an extra hour on Saturday, for a total of sixty-one during the first year, compared to the seventy-eight you've been working; there will be a further reduction in the second and third year of the contract to a nine and one-half hour day, with an extra hour on Saturday, making a total of 58 hours.

"I think you'll be pleased that we eliminated Weinstein's speedup system. Clerks will no longer be penalized because of low sales totals on the cash register. To prevent discrimination and harassment, two or more clerks will be assigned to the same key on the register. The lunch period will remain at a half hour, but the dinner period on Saturday will be extended from fifteen minutes to half an hour. Employees will be permitted to eat lunch in the store at the employer's expense, as formerly, with the understanding that a labor-management committee will make periodic checks to see that the privilege is not abused.

"There will be six paid holidays per year: Washington's Birthday, Rosh Hashanah, Yom Kippur, Thanksgiving Day, Christmas Day and New Year's Day. Anyone working on those days will be paid time and one-half. Employees with five to ten years of service will be entitled to one week of paid vacation; those with ten years or more will receive two weeks of vacation."

Eselson paused. "There is one other provision which Weinstein insisted on. He said it was non-negotiable. If we didn't agree to it, there'd be no contract. I tried to argue his lawyer out of it, but I couldn't. I'm not happy with it, but I had to accept it. Here's how they formulated it: 'This agreement will be consummated only on condition that Harry Kelber will not be rehired at Weinstein's Food Market or sent there by the union under any pretext whatever.' "

All eyes turned to me. I felt sick, betrayed. I couldn't think of anything to say. I wanted to get out of that room and go somewhere, anywhere. Sensing my shock, Eselson came up to me and put his arm around my shoulder. "Harry has done an outstanding job as your steward through all these difficult weeks. We're certainly not gonna see him penalized for his important contributions to our organizing campaign. So we've arranged for him to have a job at the Highland Dairies in Manhattan. It's a chain store we unionized two years ago. The wages and working conditions there are among the best in the industry. I guarantee he'll like it. So let's give Harry a hearty round of applause." Eselson clapped his hands and they all followed his lead. I blushed and felt the tears welling in my eyes. I was still stunned by the suddenness of the announcement and too embarrassed to say anything.

No one suggested that the strike should continue until Weinstein agreed to take me back. Eselson hadn't, nor would I. After fourteen weeks on the picketline, it would have been madness to make my case the sticking point.

There was almost no discussion when the provisions of the contract were reviewed. The men were so relieved at the thought of going back to work, they were ready to approve almost any settlement. When the vote was taken, it was unanimous for acceptance.

The snow was now ankle-deep and still coming down hard and the wind was biting. It didn't matter. No more picketlines. We were all heading for home, delighted that we could finally bring the good news to our families. Mama would kiss and hug me and have a nourishing, hot meal for me.

* * * * *

I never saw Weinstein again. All I learned about him is from hearsay. One of his clerks, whom I met at a union meeting a few months later, said Mr. W. never got over his surrender to the union. He felt his men had betrayed him, and he refused to speak to any of them except through his manager. His bitter battle with the union seemed to have broken his spirit and drained his energy. He rarely came to the store except at closing time to check the day's receipts or to talk to Louie, whose responsibilities had increased. A few weeks after the strike, much to the relief of everybody, he sold the store and moved to Florida.

7. How I Became a Communist

Eselson was right. The job at the Highland Dairies on 78th Street and Columbus Avenue was like a vacation. Just a nine-hour workday, including Saturday. I
could be home by seven and have the evening ahead of me. I'd be able to start
dating again and not feel tired all the time.

Highland Dairies was a chain of five stores, all on the West Side of Manhattan. The chain was owned by two brothers, Herb and Jerry Gaffner, both in their
late thirties, whose deceased father had been an active communist. The Gaffners
were shrewd, energetic businessmen, who had started with one small dairy four
years ago and had opened their fifth store, the one where I was now working, only
two months earlier. Herb, the older brother, a portly, good-natured man who had
studied to be an accountant, took care of the buying and pricing for the stores, as
well as its financial dealings with banks and creditors.

It was Jerry, the younger one, who actually ran the stores and with whom we
were in almost daily contact. Jerry had been a salesman for a wholesale food distributing company before it went bankrupt. He had made a point of hiring young
men in their twenties with bright, pleasing personalities like his own, who could
provide the quality service that attracted so many customers to his stores. He knew
all of his employees, about twenty of them, by their first names and enough about
their families to make pleasant inquiries about them. He was certainly a far cry
from Louie Weinstein.

The Gaffner brothers revered the memory of their father, and they had vowed,
even as businessmen, to maintain the social values he had taught them. That was
why Highland Dairies two years earlier had signed a precedent-setting contract
with Food Workers Industrial Union Local 104 that had stunned the retail food
industry. The minimum wage of twenty-five dollars was as high or higher than
many experienced grocery clerks were earning; but what created a sensation was
the reduction of the workweek to 54 hours, remarkable for those depression times.
(The communists even back then were calling for a 30-hour workweek, partly to
provide more jobs for the millions of unemployed.)

Angry competitors predicted that the stores would go bankrupt in six months.
Instead, the stores prospered. Jerry shrewdly capitalized on the contract. The morale of his well-paid employees was high, and they worked efficiently to increase

both sales and profits. With clever advertising, he attracted many new shoppers who were pleased to patronize stores that treated their workers so humanely.

For the Food Workers Industrial Union, the contract with Highland Dairies was by far the best they had been able to achieve—and without a struggle. It became their objective to make the provisions of this contract standard throughout the industry.

It was about three weeks after I had started to work for Highland Dairies that Eselson invited me to have dinner with him at a restaurant near the store. "How do you like working in a union shop?" he asked when we had ordered.

"Great. I'll have to write a letter of thanks to Weinstein for making it possible" I joked. "Seriously, Norman, I can't thank you enough for what you've done for me."

"You've earned it," he said. "We need young leaders for the future of our union, and I think you can be one of them."

I blushed with pleasure. "I'm certainly going to try to live up to your expectations. You taught me a lot."

Eselson waited until we had finshed eating before getting to the reason for his visit. "I believe you know that the Food Workers Industrial Union is a left-wing union, and that there are communists in the leadership," he began.

"Yes, I know. Weinstein himself told me," I wisecracked.

He smiled. "Did you know I was a communist?" he asked.

"I strongly suspected it, but it didn't bother me. You saw how all of us accepted your leadership and respected you."

"What do you think of the Communist Party?"

"I really don't know much about the Party, except what I've seen and read," I said. "I've come to admire their courage and dedication, but I don't know anything about their goals."

He looked at me intently. "I think you're a communist at heart. I'm asking you to join the Party." I felt his eyes searching my face for a reaction. He could see that I was startled and hesitant.

"I can't give you a quick answer, Norman. I'll have to think about it. I can tell you I admire you more than any man I've ever known except my father. I'll let you know as soon as I've made up my mind."

"Sure," he said. I think he felt disappointed that I hadn't agreed immediately. I felt embarrassed. I didn't know what else to say.

Eselson ended the conversation with an impassioned speech aimed at convincing me about the Party. It made me uncomfortable. "The world is full of men like Weinstein," he began. "They exploit and abuse working people, and think they're doing them a favor by giving them a job. Many of them are far more powerful than Weinstein. They own the banks, the factories, the railroads, the newspapers and just about everything. That enables them to control the government. They have the money to elect whoever they want, Democrats or Republicans, whoever serves them best. Now they got themselves Roosevelt for president. He's as much a capitalist tool as Hoover was. No matter what nice things he may say publicly, he'll play ball with them, you'll see." His voice rose, as he said emphatically, "The Communist Party is the only organization that fights consistently and unselfishly for the needs of the working class. I'd like you to remember that, Harry."

I promised I would. He would hear from me in a week or so.

I didn't need Eselson to tell me the country was in a state of economic chaos. The daily newspapers were full of stories that showed how badly crippled the nation's industries were; that nearly one of every four workers was unemployed and millions of others were on part time. Many of the largest banks had closed their doors, wiping out the savings of countless depositors. Farms were being fore-closed by the thousands. The number of bankruptcies was rising almost daily. The stock market showed no tangible signs of recovering from its catastrophic col-lapse. How could any thoughtful young man be expected to have faith in the capi-talist system?

I occasionally listened to Communist Party speakers at open air meetings on street corners, and while I didn't care for their know-it-all rhetorical style, I found it hard to disagree with many of the things they were saying. The obvious fact was that Big Business had been running the country, and it had fucked up everything, leaving us with breadlines, soup kitchens, Hoovervilles and no end of poverty and despair. It was clear that unless some basic changes were made, the nation might never recover from the Depression, and God knows what would happen next.

I did not know what the ultimate goal of the Communist Party was. If it was to take over the U.S. government, to establish a Soviet America, even in the dim future, I strongly doubted it would succeed, certainly not in my lifetime.

What attracted me to the communists and finally convinced me to join the Party was the strong commitment of their members, people like Eselson, to the cause of social justice and human decency. I admired their idealism, militancy, courage and selfless dedication. Even when they were clubbed and tear-gassed by the police, it didn't stop them from demonstrating at City Hall for home relief for the hungry and jobs for the unemployed.

As I began reading the Party's newspaper, the *Daily Worker,* I learned about the struggles that communists were engaged in all across the country. More than any other organization, they seemed to have become the unchallenged champion of the working class. What also interested me about the communists was the en-emies they made. There wasn't a fascist, racial bigot, anti-Semite or labor-hater who didn't declare Communism to be the main threat to civilization. I didn't buy their propaganda. If anything, it persuaded me that the Party must be doing a lot of things right to deserve such enemies.

And then there was Norman Eselson, the one communist I knew and had personally observed. I admired him immensely, not only for his competence and shrewdness, but his willingness to knock himself out to help exploited workers. Why did he do it? Not for the money. This poor, left-wing union, on principle, must pay him peanuts. He was given a tiny, crummy office and an old, battered Chevy and told to spend his days, nights and weekends, no overtime pay, to organize workers. There had to be something else motivating him. It had to be his passionate belief that he was helping to create a better world, even if he would not be around to enjoy it. That must be why he didn't complain about being overworked and underpaid.

For all my admiration of Eselson, I did have reservations about joining the Party. In all honesty, at age 20, I was not prepared to make personal sacrifices for any cause, no matter how noble. I didn't want to spend my leisure time at meetings and demonstrations and subject myself to the demands of the Party. I wanted to get some joy out of life, not waste it in struggling for a paradise that might never come. I had to think of my own future: to find a woman I could love and marry and raise a family.

But a week later, I met Eselson at the union and told him I was ready to join the Party. He was overjoyed. He gave me a warm bear hug. "That's wonderful! You've made my day! Let's have a sandwich and a coffee." He said he would arrange for me to attend a Party meeting the following Tuesday where, as my sponsor, he would introduce me to the other comrades. He called me the next day to give me the address of the meeting and told me to be there at eight o'clock sharp.

Not knowing what to expect, I was somewhat tense at my first Party meeting. Sitting in the spacious living room of a well-furnished apartment on the West Side were eight men and two women, all of them older than I, who scrutinized me closely as Eselson made a short speech in praise of my role in unionizing Weinstein's. Hy Rudnick, a ruddy-faced man of sixty with horn-rimmed eyeglasses and a bushy, gray moustache, put me at ease with his friendly smile as he introduced me to each of the comrades. Eselson, seeing I was in good hands, excused himself to go to another meeting.

The first item on the agenda, as best I can recall, was a communication from the Party's Central Committee discussing the importance of developing and supporting American-Soviet Friendship clubs. It was necessary to combat reactionary forces who were trying to reverse President Roosevelt's historic diplomatic recognition of the Soviet Union, the letter explained.

There were several announcements. A rally for passage of an unemployment insurance law would be held at City Hall that Saturday. Leaflets were available for distribution to the public. Contributions of clothing, furniture, books and other items were needed for the Party's annual bazaar during Memorial Day weekend. Comrades were urged to attend an important lecture on "New Paths of Struggle for American Labor" by Jack Stachel, secretary of the Party's Trade Union Commission. Then came a report on the unit's organizing target, one of Horn & Hardart's self-service restaurants on Broadway. We were told there had been a poor response to the leaflets of the Food Workers Industrial Union that had been handed out to employees two weeks earlier. The union had received only one inquiry. A brief discussion took place on the reasons for the poor response. One of the members, Frank, said he would check with the union on how the campaign was going at other H&H restaurants.

Party recruiting was the next item on the agenda, but no one had anything to report except Rudnick, who had convinced one of the clerks at Integrity Food Market to subscribe to the *Daily Worker.*

The "educational" that evening was on "The Party's Program for National Recovery." It had been printed as a pamphlet and been widely distributed. Every member of the unit had already received a copy. The unit's literature director handed me a copy. The discussion was led by a college-educated grocery clerk, Ben, with whom I later became friendly. When he had finished summarizing the program, there was lively debate on how best to implement the nationalization of basic industries. I didn't see how any of these people, including me, were qualified to offer expert opinions on how to do it. What could we say about transforming the banking system or declaring a moratorium on farm foreclosures except agree that they seemed worthy measures in a recovery program?

The literature director then made a pitch for a new pamphlet, "The Shorter Work Week," which, he said, was "must reading" for every Party trade unionist because it contained strong arguments for a federal law establishing the thirty-hour week. As one who was working fifty-four hours a week in a union store, I was, of course, interested in reading it. The pamphlet cost five cents. I bought five copies, partly to impress the other comrades.

Under "good and welfare," Rudnick reminded us that the Party's annual Fund Drive would begin in two weeks, and that every employed member was required to contribute a week's pay because funds were urgently needed to carry on its mass work at this "critical stage in our country's history." Unemployed members would be given raffle tickets so they could raise their share for the fund drive.

A week's pay! This was something Eselson hadn't mentioned. I could understand the Party's need for money, but a week's pay seemed too steep. Eselson wouldn't think so. He'd be disappointed in me if I didn't donate the money willingly. He had given me a job at Highland Dairies with a ten-dollar a week increase over what I had earned at Weinstein's. I couldn't refuse to meet my obligations to the fund drive without appearing cheap and ungrateful. I'd be among the first to contribute my share.

After the meeting ended, the comrades came over to me and shook my hand in congratulation. While our host served coffee and cake, Rudnick sat down beside me and asked how I felt about the meeting. It was very interesting, I said, and I could see I had a lot to learn. He told me that Eselson had asked him to "orientate" me on Party ideology. If I had any questions, he'd be available to talk to me. He gave me his address and phone number.

For the next several months, I read some of the basic works of Marx and Lenin in books and pamphlets that Rudnick lent me and some that I bought. I focused on whatever I thought could apply to the American scene. The one work that impressed me most was the *Communist Manifesto.* I fully agreed with the principle of the class struggle on the basis of historical evidence as well as my own limited experience at Weinstein's. I was fascinated by whatever I could learn of the philosophy of dialectical materialism, especially the concept of the unity and conflict of opposites. I could not understand, or found boring, some of Lenin's polemics against the philosphical idealists. I made two or three attempts to read Marx's *Das Kapital,* but couldn't get very far with it.

At Rudnick's suggestion, I took a course in political economy at the Workers School, but unfortunately, I didn't learn very much there. I could never understand the concept of the "falling rate of profit" under capitalism, and no matter how many times the instructor tried to explain it to me, he was not able to answer my questions convincingly.

What I was looking for was a blueprint, or at least guidelines, for a future Socialist America, but no one I talked to could give me enlightening answers. Most of the communists I came into contact with accepted everything the Party said and did on blind faith. Questions could be asked, but there was a limit beyond which one could be accused of being a right-wing or left-wing deviationist.

There were so many questions that were bothering me. Would the seizure of power by the U.S. proletariat, if it ever did occur, be peaceful or violent? I was told it was unlikely that the bourgeoisie would surrender its power without an armed struggle. If so, how was the Party preparing for it? I was convinced that none of the communists in my Party unit or in any of the others possessed guns or hand grenades or would know how to use them to destroy an attacking enemy if they had to. How were such people to make a revolution if it required armed struggle? And assuming they could, to what extent would American socialism follow the Soviet model? Would our economic and political institutions be dismembered and, if so, what would replace them? How would the working class control the means of production? What would happen to farmers and self-employed individuals after the revolution? And what would be the role of unions in a post-capitalist era? How would a socialist government cope with the deep-seated racism that exists in the United States? I thought that answers to these and related questions were essential if the Party was to provide clear-headed leadership toward its socialist goal.

I soon learned that even when these difficult questions were discussed, the answers were usually vague and never satisfying. It seemed there were too many immediate problems occupying the minds of Party functionaries to spend time conjecturing about the future. The Party's prime task, I was told, was to develop the class-consciousness of American workers through struggle so they would eventually carry out their historic role in creating a socialist society. When that happened, the future would take care of itself, it was assumed. The march of events would create the necessary solutions.

After a while, I grew reconciled to this view. I became so immersed in Party work and trade union activity, I could find no time for theoretical reading and thinking. In the following two years, I must have participated in scores of meetings, conferences, demonstrations, picketlines, petition campaigns, fund drives and other activities. I'm sure they all must have seemed important at the time, but now I can hardly remember any of them.

8. Adapting to a New Culture

About two months after I joined the Communist Party—it was in May, 1934—I was transferred to an "industrial unit" that met at the Party's West Side headquarters, not far from where I worked. The unit consisted of five grocery clerks, three of them. like myself, from Highland Dairies. four cafeteria workers and two bakery workers, all of us members of the Food Workers Industrial Union. Like American communists everywhere, we met every Tuesday evening for about two hours to discuss Party directives and to assess the progress of our own goals: to assist the union to organize two grocery stores and one cafeteria on Broadway.

Reading the *Daily Worker.* I was awed by the range of activities the Party was engaged in, especially among rank-and-file workers in trade unions. Day after day, I would learn about strikes erupting in one city or another: electrical workers in Toledo, truck drivers in Milwaukee, longshoremen on the East Coast, garment workers in New York, cloth dyers in New Jersey, textile workers in Virginia. In the larger strikes, almost without fail, police were brought in to use their nightsticks and tear gas against workers who violated court injunctions. And in virtually every strike, AFL "bureaucrats" in the craft unions were depicted as playing their usual treacherous role of undermining the militancy of the workers and making backdoor deals with the employers—at least that is what the newspaper reported, and I had no reason to doubt its accuracy.

What impressed me most about the Party was the remarkable energy and commitment of its members, especially in behalf of the unemployed. The Party was constantly organizing mass demonstrations and hunger marches in the nation's major cities for jobs, home relief and unemployment insurance. Communists courageously defied court injunctions banning their rallies, and they were willing to face up to police who had orders to disperse them. The Party knew how to create and sustain front organizations like the Workers Alliance, the National Congress for Unemployment Insurance, the International Workers Order for ethnic minorities, the International Labor Defense in the fight for free speech and civil liberties, tenants councils, sports and dance festivals for the youth, and public exhibitions of the work of progressive artists and writers. Wherever there was an issue of public concern, the Party would manage to establish an *ad hoc* committee to rally people for struggle. Not only the *Daily Worker,* but the left-wing weekly magazine, *New*

Masses, highly respected for its literary qualities as well as its crusading articles, continually exposed the cruelties of an immoral, exploitative economic system. I could not help but admire the humanitarian and selfless spirit the communists displayed toward working people in their pursuit of a more just society.

Until I joined the Party, I had not been interested in politics. But that changed when I became an avid reader of the *Daily Worker*. In retrospect, the Party's shrill, daily diatribes against President Franklin Roosevelt seem strange and misguided, especially since they were asserted with such strong conviction. FDR, the paper repeated, was a tool of the bankers; his National Recovery Act (NRA) was intended to enslave workers into boss-controlled unions that would undermine their wages and living standards. The President was accused of interfering in strikes on the side of the bosses and even more serious, charged with being a willing accomplice in a sinister plot to establish a fascist dictatorship in the United States. The NRA logo, a fierce-looking eagle with lightning bolts in its talons, was compared to Benito Mussolini's fasces symbol. After the passage of some of the historic New Deal legislation, the Party softened its anti-Roosevelt stand and supported him on some issues.

There was an apocalyptic tone in the eight full-size pages of the *Daily Worker* and its Sunday edition, a sense of urgency that made its readers feel morally obligated to participate in the ever-present crises of the moment. One felt guilty in not answering the call of the Party to attend a Saturday demonstration at City Hall for home relief after reading stories of people dying of starvation. How could one not come to the aid of strikers who were being beaten by police? And what about the special Tag Day to raise funds for the *Worker,* lest it cease publication next week? To be a committed Party member was almost a full-time job, I began to realize. It disturbed me. I was reluctant to have *anyone,* the Party included, make so many demands on my time and for activities that were not personally rewarding.

What impressed me—but also bothered me—was the air of certainty that Party leaders and most members displayed in dealing with any political and social problem, no matter how complex. We came to mass meetings to hear the truth from such important speakers as Earl Browder, general secretary of the American Communist Party, and prominent members of the Central Committee, like Clarence Hathaway, the Minnesota-born editor of the *Daily Worker.* Their Marxist analysis of questions that perplexed us had the ring of truth, once we accepted the fact—as we did—that there was a fundamental conflict between the capitalist class and the working class.

It was not hard to convince us that reports in the *Journal American* and other capitalist newspapers about mass starvation in the Ukraine were outright lies, designed to vilify the Soviet Union and weaken the forces of world socialism. The *Worker* in its Sunday edition frequently ran features about how life in the Soviet Union was steadily improving and how there was full employment there, in contrast to the situation in the United States.

There are various reasons why Party members were so uncritical of the views

of their leaders, some of which eventually proved false and damagingly misleading. We had no way of knowing what was really going on in the Soviet Union, and
given the choice of siding with the anti-communist press or our own Party leaders,
we obviously accepted the latter. There was no television in those years to visually
document the starvation and executions that were taking place during Stalin's forced
collectivization program. We did not believe that a Party that was waging such
heroic struggles for American workers would stoop to deception or take orders to
conceal the truth. In retrospect, I believe that few of the Party s leaders knew about
Stalin's enormous crimes. We were convinced that world capitalism was bent on
encircling and destroying the Soviet Union and that it was our duty to defend the
land of socialism against its powerful enemies. And finally, there were many members like myself who were drawn into the Party not because of any fervent loyalty
to the U.S.S.R., but because we were convinced, on the basis of our experience,
that the Party consisted of idealistic individuals who were dedicating their lives to
the service of the working class . We believed in what they were doing, and we
wanted to be part of that movement.

Personally, my interest in the Soviet Union was secondary to my commitment
to the American working class. I did not feel the same emotional attachment to it
as did so many Party members. I would have joined the Communist Party if the
land of socialism had not existed. Only dimly aware of what a future socialist
America might look like, I felt certain that it would not mirror the Soviet model.

Although admittedly authoritarian in structure, the Party maintained a highly
moral public image which attracted countless "fellow travelers" to its various causes
among liberals, particularly intellectuals and cultural personalities. The Party, whose
membership had been largely foreign-born and almost exclusively white, began to
make inroads in the black communities by launching an energetic and sustained
campaign for the release of the "Scottsboro Boys." It was a case about nine black
youths who had been convicted in 1931 of raping two white women on a train in
Scottsboro, Alabama. Despite testimony by doctors who had examined the women
that no rape had occurred, the all-white jury convicted the nine, and all but the
youngest, who was twelve years old, were sentenced to death. The Party took up
the cause of the Scottsboro Boys with extraordinary vigor and persistence. The
Worker carried almost daily stories about the world-wide attention the case had
attracted, with detailed reports of the activities of the International Labor Defense,
a creation of the Party, to organize the legal defense for the convicted black youths.
Finally, in 1935, the U.S. Supreme Court overturned the conviction, ruling that the
state of Alabama had systematically excluded black people from juries. The Party's
campaign helped win it respect from liberals and civil rights advocates and increased its influence among black people.

* * * * *

Unlike most communists who worked in private industry, I did not have to
hide my Party affiliation. The Highland Dairies manager I worked for, Mark Gross,

was a Party sympathizer and suspected that I was a communist when I was sent to his store. His main concern was that I work efficiently so that the store would prosper, and I worked hard to satisfy him. In return, I could always get a $10 contribution from him for the *Worker* Fund Drive or a few pounds of cheese and boxes of cookies for a Party conference.

Our store on Columbus Avenue represented a dividing line between two classes. On one side were the wealthier people on Central Park West, professionals and businessmen, many of them with live-in housekeepers, in spacious, expensive apartments. On the other side were the people of Amsterdam Avenue, blue-collar workers or the unemployed. Our delivery boy, Eddie, complained that the rich people rarely tipped him because he never saw them. The groceries he delivered to them were usually received by a servant who sometimes offered him a thank you. Most of the tips he earned came from the Amsterdam Avenue customers, the poor being customarily more generous.

It was Eddie who inspired us to institute what we privately called our "Robin Hood" program: to take from the rich and give to the poor. Certain customers from Central Park West were systematically overcharged and the "profits" distributed to those we knew were among the neediest. Mark was somewhat nervous about the plan but agreed to participate when we assured him it would be kept secret and would not cost the store anything.

It was my good fortune to become acquainted with Bill Albertson, a clerk who had recently been hired to work at a nearby Broadway store of the dairy chain. Bill was bright, affable and well-read, but what made him especially important to me was that he was a member of the Party's New York State Trade Union Commission. For some reason, Bill, who was about a dozen years older than me, took a liking to me and made me his protegé. It was through Bill that I gained valuable information about the Party's new "popular front" orientation, which meant abandoning the strategy of building dual unions in favor of seeking affiliation within the American Federation of Labor. The latest Party line called for various divisions of the Food Workers Industrial Union to merge with their industrial and craft counterparts in the AFL to build a united labor movement. Secret negotiations were taking place with a committee from the AFL's Grocery Clerks Union, Local 338, Bill told me. I thought the new policy made a great deal of sense but I doubted whether it could be executed, given the persistent, vitriolic hostility between the Party and the AFL leadership. I was to be proven wrong. The Party strategy succeeded brilliantly, overcoming a series of formidable obstacles. Local 104, the union I belonged to, was merged into Local 338, creating one large union of grocery employees, although tension between the two groups of union members persisted for more than a year.

Albertson, a shrewd strategist, eventually became secretary-treasurer of the merged Waiters and Waitresses Local 16, one of the largest locals in the AFL's Hotel and Restaurant International Union. As an influential local officer, Albertson was to wage a successful campaign to get rid of gangster elements that had infiltrated the city's catering unions. (Thomas Dewey, then a district attorney and later governor of New York and Republican Presidential candidate, built his political reputation on the prosecution and conviction of these racketeers.)

About September of that year, I was "elected" to the Party's West Side Section Committee at its annual convention. A slate of candidates—I was among them—was presented to the delegates who adopted it unanimously without debate. I had been notified of my nomination a week before and, of course, there was no question that I would be honored to accept. I think it was Albertson who recommended me for the post.

Besides participating in frequent meetings that seemed to last interminably, I had special responsibilities to prepare whatever leaflets had to be issued in the name of the West Side Section of the Party. I found myself spending several nights a week at Section headquarters, trying, with some difficulty, to translate Party policy statements on various issues into one-page dramatic, persuasive flyers that were distributed to the community in thousands of copies.

From the outset, I was stimulated by the assignment. I enjoyed arguing out the fine points of Party policy with Section leaders and I learned a great deal about the art of persuasion and compromise. I was less adept at using a stylus and stencil template or running the mimeograph machine, but there were always comrades available to help me.

I was now immersed in a strange world I could not have imagined even a year before. Two or three nights a week, I would work late at Section headquarters, sometimes until ten or eleven. When I was too tired to take the long ride home to Brooklyn, I slept on a battered couch in one of the offices at Section headquarters. Once in a while, I'd sleep at the apartment of my friend Gil Mason, who was also in the Section. His family had a spare bedroom and his father invited me to use it whenever I needed to. I tried not to abuse the family's hospitality.

I finally decided to rent a room on the West Side, telling Mama that I would visit her and the kids at least once a week, maybe more, and we could keep in touch by phone. Mama reluctantly accepted the idea of my moving out, but worried what would happen to me living all alone. She was not keen about my being a communist because she feared I might get beaten up. either by cops or gangsters. She kept reminding me how wonderful it would be if I married a nice Jewish girl and raised a family. It was her way of warning me not to marry a Gentile or, even worse in her eyes, a black woman.

I hardly ever saw my old friends in Brooklyn, and when I did see them on an occasional Sunday, our conversation seemed awkward and artificial. They were interested in sports and movies and dating girls and very little else. I had a new set of young friends, all of them either Party members or sympathizers, and we enjoyed each other's company.

Despite the dogmatism that pervaded the Party (it was sinful, for example, to be caught reading anything published by the followers of Trotsky), most young communists led a stimulating intellectual and cultural life. The "What's On" column in the *Daily Worker* and its Sunday edition provided a list of left-wing entertainment for almost every night of the week and especially on weekends: lectures by Party pundits and popular writers, fund-raising parties, dances, concerts, Soviet films, picnics, art shows and sport events. The nice thing about these socials was that you could invariably meet a kindred spirit who might turn out to be a future acquaintance or a good friend, even a lover. Occasionally, I went to readings of the new literary magazine, *Partisan Review*, to hear and discuss the still unpublished work of young authors.

I developed a taste for Russian movies and saw many of them that played at the Cameo Theater on 42nd Street:: *Alexander Nevsky, Potemkin, Chapayev, We Are From Kronstadt, Lenin in October* and others. The underlying theme in all of them was essentially the same: through hardship and adversity, struggle will lead to eventual triumph of the proletariat.

One evening, my friend Gil suggested we spend a weekend at Camp Unity, the communist-run resort in Wingdale, N.Y. I had never been to any camp as a child or adolescent and so had no experience in living with groups of strangers. A few hours after arriving on late Friday afternoon, I was enjoying myself immensely. I soon felt at home in the spacious dining hall and found the people at my table interesting to talk to. That night there were bunk parties that lasted past midnight, with much singing and laughter. Some couples went off to secluded spots near the lake where I assumed they had sex. There were plenty of girls around but I was still too shy to make a play for any of them.

From early Saturday morning until I left after Sunday lunch, I participated in every activity I could find time for: I played softball, went canoeing, attended a lecture on the struggle of the Asturian miners, sang in the makeshift chorus, got beaten in a ping -pong tournament, watched the amateur talent show and finally, my shyness gone, found a willing partner for some heavy petting at one of the bunk parties. I arrived home happy but thoroughly exhausted.

* * * * *

After a year at Highland Dairies, I began to get bored with my life as a grocery clerk. There must be more interesting occupations that I could qualify for. But what? I had not really given the matter any serious thought. All I knew was that I was fed up with working behind a counter, monotonously serving customers dairy products, day after day. I thought of the possibility of becoming a full-time Party organizer, but dismissed it. Even if it could be arranged. I did not have the stomach for that kind of life. I had enough foresight to know that I would be quickly burned out and would end up as an embittered failure.

I could be a writer, I thought. I had turned out some pretty good leaflets. Perhaps I could get a job as a reporter on the *Daily Worker*? I discussed that idea with Albertson. He said he'd check into it. A week later, we met for dinner and he told me there was no job for me at the *Worker,* especially since I was inexperienced. They had all the staff they needed and besides, they relied for much of their news stories on unpaid, volunteer correspondents across the country. Maybe in a few months, there might be some openings.

Seeing my disappointment, Bill came up with another possibility. "Have you seen *People's Press*?" he asked. I hadn't.

"It's a terrific, pro-labor weekly run by Frank Palmer, whom I've known a long time. I'll give you a letter of introduction to him. I don't know if he needs anyone, but it's worth a try." He wrote down the address and phone number on a slip of paper and handed it to me. Albertson's helpful suggestion started me on a career that marked a major turning point in my life.

9. *Learning to Edit a Labor Paper*

I had been waiting nervously for ten minutes in the small reception room of *People's Press* when I was finally ushered into Frank Palmer's office. As he rose from his desk to greet me, I was startled to see a huge man, well over six feet tall, with a large, round, nearly-bald head. When he displayed his broad, toothy grin, his head looked like a jack-a-lantern.

After introducing myself, I handed him Albertson's letter. He quickly read it and said, "Yes, I know. Bill called me yesterday. He thinks highly of you." I was encouraged, but only for a few seconds.

"We have a small editorial staff. We could use more people but it's all we can afford. We're on a very tight budget. If you want to work as an apprentice, we might consider you."

"I'm interested. What does it pay?"

There was that broad grin. "Nothing, I'm afraid. The only compensation is you might become a good journalist; that is, if you have the talent." He saw I was disappointed. "I'm sorry," he said, indicating the interview was over.

I hung on. "I'd like to work here," I said. "Can I work part-time?

He considered it. "Well, if you're interested, we can try it and see how it works out. Our busiest days are Tuesdays and Wednesdays. We've just gone to press. Come in next week at nine and see Alice. She'll put you to work. Here are a couple of back copies of our national edition you might look over."

My head was in a whirl as I left the office and stopped at Nedick's for a cup of coffee. What had I so impulsively agreed to? My store manager, as much as he liked me, couldn't let me take Tuesday and Wednesday off. It would mean that I'd have to give up my job. What would I live on? I thought of calling Palmer and telling him I couldn't accept.

In despair, I talked it over with Albertson. He listened quietly and then said, more to himself than to me, "It's not impossible." He telephoned Jerry Gaffner, one of the co-owners of Highland Dairies, and after a long conversation, he came back to me. "We've worked something out if you're willing to accept it." The deal was that I would be guaranteed two days a week at Highland Dairies as an "extra" on Fridays and Saturdays at seven dollars a day; Tuesdays and Wednesdays, I could work at *People's Press,* and if I could not get a hire on Mondays and Thursdays, I would be availble at union headquarters for picket duty or any other assignment. It was a crazy arrangement but I accepted. I'd have at least fourteen dollars a week income, sometimes more. At worst, It might mean cutting into my savings and stopping my allowance to Mama. I'd work it out.

Frank Palmer, I learned from Bill, was a crusader and gifted public speaker for progressive causes. He was not a member of the Party but was not afraid to share a platform with communist leaders. He was especially known for his exposés of powerful industrialists who hired gangs of thugs and scab herders to terrorize strikers. He had been an active member of the Colorado Typographical Union and felt strongly that the trade union movement needed a national newspaper if it were to provide leadership to the working class.

A couple of years back, he had started *People's Press* by convincing a small group of wealthy, socially-progressive individuals to supply the capital for his venture. He had a brilliant scheme for developing a weekly national labor newspaper with a chain of special editions in various cities across the country. Each issue would carry four or eight pages of national news and four of local news. With his extraordinary energy and salesmanship, Palmer succeeded in establishing editions in New York, Chicago, Newark, Akron, Pittsburgh, Toledo, Detroit and several other cities. The editors of these editions were, in fact, publishers. They were responsible for building up their circulation and gathering the news for their four pages, in return for which they could sell as many ads as they were able to and keep all the income. Mass subscriptions were solicited from local trade unions whose entire membership received a weekly mailed copy at the rate of "a nickel a month a member," the sales slogan that Palmer popularized. The same arrangement was accepted by several new national unions: the United Electrical, Radio and Machine Workers, the American Communications Association and the Agricultural and Farm Implement Workers Union. The national *People's Press* received all the subscription income and was able to increase its advertising lineage by offering the combined circulation of all of its editions.

For the first two months at *People's Press,* my duties were limited. Two or three times a day, I brought copy to the print shop and picked up galleys of proofs for the office. I brought lunch and a three o'clock refreshment for any of the editorial staff who requested it. I delivered copies of the paper to newsstands within a mile's radius and picked up the returns that had not been sold. But whenever I had some free time, I would watch the editors at work, listen to their comments, observe how they edited the news stories they sent to the printer. I had already taken out several books on journalism from the library and voraciously read them. My desire to become a newspaper reporter grew daily.

Finally, my day came. Ben Riskin, one of the editors who was to be my mentor, called me over and asked me to visit two bakery workers unions, Local 87 in Manhattan and Local 3 in Brooklyn. There were reports that negotiations between the two unions and the Master Bakers Association had broken down and a strike was imminent. I was to find out the latest developments by interviewing the union leaders. Flushed with excitement, I rushed to fulfill my first assignment as a labor reporter. I learned that the threatened strike had been averted at the eleventh hour by a settlement. I eagerly wrote down the terms of the contract, the names of the union negotiators and a statement from each of the union presidents. Laboriously, I typed out my notes into what I thought was a news story. When I showed it to Ben, he blue-penciled several phrases, inserted others, suggested how to dramatize the lead paragraph and ordered me to rewrite the story. I was thrilled when it appeared in the paper's New York edition as a three-inch, single-column item with a 12-point headline. I took home several copies of the paper and proudly showed my story to Mama, who bragged about me to the neighbors. I cut out the item and pasted it in a scrapbook for future stories.

Because the staff was so overworked, I found new opportunities to be helpful. I watched the daily newspapers for leads on labor stories, and Ben increasingly turned to me to cover them. In the course of several months, he introduced me to all of the skills needed to publish a newspaper. I was given practice in headline writing, proofreading, page layout and paste-up. I was allowed to spend time in the print shop watching the final page corrections before the paper went to press. Ben was a stern taskmaster and could be sharp with me when I made errors. I treasured his rare compliments.

As time passed, I found my fractured schedule intolerable. I'd wake up early, and it would be a few minutes before I figured out where I had to go or what I had to do. Was today the day I worked at Highland Dairies or was I due at union headquarters or at the newspaper? I finally decided I could no longer go on this way; I'd give Palmer an ultimatum: either he'd give me a full-time job with pay or else I'd quit. I figured I had made my work sufficiently indispensable to the newspaper so that I was in a good position to negotiate. It was risky, but I had to take the chance.

When I summoned up enough courage to approach Palmer with my request, he replied, "Let me think about it. I'll let you know my answer next week." Then he added something that almost shattered my hope: "You know we've got Katherine Beecher here working full-time without pay, and she's been very useful."

Beecher, as we called her, was a Smith College graduate from a wealthy Southern family who had become interested in unions and been recommended to Palmer, as I had been. Her work, at this point, was primarily in research and compiling newspaper clippings for possible rewriting by the editorial staff. She had never done any labor reporting, so I did not consider her a direct threat.

After several sleepless, agonizing nights, the day came when Palmer called me into his office. "You've made great progress since you've been here," he began. "Ben praises you highly. But I can't pay you a salary." Seeing the disappointment in my face, he continued, "But I've got a better proposition for you. I'm willing to give you a six-month trial as editor of the New York edition to replace Perry Sachs, who's leaving. Whatever you can sell in advertising will be yours.

The paper now carries ads worth thirty dollars a week, which you can use for salary and expenses. You'll have to submit four pages of local news on deadline and find time to sell subscriptions to unions. Do you think you can handle it?"

I was dumbfounded. I had not expected anything like this. I immediately said Yes, without a single question or reservation. I thanked him profusely. I would do my level best to justify his faith in me.

"Good," he said. "You can start with the Labor Day issue. That gives you three weeks to get settled into the job."

So I was to be an editor, in charge of my own newspaper! Not bad for a twenty-two-year-old kid!. That evening, I rushed home to tell Mama the good news. Her first reaction, after hugging me, was how much pay was I going to get. I had to explain that it depended on how much advertising I sold. She was unconvinced. *"Men kenn nisht essen fin editor,"* she exclaimed in Yiddish. ("One can't eat from being an editor.") I burst out laughing.

Labor Day 1936 was an opportunity to celebrate the National Labor Relations Act and the Social Security Act, both of which had been enacted by Congress the previous year. I worked night and day to develop feature articles that explained the content and significance of the two laws. I had no difficulty in getting the city's top labor leaders to make statements about the importance of this Labor Day and the favorable prospects for union organizing. I also wrote my first editorial in which I predicted that workers would take advantage of the new, historic labor legislation to join unions in unprecedented numbers.

In the weeks that followed, I tried to get as many local union stories as I could to fill the four pages of the New York edition. By now, I had become fairly well-informed about the city's major unions and their leaders, including the conservative, anti-communist ones in the construction industry. I was no longer shy or ill at ease about interviewing any of them. I paid particular attention to those unions that were potential subscribers. The union leaders I spoke to were very cooperative, since most of them had never been interviewed by reporters.

At this stage, most of the stories I published were detailed reports of local union activities: contract negotiations, strikes, union elections, legislative lobbying, meeting notices, testimonial dinners, conferences and obituaries. For the most part, the stories were boring for the general reader, but they contained useful information and, of course, union leaders and members were delighted to see their names in print. I had to deal with an undercurrent of suspicion that the paper was "pro-communist," so I was wary of running any story that might cause unpleasant controversy or an angry backlash that could result in unions cancelling their subscriptions. It was an enormous amount of work for a recently-tutored editor, but fortunately, I could rely on *Federated Press,* an indispensable mimeographed daily labor news service, to fill whatever gaps I had in the paper with news stories and features, and to liven up the pages with their photographs and cartoons.

The paper began to gain respectful attention from union leaders and active rank-and-filers because nowhere else could they get news of their activities. After a while, union leaders vied with each other to have their stories in the paper, and they were especially pleased when I printed their photographs. I soon learned how to exploit their vanity to gain additional unions as subscribers. I was especially proud of getting the new leaders of Plumbers Local 2, the union from which George Meany had gotten his start, to subscribe for their entire membership of nearly 4,000.

I became known as Scoop to scores of labor leaders, many of whom treated me indulgently, but some in the construction unions, I suspect, privately referred to me as the "Jew boy." I was frequently invited to union functions that provided me with free dinners and a chance to meet and become socially friendly with many local union officers.

I managed to spend some time in soliciting ads, and I was moderately successful by offering low rates. I also was able to negotiate barter deals with a typewriter company, an office furniture store and a few restaurants along Second Avenue. I allowed myself twenty dollars a week to enable me to cover my living expenses.

My connection with the West Side section of the Party vanished, and I did nothing to resurrect it. I had been told I was being transferred to a labor press unit, but I was not contacted and didn't try to find out why. My time was so completely taken up with the newspaper that even my social life was now virtually non-existent. It didn't matter. Palmer had given me a great opportunity and I was determined to make the most of it.

10. *My Work during the CIO Years*

The most spectacular and extraordinarily successful achievements in the history of the American labor movement occurred in a three-year period, 1936-1938, when I was a young labor reporter and editor. I was privileged to be involved in its high drama, both as witness and participant. It was during this time that under the leadership of United Mine Workers President John L. Lewis, the Congress of Industrial Organizations (CIO) came into existence and accomplished what had heretofore seemed impossible: the establishment of industrial unions in the auto, steel, rubber, textile, communications, meat packing and other mass production industries. Morever, the CIO welcomed into its ranks hundreds of thousands of unskilled workers, including immigrants, blacks and women, disregarding lines of color, sex and nationality.

The exciting events of those years provided a field day for *People's Press*, which used large type and banner headlines to describe them. We thrilled our readers with a vivid account of the first major CIO contract at U.S. Steel. We aroused widespread public indignation with our report on the "Memorial Day Massacre," describing how the Chicago police had shot down ten strikers and injured a hundred others as they demonstrated to unionize the Republic Steel Co. And, of course, we gave full play to the sitdown strike of auto workers in Flint, Mich.

There was one sensational story that *People's Press* in its national edition covered in greater detail than any other labor publication, thanks to Frank Palmer. Palmer had his own private connections with double informers—disreputable characters who spied on unions and supplied strikebreakers to defeat them, but who, for a price, were ready to provide information about the activities of Pinkerton, Burns and other labor spy agencies.

When Senator Robert LaFollette's Civil Liberties Committee issued its shocking revelations in December 1937 about the corporate practice of hiring labor spies from agencies specializing in industrial espionage, Palmer was able to provide additional details and fascinating insights from his own experience. It was mind-blowing to learn that a total of nearly 4,000 undercover agents had been hired to spy on union activities during the period 1933-37 by more than 2,000 of the most respected corporations in the United States. Even more sobering was the fact that stool pigeons had penetrated 90 unions, many of them becoming officers.

In one of our series on the labor spy racket by Palmer, I made a blooper of an error which earned me much ridicule and a furious dressing down by Palmer himself. We had run one-column pictures of a strikebreaker named Stinkfoot McVey, who looked like a thug, and a well-known New York labor leader, side by side, and their pictures had somehow been switched. I was the one who had okayed the page for the presses, and I was horrified when I saw the printed copy. Of course, there were immediate oral and written apologies (not to Stinkfoot) to the labor leader, fortunately a good-natured man, who treated it as a joke and forgave me. For years, the incident would be recalled with a chuckle by some of my friends in the labor press. It was an embarrassing lesson, but it taught me to check and double-check every photo in each issue to see that it matched with the caption below.

* * * * *

It was a happy coincidence that the CIO set up its regional headquarters at 1133 Broadway in Manhattan where we had our editorial offices. I quickly arranged to interview the CIO director, Allan Haywood, a United Mine Workers vice president, who was one of John L. Lewis's trusted lieutenants. Haywood was a short, sandy-haired, mild-mannered, middle-aged man who seemed miscast as a tough labor organizer. I became his sometime adviser since he knew nothing about the New York labor movement and had been told that I was highly qualified to provide him with detailed background about the city's unions and their leaders.

On any given day, the CIO's suite of offices was jammed with workers of various occupations eager to sign up, not with any particular union, but with the CIO. Those three letters had an incredible magic that amazed veteran union organizers. Frequently, the noisy crowd, mainly blue-collar workers, spilled out into the hallways and down the stairwell as they waited in line for their turn to apply. Harried secretaries worked feverishly to answer questions and process the applications, with constant interruptions by incoming phone calls. There were so many calls from workers asking to join the CIO, that overworked staff of organizers couldn't accommodate all of them. On several occasions, Haywood asked me to help out. I remember visiting a lower East Side boys' club and getting signed applications from about thirty workers employed in the manufacture of smoking pipes and cigaret holders. At other times, I met with groups of laundry workers, machinists, meat packers and chemical workers. Wherever I went, I made sure to bring along a batch of my newspapers for distribution.

One of the remarkable things about the CIO was that it gave birth to a new generation of militant labor leaders who were a far cry from the staid, tradition-encrusted AFL hierarchy. It was during this period that a number of young union officers got their start, becoming nationally prominent in later years. I can remember Leon Davis as president of Local 1199 when it was a small local of pharmacists before he helped to build it into a militant union of a hundred thousand hospital and health care workers. And David Livingston, then a 20-year-old organizer of wholesale dry goods workers, who eventually became president of District 65, nationally recognized as an important progressive force in the labor movement. In those early years, both unions were subscribers to the *Trade Union Record* and I would run weekly stories about their organizing activities.

In contrast to the fierce anti-communist attitude of the AFL's leadership, John L. Lewis welcomed the support of communists because he realized that the best of them were skilled organizers who were totally committed to building the CIO. It was at Haywood's office that I first saw and met Gus Hall, then a steel workers organizer from Ohio, later to become the diehard general secretary of the Communist Party. In those early days of the CIO, Party members began to occupy positions of leadership in the auto, steel, transportion, maritime, communications, electrical and other unions without being red-baited by Lewis or his lieutenants. I was convinced that Haywood strongly suspected that I was a communist, but it did not affect our friendly relationship.

* * * * *

By late 1938, *People's Press* was compelled to cease publication because unions that had subscribed to it were now big and strong enough to want their own publication. A new publishing company, Trade Union Service, was formed which provided printing and editorial facilities to unions wishing to publish their own newspapers. T.U.S.'s clients now included the CIO electrical, furniture, transport and communications international unions and some of their local affiliates, as well as AFL unions of machinists, teamsters and hotel and restaurant workers. In the transformation, the New York edition of *People's Press* became two independent weekly publications: *Trade Union Record,* which primarily served new CIO local unions, and the *Building Trades Union Press,* devoted to craft workers in the construction industry. I was editor of both.

Even before the change, I had hired two young, inexperienced assistants who were willing to work for as little as ten dollars a week—when I could pay them—and to endure incredibly long hours of work as part of their apprenticeship.

Howie Freeman was a Columbia University graduate, a Greek major, who turned out to have a natural talent for news writing. He was a sweet, good-natured guy, the son of a well-to-do doctor, and he didn't mind going without pay or even lending me money when I was short. He had a pixie sense of humor that was refreshing. He was a heavy cigaret chain-smoker, but I could not complain because I constantly smoked a pipe. People visiting our office in the late afternoon would remark that it smelled like a zoo.

The other apprentice was Herman Leder, completely unlike Howie. He had been a metal polisher in a machine shop, had never attended college and had no samples of his writing to show me. I don't know why I hired him; probably because I was impressed with his dogged determination and, remembering my own experience, I thought he deserved at least a trial. He was willing to take on any assignment, no matter how onerous, and rewrite a story several times until he got it right. He was so eager to work on a labor paper that he didn't mind the payless weeks. He was humorless and was often the butt of Howie's verbal jokes, but he kept working tenaciously and I marveled at his progress. In a few weeks, he was able to cover a list of unions I gave him and to write acceptable stories about their routine activities. The special quality I appreciated in Herman was his absolute reliability. He was always on time and carried out even the most tedious chores without a word of complaint.

I also hired an advertising representative, Alex Smith, a man who walked into our office and simply asked for the job. He told me he had been earning $75 a week as an ad salesman in New Jersey, but that he wanted to work for a labor publication. He didn't seem to be put off when I said we were running our papers on a shoestring and couldn't pay him a drawing account. Since we had nothing to lose, I hired him on the spot without checking his references. It proved to be a wise decision.

Smitty was bald, bespectacled and considerably older than me. Soft-spoken and reserved, he was not at all like the kind of hard-sell, high-pressure salesman I thought we needed. It took him about three months before he began selling fairly large display ads to unionized clothing manufacturers, department stores and restaurants. At his suggestion, we started a theater page, and we began to get ads from Radio City, the Roxy and some off-Broadway theaters. Howie and I became movie and theater critics under assumed names, and the free tickets we got provided our entertainment.

Our biggest advertising success was linked to the opening of the New York World's Fair on April 30, 1939. For nearly a year, our weekly paper, *Building Trades Union Press,* had been running lists of construction contracts being let at the Fair grounds. This was valuable information for building trades unions desiring to organize those jobs and for their members seeking work. It was a popular feature and served to increase our circulation substantially.

About a month before the Fair's opening, we began to prepare a special commemorative edition. Leaders of the New York City Building and Construction Trades Council provided us with laudatory statements about the Fair (some of which we wrote for them), and we also included comments from unionized construction firms. Our center spread carried photographs of carpenters, electricians, plumbers, painters and other union craftsmen working on various national pavilions. We included feature articles about the history of former world expositions and several pages of interesting data about the Fair's unusual spectacles.

In the meantime, Smitty and two other salesmen whom he hired temporarily brought in more than three times the ad lineage that we had ever published. These consisted mainly of good-will display advertisements from unions and some of the city's major construction firms.

On the day before the Fair's opening, the men who had worked on the exposition's projects were honored in a special ceremony, at which we took the liberty of distributing thousands of copies of our paper to a huge crowd of spectators. I was invited to march with a contingent of construction workers in the parade which preceded the Fair's opening. President Roosevelt and Mayor Fiorello LaGuardia addressed the crowd, estimated at one million, but I can't remember what they said. People were not interested in speeches; there were too many exciting exhibits commanding their attention. I do recall braving long lines to visit two public favorites, the Soviet Pavilion and the General Motors' "Futurama." At the end of an exhausting day, I had dinner at the Finnish Pavilion with two officers of the Painters Union, eating reindeer steak, drinking aquavit and listening to Sibelius's *Finlandia.*

The World's Fair, in addition to being billed as the "greatest exposition of all time," also marked a turning point in our fortunes. From then on, I was able to pay myself and the staff $25 a week—and without missing a payday.

* * * * *

To cut down on our living expenses, the four of us—Howie, Herman, Smitty and me—a strange quartet—moved into a four-room apartment in a run-down building on West 18th Street, not too far from our office. Our work schedule was insane and required the energy and endurance of young men like us in their early twenties with no family responsibilities. Smitty, though older, was unmarried.

On Mondays, we would start work after a breakfast of orange drink, coffee and a doughnut, price ten cents, at Nedick's. Between nine and ten, I'd go through my card file of about 150 local unions, dividing assignments among the three of us. We'd each be on the phone until noon, getting as many news items as we could and following up leads from the week before. Herman would then go to a nearby coffee shop and get us a tuna fish or ham sandwich and coffee for our lunch break, after which we would either resume our calls or go out on stories that required direct reporting. At six o'clock, we'd leave for dinner at the coffee shop (sometimes we ate at a good restaurant on a "due bill" of one of our advertisers), and from seven to nine or ten at night, we'd write our stories, and I would lay out a few of the inside pages.

On Tuesday, the routine would be repeated and, almost without fail, we would find, toward midnight, that we were short of copy to fill the pages. That meant we'd have to work through the night. Wearily, I'd begin polishing the editorial which I had drafted earlier that evening. Whenever possible, I tried to use the same editorial for both papers, but frequently, I had to write separate pieces. During the night, we would send Herman out to get coffee two or three times (and even to Times Square when I ran out of pipe tobacco and could not work without a smoke), and we took turns catnapping on our one battered couch or the floor. By nine in the morning, our work was still not done, but we had three hours before the Wednesday noon deadline when we had to submit final copy to the printers. Bleary- eyed and fuzzy-brained, we would hurry to the print shop on schedule and by five in the afternoon, we had put the paper to bed.

Somehow, we staggered home (the print shop was only a few blocks from where we lived) and each of us flopped into bed, barely able to undress. We'd wake up about midnight, raid the refrigerator (it never offered much) and go back to sleep until noon the next day.

On Friday, we were back in the office, phoning union officials for news or else rewriting items from the daily papers. We quit work at five. In the evening, we usually went to a movie and treated ourselves to a good dinner. Saturdays, we worked only until noon and took Sunday off. That's when I went to Brooklyn to see my family.

We followed the same schedule month after month, vowing to improve it, but never doing so. We led a monastic life with almost no social contact with other people. We functioned as a collective, completely dedicated to our mission. As time passed, we became more proficient at our jobs. By the end of 1939, I probably knew more about what was going on in the New York labor movement than any of my contemporaries.

11. *Covering International Crises*

Starting with the Spanish Civil War in 1936 through America's involvement in World War II, our two labor papers provided our readers with summary reports and occasional analytical features about the various international developments in those crisis-filled years. Because many of the events were charged with controversy, we faced difficulties in deciding how to present them. (If we had chosen not to publish any foreign news and stuck to narrow labor coverage, I don't think there would have been much objection from most union leaders.)

On the one hand, we had to exercise caution about not antagonizing conservative union officers who had the power to cancel the subscriptions of their entire membership. On the other hand, we felt impelled to present the progressive, though minority point of view on foreign policy issues, especially when they impinged on the well-being of working people.

After much thought, we figured out a way to resolve the dilemma. We created—and promoted—a letters column, which we called "The Reader Takes the Floor." And we also developed a new column, "Spotlight on the Issues," which scrupulously and even-handedly presented both sides of a controversial issue.

Through the letters column, we were able to spark debate on such issues as military aid to the Spanish loyalists; Chamberlain's appeasement of Hitler at Munich; the Hitler-Stalin non-aggression pact; the Soviet invasion of Finland; U.S. sale of war materiel to England; Congressional approval of the military draft, and other crises that seemed to develop week by week. When the comments on any important domestic or foreign affairs issue seemed to be lagging, we would concoct our own provocative letters, signed by "Disgusted Plumber," "America Firster" or "Better Red Than Dead" to stimulate responses, including an occasional one that strongly disagreed with our editorials. The letters column proved to be the most popular feature in the paper and, in some weeks, filled an entire tabloid page.

The "Spotlight" column was written alternately by Howie and me under the pseudonym, Jerry Goldby. We'd carefully deliberate how to write the column, especially on the more controversial issues, and it might require several drafts before we were both satisfied.

We were not always successful in pursuing this strategy. Occasionally, we received phone calls and letters denouncing us, often in foul language, as apologists for

World Communism. Several locals in the building trades threatened to cancel their subscriptions and in one depressing week, two large locals did. We also had to deal with a few angry demands that we fire Goldby. We were heartened when several readers rushed to Goldby's defense. If we had to, we were prepared to "fire" Goldby and "hire" another fictitious columnist who would arouse less criticism.

The column was better received when it presented both sides of controversial domestic issues: FDR's decision to run for a third term; the advisability of a no-strike pledge by unions; the need for AFL-CIO unity, and other talked-about topics of the day.

The toughest issue we had to deal with was the Nazi-Soviet non-aggression pact of 1939. To ordinary workers, there was not much to explain: it was an open-and-shut case; the two dictators, Hitler and Stalin, had worked out a deal to give the Nazis a free hand to conquer England and France and eventually take on the United States. Apologists for the Soviet position explained the pact as a defensive measure on the part of the Kremlin to counteract a British-French plot, hatched at Munich, to entice Hitler into a war against the U.S.S.R. They could also point to the historic record that showed the Soviet's strong, consistent advocacy of collective security at the League of Nations and thereafter.

The Soviet justification remained unconvincing within the labor movement. Despite the Communist Party's strenuous efforts, it could not find a single union leader who was willing to publicly defend the non-aggression agreement. In fact, the Nazi-Soviet pact became a hot issue in many local union elections.

Left-wing labor leaders, no matter how competent or respected, risked defeat in their bid for reelection unless they denounced the pact, which had become the red-baiting litmus test on whether they were or were not members of the Communist Party. Some left-wing union leaders denounced the Party, either for opportunistic reasons—to save their jobs—or because they strongly disagreed with its unquestioning loyalty toward the Soviet Union.

Since nearly all communist labor leaders had kept their Party affiliation secret (the Party had long ago ceased to issue membership cards) it was not hard for them to resign quietly or merely drift away.

* * * * *

Although Americans were sympathetic to the Allies when Hitler's panzer divisions stormed into Poland in 1939, the mood in the United States was strongly isolationist: our people were determined not to be dragged into another war on European soil. Memories of World War I were revived, with detailed accounts purporting to show how the munitions makers, the "Merchants of Death," had maneuvered the American people into the war for their private profit. The isolationist spirit was stoked by the America First Committee, headed by the popular hero, Charles Lindbergh. Its leadership included two progressive U.S. senators, George Norris (Nebraska) and Burton K. Wheeler (Montana), whose pro-labor records had gained them respect and influence in the trade union movement.

Early in 1940, there was a period called "the phony war," because fighting in Western Europe was at a standstill and the question was whether Hitler's next move would be against the Russians or the British. I remember being approached by a Lindbergh emissary asking whether I would take on the job of director of a labor division that was being formed by the America First Committee to organize the anti-war effort among the nation's trade unionists. I had no hesitation in turning down the offer; while at that point I was opposed to American entry into the war, I could not work for an organization that had the backing of fascist groups, both in the U.S. and abroad.

In retrospect, the American people were caught between two contradictory impulses: to want Hitler defeated and to stay out of war. After each defeat of the Allies by the Nazis in Europe and by Japan in Asia, it became less likely that the U.S. could stay out of the war. The speedy collapse of French armies during the Nazi *blitzkrieg,* the fall of Paris on June 15, 1940 and the relentless bombing of England that began in September marked a turning point in the attitude of many Americans, who now realized the growing danger of a world dominated by the Berlin-Rome-Tokyo axis. My own views had moved in that direction too.

Hitler's invasion of the Soviet Union on June 22, 1941, a gamble to seize control of the entire European continent and remove a potential military threat from the Russians, changed the character of the war. The western democracies and the Soviet communist regime were now allies with the strategic possibility of crushing the Nazi military machine in a continent-wide pincer attack from two fronts. For some Americans, the new situation served as yet another good reason for staying out of the war: Let the Nazis and communists bleed each other to death; the U.S., by staying on the sidelines and preserving its strength, could then "pick up the pieces." The American Communist Party responded to the Nazi attack on the Soviet Union by immediately abandoning its opposition to the "imperialist war" and becoming aggressively interventionist.

While anti-war forces continued to speak out, it was becoming clear that it was only a matter of time before the United States would join the war on the side of the Allies. The Japanese settled that question when on December 7, 1941, they unleashed their bombs on the U.S. naval base at Pearl Harbor in Hawaii.

Before the end of the following year, I and many of my labor editor colleagues were to become direct participants in that conflict as we were called up for military service.

12. Defending Unions Under Attack

After the passage of the military draft, the White House used every means at its disposal to persuade the major steel, aircraft and oil corporations to increase their output by offering them subsidies, loans, tax rebates and, in some cases, whole factories, including equipment and supplies. The companies put hefty price tags on the war material that was shipped to England under the "cash and carry" law passed by Congress. U.S. Steel increased its profits during 1940 by more than 1500 percent over the preceding year, and other steel companies, as well as aircraft builders, were also reporting spectacular gains. The depression was finally ending.

The nation's giant corporations, now considerably stronger than they had been a few years back, were openly disregarding basic labor legislation, confident that the Roosevelt administration would overlook their transgressions because their production was urgently needed.

On October 11, 1940, I initiated a petition of protest to President Roosevelt calling his attention to brazen corporate violations of such federal labor laws as the National Labor Relations Act and the Fair Labor Standards Act. In two weeks, my staff and I had collected the signatures of 721 New York union leaders. Stories about our petition campaign appeared in *The New York Times* and the *Daily Worker,* mentioning that it was sponsored by the two labor papers I edited: *Trade Union Record* and *Building Trades Union Press.*

The petition urged the President to issue an "executive order directing that all contracts for government purchases contain a stipulation that the contractor shall not be in violation of any provision of federal labor legislation." The list of unions whose officers had endorsed the petition was impressive and demonstrated the broad support that I and my publications had in the New York labor movement. Here is a list of some of the 84 unions represented on the petition:

Architects, asbestos workers, bakers, brewers, bookbinders. bottlers, bricklayers, brush makers, candy workers, carpenters, cement and concrete workers, derrickmen, electricians, hodcarriers, hotel workers, iron workers, lathers, lithographers, machinists, meat cutters, painters, paper workers, plasterers, printing pressmen, roofers, sandhogs, sheet metal workers, sign writers, soft-drink workers, teachers, teamsters, theatrical technicians, taxi drivers, and wine and liquor workers.

In a letter that accompanied the petition we mailed to President Roosevelt, barely a week before the crucial 1940 election, I wrote, in part:

"It is indeed shocking to see corporations which refuse to abide by the labor laws of the United States reaping the benefits of government contracts, whereas trade unions, whose aim is to improve the living standards of working people, are subjected to prosecution and indictments under a distorted interpretation of the Sherman Anti-Trust Law."

I was also involved with many unions in resisting efforts by corporate lobbyists to emasculate the National Labor Relations Act (commonly referred to as the Wagner Labor Act after its prime sponsor, Senator Robert Wagner). Big Business was charging that the law was unfair to industry and that unions had to be curbed in the interest of national defense. They wanted provisions to eliminate the closed shop and the right to strike; they sought a series of restrictions on union activities that would nullify their organizing efforts. Their prime target was to get rid of communists in unions—a group they defined in broad terms—who, they said, were disrupting the economy by politically-motivated strikes and who represented a "fifth column" that imperiled the nation's security.

The CIO reacted with alarm to what some labor leaders called a "death threat." It summoned its members throughout the country to put pressure on Congress against amendments to the Wagner Act, using demonstrations, petitions, lobbying delegations to Washington and media advertising. The AFL Executive Council, while protesting the major amendments sought by employer groups, was pleased with the anti-communist proposal, since they saw its effect as weakening their CIO rival.

To help unions in their defense of the Wagner Act, we printed a special four-page edition (a practice we sometimes followed in other critical situations) and distributed thousands of extra copies at union meetings and public demonstrations. At this time, we enlarged our mailing list to include nearly a thousand officials of construction unions across the country as a first step in our plan to turn the *Building Trades Union Press* into a national weekly.

It was not easy to counteract the high-priced professional lobbyists of the National Association of Manufacturers and the U.S. Chamber of Commerce, but the unions were sufficiently aroused to meet the challenge. We tried to be helpful by running a series of articles on the Wagner Act, seeking to refute every argument advanced by the employer groups and their allies in Congress and keeping our union subscribers abreast of important developments.

The Roosevelt administration was ambivalent about the legislation. On the one hand, it regarded the anti-labor amendments as a means to eliminate strikes and other potentially disruptive behavior on the part of unions. On the other hand, it needed labor cooperation and was reluctant to evoke the hostility of union leaders. As it turned out, FDR was able to get what he wanted, because Congress wisely refrained from enacting the amendments but found other means to restrict undesirable union activity. The employer offensive against the Wagner Labor Act was to be renewed successfully after the war in 1947 with passage of the Taft-Hartley Act.

The other critical battle—this one *within* the ranks of labor—developed during the election campaign of 1940, when Roosevelt decided to run for an unprecedented third term. There were conflicting responses to his nomination from the labor movement. A great many unions were grateful to Roosevelt for the labor and social laws enacted during his two terms as President and were fearful that a Republican administration might undo them. But others felt certain that if given a third term, he would take the country into a war they opposed; all the hard won gains of unions would be destroyed in the interest of the war effort; corporations would profiteer while workers would suffer a reduction in their living standards. I shared the same anxieties but could see no alternative to Roosevelt in the absence of a national labor party.

If the Republican candidate, Wendell Willkie, had come out forcefully for non-involvement in the war in Europe, he might possibly have defeated Roosevelt. However, Willkie was an internationalist who espoused a "One World" philosophy and was therefore no great rallying point for the anti-war forces. He had supported, not denounced, the military draft. And pro-FDR advocates made much of the fact that Willkie was the chief executive of a utility company, Commonwealth and Southern, deriding him as "Wall Street's barefoot boy," who would undoubtedly favor Big Business if elected President.

The AFL at its October convention voted to stay neutral, although a number of state and city affiliates took sides in favor of or opposed to a third term for Roosevelt. It was in the CIO that serious divisions on the third term issue occurred. On one side was John L Lewis, the CIO president, who opposed FDR's reelection and who had the support of many international unions and state and city labor councils, particularly those in which left-wing unionists were in the leadership or exercised important influence. On the other side was Sidney Hillman, president of the Amalgamated Clothing Workers, who had been appointed by Roosevelt as labor's representative on the National Defense Advisory Commission and who endorsed FDR's third-term nomination. Hillman had the support of the textile, auto, steel and rubber unions and, of course, the clothing workers. Skirmishes between the two groups took place at various union conventions, reflecting a serious split within the CIO. The stormiest and most shameful example of the Lewis-Hillman feud was displayed at the Rochester convention of the New York State CIO on September 20-21, 1940, a spectacle that I was there to report on for my newspapers.

The Hillman forces, in control of the credentials committee, realized they were outnumbered, so they resorted to the crude tactic of refusing to recognize 91 delegates from unions opposed to a Roosevelt third term while seating more than 100 recently-affiliated Clothing Workers delegates whose credentials were questionable. The credentials committee refused to budge or entertain a compromise. After a night of wrangling, the pro-Lewis forces walked out of the convention, leaving the pro-Hillman delegates to endorse FDR for a third term.

It appeared that the conflict over this issue would tear the CIO apart, but cooler heads among the international unions succeeded in their strenuous efforts to maintain labor unity. To avoid internal dissension, the United Electrical, Radio & Machine Workers, which had previously voted 300 to 1 at its annual convention against a third term for Roosevelt, decided a few weeks later to let each local union make its own decision on the issue. It was becoming clear that the public mood was shifting in favor of FDR.

On October 25, less than two weeks before the election, Lewis, in a radio address carried by more than 350 stations of the three major networks, launched his thunderbolt. "I think the reelection of President Roosevelt for a third term would be a national evil of the first magnitude. He no longer hears the cries of the people. I think that the election of Mr. Wendell Willkie is imperative in relation to the country's needs. I commend him to the men and women of labor."

To add steely emphasis to his declaration of opposition to Roosevelt, Lewis said: "If he is, therefore, elected, it will mean that the members of the Congress of Industrial Organizations have rejected my advice and recommendation. I will accept the result as being the equivalent of no confidence and will retire as president of the Congress of Industrial Organizations in November."

Like many others, I overestimated the effect of Lewis's bombshell. It did not split the ranks of labor. A majority of union members, including the vast number who idolized Lewis, could not bring themselves to vote for Willkie. Had there been a national labor party or a pro-labor candidate for President, the speech might have swayed far more union members than it did. In the end, Roosevelt received 54 percent of the vote, including mine.

Lewis, true to his word, resigned the presidency of the CIO despite strong appeals by influential labor leaders for him to stay on. Philip Murray, another Mine Workers leader and a trusted Lewis lieutenant, was elected to head the CIO.

* * * * *

The year 1941 was a turbulent one for the trade union movement. On the bright side, unemployment was reduced dramatically; between April 1940 and December 1941, the number of jobless decreased from 8.8 million to 3.8 million. The steady improvement in the labor market was accompanied by higher wages. Average weekly earnings rose from $29.88 to $36.62. Average weekly hours also increased, with the reappearance of overtime, from 39.2 in 1940 to 42.8 by December 1941.

The nation's major corporations were determined to prevent unions from organizing the vast influx of workers into industry. They stubbornly refused to extend union recognition, disregarded union wage demands and attacked the closed shop as un-American. They cloaked their anti-labor attacks in the guise of patriotism: they were fighting unions in the interest of national defense. And they flouted basic labor laws, confident that the government was on their side and they could get away with it. While wages had increased, the cost of living had risen even higher, the result of inflationary pressures and outrageous profiteering.

Unable to gain what they considered as justified wage increases, unions everywhere resorted to strikes. Work stoppages occurred in the auto industry, in shipyards, building trades, steel, coal, textiles and retail trades. The number of strikes in 1941 reached nearly 4,300, a higher total than in any previous year except 1937. More than two million workers, representing about eight percent of the nation's work force, were involved in these struggles.

Because many of these strikes adversely affected the national defense program, the federal government made strong efforts to prevent them. In March 1941, Roosevelt created a National Defense Mediation Board, representing management, labor and the public, with the right to intervene and press for settlements in labor-management disputes in defense industries. In instances when the Mediation Board failed, the government showed it was prepared to use force to prevent any disruption of war production.

In June 1941, the War Department called out 3,500 soldiers to break a strike at the North American aviation plant at Inglewood, California, The 9,000 strikers had been warned that if they did not return to work, they could be drafted into the army. In another case, the Navy Department seized the Federal Shipbuilding and Dry Dock Company at Kearny, New Jersey in a labor-management dispute that was about to erupt in a strike.

During 1941, public sentiment turned against unions, especially after the costly strike of Lewis's 250,000 coal miners. Anti-labor newspapers and employers constantly repeated their charge that the unions were putting their own selfish interests above national defense, and that a number of strikes were inspired by communists. The patriotism of workers who went on strike was put into question. Some sixteen states in the South and Southwest passed anti-labor laws and there were about thirty bills in Congress to outlaw all strikes in defense industries and to curb the power of unions. Despite strong protests from both the AFL and CIO, it appeared likely that anti-labor legislation would be enacted with public approval. The Japanese attack on Pearl Harbor changed the situation; Congress had more immediate concerns.

My newspapers were caught up in the strike wave as it developed in the New York area. I and my staff were frequently called upon by many of the smaller unions that needed help in their effort to win public sympathy for their strikes or at least to soften public resentment. We became advisers and publicists for a number of unions, including machinists, painters, butchers, department store workers, bakers, carpenters, pharmacists and others. We performed these various services without charge, but they served to reinforce the loyalty of these unions to our newspapers.

We became involved not only in strikes but also in the defense of the civil rights of unions. During the 1940-1941 Rapp-Coudert committee witch-hunts against members of the New York teachers union, we conferred frequently with Dr. Bella Dodd, the union's legislative representative, on how to persuade AFL and CIO unions to protest the committee's attempts to seize the union's membership records and to blacklist teachers it considered subversive. We were also called in by Cafeteria

Workers Local 302 to help prevent District Attorney Thomas Dewey, later to become New York governor, from destroying the union while prosecuting several of its officers, who had been indicted for racketeering.

As the federal government moved closer to a war footing, unions were urged to exercise self-restraint in their dealings with employers, no matter how serious their complaints. And because the cooperation of Big Business was needed to increase war production, the government winked at corporate violations of labor laws or evidence of outrageous profiteering. It looked like unions were going to be the first casualties of the U.S. war effort.

13. A Racket-Run Labor Convention

Of all the extra assignments I took on for unions, the most exciting one came in 1941. It involved the International Hod Carriers, Building and Common Laborers Union of America, a labor organization riddled with racketeers and gangsters operating out of Chicago and tied to the Capone mob. The last convention had been held thirty years ago, in 1911, followed by the apparent murder of the union president. A shadowy, non-elected executive board had then assumed the authority to hand-pick the international union president, their latest appointee being Joseph V. Moreschi, a Chicago union leader with racketeering connections. They had figured out a clever stratagem to avoid the expense and annoyance of holding regular conventions. Every five years the international union polled its members to find out if they wanted a convention. The final tally always showed they didn't, according to Moreschi and his henchmen who counted the votes. Thus, Moreschi was able to remain as president without ever having to stand for election.

Thanks to Westbrook Pegler, the syndicated anti-union columnist of the New York *World Telegram*, who exposed their criminal activities in a long series of columns, the officers of the international union felt compelled to hold an honest referendum of their members on March 20, 1941 on the question, "Should a convention be called this year?" This time, not surprisingly, the vote was 100,457 in favor and only 3,992 against.

The officers of New York's subway tunnel workers union, Local 147, an affiliate of the Laborers, who had been battling the mobsters trying to take over their labor organization, asked Hy Glickstein, their attorney, and me to accompany them to the convention in St. Louis, scheduled to start on September 15, 1941. They thought we could help organize the delegates to establish a democratic international union.

When we arrived in St. Louis several days before the opening of the convention, we had already made contact with progressive delegates from Minnesota, Wisconsin and California and a scattering of people from local unions in other states. That weekend, we called a meeting at our hotel, attended by about 50 delegates, at which we agreed on a program of democratic reform, giving top priority to a resolution for a biennial convention. Since this was the first convention that any of our delegates had ever attended, we spent several hours discussing tactics and parliamentary procedure. I called a press conference explaining our program, and the next day, the *St. Louis Post Dispatch* carried a front-page story that exaggerated our strength and indicated that Local 147 president Brian Feeney would be challenging Moreschi, the incumbent, for the presidency of the international union.

On the opening day, more than two thousand delegates gathered in the city's Municipal Auditorium. On a platform overlooking the auditorium sat the officers of the international union and a battery of lawyers who hovered around Moreschi, advising him on parliamentary tactics to squelch his opponents. I sat at the press table, while Glickstein was in the balcony reserved for visitors.

The first clash came over the report of the rules committee, which had engineered a constitutional recommendation that election of officers take place before any action on the resolutions. In the brief debate, Moreschi gave the floor to his hand-picked supporters, but would not recognize any known opposition speakers. Their tactic was obvious: if Moreschi could get elected before a strong opposition candidate could emerge, then he would be able to deal with the many substantive issues on his terms. The rules committee report, which had been submitted orally, was approved without most of the delegates knowing what they were voting for.

At our caucus meeting that night, we agreed that the report of the rules committee had to be challenged, and we worked out several points of attack. I spent an hour or more coaching Feeney on the speech he was to make in calling for reconsideration of the committee's report. Feeney, who was more than six feet tall and powerfully built, a sandy-haired, freckle-faced giant of a man, was greatly admired by his members for his honesty and courage in fighting the gangsters who were trying to seize control of his union, but he was inexperienced in the fine points of parliamentary procedure. We devised a plan that would give him a signal when he should ask to speak: it was to be the moment I stood up at the press table and Glickstein, sitting in the balcony, took off his jacket. Feeney was to leap up and in a loud voice, ask for the floor.

The next morning, at the agreed upon signal. Feeney rose and shouted for the floor, ready to launch into his speech. Moreschi, however, recognized a delegate from Minneapolis who, as it turned out, was making the very points on which we had coached Feeney. Meanwhile, Feeney kept insisting on his right to speak, calling Moreschi a Hitler, a Nazi and a bastard. When he refused to shut up, six sergeants-at-arms, each as tall and as powerful as Feeney, lifted him up and carried him kicking and yelling out of the auditorium.

The opposition to the rules committee report was greater than we had anticipated. Our speakers as well as several not part of our caucus were making all the objections to the report that we had suggested, and getting considerable applause. Although the committee's report was upheld, the delegates in opposition gathered about 40 percent of the voice vote, according to the reporters at the press table.

The next day, debate broke out on the recommendation of the constitution committee that officers be elected to a five-year term. Our delegates spoke for a two-year term, with officers to be elected at a biennial convention. In reply to

Morsechi's supporters, they pointed out that the AFL held conventions annually, as did many international unions. Judging from the applause given the speakers, we seemed to have gained the support of about half of the delegates. When Moreschi ordered a voice vote on the two-year term amendment, it appeared that the result was too close to call. Instead of asking for a standing vote, Moreschi, after listening to the advice of his lawyers, called a fifteen-minute recess. During the recess, his staff of tough, appointed international representatives toured the tables, warning the delegates that if they voted with the "communists," they'd lose their jobs and possibly worse. Some were promised high-paying positions with the international union if they voted right.

The intimidation worked. When the voice vote was taken, we had clearly lost, receiving no more than about a third of the votes. Shortly after, Moreschi was nominated for the presidency without opposition and elected by acclamation after a thirty-minute demonstration, during which the jubilant Moreschi forces taunted our delegates to join their snake dance around the convention hall.

With the election of Moreschi and his team of officers, the proposals for democratic reform presented by our delegates were easily defeated. So brazen were the Moreschi forces that they proposed to have a convention every five years but only if the membership approved it by a referendum vote *the very procedure by which they had avoided a convention for the previous thirty years.*

During the convention, both Glickstein and I received anonymous threats from what we assumed were Moreschi's hoodlums. Hy was denounced by name during the debate on the resolutions and I, too, was referred to as the "man in the black suit at the press table."

Frankly, I was scared. I didn't want to be maimed or killed by a Chicago gangster. Feeney saw to it that we had a bodyguard whenever we left our hotel. We could call him on the phone if we sensed trouble. We had no need to call. Moreschi had won the day, so what would he gain by terrorizing us?

When the convention was finally over, we attended a dinner with about a dozen delegates, who arranged to keep in touch with each other and vowed to continue their fight for a democratic union. I lost contact with them but remained a good friend of Feeney. Even though the union did hold a convention every five years thereafter, the opposition to Moreschi's corrupt, undemocratic regime never again attained the strength displayed at the 1941 event. Moreschi remained as president for another 27 years, retiring in 1968.

Before we left St. Louis, Hy and I, still tense and exhausted, decided to relax at a baseball game between the Cardinals and the Brooklyn Dodgers. By the fifth inning, St. Louis was six runs ahead of the Dodgers. It was time to get out of town.

* * * * *

As editor of the *Building Trades Union Press,* I was well aware that many of the craft unions were led by corrupt officials who regularly shook down construction contractors and shared their graft with racketeers, who acted as "enforcers."

Payoffs by contractors to union officials were so prevalent that it was hardly considered a crime. "This is the cost of doing business in a big city," employers would say with a shrug. They knew that their construction job could be shut down by a strike or even wrecked if they didn't submit to the payoffs. Once in a while, a union official was arrested and jailed for bribery, but it did not stop the practice.

One of the strangest stories I came across concerned the business manager of a cement masons local union. He was arrested one day when it was found that he had defrauded the widows of his members of the mortuary benefits to which they were entitled. The official had been pocketing the dues of these individuals and witholding their per capita payments to the international union. As a result, when the widows applied for benefits, they were turned down because there were no membership records of their deceased spouses at the international union headquarters. The official was sentenced to three years in jail and had to pay a huge fine. When he came out of prison, he ran for the top union office. He was elected to his old job as business manager by a better than two to one margin!

When I asked a union member to explain the vote, he said, "It's no mystery. We elected an honest guy after Tommy went to jail. He couldn't do anything for us; he didn't have the connections. Tommy's back and he'll get what's coming to us. He's a savvy guy." After two years on the job, good old Tommy was arrested once again, for attempted embezzlement of the union treasury.

It would be unrealistic to believe that among the nation's approximately 300,000 union officers there wouldn't be some who would betray their trust and commit criminal acts for personal advantage. But I had a strong hunch that, contrary to the impression created by the media, union leaders commit fewer financial crimes and for smaller amounts than business men, politicians, lawyers, bankers, stockbrokers and any other group that is subject to the temptation of available money and power.

Years later, my theory was confirmed by a report of the U.S. Justice Department. It reviewed 350,000 financial reports from 50,000 labor organizations over a five-year period (1979-1983) and it noted only 261 convictions of union officers, a rate of 0.07 percent. Two-thirds of those convicted for embezzlement stole sums no greater than $10,000 and, in some cases, less than $1,000. And according to the Surety Corporation of America, a major bonding agency, there was a significantly lower rate of embezzlement among union officers than among bankers, business executives and government officials.

* * * * *

As I enlarged my knowledge of the labor movement, I grew troubled by a dilemma which I could not satisfactorily resolve. On the one hand, I strongly believed in unions. I regarded them as greatly needed organizations whose basic mission was to improve the living standards of working people and protect them against an exploitative capitalist class. As a labor editor, I defended unions wherever and whenever they were under attack, using my skills and experience in their behalf. I unequivocally urged workers to join labor organizations, citing the many advantages of holding a union card.

On the other hand, I was fully aware of the many instances of corruption and undemocratic practices that plagued some unions. I probably knew more about what was wrong with the labor movement than most of its critics, the well-meaning ones and those, like Pegler, who were bent on destroying unions. However, if I was so committed a unionist, why did I remain silent about the abuses against the rank-and-file in some of the unions my newspaper served? Why hadn't I reported the real story of what had happened at the laborers' convention? It was a fact that I never criticized any union official, even when I knew he had committed serious errors or acted unfairly toward his membership. I never gave space to a candidate who was challenging an incumbent officer of a union that subscribed to my paper. I took pains to omit stories that I thought might anger certain union leaders, even when that information was both accurate and important. What kind of a labor editor was I?

I tried to comfort myself by saying that I was a pragmatist and that I was making the best of my available choices. What if I had proven my integrity by criticizing the undemocratic behavior of a long list of union officials? Where would it have gotten me? They could knock the hell out of me and send me to the hospital, as they would occasionally do to dissenters. But even more important, they could shut down my newspapers within a week if they so decided. All they had to do was to get a half-dozen of the large unions to cancel their subscriptions. That would teach me a lesson not to be a smart-ass critic who was causing problems.

I realized that although the *Building Trades Union Press* and the *Trade Union Record* were technically independent, they were beholden to New York union leaders for their existence. I was really publishing house organs to make union leaders look good in the eyes of their membership, whether they deserved it or not. My job, then, was to turn out the best possible house organs, finding ways to promote the principles of democratic unionism while I catered to the desires of union leaders, including the corrupt ones. Hardly an easy task.

I used to dream of editing a publication *within the labor movement* that could consistently speak the truth about unions, warts and all, and still command a respectful hearing from both leaders and rank-and-file. It was not until a half-century later that I finally decided to start such a publication on a very modest scale.

* * * * *

I believe it was in February 1942 that I first suggested to Thomas Lyons, president of the New York State Federation of Labor, that it would be helpful to him and his organization to have an official newspaper. He was interested when I explained how it could be established without too much strain on the federation's budget. He invited me to present my proposal at the state federation's executive board meeting, scheduled for May. I talked to Thomas Murray, the president of the New York State Building and Construction Trades Council, and he liked the idea.

I lobbied other executive board members and received a favorable reaction, with only a few mild objections.

To dramatize my proposal, I prepared a front page of what would be *their* weekly newspaper, *Empire State Labor.* It contained current news stories of their activities, a photograph of the top officers, a cartoon and a table of contents, head-lining the stories that would be featured on the inside of the eight-page paper. On the reverse side, in large type, I explained how Trade Union Service would pro-vide the editorial and mailing services for the newspaper at a cost that no other publisher could match. The executive board was pleased at my initiative and took time out to read the front page. It was decided to discuss the idea at the September meeting and come to a decision.

I attended the September meeting and learned that the editor of a rival labor paper, the *Trade Union Courier,* had lobbied the board members and accused me of being "tainted" with Communism. Although I had substantial support on the board, the charge was enough to table my proposal. I later learned that George Meany, a former president of the state federation and now AFL secretary-trea-surer, had told Lyons he was strongly opposed to my proposition. I knew that Meany, a staunch anti-communist whom I had met on several occasions, did not like me or my newspapers. I was deeply disappointed. I had dreamed of being editor of *Empire State Labor.* But now I had other things on my mind: I was soon to be drafted into the United States Army.

14. My Wartime Marriage

It was a lovely spring day in April 1939 when Ann Wharton walked into my office. I looked up from my typewriter to see the most beautiful woman I had ever met. My three staff members stopped what they were doing to stare at her admiringly. She wore, as I recall, a white silk tunic with multi-colored horizontal stripes, a pale-blue skirt and a broad-brimmed picture hat that framed her blond hair and pale, classic face. She was about five-foot-six.

In a soft, musical voice with a trace of a Texas accent, Ann introduced herself as the international representative of the United Public Workers of America, a CIO affiliate. I couldn't imagine anyone who looked less like a union organizer. I was immediately smitten with her.

She explained that she wanted to get help from the New York labor movement in her campaign to unionize the regional office of the Veterans Administration in Manhattan. She had been told that I was the best person to see. It was almost noon, so I suggested we discuss her problem over lunch at a nearby coffee shop.

After lunch, we continued our discussion on a bench at a local park. I gave her a long list of labor leaders to see and offered her suggestions on how to proceed. She was very grateful. I hoped I had impressed her and tried to think of an excuse to see her again.

I was able to find out that she was born and raised in a small town in East Texas. Her father, now deceased, had been a Baptist minister. Her middle name was Calhoun and her family was related to the former vice president of the United States. She also had relatives in Tennessee from where her family had emigrated to Texas.

How did she become interested in the labor movement? She had worked in Washington as a secretary in the Agriculture Department. She had helped build a local union of clerical employees in the department, and had attracted the attention of Eleanor Nelson, the secretary-treasurer of the United Public Workers. She had only recently been given the organizing assignment in the New York region. Two of her other objectives, she said, were to unionize the tailors at West Point and the production workers at Frankford Arsenal in Philadelphia. One helluva assignment, I thought. I tried to imagine the reaction of some army general when this dignified-looking woman requested a meeting to negotiate a union contract.

A week later I received a call from Ann asking whether I'd like to come to the anniversary dinner-dance that the New York locals of the Public Workers were holding at the Tavern on the Green restaurant in Central Park the following Friday. I was delighted to say yes. She added that she had drafted a press release that I might possibly use in the *Trade Union Record*. I said I'd be glad to look at it.

I enjoyed meeting her union colleagues at the dance. I was thrilled when she held my arm and introduced me as a labor editor who was being very helpful to her and the union. When I asked her to dance, she begged off; she had never learned how. I finally coaxed her onto the dance floor for a slow fox trot. I liked having my arm around her and discreetly pressed her to me. She wore a subtle perfume that pleased me, as did everything about her.

Listening to the lively conversation and laughter of the young men and women at our table of ten was a refreshing experience. For the past four years, ever since I turned 21, my social life had consisted mainly of drinking with middle-aged, male union leaders at conventions and local bars or attending their boring picnics, boat rides and dinner dances. I had had a few brief affairs, but none that were memorable. I was delighted to be here in the company of so many attractive women.

While several union members gathered around Ann to consult her about their problems, I had a marvelous time on the dance floor with one partner after another. Later in the evening, Ann showed me her press release, which listed a series of scandalous working conditions at the Veterans Administration building. I said I would consider printing it and offered some minor suggestions which she quickly accepted. When I took her home, I tried to kiss her. She gave me her cheek, but I reached for her lips. It was not a passionate kiss, but I immediately felt it was improper. Maybe I had offended her. When we parted, I thought she might not want to see me again.

All through the following week, I kept thinking of Ann. I was obviously infatuated with her, but why? She was attractive, yes, but I suspected something deeper. Could it be that she was a Christian, a blond and completely unlike any woman I had ever known? She seemed so cool and detached, I wondered what it would take for any man to arouse her passion. And I tried to imagine how she would be in bed. Although I had known her for only a short time, I felt sure she was intelligent, politically sound, competent, moral, and completely dependable— the ideal qualities I required in any woman I would ever be serious about. (To date, I hadn't had any applicants.) Ann had to be some years older than me, but that didn't matter.

And what did she think of me? It was too early to tell. I could see she enjoyed my company; why else would she have invited me to the dance? But maybe all she wanted of me was the help I could give her in her union work. How could I gain her affection?

When two weeks had passed and I had not heard from Ann, I decided to call her. She seemed glad to hear from me. She had just returned from a three-day conference in Washington and was glad to accept my invitation to have dinner at a

French restaurant on Lexington Avenue.

We enjoyed the dinner but, most of all, each other's company. While Ann described the policy conflicts at the Washington conference, our eyes smiled at each other. She explained that she enjoyed cooking but rarely had the time for it, and there wasn't much point to cooking for one.

When I took her home. this time she invited me up for a nightcap. Ann lived in a studio apartment on East 27th Street, just above the Butler Davenport Free Theater. It contained all the essentials for a professional woman: an "efficiency" kitchen, bathroom and an all-purpose room with enough space for a bed, an armoire, a dining table with two chairs, a desk and a couple of lamps.

Ann brought out a bottle of scotch and a bowl of mixed nuts, as we told each other about our families, our upbringing and how we had arrived at our present careers. Each of us had numerous stories describing the joys and frustrations of our work. We talked about the government's recent attacks on unions in the name of national defense. She said that many of her union members were being investigated by the FBI on the pretext of rooting out communist or fascist spies. There had been a policy split within the union, with some officials wanting to suspend organizing activities to avoid problems with the federal government. Ann, among others, disagreed. She was going ahead with her efforts at the West Point Academy and the Frankford Arsenal in Philadelphia. She wanted my opinion. I said I agreed with her, but she'd have difficulty in making any headway. She smiled. "We'll see." I was impressed with her calm determination.

As the night wore on, we talked about so many things that would reveal ourselves to each other. We reviewed the books we both liked: she particularly enjoyed Edith Wharton (no relation), Ernest Hemingway, William Faulkner and Sinclair Lewis. About politics, she favored a third term for Roosevelt. She knew a great deal about the Civil War and her famous ancestor, John Calhoun. Her favorite movie stars were Joseph Cotten, Robert Montgomery, Bette Davis and Irene Dunne. She liked to listen to Bing Crosby and Tony Bennett, but knew no classical music or opera. I was disappointed that she cared nothing for sports. I promised to take her to Ebbets Field to see the Dodgers and turn her into a baseball fan. She said she had neither the time nor desire for physical exercise, but she managed to stay healthy and maintain a trim figure by eating health foods like wheat germ, dessicated liver extract and a variety of vitamins.

By now, it was well past midnight. We had gone through a half bottle of scotch (Ann could hold her liquor) and we were both pleasantly relaxed. We hadn't noticed that it had been raining. Now, the downpour had become heavy, with a strong wind whipping sheets of rain against the windows. The lightning and thunder upset her. Ann suggested that I spend the night at her place, and I readily agreed, although the apartment I shared with my three staff workers was only a few blocks away.

In the morning, she shook me by the shoulders while I was still in bed. She was fully dressed. "Breakfast is ready." On the dining table were orange juice, scrambled eggs, bacon, toast and hot coffee. I was overwhelmed. I hadn't been treated this way since I was a child under Mama's care.

"I've got to rush to the office, Harry," she said. "Stay as long as you like." I told her that I too had to get to work and would leave shortly. She kissed me on the cheek and left.

I lay there in a daze, with a wonderful feeling of well-being. I was in love with this tantalizingly beautiful woman—and a union organizer. I was sure she was falling in love with me. I dressed slowly, made the bed and washed the breakfast dishes. I returned to my office thinking what a lucky man I was.

Several days later, Ann invited me to dinner. She had prepared a delicious meal of lamb chops, vegetables, salad and fruit compote. Afterwards, since it was a lovely, warm evening, we went for a long walk, hand in hand. When we returned, we understood that I would stay for the night.

Within a month, I moved in with Ann. Hadn't she said "stay as long as you like," I reminded her jokingly. As the weeks passed, we grew fonder and more considerate of each other. We were both deeply involved in our work which, in Ann's case, required a lot of out-of-town travel. However, we managed to set aside enough time to be with each other. We had many friends, mostly her union associates, that enabled us to enjoy as active a social life as we wanted.

* * * * *

In April 1940, a year after we had met, we eloped to Havre de Grace, Maryland, a famous horse-racing town, where the local justice of the peace married us. We spent our one-day honeymoon eating at an expensive restaurant and visiting the race track where we won ten dollars. We returned home, a happily-married couple, and then plunged back into our work.

We spent a lot of our spare time, mostly on weekends, looking for a larger apartment. It took us weeks to find a one-bedroom rental that was spacious, fairly priced and convenient to both our offices. It was on Lexington Avenue, barely one block from where we were living.

The furniture we bought (some was given to us) could be charitably described as eclectic. Neither Ann nor I had any talent for interior decoration, but we were comfortable, especially since we could have a large desk, a typewriter and a file cabinet at one end of our living room.

I had been debating for some time whether to tell Mama that I was married, and I couldn't bring myself to do it. She had a bad heart and I didn't want to upset her—as I knew she would be—if I told her I had married a *shiksa*. Ann told me I was wrong—in fact, she resented my attitude—but couldn't change my mind. We finally agreed that I would tell her before the end of the year. In the meantime, I phoned Mama at least once, sometimes twice a week, to inquire about her health and tell her how busy I was. I also made it a point to visit the family everytime that Ann was in Washington, Philadelphia or some other city on a union assignment. As it later turned out, I misjudged my mother's reaction to Ann, and I apologized to both for my shameful behavior.

Ann had no such problem. She invited her mother to come up from Texas and spend a week or two with us. I readily agreed, but I was somewhat nervous about how it would work out. The first thing I noticed about Katie, Ann's mother, was her pleasant, careworn face and her thinning gray hair through which I could see her scalp. She was a broad-framed woman, on the plump side, with the shrunken height and slightly hunched shoulders of an arthritis victim.

On the first day of her visit, Katie and I were formal toward each other. I wondered what she thought of her daughter marrying a New York radical and, to boot, a Jew. Was she an anti-Semite and being civil-mannered to avoid giving Ann pain and embarrassment? It was not a question to ask. Whatever her views, we soon became quite friendly. I found time to take her to the Museum of Natural History, to Chinatown for lunch, and window-shopping along Fifth Avenue. I could see she really didn't care much for sight-seeing. It was too fatiguing for her. "I'm a homebody," she said.

About the third day, I found one unexpected source of entertainment that pleased her immensely: Chinese checkers. While Ann prepared dinner, we'd have a game, and usually one or two after dinner. When she was not playing with me, she would try to figure out winning tactics on her own. She focused intently on the board, especially toward the end of a game, and she beamed with pleasure whenever she won which, I saw to it, was quite often. She also liked going to the movies, and Ann and I would take her to entertaining ones that did not contain embarrassing love scenes or terrifying violence.

Once in a while, Katie would talk about herself and her family. In her low-pitched Texas drawl, she would describe the years she had worked on a farm that harvested pecans; how she had saved enough money to acquire a few lots of farm property and was now in the real estate business. She had raised four children: Ella, the oldest, was a school teacher in Houston; Ann was the second oldest; then there was Connie, who had married Stu, a chemist, and lived in Maryland. Her one son, Ivan, ran a mink farm in Louisiana. She wanted to know about me and my family. She was especially interested in how we had survived the early years of the Depression, comparing our experience with her difficult time.

She stayed on for a month and before she left I was calling her Mom and felt quite at ease with her. Ann and I promised to visit her next spring. She said she was sorry she had not met my family on this trip (I had offered some lame excuse for not arranging it), but I promised to send her pictures of them.

* * * * *

A week after Ann's mother returned home, Congress passed the military conscription bill. Suddenly, I realized that I, too, among the millions of Americans, could be drafted for a war which I then opposed. A month later—it was mid-October, 1940—virtually every newspaper in the country carried front-page photographs of Secretary of War Henry L. Stimson, blind-folded, plucking the first numbers from a fish bowl that would determine the order in which men would be drafted into the army.

I can remember sitting with Ann at a coffee shop near our house with the early edition of *The New York Times*. Nervously, we checked the long lists of draft numbers to see where mine was located. I was lucky; my number showed up in the lower half of the roster. It appeared that I would not be conscripted for at least a year. I might even be exempted as a married man. We breathed a sigh of relief and decided to celebrate by taking the day off.

The year 1941 was a worrisome one during which Ann and I felt under constant strain. With the election of President Roosevelt for a third term, we were convinced that it was only a matter of time before the country would be plunged into the war. While the daily newspapers and radio stations vehemently denounced the many strikes that were erupting all over the country as "sabotage" and their leaders as "traitors," I was giving them my editorial blessing. I was warned that if I continued to support the strike movement, I might end up in jail or the army. These warnings convinced me that the U.S. was becoming a "garrison state" and that the government was trying to put unions into a straight-jacket so they couldn't protest corporate profiteering or the decline in workers' living standards.

Ann's problem was tougher than mine, by far. She and her colleagues had to contend with a rising clamor that the United Public Workers represented a potential danger to the national security. It was not hard to convince many people that the union, whose members worked in federal and state government offices, might be harboring nests of spies passing classified material to foreign countries, Some right-wing organizations were demanding that the union turn over its membership lists to the FBI for screening. Under such pressure, many federal employees resigned from the union rather than face the prospect of continued harassment about their patriotism.

Ann's new top priority was to stem the exodus of union members in the New York metropolitan region—a difficult job. We spent many long hours talking about it. Although she had negotiated a favorable contract for the West Point Academy tailors, a group there wanted to pull out of the union.

To save union expenses, Ann decided to use our apartment as her office. After some delay, we managed to get her an additional phone. With the help of a part-time secretary and an occasional volunteer, who typed memos and served as a courier to and from various locals, Ann worked from eight in the morning until late at night, conceding an hour or two to have dinner with me and relax. I really did not care for this arrangement, but I felt I couldn't object.

I now had a first-hand opportunity to see how she worked as a union organizer, and I was amazed at her efficiency. What was most obvious was that she wasted no time. She planned her day's work methodically the night before, allowing some time for unexpected developments—and she kept to her schedule. In phone conversations and at meetings, she was impatient with small talk and irrelevant comments—an attitude that could sometimes be irritating and counterproductive, but which she would not, probably could not, change. Her major strength was that she could immediately see to the heart of a problem and could quickly, point by point, set out the options to respond to it.

At least twice a week, sometimes on weekends, she held meetings at the apartment. One of her serious faults at these meetings was that she wouldn't really listen to what other people were saying. She knew what she wanted, and the fact that she was most often right in her judgments didn't make this less of a failing. Despite her generally mild manner, she could be so dominating that few people were ready to challenge her.

At the end of a day of frustration, she'd sit in an armchair, grim and exhausted, with a scotch in her hand. When I'd say she was losing her sense of humor, she'd smile and respond, "What's there to laugh about?" At one point, when she was in despair because one of the New York locals had seceded from the international union, I persuaded her to take a long weekend with me at a pleasant resort in upstate New York. It made me happy to see her discussing, and even joking, about other things beside those damned government unions. Reinvigorated, we agreed to do this at least once every two months.

Our country's formal entry into the war the day after Pearl Harbor proved at least a temporary blessing for the Public Workers. Like other unions, it pledged unstinting loyalty to the government at this time of national crisis. Responding to President Roosevelt's call for labor cooperation, the union declared that its members would be a valuable stabilizing, morale-building force within the government. Its leadership was ready to work with federal officials on programs to inspire greater efficiency and productivity.

The pressure on Ann eased off, but not completely. The union's tactic was enough to stem further losses in membership but not to regain those who had left the previous year. The union was confronted with other difficulties: it had serious financial problems and had informed its staff people that their salaries would be *temporarily* cut by 10 percent, and that, unless the situation improved, there might have to be layoffs. To make matters worse, an opposition faction had developed on the West Coast that accused the national union leadership of being fellow travelers and dupes of the Communist Party, and it announced it was preparing a "pro-American" slate of candidates for the union's next convention.

Ann agreed with me that there was not much of a future for her as international representative of the Public Workers, and that she had better start preparing now for a new job and possibly a new career. Could she get a position with another union? Not likely, I said. From my observation, unions weren't hiring anyone, and if they were going to, it would be someone from their own ranks with a knowledge of their industry. I suggested she try canvassing some of the city's progressive organizations that might be interested in an experienced organizer like her. Anyway, there was no rush. If Ann left the union, she could take a few months off to look for work that suited her. We had enough savings to handle that contingency.

In October, 1942, the local draft board classified me as I A and said they would inform me when and where I would be inducted. Frankly, I was not eager to go into the army. I wanted to stay with Ann and continue my work as a labor editor, which I thought could be more important for the war effort than anything I might accomplish as a soldier. I did try, as a married man, for a postponement, but to no avail. The three members of the draft board listened attentively to my appeal, but two days later, I received their letter of rejection. I was told to report to the induction center at Fort Dix in New Jersey on November 4.

A week before my induction, Ann informed Eleanor Nelson, the secretary-treasurer of the UPW and a good friend of ours, that she wanted a leave of absence, as of the first of the year. She planned to find some low-pressure secretarial work to earn some money and have enough free time to visit me wherever I would be stationed. With the army allotment I would be sending her, she was sure she could manage. She knew how to live frugally.

While I was at Fort. Dix and Atlantic City for army training, Ann visited me on weekends, when I managed to get a 24- or 48-hour pass as a married man. The weekend before I completed my basic training and was to be assigned to a permanent outfit, Ann visited me and over lunch, looking as happy as I had ever seen her, broke the news that she was pregnant. We had been talking about having a baby for some time. Ann, at 37, did not want to wait for the end of the war, whenever that would be. I was less eager and uncertain about taking on the responsibilities of parenthood. Ann was disconcerted that I had not greeted the news with enthusiasm. I had to assure her that I really wanted the baby and that I would make a loving father. It occurred to me that if I were killed, at least I would be leaving a living memory to Ann and Mama. That evening, we went to one of the best restaurants in Atlantic City to celebrate.

We phoned Ann's mother, who was delighted and immediately agreed to stay with her until the baby was born. Ann had found a part-time job as a copywriter in a small advertising agency; she planned to work there until a couple of months before the baby was due, sometime in June. If I were not overseas by then, I would arrange to get "compassionate leave" to be present at the baby's birth. We agreed that if it was a boy, he'd be named Adam (my choice); if a girl, she would be Kathryn (Ann's choice). We promised to keep in touch by letter and phone at least twice a week as soon as I found out where I was to be stationed. I did not call Mama to tell her the news; that could wait until the baby was born.

* * * * *

Early in June 1943, I heard rumors that my outfit, stationed in Albuquerque, New Mexico, was about to be moved to a port of embarkation (P.O.E.). Whether we were headed for the West Coast or East Coast P.O.E. became an obsessive subject for discussion and betting. Most of the men, like myself, hoped we'd be assigned to the European Theater of Operations (E.T.O.) rather than the Pacific, and we preferred to be stationed in England rather than in Italy, where U.S. forces were engaged in fierce fighting with German troops. The military command was not asking for our preferences.

On the day I put in for a five-day pass to be with Ann at the baby's birth, our outfit was suddenly put on alert. All leaves were cancelled and no one, except specially authorized personnel, was permitted to leave the airbase. My request for a five-day leave was dismissed, but I was permitted to make a weekly phone call to Ann. On one of my calls, I was able to reach Ann at Beth Israel Hospital to learn that two days before, on June 17, she had given birth to a beautiful seven-pound girl, our daughter Kathryn, and that she and the baby were doing fine. I was a father!

The mystery about my outfit's future destination cleared up early in September when we were loaded onto a train for a three-day trip to New York. With persistent effort, I was able to get a five-day "hardship" leave, subject to recall, to see Ann and our six-week-old Kathy. I was overcome with joy and happy tears as I stood beside her crib, watching our little red-haired baby and then cradling her in my arms. I now really felt like a parent! Ann looked tired but happy. She was suffering from a bad cold and did not want me to get too close to her. I would have loved to take her and the baby away for a long, restful weekend, but there was no time for it.

By coincidence, my younger sister, Julia, was being married that weekend to Bernard Tursky, a nice young man who worked in a neighborhood grocery store. My younger brother, Marty, who had lied his way into the regular army at 17, could not attend the wedding. He was fighting as an infantryman in Italy after participating in the African campaign.

The family had not expected me to attend and were overjoyed to see me after my absence of nearly a year. In my uniform, I was almost as much the center of attraction as the bride and groom. It was good to see them all on this happy occasion. Mama cried with tears of pleasure. She kept kissing and hugging me, stopping only to accept the congratulations of relatives and friends. She had spent a week preparing all the food for the wedding and, of course, there was more than enough for everyone.

I had thought that this week would be an ideal time to tell Mama I was married and have her meet Ann and Kathy, but once again I found a pretext for covering my moral cowardice: I ought not risk upsetting Mama in her moment of happiness. The following day, I said farewell to Ann and the baby, promising to write as soon as I had arrived at my destination. I had the comfort of a snapshot of Kathy in my wallet.

15. *Three Years in the Army*

It took me some time before I could adjust to Army life. I had never liked being part of a herd. At the very outset, I felt outraged at the incessant effort to dehumanize me and, as I was told, to transform me into a "cog in a fighting machine." After a few days at Fort Dix in New Jersey, where I was subjected to aptitude tests, I was "shipped" to Atlantic City for preliminary basic training prior to my permanent assignment. I felt silly doing close-order drill on the boardwalk to the barking commands of a sergeant, while tourists watched us as though we were part of their entertainment. I hated to salute officers whom I neither knew nor respected simply because they had a couple of silver bars or an eagle on their uniforms. I'd grit my teeth in anger at some officious lout of a non-com inspecting my bed to see if I had made it properly, including the hospital corners, and having the authority to deny me a weekend pass if he was not satisfied. What in hell did this have to do with the war against fascism! When Ann came to visit me on weekends, I felt uncomfortable in my ill-fitting dress uniform. I looked and felt like a hotel doorman.

I guess I was angriest when, in a formation of about forty privates, I and three others were singled out at random for K.P. duty, not for an ordinary meal but for Thanksgiving Day lunch and dinner. We were sent to a huge mess hall, where I stood on the serving line, dishing out mashed sweet potatoes and cranberry sauce. The line of soldiers seemed interminable. My right shoulder and wrist ached from the repetitive motion. Toward evening, I was transferred to work at the "China clipper," a huge automatic dish-washing machine. It was about midnight when, after we had cleaned up the kitchen and the dining hall, we were finally released so we could stagger back to our hotel and flop into bed. Not a word of praise or thanks.

Fortunately, the tedium and absurdity of my life at Atlantic City appeared to be coming to an end when my detachment received the news that the following day we would board a train that would take us to our permanent outfit. I was in line to answer roll-call at six the next morning, my two duffle bags bulging with my belongings. It was a mile and a half march to the railroad depot, and with every step, the bags felt heavier and heavier. Almost at the point of exhaustion, I finally reached the railroad station. There must have been at least several hundred men in the contingent. As they were counted off, they boarded the train. When there were only a few of us left on the platform, the lieutenant in charge held up his hand and said, "That's it. You guys better get back to the base." We were "supernumeraries" who, we were told, would have priority in the next shipment. As we sweated our way back to the hotel, we cursed the fuckin' stupidity of the army and its indifference to personal feelings. Little did we know (I learned this a long time later) that the outfit we missed joining was an infantry regiment that fought at Iwo Jima and suffered among the worst casualties of the war.

I was amazed to see what little interest I now had in what was going on in the labor movement. When Ann brought me copies of my newspapers, I looked through them casually and uncritically, without the feeling that I was still the editor, with my name still listed on the masthead. The staff was doing fine without me and the world out there was going ahead with its business. I was in a strange, eventually dangerous new environment and I would have to make many adjustments to survive in it.

* * * * *

I finally got to my permanent outfit, the 43rd Air Depot Group of the Army Air Force, stationed at a base outside of Albuquerque, New Mexico. None of us had the slightest idea that, in nearby Los Alamos, scientists were working to perfect the first nuclear bomb.

I liked the basic training program: the strenuous morning calisthenics, the rifle range, the long hikes up the Sandia Peak, the obstacle course and the various war games we played, sometimes under real rifle fire. In a couple of months, I qualified for marksman with the M-1 rifle and carbine, and could quickly and methodically take apart, clean and put together each of the weapons. Although I was nearly twenty-nine and one of the oldest men in the outfit, I could run the obstacle course, including the climbing of a high wall, in as good a time as most of the others. I was becoming lean and strong and felt good about my muscular body.

The colonel in charge of the outfit had been a successful shoe manufacturer in Boston. To compensate for his civilian background, he acted like a military martinet. He enjoyed marching us in the rain, anything to toughen us. The gas mask drills he put us through in the Sandias low hills were more like punishment than training. He was a mean disciplinarian and he'd punish his men for the slightest infraction of his arbitrary rules, usually by cancelling their off-base passes or putting them on latrine duty for a week or more. For some reason, the colonel took a liking to me. He said he needed an "intellectual" like me to talk to because, as he confessed, military life was dull and limiting. I was amazed to see how pleasant and friendly he could be in private conversation.

One day, he told me he wanted the outfit to have a magazine; it would be a good way to build morale and develop a sense of mission among the men. If I would agree to edit it, I would be relieved of all other duties. He had already arranged to have a print shop in town produce the magazine. I strongly suspected that he hoped to use it for self-promotion, but I eagerly accepted the offer. I enjoyed the freedom and perks of publishing *Spotlight* and used it for my own self-promotion as well. My feature articles on the mess sergeant and supply sergeant earned me their gratitude and much more. I could requisition any article of clothing or equipment merely by walking into the supply room, and I enjoyed special treatment at the mess hall. When, after three monthly issues of the magazine, it earned a special commendation from Army Air Force headquarters in Dayton, Ohio, the colonel was so pleased that he promoted me to corporal.

Colonel Burstein even organized a small marching band after checking the records of the fifteen hundred men under his command for anyone who played a musical instrument. He had one of the musicians compose a song, "The Fighting 43rd," and ordered me to write the words to the tune. It was a horrible song with my corny lyrics to match, but he was proud of it. To my dismay, he commanded the men to memorize the words; failure to do so would mean cancellation of their weekend pass. He even forced them to sing it during our marching drills. I was deeply embarrassed and apologized to anyone who would listen. For weeks, I was on the shit list of the men in my squadron.

For the most part, we led a regimented existence, even to complying with instructions on the uniform of the day. About half of our scheduled time was spent on learning the art of war, including how to shoot and bayonet an enemy, while building up our stamina for survival under battle conditions. Several hours a day, we worked in huge hangars, containing stockpiles of air corps supplies, from aircraft engines, parachutes and pilot's flight jackets to gloves, flashlights and various sizes of tools, screws, bolts and gaskets. All items, including their description and quantities, were entered manually on inventory stock cards which it was our responsibility to keep up-to-date. We had to learn the location and storage handling of each item, and to master the complex paperwork involved in shipping and ordering. We were constantly reminded that we were an essential part of the Air Force and that combat pilots were depending on us to keep them flying. It was also explained to us that we had to be in combat-ready condition for future operations overseas in case the enemy attacked our supply depot.

To keep us physically fit for battle, the colonel periodically would arrange what he called "war games." The one I shall never forget was an operation in which our group of squadrons was supposed to storm on foot a fortified position of the enemy about five miles away and capture its defenders.

We started out one morning in formation, each of us carrying a full field pack weighing about 50 pounds, a canteen of water and our carbines. We were in desert country where the temperature on that day was close to 110 degrees and there was no shade, not a building or a tree in sight.

As we trudged along the sandy road, "enemy" planes roared overhead and began to "bomb" us with bags of flour. If we were hit by the flour, we were "dead," out of action. To escape that fate, we ran for cover where we could find it, behind a boulder or into the ditch alongside the road, or just lay flat on the ground, praying not to be hit. The bombing raids continued every ten minutes, inflicting many casualties.

Meanwhile, more and more soldiers were reaching the point of exhaustion under the blazing sun. You could fry an egg on the top of our helmets. Having drunk all the water in their canteens, men were pleading for more, but there was none to be had. One man, in a state of delirium, snatched the chaplain's canteen and gulped down whatever water was left in it before anyone could stop him.

Every hundred yards or so, a group of soldiers would faint or become delirious and had to be picked up by the medics on stretchers and deposited in the accompanying "meat wagon." I endured the heat and the bombing until we were about a mile from the "enemy" before I collapsed and was brought back to our improvised hospital. I and all the men around me were badly dehydrated and moaning for water. The medics moistened our fevered lips and put cold compresses on our foreheads; we rested on cots under a huge open tent until the exercise was officially over, when we were brought back to the base.

We later learned that a bedraggled, completely exhausted remnant contingent of our men had staggered into the enemy stronghold where they were cheerfully greeted by the defenders, who invited them for lunch.

There was an investigation of this incident by a representative of the Adjutant General's office during which the men complained vehemently about the colonel's behavior. He was subsequently removed as commanding officer and replaced by a regular army captain who was to lead us overseas.

* * * * *

After eight months of training in Albuquerque, we were sent to the Port of Embarkation in New York. Less than a week later, on September 20, 1943, our outfit and many others were loaded onto the *Queen Mary*, sailing the Atlantic toward England. German U-boats had been torpedoing American ships, and we worried that we'd be among the next victims. At least once a day, we had boat drills, and we were never sure whether it was an exercise or a response to a submarine attack. During the day, we scanned the water to see if any pipes were protruding, signaling the presence of a Nazi U-boat.

Between 10,000 and 15,000 soldiers were packed on the ship, with a dozen men crammed into each stateroom that in peace time was occupied by a couple or single person. We slept in metal bunks piled four high; they could be folded flat against the wall when not in use.

Meals were served in three shifts, family style. The food was horrible, especially the kidney stew. I existed mostly on K-rations and a few chocolate bars. Many of us spent the trip sleeping on the floors of the ship's ballrooms, with fancy chandeliers swaying overhead.

At the end of the uncomfortable six-day trip, we arrived on a stormy night somewhere in Scotland, dripping wet as we debarked for shelter. We were each given a clump of fish and chips wrapped in wet newspaper, and a cup of steaming coffee. We quickly fell asleep on metal beds, too exhausted to take off our wet clothes. We looked and felt like a miserable lot. The next morning, another rainy day, we were flown to our air base in England, near a town called Wantage. It consisted of an airfield for servicing planes, a few huge hangars containing aircraft supplies, and a large number of quonset huts where we were quartered.

For six weeks, we were forbidden to leave the base to go into town, why I could not tell. It rained incessantly and we rarely saw the sun; we sloshed around in mud with our heavy boots, as we went about our duties. The quonset huts were damp and bone-chilling cold. None of the ten men in each hut, I included, wanted to get out of bed at six in the morning to light the pot-bellied stove. To make matters worse, the only meat we got at meals was one frankfurter apiece. We were told that U-boats had torpedoed the ships carrying our food supplies from the United States. (We were enraged to learn several weeks later that two army majors had sold several truckloads of meat on the black market,)

My low spirits got a lift when I found out that our base was not very far from Oxford. With my first pass, I went to see the famous university, a mass of dreary-looking gray buildings with cobblestone courtyards. I tried to meet the dean of Ruskin College—I had heard a great deal about its labor programs—but managed to talk only to a group of three undergraduates who were relative newcomers and did not have very much to tell me about the curriculum. I enjoyed walking around the town and stopping into a pub to have a pint and watch men playing darts. I also got myself invited to lectures at the English Speaking Union. The cultured, informed speech and spontaneous wit of their speakers were a delight, especially as a relief from the obscenities and complaints that passed for conversation back at the base. I thought how wonderful it would be if I could study at Oxford as a Rhodes Scholar.

Fortunately, there were a few men in the outfit that I enjoyed talking with. I was especially fond of John Howard, an English teacher from Portland, Oregon; Dwight Holmquist, a fun-loving college student from Minneapolis, who was our supply sergeant, and Murray Weiss, later to become editor of the European edition of the *Herald Tribune.* At least one evening a week, a half a dozen of us would meet in the supply room to discuss the war, sports or whatever else was on our minds and to tell each other stories about our lives and experiences back home.

On one of my weekend leaves in London, I toured the bombed-out sections of the city and was aghast at the amount of destruction. I tried to imagine what it was like to endure the bombing, day after day, not knowing each time whether you'd come out alive. Toward evening, after a few scotches at a bar with some other G.I.'s, I went to the Red Cross building where a dance was being held. I hadn't been close to a woman for months and I needed the physical contact, even if it was only during a dance. On the third dance, I found someone I really liked: she wore the uniform of a WAVE and had been a school teacher in civilian life. She was bright, shapely and a good dancer. She gave me her address and phone number—she lived in Swinton, not too far by train—and I said I'd get in touch with her.

Back at the base, I cooled off and never did call her. I was scared of complicating my life with Ann and becoming infected with syphilis or gonorrhea, whose effects were displayed in nauseating detail in the sex education films we were required to watch.

* * * * *

During the early months of 1944, we worked long hours to supply the needs of many combat squadrons attached to the Eighth Air Force. We continued to hear rumors that any day now, General Eisenhower would launch an invasion of the continent, and that would mean the beginning of the end for Hitler. We did our best to see to it that no plane was down for lack of spare parts.

On the morning of June 6th, I stood at the entrance of my quonset hut and looked up at the sky to see a continuous flow of planes and gliders heading toward the Channel. This was D-Day! I'd had a premonition that the Allied invasion was imminent because of the unusual increase in orders for engines and spare parts the previous week.

In the early hours of the invasion, there was little we could find out as we waited, tense with anxiety, for official reports of the landing. That same evening, I received orders to lead a convoy of a dozen trucks loaded with spare parts for aircraft to Southampton, a key staging area for Allied troops. Southampton had been virtually flattened to rubble by the persistent Luftwaffe bombing. Only a few buildings remained. When we arrived there the next day, we saw several troop-ships returning from the French coast with their cargoes of American casualties. I gazed with horror at the grim parade of men, most of them much younger than me, with bandaged heads and missing limbs, still capable of walking slowly down the gangplank. I was close enough to see the fear and pain in their eyes. Behind them were stretchers bearing the badly wounded and finally the black body-bags of the dead. This was my first direct experience with the horrors of war. It stunned and scared me. For the first time since my induction, I had a clammy fear that I would not come out of this war alive.

A few days later, still possessed of my gloomy forebodings, I decided to tell Mama about my marriage and daughter. I wrote her a long letter in Yiddish, explaining that since I did not know what the future might hold, I wanted her to meet Ann and Kathy. I said I was sure she'd love her little granddaughter. I told her a great deal about Ann and why I loved her. I pleaded with her to have enough faith in me to accept that I would pick a fine woman as my wife. I apologized for not letting her know sooner. I ended by telling her that if she loved me and wanted me to be happy, she would have to love my newly acquired family. I gave her Ann's address and phone number and urged her to visit her as soon as possible. At the same time, I asked Ann to get in touch with Mama. I had finally taken the plunge but I was not sure how it would work out.

A few weeks after American troops occupied Paris, the 43rd Air Depot Group was ordered to set up operations at a base in France. The trip across the Channel on a barge-like landing vessel was horrendous. We were packed in so tightly that we had to stand motionless the entire time and had no space to remove our heavy back-packs. When we approached land after what seemed an eternity, we had to wade ashore in waist-high water. We spent a day at Saint Lô, a town whose bullet-riddled buildings were the scene of fierce fighting in the early days of the Allied landing.

Walking around the town, I decided to drop in at a barber shop for a shave. The barber, without my asking, assured me that he hated the Boche, had never had any sympathy for the Nazis and was delighted that the Americans had arrived to liberate France. He insisted on a toast to *Les Americains*, offering me a well-filled glass of calvados. After finishing the drink, I was thoroughly anesthetized. I felt him scraping my face with what must have been a very dull, if not rusty, razor, but I was too drunk to complain. There was a young woman in the shop who asked, *"Voulez vous coucher avec moi?"* which, with my high school French, I was able to understand but in no condition to respond to, even if I had agreed. From Saint Lô, we were taken by airlift to our new base near the town of Coubert, some 18 kilometers from Paris. To our surprised delight, our supply squadron was quartered in a château, which a few months earlier had been occupied by Nazi troops. After our experience with quonset huts, we regarded this as luxurious living.

For lack of anyone better suited for the job (I, at least, had three years of high school French and held the rank of sergeant), our commander appointed me "liaison non-commissioned officer" to the residents of Coubert. In that capacity, I met the town's mayor, Madame Courjou, a widow in her mid-forties and a staunch communist. At our first meeting, I was able to comprehend, more from her tone than her words, that she considered the behavior of the American soldiers she had seen as contemptible. She thought it disgusting that Americans expected to buy the affections of French girls by offering them cigarettes, candy bars and nylons. Madame Courjou was especially concerned about her two daughters, Geneviève, about twenty-two, and Yvette, hardly more than sixteen. I assured her that our commander was as eager as she was to avoid unpleasant incidents, and that any offensive behavior by our soldiers would be punished.

The mayor's frosty attitude toward me gradually grew cordial when we became better acquainted and found we shared similar views on many political issues. She was particularly pleased when I told her how much I admired the role of the French communists during the Nazi occupation. On several occasions, she invited me to her modest house to meet some of her friends, once to a discussion of the political situation facing France. I was the only American at the memorial to honor her husband, the former mayor, and more than a score of residents, who had been killed just a year before by the Nazis. The ceremony, held in the town cemetery, was simple and rather brief. After each name was read from a roll-call, the spectators chanted, *"Mort pour La France!"* Flowers were then laid on the graves of the victims. I felt awkward standing there, not able to share their grief or imagine what it was like to live under the Occupation.

Madame Courjou had forbidden her daughters to have dates with American soldiers but, of course, that did not apply to me. Geneviève, the older one, liked me and sent me flirtatious signals whenever I visited. She was of medium height, dark-complexioned, with long, black hair done up in ringlets. She was not especially good-looking except when she became animated, and then her dimpled smile and expressive eyes made her attractive. She was college-educated and was planning to go to Paris next year to study law.

Geneviève and I became better acquainted at an American Red Cross dance for soldiers and townspeople. We had several dances during which she excited me by squeezing my hand and pressing against my body. Later, we went out in the courtyard where we embraced and kissed. On a weekend when I told Geneviève I'd be in Paris, she happened to mention that she'd also be there, visiting a girl friend and doing some shopping. She showed up at the Red Cross building where I was staying and invited me to visit her friend that evening. She was alone in the apartment when I got there. As soon as I entered, she put her arms around me and kissed me passionately. "Harry, I love you," she said in English. Suddenly, I felt as though I had been ambushed.

Geneviève was disappointed at my cool response. "I thought you loved me," she said. "My friend won't be back to Monday. We have the whole weekend for ourselves. I want you to know that I've never slept with a man. You'll be the first."

Instead of exciting me, her open invitation cooled me off. I had never slept with a virgin and, unlike some men, I had no desire to. I had done nothing wrong but I was beginning to feel guilty. How would I be able to face Madame Courjou if she found out I had deflowered her daughter! And why would I want to cheat on Ann? Perhaps, if she had been prettier and more seductive, I might have felt less moral.

"Listen, Geneviève," I said. "I'm a married man and I have an eighteen-month-old daughter." Her initial shock quickly turned to anger. "Why didn't you tell me this before?" she shouted, her eyes flashing. "Why didn't you wear your wedding ring?"

"I don't have a wedding ring. I never intended to keep my marriage a secret. The men in my outfit know I'm married. Anyhow, Geneviève, I'm very fond of you, but I don't want to get into bed with you. I'm sure we'd both regret it in the morning. Let's remain good friends."

She stopped her sobbing. "I guess you're right, Harry. I wish you and your wife and daughter a long and happy life."

I invited her out for dinner, but she refused. I could see she wanted me to leave. I did not kiss her goodbye. On the way back to my room at the Red Cross, I wondered about Geneviève. Did she really love me or had she hoped to entrap me into marrying her and bringing her to the United States? The latter was possible. It was happening to other G.I.'s. I resolved to see her as little as possible, and never alone.

By the middle of December, we received the disquieting news that the Germans had launched a counter-offensive designed to split the allied armies. We got a brief taste of it when three enemy planes bombed the outskirts of Coubert, destroying farm property but costing no lives. We were commandeered to improve the air-raid shelters of the townspeople who were becoming increasingly jittery as the German armies advanced. Fortunately, by mid-January, the Allied armies were once again on the offensive. It now looked better than ever that it was only a matter of time before Hitler's armies would be crushed in a powerful Russian-American pincer.

* * * * *

Later that month, I was told by my commanding officer that I was being transferred to the 109th Bombardment Group at an air base near St. Denis, about fifty kilometers north of Paris. I had been selected to serve as the group's public relations specialist because of my newspaper background.

I hated to leave my outfit; there were several men I had become fond of and hoped to see after the war was over. I managed to get a few of them together for a farewell party. We exchanged addresses and phone numbers and promised to remain in touch. (I actually did correspond with several of them after the war.)

When I reported to my new commanding officer, a colonel with an impressive record as a combat pilot, he explained what my duties were. Picking up a sheet of paper on his desk, he pointed to a table of figures. He showed me that our outfit was on the bottom of a list of eight combat groups in the U.S. Ninth Air Force in terms of press releases and photographs that were being sent back to the States to build morale on the home front. "I want you to get us into the top three," he said. "Whatever you need to do the job—staff, supplies, transportation—you ask for it and I'll see that you get it." He handed me the paper. "I'm counting on you to deliver. Any problems, let me know." I saluted and left in somewhat of a daze.

I examined the report with curiosity. The top combat group had sent out thirty-five press releases and seventeen photographs, compared to our eight releases and five photos. A few hours later, I came up with a plan which I discussed with my assistant, Corporal Tim McCarthy, who thought it was brilliant.

The next morning, I asked the colonel for three men who could type; by noon, they reported to me for duty. I had them type several bits of selected information about the background and record of the members of each combat crew on 3 x 5 cards. This data could then be typed into the appropriate blank spaces of a master press release I planned to design. Every time a squadron returned from a bombing mission, either I or Mac was there at the debriefing session to get the names of the crew and any unusual happening. Then we'd rush back to our office and have our typists prepare a press release about each of these crew members using the data in the card file. We did just enough of these to assure that we'd be somewhere near the top of what Mac and I called the "racing form."

When the monthly report came out, our combat group was in first place in the number of press releases distributed to the men's hometown papers, but we still lagged in our output of photographs. The colonel was delighted and indicated that both of us might soon have a promotion in rank.

To boost our picture production, I came up with another idea that required unusual cooperation. When I hesitantly presented it to the colonel, he exclaimed, "Excellent! We'll do it!" Two days later, he ordered the entire crew of several bombers to stand alongside their aircraft while a photographer took their pictures and we jotted down their names. We were now able to send batches of individual and group photographs along with our press releases to newspapers in the States. And, as we anticipated, when the next monthly report came out, we were at the top of the list in photos as well as press releases.

Public relations officers from other groups found out what we were doing and prepared to beat us at our own game. However, we had another plan that enabled us to maintain our first place position. We had our crew members give us the names and addresses of their high school or college, church or synagogue, or any organization to which they belonged. We used this information to multiply the number of press releases we could put in the bulging mail bags for air shipment to the U.S.A. If the Army Air Force wanted to cheer up the folks back home, we were certainly doing our part—and enjoying the game.

The outflow of press releases reached such a torrent that U.S. daily newspapers were outraged at the unpublishable "garbage" they were receiving in the guise of press releases, and they urged the military to enforce some measure of discrimination. Not much changed. All of us continued to fight for top positions on the monthly "racing form."

Our final effort (Mac and I called it the "big bang,") came about two weeks before the Germans surrendered. General Eisenhower had sent our Air Force group a "special commendation" for its contributions to the Allied war effort. We decided to quote Ike's expression of gratitude in individual press releases about each of the several hundred crew members. It was a silly thing to do, but it did reveal how absurd and wasteful the military could be. At any rate, I had made the colonel happy. I never found out whether he got his promotion. I hoped not.

* * * * *

It amazed me how seldom I thought about life back home. I corresponded regularly with Ann and Mama, but hardly anyone else. I didn't hear much from the staff back in New York and, surprisingly, I didn't seem to care. My work and my friends were here at this airfield; this was the real world I lived in; we were winning the war and what was happening three thousand miles away somehow didn't seem important.

That changed for me on April 12, 1945, when the news came over the loudspeaker that President Roosevelt had died. We stopped everything and stood at attention in shocked silence, as taps were played and the headquarters flag was lowered to half-mast. I felt genuine grief about the loss of FDR. Suddenly, I was homesick. I wanted to get back to work on my newspapers. I was eager to be involved with the labor movement once again when it would be grappling with new problems, enormous ones, after the war. I found myself reading and listening to every scrap of information I could get about what was happening in the States.

My thoughts about home grew considerably stronger on May 9th, when we heard the news of the German surrender. We celebrated with several cases of champagne which had been set aside for just this occasion. What mattered most for us was how soon we could be sent home.

The military had worked out a complex system of points under which men who had been drafted could qualify for return to the United States and be discharged. Because of the limited available transportation, those with the most points would be shipped home first. Everywhere, the men were busy calculating their points and anxiously comparing them with each other. As a married man with one child and two and a half years of military service, more than half of it overseas, I figured I was fairly high on the list to be sent home. But weeks went by and nothing happened. Morale was at a low point and some of the men were muttering rebellion. We had little to do except wait for orders to depart, but where were those orders?

One day, late in July, when we heard that our departure was already scheduled, the entire outfit was loaded into trucks at six-thirty in the morning, before breakfast, for a drive to an undisclosed destination. After an hour's ride, we stopped and were herded into a theater to see a movie. When the title, "Two Down and One to Go," appeared on the screen, there was a mixture of wild yells, hoots and groans of protest. Men were rising from their seats and angrily shaking their fists at the screen. The thought of being shipped to the Pacific seemed unbearable. We were on the verge of rioting when the commanding officer, after several minutes, managed to restore order by telling us that at the end of the film he would announce some good news that we would all appreciate.

The film started by soft-soaping us: a general appeared on the screen to assure us that the American people were proud of the marvelous job we had done in defeating the Nazis, and the nation would be eternally grateful to us. Then came film clips of our successful bombing of German installations and the arrival of American troops in Paris. And now, the commentator came to the film's message: Japan was still battling our soldiers in the Pacific, and the United States would never be safe until it was defeated. We were now shown film clips of Pearl Harbor and the Battle of Bataan. The final scene was a speech by another general telling us that the American people were counting on us to "finish the job."

After the film, the commanding officer informed us that we would be departing for an embarkation point in Hamburg and leaving for the United States within a week on a fleet of Liberty ships. When we arrived in the United States, we would be assigned to an airfield indefinitely—it might be months or sooner—before we were sent to the Pacific Theater of Operations. We greeted the news with cheers: at least we were finally going home—all of us, regardless of how many points we had. As for fighting Japan, that was in the future; if we were lucky, we might not have to go.

The next few days were busy ones for all of us. With all the mementos and gifts we had accumulated, we had to decide what to take with us and what to leave behind. We had been told that our baggage would be limited to what we ourselves could carry up the gangplank. One of the difficult decisions I had to make was to abandon several items like a Luftwaffe cap, a hand-woven Belgian tablecloth and a toy music box in favor of the large and heavy two-volume set of paintings from the Louvre.

Our commanding officer had not lied to us. We did get to Hamburg where we spent three miserable days in a compound with poor food and not much to do except play cards. We boarded the Liberty ship on July 30th for what was to become a historic 13-day trip. The first few days were uneventful. Just about everybody, including me, had gambled away most of their pay in poker games; by then, a huge amount of money was in the hands of some twenty men, who were gathered around three tables with thousands of dollars piled in front of each player. A ring of onlookers, the previous losers, stood behind the gamblers, watching the betting in fascination. Each pot contained several thousand dollars. Several of the players had hired soldiers as bodyguards to protect their winnings. I was reduced to playing chess and cribbage for a few francs which I was bringing back as souvenirs.

Because of my public relations experience, the commanding officer had arranged to have me assigned to the ship's radio transmission room. If there was an important but unclassified news bulletin, I was to broadcast it to the men over the loudspeakers. On the evening of August 6th, while we were on the high seas about half-way home, I was handed a message that an atom bomb had been dropped over Hiroshima in Japan. When I announced the startling news, there was an explosive roar that reverberated throughout the ship. Happy-faced men were hugging each other with glee. Some went down on their knees in silent prayer. We were going to come out of this war alive! Not a thought about the Japanese men, women and children who were incinerated!

For the next few days, I was probably the most popular man on the ship. Wherever I went, men would be asking me, "Anything new?" I was now instructed to broadcast whatever news I could obtain twice a day. Two days later, on August 8th, I was able to announce the heartening news that the Soviet Union had declared war on Japan. And on the following day, I reported that a second atom bomb had been dropped on Nagasaki.

When we landed in New York on August 12, 1945, we knew that the war would be over in a matter of days. We let out cheers of joy when we sailed past the Statue of Liberty and saw the New York skyline. On August 14th, while we were lined up in formation at a railroad station waiting to go to Westover Field, Massachusets, we were told that Japan had formally surrendered.

I was under the impression that now I would be discharged immediately. The war was over and the army had no further need of my services. I was mistaken. I had to remain at Westover for more than two months while I tried vainly to hurry the process of my discharge. During this ordeal, I was assigned secretarial jobs, including interviews with men applying for their separation papers. Finally, on October 27th. I was processed out of the army, with three hundred dollars in severance pay. I felt like I had been let out of prison. Three years of my life gone by. I was impatient to get back to the real world.

16. Returning to Labor Activity

I arrived on a rainy Saturday morning to our new home, a six-room, rent-controlled railroad flat on West 70th Street that Ann had been able to get through her friend, Barbara Tabb. Ann had already put me on notice that we had tenants—a Chinese woman, a scientist named Darren Chen, and her two-year-old son, Billy.

Ann greeted me at the door, with little Kathy standing beside her, looking up at me quizzically. I restrained myself from lifting her up and dancing her around in my arms because I was afraid it might startle her and she would cry. We'd get to know each other soon enough. Ann looked pale and tired. It had been a tough two years for her while I was overseas.

It was not a great homecoming. There were no friends to welcome me. No party had been planned. I took off my rain-soaked uniform and got into some civvies that were hanging in the closet, while Ann made breakfast. As I shaved, Kathy watched me intently, then ran off to Ann. This was a new experience for her—and for me. Every time she came back, I made a funny face at her, and she smiled. It was our first father-daughter game.

I met Darren and Billy later in the day. She was a short, intense woman who spoke in clipped sentences. When she laughed (she found so many things amusing), her body would shake and her eyes twinkle. She was working in a lab at Mt. Sinai and planning to go back to China after her training. I liked her and felt no strain about adjusting to her presence. Billy was an adorable but mischievous two-year-old with a disarming grin. He would be a nice companion for Kathy.

The weather cleared up on Sunday. I was able to take Kathy and Billy to the playground in Riverside Park. They played beautifully together. I was beginning to enjoy being a father. But as much as I liked Darren and her son, I was unhappy about living in the same apartment with another family. I had more than enough of communal living in the army, and I wanted privacy. There were now five of us, instead of two, living together; I told Ann it would be hard for me to get used to it. She explained that she had been strapped for money, and that Darren helped pay the rent. When I got back to work and earned a salary, we could arrange to have the apartment for ourselves.

On Monday, I received a series of bewildering shocks when I walked into the headquarters of Trade Union Service where my editorial offices were located. A strange person at the reception desk asked me who I wanted to see. I explained, with annoyance, that I worked there. She gave me a blank stare. I went to my office to find a young woman sitting at my desk. She apparently knew who I was and seemed embarrassed. Confused and angry, I rushed to a rear office to see Vic Levitt, the president of T.U.S., and find out what the hell was going on.

Vic was delighted to see me. After we had embraced affectionately, he brought out a bottle of scotch to celebrate my homecoming. "I've got some bad news to tell you," he said apologetically, "but before I do, I want you to know you've got a job here as long as I'm running the company."

I braced myself for a shock, not knowing what to expect. Had T.U.S. lost its bread-winning publication, *UE News?* Had I been removed as editor of the two labor papers I founded seven years ago? What had happened to my staff?

"Sorry, Harry, but we've had to fold your papers. We stopped publishing the *Trade Union Record* in March of last year. We tried to continue the *Building Trades Union Press* but it became financially impossible. The cost of newsprint and mailing went sky high, and we had no alternative but to make some adjustments or else face bankruptcy."

I was stunned. I couldn't believe it. "Why wasn't I told about this?" I asked, almost in tears.

"There was no point in upsetting you. What could you do about it? We tried to get financial support from some of the unions to save your papers, but they, too, were cutting back on expenses." Vic reached toward me and put his hand on my shoulder. "Look, Harry, it's not the end of the world. Now that you've heard the worst, let me give you some good news.

"The good news," he said cheerfully, "is that we've arranged to provide editorial and printing services for several important unions, and there'll be more than enough work for you. I want you to take charge of the editorial department. There's no rush. Why don't you take a vacation for a couple of weeks or as long as you like ? The job will be waiting for you."

I returned home terribly depressed. I couldn't sleep. I'd wake up at two in the morning and go out to walk along Broadway or I'd sit in the kitchen reading and drinking coffee. At Ann's suggestion, I went to see her doctor for a checkup. He told me I had hypertension and prescribed some medication. He mentioned that he was treating several veterans with the same psychological problem: they had returned to their civilian jobs too quickly. He advised me to take a vacation and mentioned that two of his patients had gone to Mt. McGregor, a rest and rehab center for veterans in upstate New York, where they had stayed for a month without charge.

I checked with the Veterans Administration and found out how to get in touch with the Mt. McGregor facility. When I called, they put me on a waiting list and said they would notify me when an opening was available. A few days later, to my surprise, I received a phone call saying I could come the following Monday; they were opening up a new dormitory building where I would stay. Ann agreed I should go; she thought it would help me.

It was early in January when I arrived at Mt. McGregor. It was a cold, sunny day; the air was invigorating. I had to go through a processing assembly line, just like in the army before I was assigned to my own room. It was small, clean and had a picture window. I was pleased because I had a good view of the surrounding area and the valley below.

There were several hundred vets at the center, including some from World War I and one old geezer, barely alive, who had fought in the Spanish-American War a half century ago. For several days, I kept to myself, taking walks along the trails, reading. listening to classical music, napping and reporting for meals and snack-time. I had brought along an anthology of modern poetry, a volume of Shakespeare's plays, a couple of novels, a book of chess games and a thick notebook in case I was inspired to write a short story or a poem.

In the evening, there usually was a program of entertainment in the center's theater. It consisted either of an old movie, a standup comic, a pop singer or a jazz combo, but the one nightly feature that the vets enjoyed most was the bingo game that followed the entertainment. The competition excited them, especially if they won a prize, such as a shaving kit, a set of handkerchiefs, a pair of ties, a box of candy or a book. I found it boring, but there was not much to do in the evening except to read or find a partner for a chess game.

I started to write a story about a labor spy operating within a union and how he was exposed while trying to break a strike. I worked on it mornings, but did not get very far with it. I told myself I'd finish it when I got home. By the third week, I'd had enough of Mt. McGregor. I could have stayed another week, possibly longer, but I felt fully relaxed and was eager to get back to work.

* * * * *

On the first few days after my return to Trade Union Service, I found I had not lost any of my journalistic skills. I missed working on my own labor papers, but I soon found pleasure and excitement in editing the newspapers of several unions. Within a month, I was editor in fact if not in name, of the official publications of the United Furniture Workers and two of its local affiliates; I was also putting out the monthly newspaper of the bakery workers union, and the large over-the-road teamsters local. There was enough work to keep me and one of my former staff members, Howie Freeman, on the payroll. However, it took many months before I became reconciled to the loss of my two papers.

As busy as I was, I found time to renew my pre-war relationship with many labor leaders, both progressive and conservative, who were caught up in difficult struggles. Corporations everywhere were taking advantage of shortages in consumer goods to reap huge profits, while refusing wage increases to their employees to compensate them for their loss of purchasing power during the war. Runaway inflation had outpaced the modest pay raises that unions had won under the War Labor Board's so-called "Little Steel Formula." There was hardly a union that was not involved in a strike or considering one.

To help the striking unions, I developed a Union Action Kit, consisting of a package of ten postcards, each containing a satirical illustration by Fred Wright, the popular labor cartoonist. On one side of the postcard next to the cartoon was a tightly written statement explaining why the workers had gone on strike. On the back of the card was a brief printed letter to the company, asking it to negotiate with the union. Strikers were instructed to pass out the postcards to family members, friends and neighbors, urging them to sign the cards and mail them to the company. Among the unions that liked the "double action" kits and bought thousands were the American Communications Association, Packinghouse Workers, Furniture Workers and United Electrical Workers.

* * * * *

It was early in April, 1946 when I received a phone call from Sir Anthony Jenkinson, the radical scion of a wealthy British family, who asked to see me. He was a tall, homely, giraffe of a man, who disdained his title and background and preferred to be called Tony. When we met over drinks, he told me he was looking for a managing editor of *Allied Labor News,* a worldwide labor press service that he had established in 1943. He had heard I might be the man for the position, and he wanted to know if I was interested. ALN had correspondents in major capitals of the world, he said. As he saw it, international labor solidarity, particularly among the allied countries, could play an important role in promoting world peace and in raising the standard of living of workers in all countries. ALN could serve as an informational connecting link among the various labor movements. If I accepted the position, I would be in charge of the New York office, from which I and a staff of two other journalists, would mail out a twice-weekly news service to American subscribers.

I was excited by the possibilities. I told Jenkinson that I would give him my answer in a few days, although I had already made up my mind to accept. Vic, who was one of my closest friends as well as my employer, didn't want me to leave, although he recognized the importance of the new job. He said, "Let's call it a leave of absence. You never know how things may turn out. If you ever want to come back, there'll be a place here for you."

Jenkinson was at the ALN office when I arrived for my first day. He introduced me to Gladys Carter, one of the editors, and Marguerite Moorman, a black woman, who was both secretary and office manager. Another editor, Herman Starobin, would be at the office the next day. After briefing me on some financial matters (I believe my salary was somewhere between $75 and $100) and providing me with authority over the bank account, he said he had to rush back to England to make some changes in ALN's London office, after which he planned to go to India, China and Japan. I was very impressed. As managing editor, I imagined I'd be able to find reasons to travel abroad—and at ALN's expense. I thought I had worked myself into a good deal.

I fully agreed with Jenkinson that this was an opportune time to develop a world-wide labor news service. The United Nations had come into existence the year before and it was headquartered in New York City. Obviously, it would be a valuable source for news and new subscribers. Even more important, the World Federation of Trade Unions (WFTU) had also been created in 1945 under the auspices of the British Trade Union Congress, the All-Union Central Council of Trade Unions of the Soviet Union and the Congress of Industrial Organizations (CIO), representing the American labor movement.

ALN's goal, as I saw it, was to become an indispensable news and information service for the WFTU through our global network of correspondents. By maintaining a close relationship with WFTU leaders, we could develop contacts with union officials in scores of countries and expand our list of international subscribers. There appeared to be no end to the possibilities.

Almost from the start, there were more mundane matters that required my attention. The several thousand dollars that Jenkinson had left me in our bank account was soon spent on salaries and office expenses. When I teletyped him for additional funds, his quick response stunned me. He had no more money to invest and I should close the office. I suggested we negotiate a bank loan. His response: No loan; close the office. I teletyped back that ALN was too important to be shut down. He answered: "I'm ordering you to shut it down." I replied: "I won't." We continued this stand-off exchange almost daily.

Although I hated fund-raising and had never been good at it, I now had to spend most of my time looking for "angels" who would subsidize us. Communist Party leaders thought that ALN was worth preserving and suggested some rich Party sympathizers who might be willing to contribute. I had lots of competition. Wealthy "fellow travelers" and liberals were being beseiged by fund-raisers whose causes were much more appealing than mine. I had to endure some very obnoxious people who held out promises to contribute and, after several meetings, changed their mind. There were individuals who, for a paltry donation, wanted a voice in ALN's editorial policies.

Despite the constant frustration, I persevered and raised enough money to keep us going for several months—but only if we operated on an extremely tight budget, requiring all of us to take pay cuts. This also meant that we would have to persuade our correspondents to forego, for at least several months, the pay that Jenkinson had promised them. We appealed to their sense of commitment to what ALN stood for. Most of the correspondents (they had other jobs that earned them a living) agreed to continue, and we tried to find replacements for the few who quit. In one case, the Indian correspondent, a fine journalist, said he would keep sending us his articles without compensation if we supplied him at least with the postage.

Disheartened as we were, the small ALN staff continued to get out the news service on schedule. Gladys did most of the rewriting, Herman covered the United Nations and I wrote a regular column and an occasional story about the American labor scene for foreign subscribing organizations.

We finally reached the point where, despite our efforts, ALN was financially bankrupt. Rather than fold, we negotiated an arrangement to have *Federated Press,* a domestic labor news service founded in 1919, take over ALN with two of our staff members, Gladys and Marguerite. ALN continued to serve a limited number of subscribing labor publications until several years before *FP* shut down in 1956.

I returned to my job at Trade Union Service in May 1947, just when the labor movement was engaged in a bitter but losing fight to prevent Congress from passing the Taft-Hartley anti-union amendments to the Wagner Labor Act. Although I and other labor editors wrote numerous leaflets, articles and pamphlets denouncing the drastic anti-union restrictions of Taft-Hartley (unions called it the Slave Labor Act), it was to no avail. Public opinion, angered by the rash of strikes of the past year, was overwhelmingly in favor of curbing "Big Labor." So strong was the prevailing anti-union sentiment, that Congress was able to pass Taft-Hartley even over President Truman's veto.

Among the new law's provisions was one that required union officers to file affidavits affirming they were not members of the Communist Party and had not been during the preceding twelve months. The law further stated that a signatory must also certify that "he does not believe in, and is not a member of or supports any organization that believes in or teaches, the overthrow of the United States Government by force or by any illegal or unconstitutional methods." If they failed to do so, their union would be deprived of various protections under the National Labor Relations Act and it would become more difficult for them to organize new members.

The clear intent of this provision in the law was to cripple the labor movement, by going after left-wing or communist labor leaders who had been infusing militancy into unions and provoking the post-war strike wave. When John L. Lewis and officers of the International Typographical Union, who could hardly be accused of being communists, refused to sign the affidavits on principle, it made it a lot easier for labor leaders suspected of being communists to take the same position. Moreover, since virtually all unions in both the AFL and CIO opposed the law as a whole, left-wingers made only a muted effort to focus on the anti-communist issue for fear that their opposition to this clause in the law would be construed as proof they were pro-communist.

I was intensely interested in how many unions and their officers were signing the affidavits and managed to get some figures from the regional office of the Labor Department which I publicized. Nearly a year after the passage of Taft-Hartley, of the 60,000 unions that had been requested to comply with the provisions of the law, only a fraction actually signed the anti-communist affidavits. Here is the breakdown:

CIO: 421 local unions and 206 officers.

AFL: 3,192 locals and 474 officers.

Unaffiliated: 694 locals and 5,681 officers.

Clearly, most of the nation's local unions were refusing to sign the anti-communist affidavits, mainly, I believe, because they did not wish to show their compliance with a law that took away many of their basic rights while expanding the rights of employers. Nevertheless, this matter posed a serious dilemma for union leaders who were communist or whose behavior could be described as pro-communist. To sign or not to sign? In either case, their opponents could make this an issue in union election campaigns, causing them much embarrassment. It was hard to prove that anyone had been a "card carrying" communist, because there were no cards or other documents to attest to their membership. What was acccepted as proof was circumstantial evidence that a labor leader had followed the Communist Party line in instance after instance, primarily on foreign policy.

In the United Furniture Workers, whose official newspaper I edited, there was strong disagreement between the president, Morris Pizer, and the secretary-treasurer, Max Perlow, about signing the anti-communist affidavit. Pizer favored signing, while Perlow was opposed. I customarily wrote each of their columns after they indicated orally what they'd like to say. They were frequently delighted at how well I expressed their opinions when they reviewed my handiwork in print. Now I had the schizophrenic task of writing pro-and-con columns on the same issue. Each of them thought I had done a better job for the other. To cap it all, I was instructed to write an editorial on the importance of maintaining unity.

Pizer won the preliminary battle when the General Executive Board voted 14-13 to instruct the officers to sign the affidavits. However, at the union convention three months later, the delegates, to my private delight, reversed the Board's action by a roll-call vote of 22,497 to 17,164. Fortunately, both top officials had the good sense to patch up their differences, at least publicly, in the interest of unity.

The officers of the UE, the other union that I had a close relationship with, had no problem about refusing to sign the affidavits; they received overwhelming support for their decision at the union's 1948 convention.

* * * * *

But there was another issue that caused considerable dissension within the ranks of the labor movement. Hardly two years after the end of the war, the United States and the Soviet Union were locked into a power struggle over the fate of Greece and Turkey, whose governments were in danger of being taken over by a communist-supported guerrilla movement. To prevent the two countries from falling into the Soviet orbit, Congress voted some $700 million in aid to their beleagured governments.

When the United States proposed the Marshall Plan to finance the reconstruction of Western Germany and invited the Soviet Union, among twenty-two other nations, to join a consortium for that purpose, the Russians withdrew and denounced the effort as a plot to establish American hegemony over Europe. The communist coup in Czechoslovakia in March 1948 and the possibility that the Communist Party of Italy might win the forthcoming election and take control of the country heightened the tension between the superpowers. The World War II alliance between the foremost capitalist and communist powers was unraveling to be replaced by the Cold War that was to dominate our lives for the next 40 years.

In this titanic struggle, the leadership of both the AFL and the CIO supported the Truman Doctrine and the Marshall Plan. The CIO's left-wing leaders, under the influence of the Communist Party, opposed the Marshall Plan on the grounds that it was dangerous to build up West Germany so soon after the end of the war and besides, the enormous financial outlay was too great a burden on the American people and the money could be better spent at home. As plausible as these reasons sounded, they could not hold up when subjected, as they were, to a barrage of red-baiting.

It was difficult for left-wing union leaders to deny the charge that they were following the Communist Party line and that American communists were "taking orders from Moscow." A "cold war" was also developing within the CIO, with the left-wing unions in an uncomfortable minority position.

Another major source of friction within the CIO arose during the 1948 presidential election. With the active support of the Communist Party, leaders of several unions under its influence endorsed the Progressive Party candidacy of Henry Wallace, a former U.S. vice president under FDR, in conflict with the official CIO position, which favored the reelection of President Truman. I attended several meetings of left-wing activists at which the issue of a third party was hotly debated; the decision to support Wallace was far from unanimous. Critics pointed out the risk of deepening the division within the CIO and their belief that no third party candidate could win. Third-party advocates argued that Truman had become deservedly unpopular, that the Republican candidate, Governor Thomas Dewey, had little labor support and that Strom Thurmond, a southern governor and a racist on the States Rights Party, would run poorly. In a four-way race, they said, Wallace could emerge a winner. Even if Wallace did not win, the new Progressive Party could become the balance of power and a political force for the future. I was persuaded that this was the best option under the existing unfavorable conditions. I could not see myself supporting Truman or abstaining from voting.

Although UE President Albert Fitzgerald was co-chairman of the Wallace Election Committee and most of its officers were openly in favor of the Progressive Party candidate, the union at its 1948 convention refrained from endorsing any presidential nominee, giving the locals a free hand to make their own choices. The purpose of this political tactic was to avoid giving the pro-Truman forces on the CIO Executive Board another pretext for attacking the union.

We at Trade Union Service had a personal stake in the Wallace candidacy because we were publishing a substantial amount of Progressive Party leaflets and a series of four-page newspapers for regional distribution, some of which I wrote and edited. The Wallace campaign provided a springboard for the creation of the progressive *National Guardian*, which also was published in the T.U.S. printing plant.

The Wallace platform was strongly pro-labor and favored a peaceful accommodation with the Soviet Union, in contrast with Truman's conservative domestic program and cold-war foreign policies. With hordes of young people flocking into the campaign and signs that Truman was being disavowed by influential Demo-crats, our hopes for a good showing by Wallace began to blossom.

We could not have miscalculated more abysmally about the outcome of the election. At a "victory" celebration at the Park Avenue townhouse of the Progres-sive Party, we were shocked into disbelief when the results were announced. That Truman defeated Dewey was no major surprise. But what absolutely stunned us was that Wallace came in *fourth*, behind Thurmond, with *less than two percent of the popular vote and not a single electoral vote!*

The Wallace debacle was irrefutable evidence that the Progressive Party and its left-wing adherents were out of touch with the rank-and-file of the labor move-ment. Even before the 1948 elections, the left-wing forces had suffered serious setbacks in important unions where they had occupied high positions. In March 1946, Reuther won the presidency of the United Auto Workers over R.J. Thomas, the candidate of the union's left-wing. In the National Maritime Union, Joe Curran, its president, broke with his pro-communist associates in the leadership and be-came an ardent red-baiter, as did Mike Quill, president of the Transport Workers.

Red-baiting was now being introduced into the CIO after years of collabora-tion between moderate and pro-communist unions. The CIO leadership became as heavy-handed as their AFL counterparts in stamping out opposition to their poli-cies. It lifted the charters of progressive CIO industrial union councils in New York and several other cities because it disapproved of their actions. It fired staff people who were thought to have pro-communist ideas or associations.

As a member of the representative assembly of the New York Newspaper Guild, I witnessed the new, destructive witch-hunt tactics which the national CIO was encouraging. At a stormy meeting of the Guild, Jack Ryan, the union's execu-tive vice president, was heckled repeatedly to state whether he was or was not or had ever been a member of the Communist Party. When he declined to answer this question as an invasion of his privacy, this was advertised by his opposition as proof that he was indeed a communist. In the election that followed, Ryan was soundly defeated, despite his reputation as an excellent union leader.

The single most important target of the anti-communist majority on the CIO Executive Board was the UE, the largest left-wing union, with 600,000 members. James B. Carey, the secretary of the national CIO, had been the first UE president, but he had been ousted at the 1941 convention in favor of Albert Fitzgerald. With the support of a small group within the union and the assistance of an outside organization, the Association of Catholic Trade Unionists, Carey had tried, thus far unsuccessfully, to regain the presidency. Operating with strong allies within the CIO Executive Board, he saw fresh opportunities to return to power.

His strongest allies were Walter Reuther, president of the United Auto Work-ers; Phil Murray, president of the CIO, and the officers of Murrray's union, the United Steelworkers of America (USA). There were much more practical issues at stake than ideological differences in the CIO Board's attack on left-wing unions. Reuther got the Board to order the 50,000-member Farm Equipment Workers to affiliate with his union on pain of expulsion. Similarly, the Mine, Mill and Smelter Workers were ordered to merge into the Steelworkers. The two unions, with left-wing leadership, refused to comply, considering the CIO order a brazen violation of their autonomy.

At the same time, CIO staffers, with the approval of Carey and Murray, were assisting UAW and Steelworkers organizers to conduct raids on UE locals and shops. In its formal complaint to the CIO Board, the UE cited 456 raids on its jurisdiction, of which 92 percent had been defeated. It finally reached the point at which the UE was compelled to say it was witholding its per capita payments until the CIO leadership called a halt to the raids and ceased interfering with the autonomy of affiliated international unions.

The CIO Executive Board responded by chartering a new union, the International Union of Electrical Workers (IUE), with Jim Carey as its head. To give legitimacy to the new union, which then had no members and no constitution, a number of important government officials were invited as speakers to a convention organized by Carey.

Finally, at its 1949 convention, the CIO carried through a massive purge of eleven of its affiliated international unions, including the UE, representing about one-fifth of the total membership. The grounds for the expulsions were that these unions had shown a consistent pattern of following the Communist Party line dating back to the Hitler-Stalin Pact. In reply, the defending unions insisted in vain that the CIO was a federation of autonomous unions, and their members had a right to formulate their own policies without interference from the CIO Executive Board.

I and my colleagues at Trade Union Service followed the conflict between the UE and the CIO leadership closely and with anxiety, because the *UE News* was our biggest customer. If the UE were to suffer severe losses in membership, it would seriously damage our financial stability.

I had personal reasons for feeling upset about the unjustified attacks on the UE. I had known its leaders since 1937 when the union first received its charter from the CIO. I had worked closely over a period of ten years with the editor of the *UE News,* Tom Wright, a dear friend, who kept me informed of the reasoning behind UE policies and tactics, including some of the internal debates. At no point did I think the UE should have—or could have—acted differently without losing its identity as an outstanding democratic union.

I had an especially high regard for James Matles, the union's first director of organization, whom I considered to be one of the most brilliant organizers in the labor movement. Friend and foe respected him as a shrewd, tough and meticulous negotiator and a man of unquestioned loyalty to working people. More than any single individual, it was Matles who helped build the UE into a union of 600,000 members. Even during the union's difficulties with the CIO, Matles employed his skills to win favorable contracts at General Electric, Westinghouse and other giant companies. When we became good friends, we were both pleased to discover that our families came from the same town in Romania.

Given the anti-communist climate in the country and the CIO's financial and staff support, as well as assistance from U.S. government agencies, the IUE was able to make successful raids on the beleaguered UE. It was heartbreaking when the entire District 4, consisting of all locals in the New York metropolitan area, abandoned the UE to join the IUE. Union leaders who had worked together for years and had close personal ties were now bitter enemies. I had friends in both camps, but my allegiance was to those who remained with the UE, even though its membership eventually shrank to less than 70,000.

By 1950, the CIO had completely purged the organization of communist influence, but in doing so, it largely destroyed the inspiring militancy that had characterized it in the early years of its existence. It is worth noting that when Senator Joseph McCarthy launched his anti-communist investigation during the early 1950s, he paid little attention to the labor movement because the CIO had already done his work for him.

The CIO was now as thoroughly bureaucratized as the AFL, from which it had rebelled a dozen years earlier. Its fratricidal campaign had cost it the loss of countless seasoned organizers. By insisting on conformity from the state and local industrial union councils, it inhibited the kind of grass-roots initiatives that had made the CIO such a dynamic organization. Anti-communism could provide the means for eliminating left-wing opposition within a union, but it had no value whatever in a campaign to organize new workers.

As for the Communist Party, having lost its influence in the labor movement, its formerly powerful mass base, it ceased to have any impact whatever on the national scene. The capitalist press and reactionaries in government had succeeded in stigmatizing the Communist Party as a subversive, traitorous organization, so that its once broad influence among liberals and "fellow travelers" all but vanished. I found myself regretting that.

Normally optimistic, I was full of foreboding about the future of the labor movement. I could see the growing signs that national union leaders would be giving unqualified support to the developing Cold War with the Soviet Union, and that it would have disastrous consequences for working people. The groundwork had been laid for crushing any labor opposition to U.S. foreign policy. Conformity, in the name of unity, was now the hallmark of the nation's unions.

I felt that this was no longer the labor movement I had worked in and been proud to be a part of.

17. An Unhappy Time

Our family suffered a severe blow when Mama died suddenly on July 16, 1946, only about nine months after I had been released from the army. She had been visiting my two sisters in Boston and was returning home when the accident occurred. Hurrying to catch a train, she tripped and fell down a flight of stairs, where she lay unconscious. Taken to Boston General Hospital, she remained in a coma for a few days and then died. The doctors said she had suffered a heart attack, whether before or after the accident they could not tell, nor did it now matter. I rushed to the hospital and stood beside her bed, hoping she would open her eyes and say a word. She never did. All I could do was to stare at her pale face, kiss her cheek and weep. She was 62 years old.

My consolation was that she had experienced the joy of loving and being loved by her granddaughter. In my first post-war visit to Mama, I begged her forgiveness again and again for being so stupid as not to tell her about my marriage. She was so happy to see me that she forgot to scold me.

It was a happy moment when Ann, Kathy and I visited Mama in her apartment on Coney Island Avenue in Brooklyn. I noted how friendly Ann and Mama were and how they had warmly embraced. Mama rushed to the bedroom to bring out some new dresses she had made for Kathy. She had taught her smart granddaughter several Jewish expressions which Kathy was able to repeat on request. "That little Kathy is my joy. She is such a charmer," Mama said in Yiddish.

From my older sister, Lee, I learned what had happened after Mama received my letter from France about my secret marriage. That same day, Mama had called Ann and invited herself over to our apartment. I can imagine how she felt when her critical, inspecting eye surveyed the habitual disarray in each room. The two women at first greeted each other with some reserve, but after Mama had picked up Kathy and was hugging and kissing her, with tears of joy streaming down her cheeks, Ann felt a lot friendlier toward her.

Ann and the baby visited Mama many times and she also met my two sisters and other relatives and friends. Mama made Kathy a wardrobe of dresses, blouses, overalls, skirts and even a pair of riding jodhpurs. Our daughter was probably the best dressed two-year-old in New York.

Ann, basically a reserved person, responded sympathetically to Mama's warm, emotional personality. She was gracious enough to let Mama take Kathy for a week-end from time to time, even permitting her to wear a golden necklace with a Jewish star, which Mama had bought. I wished Mama had not been so aggressive in her personal campaign to educate Kathy in the Jewish faith. Neither Ann nor I was religious, and we had agreed that our child would not be indoctrinated in any religion but would make up her own mind in her own time.

* * * * *

However, there was also sadness and disappointment in Mama's final months. She had become hysterical when she first learned that her younger son, Marty, had been sent to an army prison camp on charges of desertion. It appeared he had walked out of his outfit in Italy and stayed AWOL for 13 days. When he voluntarily turned himself in, he was court-martialed and sent back to the States as a prisoner in the Disciplinary Training Corps. He had been offered the option of joining an army unit that was fighting the Japanese in the Pacific or serving a two-year prison term and receiving a dishonorable discharge. He told the authorities he had had enough of fighting.

Marty's girl friend, Bea, visited him at Fort Leavenworth, Kansas, where he had been transferred. She reported that he was in good health and that they had made plans to marry when he was free. It was too much of a trip for Mama to make, but when Marty was transferred to another camp in Pennsylvania (I forget the name), Mama and I went to see him. Except for her infrequent visits to Boston to see her two daughters, she had never been outside of New York City.

Marty had always been a problem for Mama. He loved her but was too strong-willed to listen to her. He had enlisted in the regular army when he was seventeen by lying about his age. We had tried hard to dissuade him, but in vain. He was a high school dropout without a job, and he wanted adventure. He was shipped to North Africa where he got more adventure than he had bargained for as a fighting infantryman. Physically strong and hot-tempered, he broke the nose of a soldier who had called him a Jew bastard. He was put in prison, but soon released when his outfit was ordered to Italy to support U.S. troops at Anzio. It was shortly after that he decided to go AWOL.

Our thirty-minute visit with Marty, after a long tiresome train ride, was emotionally exhausting for Mama. Marty looked thin and pale, had grown a moustache, but otherwise seemed in good health and, of course, he was glad to see us. Mama felt relieved when he told her they had reduced his prison term by a year because of his combat record, and he would be home in August.

The same month that Marty came home, he was married to Beatrice Moskowitz, his longtime girl friend who had remained steadfast despite his tendency to get into trouble. Bea became a close friend of my sister Julia when they were in nurses' training together. Through her, she had become acquainted with Marty and conducted a long correspondence with him while he was in the army.

We felt it was too soon—only a month after Mama's death—to have a wedding, but Marty was insistent. He was in a terrible emotional state and he needed Bea to provide him with loving support.

Ann and Kathy attended the wedding. Our daughter, wearing one of the dresses Mama had made for her, added some joy to what was a bitter-sweet occasion as she flitted around the room, enjoying the attention she was getting. I was Best Man, and I was pleased to see Marty married to a woman I hoped would give him stability. And even more pleased when my hopes came true.

Shortly after my return to civilian life, I woke up one morning to admit what I had been feeling for some time. I was no longer in love with Ann. Yes, I respected her, was fond of her, but I did not want to live with her. I did not want to be married. There was no other woman in my life. I simply needed to be free to do what I wanted when I wanted.

Ann was not as attractive to me as in the pre-war years. The difference in our ages and our temperaments was now self-evident and it bothered me. She no longer had the glamour of a union organizer nor, for that matter, did I as a former energetic labor editor. All the joy and fun had been drained out of our marriage, and I saw no hope of rejuvenating it. So what should I do?

For two years, I resisted the idea of a divorce or even a separation. I did not want to hurt Ann. As unhappy as I was, there would be greater unhappiness in a breakup, I told myself. Kathy was our common interest, and we wanted her to grow up happy and well. There were several children of her age in our building with whom she played; for her sake, we became friendly with their parents. In fact, we spent two weeks with one of the families at a camp site in Riverhead, Long Island, where we all had a delightful time. Kathy got along beautifully with the two Douglas boys. Ann and I enjoyed being with each other. It was almost like old times.

But it really wasn't. I'd frequently stay out until late at night, drinking at the Newspaper Guild bar because I could not bear going home. Finally, I told Ann I wanted a separation; I was unhappy and I needed to be on my own for a while. She didn't try to dissuade me or display any emotion, except that by the peculiar way she pursed her lips, I could tell she was deeply hurt.

Through the latter part of 1949 and all of the following year, I lived alone, and I didn't like it. I found a room in a cheap boarding house and felt miserable coming home late at night. I missed Kathy and tried to spend part of each weekend with her. I would mumble some excuse when she asked me why I was not living with her and Ann.

As unhappy as I was with the separation, I knew I did not want to get back with Ann. I did not have a steady girl friend, nor did I get involved sexually with any of the young women whom I would see regularly at the Guild bar. For the first time in my life, I was not pleased with myself. I was only 34 and felt I had no future except editing publications of unions that were increasingly conservative. In June, 1951, I received the final papers of my divorce from Ann. The basis for the divorce was the phony story that I had committed adultery, and that investigators hired by Ann had found me in bed with another woman in a seedy hotel in Manhattan. Our lawyers said this was the most accepted reason for granting a divorce rather than incompatibility. Ann and I reluctantly agreed to the scenario as long as we didn't have to be present in court.

Ann was a woman of great pride. She refused to challenge the divorce. If that's what I wanted, then I should have it. She hoped we could continue to be good friends. She said she didn't want any alimony for herself, but accepted my allotment of $30 a week for Kathy. As to our common property, which actually was not very much, I left everything to her except some clothes, books and a few personal items. I could visit Kathy whenever I wanted to and spend vacation time with her. Ann and I took pains not to give each other any reason for complaint or bitterness, although it was clear that she had the worst of this "amicable" divorce.

I was sorry for Ann. Unable to get a job with a union or progressive organization, she had decided to start her own public relations firm. By working hard and with sheer persistence, she had managed to get a handful of accounts that paid very little for her services: a cabaret singer, a new toothpaste company, a furniture store and a portrait photographer. The one advantage of the job was that she could work at home and have a flexible schedule. All her clients made excessive demands on her which she tried hard to comply with. Each time she thought of quitting, she would come up with a potential client or two with a substantial advertising budget, and she would be encouraged to continue. With my $30 weekly stipend for Kathy and by living frugally, she managed to make ends meet, barely.

My estrangement from Ann had not been based on any involvement with another woman. During the period of our separation, I had no "affairs" or strong interest in forming a serious attachment with anyone; the furthest thing from my mind was the thought of getting married again. I had not a dime in savings and my future was uncertain. It might take years, if that, before I could earn a livelihood as a printer, which was what I had decided to become. I was no great "catch" for any woman who might regard me as a prospect for marriage.

* * * * *

As a born-again bachelor, I arranged to live wth Sam Rubenstein, who had a penthouse apartment at the Amalgamated housing project on Grand Street. Sam was shop chairman at the *Jewish Day,* and we had become good friends through our activity in the Newspaper Guild. Sam's spacious, well-furnished apartment had Brueghel paintings, large and small, in every room. He was a party-loving, gregarious man, which may explain why he was so fond of Brueghel. All of his rooms, including the bathroom, were wired for classical music, which he played continuously.. On a sunny Sunday morning, I would find Sam on the terrace, letting down a small basket on the end of his fishing line to an ice cream vendor twelve stories below and then reeling up his purchase.

Sam loved giving fund-raising parties for one cause or another; the people who came to his lively soirées were mostly Guild members and their friends. I enoyed the parties, but wasn't sufficiently interested in any of the women to invite them to sleep over. I stayed with Sam until my new career took me elsewhere.

* * * * *

Fortunately for me, I was able to develop a social life as part of my activity in the Newspaper Guild. In 1949, I was named campaign manager of a rank-and-file ticket that was challenging the conservative union leadership. In that capacity, I became better acquainted with a lively group of women and men from various newspapers and magazines who were strong supporters of our slate. After our caucus meetings, a few of us would gather at Hector's cafeteria on Broadway and 44th Street for coffee and conversation or congregate at the Guild bar. Although I was at least several years older than nearly all of them, I was glad to be accepted as part of the group. It was perfect therapy for my fractured self-esteem. We lost the election, but the warm camaraderie of our set continued for many years after.

Of all the young women I met, I was most attracted to Miriam (Mim) Kolkin. I had first met Mim in 1947 at *Federated Press.* the labor news service, where she was chief editor. She had worked there since she had graduated from Hunter College at nineteen. It was not love at first sight, or even second, for either of us. We worked together briefly as volunteers on a new left-wing monthly magazine, *March of Labor.* I could tell she was a competent journalist and more politically-focused than any of the women I had met. I'd see her from time to time at union meetings or at social gatherings of mutual friends, but never alone or intimately until the summer of 1950. As I grew to know her better, I admired how even-tempered, low-keyed and unassuming she was compared to me and some other left-wing people I knew. I found I enjoyed being with her: she made me feel comfortable and youthful. She was 28, eight years younger than me, and the kind of stable, non-threatening companion I needed to help me through the emotional crisis I was enduring. We were never at a loss for things to talk about in our long walks or while having a meal at some cafeteria. Our political views generally coincided, and even when we disagreed, we were never quarrelsome or offensive toward each other.

Mim was an attractive woman, of medium height and with a trim figure. I liked looking at her face, especially her blue eyes. I began to fall in love with her. I wasn't quite sure how Mim felt about me. One of our mutual friends, Gladys Bentley, a veteran member of the Newspaper Guild, had warned her not to get involved with me. She said I was a flighty, irresponsible *luftmensch* who did not have much of a future.

Mim lived alone in a three-room apartment on East 12th Street. She had been a "red diaper" baby. Her father was Alex Kolkin, a founder of the U.S. Communist Party and currently a leader of a rank-and-file group in the International Ladies' Garment Workers. He had left his family to become a union organizer when she was a child, but she saw him occasionally. Her mother had died of breast cancer in 1948. Mim's older brother, Al, lived with his wife, Lucy, in Brooklyn. She profoundly loved her mother and Al, who both worked to support their small family and made it possible for her to get a college education.

Although we had never said a word about marriage, I assumed that Mim was getting serious about me when she invited me to a large family Thanksgiving Day dinner at the home of Lucy's parents in Bensonhurst. I found myself under critical inspection by assorted uncles, aunts and cousins who assumed that Mim and I were engaged. I wondered whether Mim had told them I was a divorced man with a small daughter and eight years her senior. I managed to get across the idea, without putting it into words, that Mim was my friend, not my fiancée. I spent most of the evening, trying to charm Lucy's aunts and uncles and discussing gin rummy and poker with her mother.

My relationship with Mim had its ups and downs and there'd be months when we wouldn't see each other. She had other men friends. But in the summer of 1953, when we were getting close again, Dave and Naomi Fisher, our longtime friends, who were married and living with their son, Paul, in Schenectady, invited Mim and me to join them on a 10-day vacation trip to Canada. We both accepted, realizing that this could turn into our pre-marriage honeymoon. We traveled by car, with Dave doing all the driving and enjoying it.

One of the towns where we stopped for lunch on our way to the Canadian border was Hanover, New Hampshire, where we briefly toured the Dartmouth College campus and saw several works of David Siqueiros, the famous Mexican painter. We had an enjoyable time in Montreal and Quebec, seeing the historical sites, dining at several good restaurants, browsing in book stores, shopping for gifts and even going to the race track where we lost the small amount we had set aside for betting. By then, we were very much in love and felt like a married couple.

On the way back to the States, Mim and I asked to be dropped off at Lake Placid where we planned to spend a day or two to wind up our idyllic vacation. There was not much we wanted to do except be alone with each other.

That evening at Lake Placid, we had a serious talk about our future. We were in love with each other, but what about marriage? Mim was ready for it, but I wasn't—at least not until I could get a steady job at decent wages in my new career as a printer. I'd have to work out-of-town for a couple of years to get the experience before I could apply for membership in the New York Typographical Union. Was she willing to wait?

Mim didn't respond or offer alternatives. On the train trip home, she was sad and contemplative. For me, it was the climax to the unhappiest period of my life.

18. A New Career as a Printer

The red-baiting campaign of Senator Joseph McCarthy was gathering momentum, and Trade Union Service was being smeared as a pro-communist publishing company. As a result, we lost several important labor papers, as well as the official organ of the National Association for the Advancement of Colored People (NAACP), a very substantial account. The *National Guardian* was unable to pay its printing bills, and we could no longer afford to subsidize it. The circulation of the *UE News* had been cut in half and was still dropping. T.U.S. was in desperate need of new customers which, in the current political climate, were hard to find. Although I, as the oldest employee, had top seniority and would be the last to be laid off, I now felt that T.U.S.'s days were numbered, and I had better start looking for another job. It would have to be in the editorial field, I thought, because I had no other occupational skills that could command a decent salary.

One day, after I had completed my editorial work on the *Furniture Workers Press,* the international union president, Morris Pizer, called me into his office and informed me he was going to hire a full-time editor who would also handle public relations for the union. I could have the job if I wanted it, but only if I were to announce publicly that I was resigning from the Communist Party. He said that given the situation within the CIO, he couldn't afford to have a communist—or anyone suspected of being a Party member—on the union payroll. I told him he could take his job and shove it. No one was going to put a padlock on my mind.

I brooded over the matter for days. What options did I have for maintaining my intellectual integrity? Where could I get a job in the newspaper field with my left-wing background? There were no openings within the labor movement for reporters or editors, and which union would dare to hire me, even if there were?

One day, I suddenly hit on a possible solution. It startled me. *I would become a printer! I would be a blue-collar craftsman and remain in the labor movement without compromising my ideas!* Here was an occupation in which competence was judged by how many galleys of type a worker produced and how error-free they were, not whether his ideas or outside behavior were acceptable to an employer. Over the years, I had worked with union printers in various composing rooms, so I had a good idea of the work they did and the skills they used.

I discussed my decision with Murray Melvin, the foreman of the T.U.S. composing room, who was also a longtime friend, and he agreed to help me, although he warned it would be a difficult undertaking. The International Typographical Union required a six-year apprenticeship to attain the status of a union journey-man printer. The I.T.U.'s comprehensive program was meant for eighteen- or twenty-year-olds, not for a man like me who was about twice that age.

If I wanted to become a printer, Murray said, I'd have to learn the trade by knocking around in non-union shops, probably outside of New York. He volun-teered to give me some preliminary lessons on how to set type on a linotype ma-chine, but it would have to be done surreptitiously, after the regular union typeset-ters had gone home. (He risked a fine by the union, because it was a violation of the contract for anyone but a union member to work at the machines.) He also lent me his six-volume set of instructional material used in the I.T.U. apprenticeship program, which I began to study assiduously. I rented a linotype keyboard and spent hours practicing the fingering of the standard typesetting machine.

Weeks, and then months, went by and I still had insufficient knowledge and skill to try to get a typesetting job in a non-union shop. By then, Murray would let me work alone in the composing room late at night. Sometimes, I worked on "live" copy for our publications. He was patient with me whenever I screwed up the machine with a hot metal "squirt" that required him to spend time repairing it.

Periodically, I was discouraged and depressed at the thought that I might never develop the skills to become a full-fledged printer. I don't know what I would have done if I had not had my editorial job to fall back on and was not drawing a regular paycheck.

Finally, when I thought I was sufficiently skilled, I sought night-shift work in non-union print shops. When I did find an occasional job, I was fired, often on the first or second day, because I wasn't productive enough. But I was not discour-aged; I was improving my skills and broadening my knowledge of printing with each job.

* * * * *

In mid-August, 1953, a "Help Wanted" ad in the Sunday edition of *The New York Times* caught my eye. The Dartmouth Printing Company in Hanover, New Hampshire, needed a skilled linotype operator; the pay was $75 a week plus benefits.

I called the phone number in the ad and promoted myself as a competent typesetter who also had extensive editorial and proofreading experience. The voice on the other end sounded pleased. I was told the job included putting out the daily Dartmouth student newspaper and that my editorial experience would be an asset. I was asked to report for work the week after Labor Day on Monday at 8 a.m.

Vic Levitt, my employer at Trade Union Service, did not try to dissuade me from leaving my job. It made it easier for him to deal with the painful task of laying off another employee because of a further decline in business. He arranged a going-away party for me at which I was presented with an expensive brief case.

Vic said I would receive two weeks' pay for every year of service in accordance with the T.U.S. contract which I had helped to negotiate a few years earlier. In my case, severance pay amounted to 32 weeks' wages, a sizeable sum, which would be paid out in installments.

I had dinner with Mim and told her the news. I mentioned that the printing plant was located in Hanover, where we had stopped on our recent trip with the Fishers. She was glum, and we were both uncomfortable. There was not much more to be said, certainly no talk about marriage. I promised to write and hoped she would answer.

The day before I was to leave, I had an anxiety attack. Could I really hold down a job as a skilled typesetter? What if they fired me, and I had to return home as a failure? What was I going to do in a strange, small town, away from Mim and all our friends? I went to a local bar and had a couple of Manhattan cocktails. It calmed me down. I convinced myself it was too late to back out. I had told too many people that I was going out-of-town on a new job, I'd have to do a lot of explaining as to why I changed my mind, and none of it would do me credit. And if I did not take the job, I'd be throwing away the nearly two years I'd spent learning to be a printer. My confidence returned. I wanted that $75-a-week job, and I'd do everything possible to hold onto it.

* * * * *

I arrived in Hanover the night before I was to report for work at the Dartmouth Printing Company. I treated myself to an expensive steak dinner at the restaurant where Mim and I had lunched with the Fishers on our way to Canada. Afterwards, I went to my hotel room where I planned to get a good night's rest, but I was too tense to sleep. I lay awake, thinking that perhaps I had acted rashly in coming there; I wasn't skilled enough. After all, I had never had a full-time job as a linotype operator. How much could I lie to the employer when he would ask me about my previous experience?

I dozed off intermittently, and finally got out of bed at six-thirty in the morning, still tense. I had breakfast at the local diner, and dawdled over an extra cup of coffee, so that I could arrive at the printing plant precisely at eight o'clock, the hour of my appointment.

Mr. Foley met me in his glass-enclosed front office. He seemed friendly as we shook hands. He looked like my stereotyped image of a small town businessman, a loyal member of the Elks or Rotarians. He was a man of about fifty, of medium height, a round, ruddy face, bespectacled, thinning black hair and a pot belly. He was smoking a pipe, and I recognized the aroma. I got a smile out of him when I asked if he was smoking Edgeworth tobacco. I had guessed right. We spent a few minutes talking about the quality of various brands of pipes and pipe tobacco. I began to feel relaxed. He asked about where I had worked and on what type of publications. I mentioned a few non-union print shops where I had put in a total of six years, working mostly on newspapers. He seemed satisfied. He showed me about the composing room and introduced me to the four operators at their machines. I could see, by glancing at their hands while they worked, that they were far more competent than I was.

Foley told me that I would be working the night shift. The hours were from 5 p.m. to 1 a.m., with occasional overtime. I was to report to Leo, the foreman, at 4:30 p.m. to get my assignments for the night's work. He suggested that I stay at Mollie's, a boarding house a few blocks from the plant, where I could get a clean, reasonably-priced room. Most of his employees either brought their lunch or ate at the all-night diner down the block.

I moved my bags from the hotel to Mollie's and met Mollie herself. The room she rented me was clean, sunny and comfortable. In a few minutes, I was fast asleep, and I didn't wake up until I heard my alarm clock ring. I had a half hour to get dressed and hurry down to the plant.

Leo, the foreman, was a mean-faced man in his late fifties, who had been working in the plant for more than twenty years. I immediately sensed his hostility toward me. I strongly suspected he didn't want me to work there and would look for an opportunity to fire me. My intuition was confirmed, when he brought out a table of statistics requiring complex formatting, and told me to reproduce it according to new specifications. It was hardly the kind of work to give even an experienced typesetter for his first day on the job. I said I hadn't worked on tabular matter for some time; did he have any straight copy that I could typeset until I could get used to his linotype machines. He dismissed my request. "Do the best you can, and when you're done, you can start on this copy," he said, handing me a sheaf of typewritten pages, and then walked away.

There was only one other operator on the night shift besides me. Dick Jones briefly introduced himself and went to work at his machine. I worked for more than an hour on the table, and was having great difficulty aligning the figures in each of the columns. Dick saw me struggling, came over to my machine, and suggested an easy way to do the headings over each column and how to handle the various footnote references that cluttered the table. He had apparently done dozens of these tables and knew how to apply time-saving techniques.

By the time of our dinner break, I had completed only about two-thirds of the table and felt mentally exhausted. At the diner, I confided to Dick that I desperately needed the job, and was worried that I would not have time to reach an acceptable level of competence. I guess he sensed my agony and felt sorry for me. How grateful I was when he volunteered to help me make up the shortage in my night's quota of type! He finished my table, while I set some straight matter for a publication he was working on. He was quite willing to work with me for an hour past quitting time so that my output would represent a respectable night's work. I kept thanking him every few minutes.

I can only speculate about why Dick was so helpful to me. Perhaps he read the agony in my face and felt sympathetic. Or he was naturally a kindly man. Or this was a way to display his mastery on the linotype. What is undeniable is that if he hadn't helped me, I would have quit or been fired, and that probably would have been the end of my career as a printer. I don't know what I would have done then. Years later, I was able to help him get a position he strongly wanted and that changed *his* life.

After the night's work, we went to the diner. He had a couple of beers and I had coffee and a muffin. He didn't say much about himself, and I was reluctant to press him. He had been working at the plant for four years, and was the highest-paid operator. Foley had promised him that he could become foreman when Leo retired the following year. He mentioned the various magazines and catalogs the company was printing and responded to my many questions about *The Dartmouth,* the daily student paper on which I would be working.

Dick was about 30 years old, brown-haired, nice-looking and a bachelor. His parents and two brothers lived in Belfast, Maine. He apparently was not interested in what was going on in the world, rarely read newspapers and had no strong political opinions. He was a practicing Catholic and considered himself a Republican. As I was to find out in the following days, the only subject that he was keenly interested in was printing, about which he had a lot to say and was pleased when I turned out to be a good listener. Dick also lived at Mollie's, in a room across the hall from mine.

On my second night at the plant, I met two of the student editors from *The Dartmouth.* Several of their headlines didn't fit, and I was able to rephrase them so they did. Their writing was sloppy—frequent mistakes in grammar and spelling—which I corrected while transforming their copy into metal type. They thanked me profusely. It was time-consuming, but I felt that if I could make them dependent on me, it would help to solidify my hold on the job. Dick understood what I was doing and approved. Again, he said he would produce additional type to cover me.

Toward the end of my third day, Leo dropped into the plant and spent a few minutes watching me work. He made me nervous. The following morning, I received a phone call from Foley. He asked me to come in at four o'clock; he had something he wished to discuss with me. I smelled trouble.

Foley, grim-faced, came straight to the point. "You're not an operator," he began. "You lied to me. You're still a learner." He said he was aware how I had helped the students on the paper, and that was why he was offering me the following proposition: He would put me on trial for two weeks at $45 a week, retroactive to my first day on the job. At the end of that time, if my work improved sufficiently, he would make some "adjustment" in my wages. If it didn't, then he would dismiss me. That was the deal, take it or leave it. I swallowed hard and took it. Somehow, I now felt more relaxed. I was certainly worth $45 a week and I was confident that I could improve my output sufficiently to keep my job.

Aside from Dick, I had not a single friend among the forty employees. I was the only Jew in the plant, and it didn't help that I was from New York City, that sewer of crime and radicalism. On some mornings, I could hear Mollie's loud, gossipy voice on the telephone, reporting to one of her confidantes on how that

"Jewish fella from New York" was doing at the plant, including the difficulties I was having.

With each issue of the newspaper, I became more proficient. My speed was increasing; I was producing more galleys of type and, what was equally important, the number of errors per galley had decreased substantially. I knew Foley was checking my proofs daily, but I was no longer nervous about it.

At the end of the two-week trial period, Foley told me he was raising my pay to $60. But why not $75, I asked. The blunt reply: I wasn't worth it.

By mid-November, I confronted Foley with a demand for a $15 raise. I told him it was not only the money but also a point of honor with me. I felt I was now a sufficiently skilled linotype operator and wanted the $75 a week for which I was originally hired. I would not work for less. I was surprised when he agreed without an argument. We shook hands. I think he liked my spirit.

I had been in Hanover for two and a half months and had almost no social life. Through the students at the newspaper, I was able to make contact with a music professor at the college, who allowed me to sit in on his classes. I was able to rent a clarinet and start music lessons. I had a spacious practicing room in one of the turrets of the liberal arts building where I would be permitted to spend an hour each day in the early afternoon. I was even considering the possibility of matriculating at Dartmouth if they would accept me.

I had no car and was dependent on Dick to guide me around town or to take a trip to a neighboring city. Dick had no interest in the theater, concerts or literature. His one hobby was golf; I would sometimes caddy for him. Otherwise, the only relaxation he wanted was to go to a bar and have a few beers.

I learned that he had courted a young woman, a high school friend, in Belfast, but that she had jilted him. In Hanover, he was considered the most eligible bachelor in the non-collegiate community, but had not found anyone to fall in love with, despite the many blind dates arranged for him.

We spent some of our waking hours each day talking about printing. I had brought along the I.T.U. volumes on apprentice training and an illustrated history of typesetting machines, type fonts and printing presses. Dick was fascinated by the books and spent hours reading and discussing them. I was bored by his one-topic conversation, but tried not to show it. He was being so helpful to me that I didn't want to offend him. He wasn't great fun to be with. He was, I found out, an alcoholic, and when he had too much to drink, he would become surly and belligerent.

As my job became more secure, I had more time to feel lonely. There were nights I wished I was back in New York. I missed Mim. I was lovesick when I received her letters. When I wrote to her, I had not much to say about my future plans, because I hadn't made any. I couldn't say whether I intended to settle down permanently in Hanover (I *could* adjust to life in a college town) or return to New York in a year or two. With my improved skills as a printer, I could probably get work in many cities if I so desired. In one of my letters, I wrote that I hoped to be in New York during the Thanksgiving Day weekend and would like to see her.

Mim and I met in a restaurant on 57th Street on the Friday evening after Thanksgiving Day. We were so happy to see each other, we hugged and kissed for several minutes before sitting down at the table. I had not come with any intention of proposing marriage. I was just lovesick for her and could feel her responding to me. Halfway through the meal, after I had toasted her with a couple of Manhattan cocktails, I found myself blurting out a marriage proposal. No speeches or preambles; as best as I can remember, it was:"Mim, I love you. I want to marry you." She didn't have to say Yes; the answer was in her face. We were both glowing with happiness. All my uncertainties had vanished. The important new factor was that I now was confident I could earn a living in an occupation I liked.

We took a cab and went to her apartment, holding hands and kissing all the way. We spent the weekend, not doing anything special except acting like a married couple. We had many problems to work out; the most immediate one was an agreement on a wedding date. I originally suggested that we have the wedding next June, when I would have been able to save some money and could come back to New York as an I.T.U. member. Mim didn't want to wait that long. We finally agreed on a date: January 2, 1954.

If Mim had been willing, I would not have minded our settling down in Hanover. It was a pleasant college town, free from the crime, violence and poverty of New York. A much better place to raise children. But Mim did not want to give up her job at *Federated Press*. I sensed she would be unhappy living in Hanover, away from her friends and the excitement of city life and politics. We agreed to live in New York.

The toughest question was how and where to live during the six-month period between January 2, our wedding day, and June, when, hopefully, I would be ready to return to New York with a union card in my pocket. We didn't settle that problem except to agree that, if possible, I should try to return to New York permanently by the end of April, instead of June. In the interim, we would somehow manage to see each other every week or two. That very Sunday, we had our first taste of separation when I took the red-eye train back to Hanover.

* * * * *

One of the crucial problems I had to solve was getting a union card in New Hampshire, which I could then use as a "traveler" to become a member of the powerful New York Local 6 ("the Big Six") of the International Typographical Union. I made inquiries and learned that there was a small I.T.U. local in Laconia, about ninety miles from Hanover, where I could apply for membership. Working out the logistics turned out to be only one of my many problems.

That New Year's Eve, our many friends gave Mim and me what turned out to be a wonderful wedding reception at the home of Ann Samberg in Woodside, a community in Queens. It was a memorable prelude to our marriage, which was to take place in two days. The previous night my brother Marty had tossed a "bachelor's party" in my honor; we played poker until two in the morning. I had incredible luck, winning large pots on cards that I should have folded. Marty was very pleased; it was a substantial, if unexpected wedding gift.

Our Saturday afternoon wedding took place in Greenwich, Connecticut, because, for some reason I could not understand, I was forbidden, as a divorced man, to be married in New York City. It was a simple wedding, officiated over in his living room by a justice of the peace who also ran a children's clothing store. We had agreed to invite only the members of our immediate families. On Mim's side, there were her father, Alex; Al and Lucy, and their two young daughters, Margie and Judy. On my side, Marty and his wife, Bea, and my two sisters, Lee and Julia. The ceremony took but a few minutes, after which we all went to Manero's for a steak dinner. Her father picked up the tab.

There was no time for a honeymoon. Instead, we went back to Mim's apartment in Brooklyn Heights for the remainder of the weekend. Mim had a bad cold, and both of us had to be back at work on Monday. We agreed that I'd return to New York the next weekend or the one after that and, in the meantime, we'd be in touch with each other by phone several times a week.

* * * * *

Early in January, I contacted the secretary of the I.T.U. Laconia local who said he needed proof that I was a skilled printer before accepting my application. I had no evidence to offer except that I was working at the Dartmouth plant, which was non-union. He said he could send one of his officers to the plant to see if I was actually working there, and to examine my skills. That raised a difficult problem for me. If Foley got wind that a union organizer had come to his plant to see me, he'd fire me instantly. I explained my predicament and asked the union official if he could come to the shop late at night. He agreed. I had to tell Dick what I was doing. He did not want to have anything to do with the union, but he wouldn't tell Foley about my arrangement.

My meeting with the official from Laconia went smoothly. He came at about ten at night, watched my work for a few minutes, asked me some questions, and then left, saying he would file a favorable report. The next step was to have the local union committee act on my application, after which I would be summoned for my induction. I would be notified by mail about the date.

In March, I finally received word that I was to appear before the executive board in Laconia for the formal induction ceremony. The question now was how to get there. Dick agreed to drive me to a station where I could get an early morning train to Laconia to arrive in time for the executive board meeting.

The noonday meeting with the board had to be delayed because there was an insufficent number of members for a quorum. One of the board members was dispatched to check a local bar where he rounded up two others, but they were still one short of a quorum. The chairman suggested I come back next month because he couldn't go ahead illegally. I thought I would burst with frustration. I pleaded with them to get past the minor technicality and induct me. I was so desperate, I offered to try to organize my shop, if I could only get the proper credentials as an I.T.U. member. I think that argument influenced a few of the board members in my favor.

There was some discussion as to what was the proper induction ritual. Apparently, the international union had made some changes in the ritual which appeared confusing to one board member. He raised a question: Would my induction be legal if I were sworn in under the wrong ritual? Board members responded to the question with differing opinions. I realized that if the discussion went on much longer, I would miss my train and get back to my job several hours late; I would have to make up a lame excuse to explain my absence. Finally, after listening to my earnest plea, they agreed on the latest version of the ritual, and I was inducted into the union. One of the men said it was common practice for the new member to buy a round of drinks after his induction. I told them I had to catch a train, but I left a ten-dollar bill to celebrate the occasion.

God, how relieved I was! I would have liked to have had my union card in hand, but they informed me it would be mailed to me in April after my membership was reported to I.T.U. headquarters in Colorado Springs. Mim was delighted when I told her that I was getting my union card, and that now I could return to New York permanently by the end of April instead of June.

During our four-month separation, Mim and I saw each other on the average of once every two weeks. I'd come to New York, weary after a night's work and a long train ride; I'd spend part of Saturday sleeping; in the evening, we'd go to a movie or visit friends, and Sunday afternoon, I'd kiss her goodbye and head back to Hanover.

We had two lovely weekends in Springfield, Massachusetts where we attended the concerts of the Cleveland Symphony Orchestra, then under the direction of George Szell. I remember the program of one of the concerts, which consisted of tone-poem pieces: *La Mer, Daphnis and Chloe,* and *The Firebird Suite.* After the performance, we were thrilled to see Szell close up, standing with us in the buffet line at our hotel.

In February, Mim came up to Hanover for the weekend when Dartmouth held its annual Queen of the Snow Carnival. Dick and I had helped the student editors put out a special edition for the occasion. Late that night I prevailed on Dick and our pressman, George, to help me with a remake of the front page with a boxed story, headlined "Mim Kelber to Hit Campus Soon." The lead paragraph read:

"Mim Kelber will make her first visit to Dartmouth on Lincoln's Birthday, college president John Dickey announced today. The well-known newspaper reporter will be among several honored guests at the college's annual Snow Carnival."

Mim met Dick and Mollie and was able to compare her present impression with my description of them in my letters. I think her visit, while she enjoyed being with me, confirmed her decision to stay in New York.

On the day I received my union card from Laconia. I told Foley that I planned to leave in April. He was ready to offer me $90 a week to keep me, but I explained it wasn't a matter of money. I didn't tell him about my union card.

He gave me a party at the shop, where I was congratulated by each of the employees, several telling me they were sorry to see me leave. Foley gave me an extra week's pay and said I could come back at any time, a job would be waiting for me. The "Jewish fella from New York" had made good. Mollie hugged me and said what a lovely wife I had as she turned her head toward Dick.

I was also pleased at the surprise dinner the editorial staff of *The Dartmouth* gave in my honor. There were several humorous anecdotes about the editorial disasters that I had prevented. There was applause when one of the editors said I should be made a professor in the Journalism Department. They gave me a Dartmouth senior pin and a freshman beany cap as mementos.

I had a final dinner with Dick at the best restaurant in town. I told him how much I appreciated his friendship and invited him to visit us in New York whenever he could come. We promised to write to each other.

I was saddened to leave Hanover. It had been an exciting eight months with a great many anxieties but also satisfactions. Just about everything had worked out well for me. I had been extraordinarily lucky. Unlike Mim, I enjoyed the leisurely pace of life there. If she had wanted to move to Hanover, I'm sure she could have gotten some editorial job at the college, but it couldn't possibly compare with her work at *Federated Press*. And she would miss her friends and the political activity which was such an important part of her life. I suddenly realized that I had thought very little about the labor movement and the Communist Party, and they didn't seem to matter in the kind of existence I was leading. That, I guessed, might change when I returned to the city.

It was a beautiful spring afternoon when I boarded the train back to New York. This chapter of my life was closing, and I had no clear idea of what lay ahead.

19. The 114-Day Newspaper Strike

As soon as I returned to New York, I deposited my traveler's card at Local 6 headquarters, permitting me to work in union print shops within the city. For about three months, I was sent out by the union House of Call to a variety of short-term jobs as a replacement for members who had gone on vacation or were ill. My first job was at a greeting card company where I typeset announcements for births, weddings, bar mitzvahs and the like. It required constant changing of 60-pound metal font "magazines" for each line or two of fancy type I used. At the end of a seven-hour shift, my arms felt like lead while my fingers were hardly exercised. The job, fortunately, lasted only three days.

I was determined not to complain at whatever job I was assigned, and to do my best to satisfy my employers. I thought that if I had a good work record, it would help me get a steady job later on. I spent a week at a shop that printed Schrafft's daily menus; I set news copy at *The Wall Street Journal* for several days; I worked for a company that published catalogs; I was sent out to ad shops, which required printers with great composing skills and knowledge of typography, and to legal shops where the employers demanded so many galleys of type that I was stretched to the limit. In many of the job shops, four hours of overtime per night was standard. I admired the stamina of the men who could work that much overtime, night after night, some of them for years, but that was not the kind of life I wanted.

Almost all the jobs involved night work. I actually preferred it for several reasons: it was easier to get work when compared with the day shift; the employer rarely showed up to hustle us; the workplace was more relaxed; the night foremen generally were less demanding, and occasionally, when we had done our night's work, we were sent home a half-hour or an hour earlier. And the night differential pay, amounting to 10 percent over the day-shift scale, was also an important inducement. Of course, there were disadvantages. Mim wasn't happy about giving up our evenings together and limiting our social life to weekends. But that was one of the compromises we had to make. She was active in the Newspaper Guild and the anti-nuclear movement, and was also a prodigious reader. When I'd get home long after midnight, I'd often find her absorbed in a book. We'd have tea and catch up on the day's events. At the end of three months, I had acquired job experience on virtually every kind of printing. The union's employment director was pleased with my work record and was beginning to send me out on better jobs and for longer durations.

But there was a serious problem that nagged me at the outset, especially because it was outside my control. The I.T.U. constitution required that the name of every new member be published in *The Typographical Journal* for three successive months. During that probationary period, any member could raise questions about the character or skills of any of the new inductees. The provision was designed to bar former scabs, communists and those with substandard skills. I was potentially vulnerable on two of these counts. Some union printer could charge me with being a communist, which would require an investigation and hearings that might or might not condemn me. Suspicions could also be raised about my printing skills since I had not come into the union through the usual six-year apprenticeship program, but had "stolen" my training in a non-union shop. In actuality, I had been working "at the trade" only for a total of eleven months. It was in my favor that I was listed as a linotype operator and not solely a proofreader. I was relieved when, at the end of the three-month period, no complaint had been lodged against me, and I became a full-fledged member.

That September I put in my union card at Fairchild Publications as a substitute printer. The company published *Women's Wear Daily* and several weekly tabloids geared to supermarkets, electronics, shoe and other industries. As a sub, I had to show up at the start of each night shift; if I were needed, I would be put to work; otherwise, I would be dismissed for the night. It was a system that assured an employer enough skilled printers, if and when he needed them.

Because this was the busy season at Fairchild, I could count on a minimum of three days' work a week and frequently five. I liked working at Fairchild and enjoyed the camaraderie among the operators. Besides, it was only a twenty-minute subway ride from where we lived.

I no longer had to worry about proving my competence. I could produce enough galleys of straight-matter type to please the plant superintendent without feeling any pressure. And I could look forward to the time, possibly in a year or two, when I would have a "sit" (situation) and become a permanent employee.

Fairchild was a very prosperous firm. I was now forty years old, and I felt I had a secure economic future.

* * * * *

In the next three years, we became a family. Karli was born on May 8, 1955 (Mother's Day) and Laura on August 29, 1957. We were living in a six-room, second-floor apartment in an old building at 1 Clark Street in Brooklyn Heights, adjacent to the Promenade. Our rent was $126 a month, a bargain even in those days. From our picture windows in the living and dining room, we could look out across the East River and have a grand view of the New York skyline.

By then *Federated Press* had folded. Mim got a part-time job editing books and writing dust jackets for a "vanity" publishing company, work which she could do at home and on her own schedule. Later, when our kids were in elementary school, she took a full-time job as editor of a dental publication, followed by work on a pediatrics newspaper. She earned enough money so we could hire a house-keeper two days a week. Kathy divided her time between our place and the small house in Queens Village that I had helped Ann to buy.

We led a fairly comfortable middle-class existence. Some of our close friends from the Newspaper Guild days lived nearby. Through our activity in the parent-teachers association, we became friendly with several other progressive families in the neighborhood who were to constitute a large part of our social life and had children about the same age as ours. Every summer in those early years, we rented a house for a month, either in Shelter Island or Fire Island.

While enjoying our family life, Mim and I found time and opportunity to become involved in the anti-war and civil rights struggles of the 1960s. We had dropped out of the Communist Party in the 1950s during the shock waves that followed Nikita Khruschev's stunning (to us) revelations about Stalin's reign of terror. Neither the die-hards, such as Mim's father, nor the would-be party reform-ers made much sense to us. The C.P. was in such disarray that we'd had no affilia-tion with any organized party group for years. Some time back, I had sent the party's central committee a long critique of its policies and recommendations for a program that would provide much-needed leadership for working people, but never had any acknowledgement that it had been read or even received. We were no longer communists but we retained our basic beliefs and opposition to predatory capitalism and Cold War militarism.

Early in the decade, Mim, along with other progressive women, was a founder of Women Strike for Peace, whose principal focus at that time was to compel our government to ban further nuclear testing because there was evidence that nuclear fallout was contaminating the milk supply with cancer-causing strontium 90.

While supporting the developing civil rights movement for racial equality, Mim and I became deeply involved in a community conflict over school integration, an issue that directly affected our children. The Board of Education had proposed a plan to pair P.S. 8, a predominantly white school which our children were attending, with P.S. 7, a school in an adjacent community whose student population was al-most entirely black. Children from both communities would attend P.S. 8 kindergar-ten and the first four grades and then switch to P.S. 7 for the last two years. Bussing was involved. It was an issue that had the Brooklyn Heights community in turmoil for months and caused the breakup of some longtime friendships. Mim and I were strong supporters of the pairing.

Although the school pairing proposal was approved at a stormy meeting of the P.T.A., we realized that the integration plan would prove to be a failure unless we could demonstrate an improvement in the education of both white and black children. A racially-integrated board was formed that succeeded in enlisting the assistance of Brooklyn College educators. It also organized volunteer teachers and clerical support for the two schools from both communities. I volunteered to teach a math class Friday mornings to third-graders and Mim became co-editor of the P.T.A. newsletter.

Our children grew up as "red diaper" babies. Even as infants, they were taken to the various meetings, demonstrations, picketlines and fund-raisers that were part of our activities. As they grew older, they would listen to the political discussions at the dinner table or when we had friends over for Sunday brunch. Our kids learned how we felt about the Vietnam War, President Nixon, the Pentagon, the FBI, civil rights, nuclear testing and other subjects that deeply concerned us. We were pleased that they retained our progressive values and attitudes as they grew into adulthood.

* * * * *

On December 6, 1962, a strike by New York Typographical Union No. 6, of which I was a member, and a lockout by the Publishers Association of New York City combined to shut down all nine city daily newspapers. I was then working as a linotype operator at the *New York Post*. I remember the tension and uncertainty we felt as we waited at union headquarters for a telephone call that would inform us whether the strike was on or a settlement had been reached. When the midnight strike deadline had passed and was extended by the negotiators to 2 a.m., we felt that an agreement was in sight. Although picket signs and other preparations had been made, no one, including the publishers, expected the printers to strike. After all, the "Big Six" was a conservative union that had not shut down a daily newspaper in 87 years.

One of the critical issues in the strike was the refusal of the printers to allow *The New York Times* to introduce computerized typesetting machines before coming to an agreement with the union on all questions pertaining to their operation. The union's president, Bertram A. Powers, realized that technological change in the printing industry was inevitable, but he insisted that his union members should not be victimized by automation, but should have a share in its benefits.

Despite repeated warnings by Powers that the union's strike threat was no bluff, readers and advertisers were caught by surprise, and the publishers received the news in stunned silence when the typographical union announced a walkout at the four newspapers that had the financial resources to withstand a strike without closing down permanently: *The New York Times, Daily News, World Telegram and Sun,* and *Journal American.* By permitting the five "marginal" dailies to continue publication for the duration of the strike under the terms of the old contract, the printers could not be charged with depriving the reading public of a daily paper. The strategy was also aimed at causing division within the Publishers Association and creating pressure for a settlement.

The publishers immediately parried the union's maneuver. Three hours after the strike began, the *Herald Tribune, Mirror, Post,* and Long Island *Star Journal* announced they were suspending publication for the duration of the strike. The union's selective strike tactic was branded by the employers' group as "a deliberate device to whipsaw the struck papers into making excessive concessions." The lockout on these four newspapers affected not only printers but all other newspaper employees. The publishers counted on maximum public pressure, generated by a complete news blackout in the city, to force the union into a quick and less costly settlement.

On the day the strike was called, I was asked by Powers to be editor of the daily strike bulletin: it was important to keep the members informed of the progress of the struggle and to bolster their morale in the face of anticipated difficulties. Although I had been told that Powers was a tough taskmaster to work for, I agreed to take on the job. If he was nasty to me or fired me, I had nothing to lose. I could always go back to my picketing assignment at the *Post* and receive my strike benefit pay. As it turned out, Powers and I got along very well, even in the high pressure, unpredictable situations with which we were confronted almost daily. I don't remember ever being rebuked, either publicly or privately, for anything I wrote in the daily bulletins to the strikers.

Local 6 was the target of criticism from the very first day of the strike-lockout. Department store owners angrily charged that the newspaper shutdown was ruining their pre-Christmas sales. The families of less union-conscious newspaper workers blamed the printers for depriving them of paychecks during the holiday season. The public, denied its daily papers, angrily demanded an end to the strike.

As the days passed, the chorus of complaints rose in volume and included proprietors of theaters, hotels, restaurants, newspaper vendors, stockbrokers, shipping companies, employment agencies and advertisers of every description, each citing inconvenience and hardship as well as the damaging effect of the strike on the city's economy. Even the Dog Owners Association of America, on behalf of countless dog owners with puppies in the housebreaking stage, wired the union that "dogs are in desperate need of newspapers. Please believe us: magazines won't do." The focal point of public indignation was Powers, the union president. He earned a public rebuke from President John F. Kennedy, who demanded that the newspaper dispute be submitted to binding arbitration, a proposal the union rejected. *Time* magazine ran a cover portrait of Powers, picturing him looking grim and menacing, beside a huge monkey-wrench between two rolls of newsprint.

From the outset of the newspaper shutdown, Local 6 faced three potential dangers, each of which could compel it to accept an unsatisfactory contract: (1) the I.T.U. strike benefit fund would be unable to provide the required benefit payments in the event of a long struggle; (2) other newspaper unions might withdraw their support, leaving the printers in an exposed and isolated position, and (3) a government sponsored "third party" might intervene to recommend an unpalatable settlement which the printers would be pressured into accepting. At various stages in the 114-day strike-lockout, each of these dangers was thrust into prominence, and they were often intertwined to intensify the union's difficulties.

There was also the potential threat that the newspaper owners would attempt to publish their papers by importing scab printers from other cities. When rumors spread that the *Times* was seriously considering such a move, the one million-member New York City Central Labor Council responded by staging a "Back the Printers" rally, featuring a two-hour demonstration of 25,000 unionists around the *Times* building—probably the largest picketline ever conducted in New York City.

Writing the daily strike bulletin—a mimeographed legal-sized page or two—was frequently a nerve-wracking task. Normally, I checked the day's news items with Powers, but there were times when he was not available and I had to make decisions on my own before the five o'clock deadline. There were all sorts of problems requiring policy positions that had to be taken quickly: the persistent danger that the fragile unity of all the newspaper crafts would fall apart under the divide-and-rule tactics of the publishers; the worries that fact-finding panels and third-party groups would attempt to impose a settlement on the printers, who insisted on direct contract negotiations with the publishers, or the possibility that the printers themselves would grow weary of the struggle and capitulate. One of the principal tasks of our daily bulletin was to maintain striker morale as week after week went by without a contract.

My job was made more difficult by the constant interruption of phone calls from out-of-town and foreign reporters who, unable to reach Powers, were referred to me. And there were calls from politicians, businessmen and officers of other unions demanding to know when the damn strike would be settled and why were we inconveniencing an entire city for our selfish ends.

Day by day, I chronicled the twists and turns of the strike. There were several 24-hour meetings at City Hall where Mayor Robert Wagner and his aides sought tenaciously to effect a settlement. There were scenes of high drama, as when the printers, on the 100th day of the strike, in a secret ballot vote, rejected a tentative contract recommended to them by Powers and the negotiating committee after a stormy four-hour debate. And then the climax—a dramatic membership meeting at Madison Square Garden when a slightly revised contract was finally accepted by a secret-ballot vote of 2,562 to 1,763.

After sixteen weeks of bitter conflict, the city's daily newspapers were back on the streets on April 1, 1963. The printers were victorious on the three issues they had fought for as a matter of principle: (1) a common contract expiration date for all ten newspaper unions so that it would make it more difficult for publishers to play off one union against another; (2) a 35-hour week, achieved by reducing working hours by 15 minutes a day from the preceding contract; and (3) the right to share in the savings that would result from the use of automated typesetting. The "economic package" which the union gained in the final settlement was calculated at $12.63 a week per employee over a two-year period compared with the publishers' "last and final offer" of $10.29 on the eve of the strike.

Since the contract contained an extraordinary provision guaranteeing their printer employees a lifetime job, the *Times* had to rely on staff attrition and "buyouts" to get rid of a large portion of its composing room work force who were no longer needed. For older employees, a buyout could amount to as much as $ 50,000 or more. The newspaper's management offered other inducements to their printers, such as a year's paid leave to seek another career, with the option to return to their jobs at the newspaper if they so chose. Over the years, the *Times,* through its various enticements and its prerogative not to replace any printer who retired, quit or died, was able to reduce its composing room staff from well over one thousand to fewer than two hundred.

* * * * *

Writing the daily strike bulletin for a period of nearly four months was a rewarding, if exhausting, experience. I had an insider's view of Powers' brilliant leadership and learned a great deal about strike strategy. I felt a new sense of pride in being a member of this union, founded in 1850, and now knew first-hand why the "Big Six" was considered one of the most democratic local unions in the United States.

I was glad to get back to my linotype job at the *Post,* where I remained an active member until I left the newspaper in September 1965 to pursue a new career. Two years later, my book, *Union Printers and Controlled Automation,* which includes a chapter on the 114-day newspaper strike, was published by Macmillan's The Free Press.

20. Helping Doctors Get Social Security

It all began during a pleasant conversation I had with Dr. Harold Aaron, my physician and longtime friend. Harold was a distinguished doctor who had designed and was administering the medical program of a large union, District 65 of the Retail, Wholesale and Department Store Employees. After examining me, he mentioned that he was national chairman of the Physicians Forum, an organization of progressive-minded doctors. He and members of his committee were planning to hire a part-time educational and legislative director to initiate a campaign for social security for physicians. Candidates would be interviewed by appointment the following week, and would I care to apply. I said I was interested. It would be nice to supplement my printer's pay, and I could afford the time to "moonlight" on another job, especially if it was challenging.

The three-member committee that interviewed me consisted of Dr. Aaron, Dr. Edmund Braun and Dr. Walter Lear. They said that they wanted to conduct a national educational campaign to convince physicians that it was in their interest to support legislation providing them with social security coverage. I was told the part-time job included fund-raising for the campaign, since the Forum operated on a tight budget. The pay would be $50 a week.

I explained that I had extensive experience in putting out newsletters and other printed matter, that I could give them references from a number of organizations I had worked for. I thought it would be a difficult job, but I assured them that if they hired me, I would work efficiently and responsibly. They had me wait in the anteroom while they discussed my candidacy. In a short while, they called me back. Harold was all smiles.

"We want you for the job. When can you start?"

"Next Monday," I said, smiling back and shaking their hands.

I would have liked to think they were impressed by my ability and sincerity. Perhaps, but the more likely reason they hired me was that they couldn't get anyone else to work for so little pay and to take on a monumental assignment without staff or resources and almost no chance for success. I had probably come across as too eager; they must have figured that I would work full-time for part-time pay.

Whatever their reasons, I was pleased to be hired. We could use the extra income. I would have the experience of directing a challenging campaign from the very beginning. It would be interesting to work with doctors, whom I had always regarded with awe. And if they should become dissatisfied with my work, the worst thing they could do to me was fire me. I wasn't depending on them for a livelihood.

My first task was to understand the issue of social security, about which I knew very little. I studied the provisions of the Old Age, Survivors, and Disability Insurance (OASDI) Act to understand the three-way coverage it offered: life insurance, disability benefits and retirement income. I read back issues of the *Journal of the American Medical Association (JAMA)* to find out the basis for their opposition to social security. I tried to find out why Congress had included lawyers, dentists, bankers and other self-employed professionals under social security, but had slammed the door on physicians. I interviewed doctors to elicit their reasons for favoring or opposing coverage. Within three weeks, I knew enough about the subject to talk and write intelligently about it.

Meanwhile, Drs. Braun and Lear had decided that what the Forum needed and wanted was a high-powered advertising agency that could take charge of the campaign and whip up support in Congress. They met in Washington with the president of an agency that had been highly recommended to them. In the course of a two-hour meeting during which he called in staff members to discuss the issue, the agency head concluded it would take $100,000, at an absolute minimum, just to get the campaign off the ground, and it might require a half-million dollars over a two-year period to build up significant support in Congress. He reminded the two doctors that the AMA could spend millions to defeat a social security bill. Obviously, the Physicians Forum could not raise that kind of money, so no deal was struck. A week later, the Forum received a bill from the agency for $3,000 for "out of pocket" expenses—an amount greater than my projected annual salary. Braun and Lear decided to stick with me. At the end of my first month, I had prepared a low-cost brochure, consisting of four pamphlet-size pages, printed sparingly in black ink on gray paper. Its front-page headline read:

NINE SOUND REASONS
Why Physicians <u>Need</u> —And Can <u>Get</u>
Social Security Coverage.

On the inside pages were the nine best reasons we could think of, stated clearly and succinctly. The back page featured a strong appeal for funds and a coupon. Since we did not have the money to pay the postage for a national campaign, we limited the first mailing to three states: New York, New Jersey and Connecticut.

To our surprise and great delight, we received more than 300 responses, containing contributions of from $10 to $100, and a couple of checks for $500, far more than the cost of the mailing. Apparently, our nine reasons had struck a responsive chord among a cross-section of physicians. Encouraged, we mailed out the same brochure to all physicians in California, Washington State and Oregon— and once again, the contributions and letters of support came pouring in. We now were able to undertake a national mailing, which brought us donations from approximately 5,000 physicians.

On the basis of our expanding list of supporting physicians, we were in a position to organize a National Committee on Social Security for Physicians, consisting of 60 doctors from 43 States. When their names appeared on our new letterhead, the AMA put pressure on all of them to resign. The handful who did were easily replaced.

The AMA's *Journal* repeatedly denounced the concept of social security for physicians, declaring it would trap doctors into accepting "socialized medicine," with serious consequences for the medical profession and its practitioners. In its issue of July 21, 1956, *JAMA* had reported that polls in 34 state medical societies showed that its members were opposed to being included under social security, most of them by large majorities, while only three medical societies were in favor.

We now faced what seemed to be an impossible task. Could we reverse the results? It seemed unlikely, but we had nothing to lose by trying. With some of the money from our mailings, we began to publish a newsletter that we targeted at state medical societies scheduled to hold their annual conventions and conduct new polls of their members. Our focused campaign on state societies succeeded: poll after poll by the societies showed that physicians, especially those in the larger states, were voting in favor of inclusion under social security, to the consternation of AMA leaders.

By June 29, 1958, Dr. Aaron, speaking as chairman of the national committee of physicians, was able to tell the Senate Finance Committee that a tally of 27 statewide polls on the social security issue showed:

• 19 States, representing 126,462 physicians or 64 percent of the nation's total, were in favor of social security coverage;

• 6 States, representing 18,266 physicians or 9 percent of the nation's total, were opposed to coverage;

• 2 States, representing 4,531 physicians or 2 percent of the nation's total, were in favor of voluntary coverage only.

The Senators were given a tabulated breakdown of the various state polls. Dr, Aaron also noted that the trend among physicians was confirmed in an independent national poll by the magazine, *Medical Economics,* which showed a nearly two-to-one majority in favor of coverage.

Our lobbying campaign impressed the members of the House Ways and Means Committee. At committee hearings in June 1958, one member stated:

"I want you to look at this pile of correspondence that has come into the Ways and Means Commitee in the past few days. That represents letters, telegrams, communications from all parts of the country, in fact every State in the Union, showing that 2,163 doctors are in favor of being covered under social security and only 135 are opposed to it."

Although neither of the two houses of Congress voted in favor of including doctors under social security in the 1958 session, we were not too disappointed. We had conducted a fairly good campaign and made substantial progress, and we hoped to make even more in the next session of Congress—and we did.

In the 1960 congressional session, the House approved H.R. 9925, a social security bill for physicians, introduced by Rep. Thaddeus Machrowicz (Dem., Mich.). However, a companion bill in the Senate (S. 1025), introduced by Sen. Thomas Dodd (Dem., Conn.) never got past the Finance Committee.

In its August 20, 1960 issue, *JAMA* bragged that the AMA lobby had success-fully achieved its objective. It said that Sen. Harry Byrd (Dem., Va.), chairman of the Senate Finance Committee, had made a decision to kill the Dodd bill "because the American Medical Association had requested the action."

To prevent physicians from becoming demoralized and dropping out of the campaign, we proposed a series of actions that we hoped would put the AMA on the defensive, including a legal suit charging the AMA with wilfully depriving physicians of the protection and benefits of social security. We had letters by emi-nent physicians published in *The New York Times* and in newspapers in other key cities, arguing the case for social security coverage. And we had state delegations of physicians go to Washington to lobby their representatives.

* * * * *

In the spring of 1964, the chairman of the Forum's finance committee, asked me to take a 50 percent cut in salary, from $200 a month to $100, because he thought there was less need of my time and activity. Although I felt it was an outrageous request, I reluctantly agreed. After working seven years on the cam-paign, I did not want to leave, just as it was nearing a successful climax.

Soon after, the House passed legislation extending social security coverage to physicians by a roll-call vote of 388 to 8. It was also clear that the Senate would approve a similar bill by a wide margin.

Instead of congratulating me for my efforts and rescinding the wage cut, the finance committee chairman arranged to have me fired by misleading the board of directors into believing that the separation was by mutual agreement. I decided not to get into a messy fight to save my job and to leave with my dignity unimpaired. Shortly after, I received this unsolicited letter from Dr. Ira Shamberg, then chair-man of the Committee on Social Security for Physicians:

"For the past seven years, you have carried out the functions of Public Rela-tions man for the Committee on Social Security for Physicians expertly and with a high degree of professonal know-how. You were not a secretary, performing tasks assigned to you by the chairman of the committee, but worked on your own initiative in a dynamic, creative and imaginative way. The caliber of your work was very high. The amount of money brought in by your Social Security newslet-ters from physicians throughout the country and the imprint of the committee's point of view on Congress are both testimony to your expertise.

"To my knowledge, your personal relations with all of the members of the Committee and of Physicians Forum were cordial and cooperative. The friendly and congenial atmosphere created was essential for the Committee to be able to carry on its educational fund-raising and lobbying activities.

"I knew nothing of the plans of the Physicians Forum, apparently made at a meeting of the finance committee prior to the Board of Directors meeting in December, to eliminate your position, and I believed what the entire Board was told at our meeting in December that your separation from the Committee on Social Security for Physicians was mutually desired by you and by the Physicians Forum. Had I had any inkling at the meeting that the decision was a unilateral one, I would have fought for your retention.

"I greatly regret your separation from the Committee, both because I enjoyed working with you, but more importantly because I feel our chances of getting social security for physicians in the current session would be greater if you, with your enthusiasm, experience and abilities, were working with us this end."

The bill to include physicians under social security finally was approved by Congress and became law in 1965.

In calm retrospect, I believe I owe the Physicians Forum a debt of gratitude. Their officers gave me an opportunity to conduct a campaign on an important social issue. I developed skills in organizing, lobbying, speech-writing and fund-raising, all of which I was later able to use in the service of the labor movement.

If only the AMA had known that its principal adversary was a part-time employee of the Physicians Forum, earning $50 a week, when paid; that he made his living and spent most of his waking hours as a full-time printer; that he had no staff and no funds to conduct the campaign except what he could raise; that he worked out of his apartment, while his two young children demanded his attention, and that he turned out the copy for a stream of newsletters, memos and other materials on a battered manual typewriter, most of it done at odd hours.

One of my fondest memories is of my daughter Karli, then nine years old, answering the phone and calling out, "Daddy, it's Senator Dodd!"

If I had known in advance what it would be like to conduct this important national campaign, I would have gladly worked for nothing.

21. Earning My College Degrees

From time to time, I had thought about going back to college, but always dismissed it. It was 28 years since I had set foot in a college classroom—it was at Brooklyn College—and the memory was still painful. The idea of sacrificing one or two evenings a week over a seven-year period to earn a degree seemed absurd. I hadn't needed a college diploma to earn a living as a labor editor or printer. Why did I need a degree now, and what would I do with it?

In the autumn of 1959, I received a brochure describing an unusual educational program, designed for successful professional people who, for whatever reason, had never earned a college degree. Under the Special Baccalaureate Program for Adults, sponsored by the Ford Foundation, it was possible for individuals to earn a four-year baccalaureate degree in three years.

That was not the only feature that attracted my attention. It was the quality of the educational program that excited my interest. In the main, it consisted of three survey-type seminars: the Humanities Seminar would cover history, literature, philosophy and art; the Social Science Seminar, sociology, anthropology, psychology and political science; the Natural Science Seminar, biology, chemistry and physics. The seminars would be conducted at Brooklyn College with outstanding instructors chosen also for their ability to communicate with adults. Students would attend four-hour evening classes twice a week. Each seminar was worth 18 college credits. The program would be limited to thirty students who were equipped to benefit from the high-level instruction. They would be selected on the basis of a comprehensive written examination and an oral interview.

Upon completion of the three seminars, students would have an opportunity to acquire a maximum of 48 college credits for "life and work experience," based upon documentation, testing and interviews with faculty. In the final phase of the program, students would concentrate on a major subject in a series of required courses. As outlined in the program, a four-year Baccalaureate of Arts or Science could be earned in three years if students completed each of the requirements.

I took the written exam along with several hundred other applicants. It was a stiff test, requiring substantial knowledge of math, literature, history, science, music and painting. I thought I did poorly, and my only consolation was that everyone else taking the test felt the same way. Almost two weeks later, when I had just about given up hope, I received a letter saying I was accepted.

The instructor of the Humanities Seminar was Professor Ruth Kriesberg, a young, vivacious, broadly knowledgeable woman whose bubbling enthusiasm for everything she talked about captivated the class. She had an ample supply of provocative questions, each of which immediately ignited debate from her articulate and highly opinionated students. This was no ordinary class of college students: there were several successful businessmen, a couple of professional artists, some housewives, a magazine writer, a hospital administrator, a union leader, a machinist, an insurance salesman, a furniture store manager, a social worker, and a few others whose occupation I can't recall.

The course began with readings on ancient Egypt and Greece. We were required to go to the Brooklyn Museum to examine Egyptian and Greek sculpture and artifacts, and to read at least one play each of Aeschylus, Sophocles and Euripides. We spent a week on Plato's *Republic*. We heard a guest lecturer discuss the rise of Christianity and the role of the Church and saw slides of medieval Church art. In addition to our extensive readings, we had to write short papers each week. Our homework assignments required many hours of preparation, but I never heard a single student complain.

There was no particular structure to the seminar. It consisted mainly of what Professor Kriesberg liked and to which she could bring her infectious exuberance. One week, we would read the morality plays of the Middle Ages and essays on courtly love; another week, we would talk about the nature of Romanticism and read the poems of Keats and Shelley. She invited a professor of music to talk about Bach, and we listened to recordings of the Brandenberg concertos. She had her husband, Irving Kriesberg, an artist, lecture us with slides on the works of some of the leading Abstract painters, after we had been to the Metropolitan Museum of Art to examine the Impressionist collection.

If the purpose of the seminar was to broaden our intellectual horizons and to have us continue our pursuit of knowledge, it succeeded admirably. During the seminar, I found myself visiting the Cloisters and also writing a paper on Roman doorways. Under Kriesberg's guidance, I developed an interest in Greek and Roman literature and filled a looseleaf notebook with my comments on the plays of Euripides, the poetry of Ovid and Catullus and the comedies of Plautus and Terence. I also read a collection of Elizabethan plays and wrote short reviews of each.

I can't remember how I found the time--with my job as a printer and my work for the Physicians Forum--to complete all these reading and writing assignments, but I did, because I so thoroughly enjoyed doing them.

My Social Science seminar was not quite as exciting because our two professors, while well-versed in their subjects, were rather dull. Like the Humanities seminar, it was mainly a "tip of the iceberg" survey of several academic disciplines. We read essays by outstanding theorists in psychology, sociology, anthropology and political science, amplified with lectures by our instructors, but there was little of the animated discussions that we had during the Humanities classes.

The one exception was our study of social revolutions, in which we examined the British, American, French and Russian revolutions, and tried to decide what factors they had in common. To guide us in our analysis, we were given a theoretical model that was supposedly applicable to any social revolution. It provided a detailed description of the revolutionary process at every stage of its development. I wrote an ambitious term paper on the American Revolution, based solely on the theoretical model.

The Natural Science Seminar was by far the most difficult for me and my classmates. Our instructor was an Italian physicist, a highly-educated, but arrogant scientist, who was not overly concerned about whether we understood his abstruse lectures. Fortunately, we had excellent survey textbooks in biology, chemistry and physics, which enabled most of us, through diligent study, to gain some basic knowledge of the three sciences. Because there was so much to learn, he agreed to meet with us for several weeks during the summer recess and to allow time to review topics that needed further explanation.

What I remember most vividly about the seminar was the professor's weird final examination. He gave us a 48-hour weekend take-home test of eleven of the toughest questions I had ever seen. He did not seem to care whom we consulted to get our answers. Here are two of the test questions for what was supposed to be an undergraduate survey course in science:

"Explain in terms of quantum theory the regularities of Mendeleyeff's table of elements."

"Discuss quantitatively the relationship between Bohr's atomic model and de Broglie's theory, and indicate the physical meaning of the result."

I tried to limit my "cheating" to only two of the eleven questions by consulting a physics professor and a chemistry professor at Brooklyn Polytechnic Institute whom I knew, but they were not very helpful. I managed to answer all eleven questions, including some complex mathematical ones, by spending all my waking hours of the weekend wrestling with them and having long telephone discussions with my classmates. Fortunately, the professor charitably graded us "on the curve," so I received a satisfactory mark.

I have saved this remarkable test and my surprisingly well-researched answers in twenty typewritten pages as one of my most cherished memorabilia. Reading my test paper, I am amazed at how much I knew at the time about some of the advanced scientific theories, including atomic physics. I am grateful to the professor for choosing not to water down the content of the course to an undergraduate level. I also have to confess that there is much that I have forgotten.

Having satisfactorily completed the three seminars, I applied for credits based on my work experience. The faculty committee readily agreed that my 17 years as a labor reporter and editor were worth six credits in journalism and that my work for the Physicians Forum qualified me for three credits in political science. I passed examinations in economics and the history of American trade unions for six credits, and I was awarded three credits for my knowledge of typography. I submitted a small collection of my poems that were favorably received for three credits. I was given the standard eight credits for my three years of military service in World War II.

For my major in American Studies, I was placed in an Honors Class of day-time undergraduates, all of whom were young enough to be my children. The instructors were Professor John Hope Franklin, the outstanding black historian, later to become head of the History Department at the University of Chicago, and Professor Henry Dietz, chairman of the Philosophy Department. In this one-year course, requiring eight hours a week of classroom work, we were given a reading list of more than 80 works by distinguished American authors in fiction, history, philosophy, sociology, religion, education, poetry and drama, arranged in roughly chronological order, from colonial times to the 1940s. The readings and class discussions provided me with a solid foundation for my graduate work.

In June 1962, I received a Bachelor of Arts degree, *summa cum laude,* and immediately enrolled in the American Civilization graduate program at New York University for the fall semester. In 1963, I won a New York State Regents Fellowship in a competitive examination. It was worth a total of $4,000 and enabled me to take two days a week off from my night-shift job as a printer at the *New York Post* to attend graduate courses at N.Y.U. and complete the 30 credits I needed for a Master's Degree in American Civilization in one year.

My thesis paper was on *"Fincher's Trades' Review*: An Influential Labor Newspaper of the Civil War Period." Jonathan Fincher was a remarkable labor leader and an astute, highly-literate editor, whose news stories described the economy and the lives of working people more graphically than any of the accounts I had read in the histories of this crucial period. I enjoyed doing this paper because, as a former labor editor, I tried to imagine how I would have handled the news reporting, page makeup and editorials if I had been in Fincher's place.

I had no trouble in reaching a decision to apply for admission to the doctoral program in American Civilization or keeping up with my course work after I was accepted. My extensive readings during my undergraduate American Studies program had provided me with sufficient knowledge to coast through several courses.

In 1965, my final year at NYU, I took ten specialized courses in American history and literature to complete my class requirements for the Ph.D. I had no problem with the written examinations for the doctorate, but it was the oral exam that almost caused me to have a nervous breakdown.

I had to appear before a panel of six professors, each of whom could question me for 20 minutes in the area of their expertise. Three of the professors would interrogate me on colonial, 19th century, and modern American history; then the other three would take turns to probe my knowledge of colonial, 19th century and modern American literature. If I failed the orals, that would be the end of my quest for a Ph.D. Theoretically, I could wait a couple of years after a failure and try again, but I knew I'd be too discouraged to do that.

I had heard that the colonial literature professor on my panel took pride in jolting students with absurd questions. (Example: "Name two 17th century preachers at the First Unitarian Church in Boston.") and he openly boasted how many he had caused to fail. I had also angered a professor of 19th century history by challenging a comment he made when I attended his class. I discovered, to my horror, that he would be a member of my panel. I realized that they could ask me anything they wished. It was going to be an intellectual hazing. How could I prepare for it?

For two months, I spent every hour I could spare to write down on 3 x 5 cards whatever facts I could gather on American history and literature, catalogued chronologically. I amassed several hundred of these cards. I would review the cards at every opportunity, even during walks on the Brooklyn Heights promenade. I put the information on my tape recorder and played it back while eating or resting. I was getting so short-tempered that in the last week before the orals, Mim and the children went off to Asbury Park so I could study without interruption. By the time of the exam, I had lost close to ten pounds and was tense and irritable.

I don't know how to explain it, but I was calm and clear-headed when I walked into the room where the six professors were gathered. I was all prepared for the colonial history professor, answering his trivia with some additional ones of my own, including comments about the sermons of particular preachers. I felt like a baseball batter at the plate; they were throwing me fast balls, curves, sliders and change-up pitches: "Name six works on colonial history and describe their differences." "Can you paraphrase the last paragraph in *Sister Carrie?*" "Discuss the rise of nationalism in the 1820s." "Who were the vice presidential candidates in the elections of 1872?" "Discuss Western expansionism." "What did Walt Whitman have to say in his *Democratic Vistas?*"

I did quite well on the broad, general questions and admitted ignorance on no more than two that dealt with trivia. I spoke slowly and deliberately, and paused thoughtfully for a few seconds after each question. This limited the number of questions each of them could ask.

When they had finished with me, they told me to wait outside in the hallway while they discussed my performance. As the minutes slipped by, I became more certain that I had failed. After nearly a half hour, which seemed like an eternity, they called me in. The chairman of the panel, Professor Henry Parkes, announced that I had been approved. Each of the panelists shook my hand and left, without further comment. My ordeal was over. I was too exhausted to feel elated.

All that remained for me to obtain my Doctorate was to submit an acceptable dissertation. This is the toughest requirement, one on which many students spend from three to seven years, frequently giving up in despair. Colleges are filled with junior instructors with ABD's (All But Dissertation).

For my dissertation, I chose a topic about which the committee assigned to me knew nothing, while I was well-informed: "The Response of the New York Typographical Union No. 6 to Technological Changes in the Printing Industry Since 1947." I had originally intended to do my dissertation on "Automation and the Labor Movement," but my adviser, Professor Vincent Carosso, suggested it was too broad a topic; I could avoid difficulties in research and writing by limiting myself to one industry and a restrictive time frame. His advice made good sense.

Selecting the printing industry for my dissertation gave me several advantages. I could avoid expensive travel time; almost all the research material I would have to review was readily available in New York City. I could draw on my personal experience in the citywide newspaper strike two years earlier over the issue of automation. I had also participated in a three-week study at the *New York Post,* which measured the amount of labor hours saved by the introduction of computerized typesetting machines. My research included a visit to the I.T.U. Training Center in Colorado Springs, where I was able to study the latest computer-driven printing equipment. For background material, I had access to union records dating back to the 19th century, so I could describe the impact of the Mergenthaler linotype machine in 1886 on the employment, wages and working conditions of printers. I made several trips to the composing room of *The New York Times* and one to the *Washington Post*, where I could see the computerized typesetting equipment in operation. I examined union contracts that contained provisions about the introduction and use of automated machinery, and I interviewed many employers and union members to get their reactions.

With all that information at hand, the actual writing of the 348 pages (I typed the entire manuscript on my manual typewriter) took not quite three months. The most bothersome part was inserting footnotes at the bottom of each page (there were at least one or two per page) and doing them in the rigidly prescribed method. My selected bibliography ran to seven pages.

Normally, the author of a dissertation has to defend his thesis before a faculty committee. In my case, there was no one sufficiently knowledgeable about the subject to challenge me. Members of the committee had read my manuscript and found it well-written and its style academically acceptable.

I was awarded the degree of Doctor of Philosophy by New York University in February 1966. I had gained my B.A., M.A. and Ph.D. degrees in less than six years.

* * * * *

What now? At age 51, should I be thinking of a new career as a college instructor, with all the problems, heartaches and low pay of a beginner? Or should I stay on in my secure position as a night-shift printer at the *New York Post?* I had a wife and two growing children to consider. I decided to play it cautiously: I would not give up my printing job until I was actually hired by a college.

22. *My Debut as a College Professor*

It was sometime in July 1965 that I read an ad in the Sunday issue of *The New York Times* about openings for an English and a history teacher at New York Institute of Technology. I called the next day and was invited by Dean Ted Steele to come in for an interview.

I know of no college anywhere that would ever hire a faculty member on the basis of a single half-hour discussion with an applicant, particularly someone who was unknown and came off the street, as it were. Yet that was how I was hired.

I began the interview with Dean Steele by telling him I could serve the college as a " two fer." I could, and would be willing to, teach any English or history course in the college curriculum—a brash statement, since I had never taught any college course before. He seemed impressed, probably figuring that he would be saving the salary of one faculty member if he hired me.

I told him I had completed all my course work and submitted my dissertation for a Doctorate in American Civilization from New York University. That turned out to be a big plus, since almost none of his faculty members had a Ph.D. Nor did it hurt that he was an alumnus of NYU. I did not submit any résumé, nor did he ask for one; nor was I asked to appear before a faculty committee for approval.

Steele had been an outstanding chemical engineer who also had extensive knowledge of other technical fields. He had little experience or taste for academic affairs, but he was a practical, no-nonsense type of administrator. He saw me as a satisfactory answer to his problem, and was glad to have it settled, so he could move on toward more important, pressing matters. I believe what convinced him to employ me was that I came across as a mature, articulate individual who could handle a class of students. Besides, this was a *technical* school, and the only reason it offered liberal arts courses was to get college accreditation.

We spent the next twenty minutes in a give-and-take discussion on the content of my contract, and reached agreement on the following terms:

Starting on September 1, 1965, I would be a full-time Assistant Professor of Humanities at a salary of $8,000 a year; on January 1, 1966, by which time I would have received my Ph.D. diploma, I was to be promoted to Associate Professor with a salary of $8,700 a year. I would be teaching a total of 15 hours a week for whatever courses the college assigned me, and I would be available for a minimum of five office hours for student counseling and administrative matters.

I could hardly contain my feeling of elation. I rushed home to tell Mim the good news. I would now be called "doctor" and "professor"! What a change from yesterday when I was just a blue-collar printer. I was now part of the world of academia, with new responsibilities but also new opportunities.

On the first of September, I formally resigned my printer's job at the *New York Post*. The night-shift men, with whom I had spent more than ten years, gave me a party and an attaché case as a going-away gift. I also received an Honorable Withdrawal Card from the International Typographical Union, which would allow me to return to the printing industry if I failed in my teaching career.

* * * * *

The Old Westbury campus on Long Island to which I was assigned was situated on the beautiful, spacious Whitney estate which the Institute had recently bought and was transforming into a college complex. The large stables, once occupied by race horses, had been converted into classrooms, and a number of new structures had been built to house administration offices and various college services. Unlike the Institute's New York "campus" in Manhattan, it provided students with an idyllic setting with acres of well-kept, grassy fields and shade trees. I was pleased that this was the college's first semester there; I was getting in on the ground floor; I was confident I could play an important role in its development and, at the same time, advance my career.

I shall never forget my first contact with the students. About 300 freshmen—only a small percentage were women—stormed into one of the large halls, pushing around the movable metal chairs and raising an awful racket. The microphone at the front of the hall was not working so I had to shriek to quiet them and arrange them in some kind of order. They were there to take a placement test of their competence in English grammar.

As befitting a technical college, students had to answer the multiple-choice typewritten questions on computerized punch cards, which could then be run through a machine for sorting and grading. Several colleagues and I who were serving as proctors were besieged by a line of students who had made mistakes in filling out the cards and required new ones, or who needed pencils with sharp points or erasers. But that was the least of our problems. It seemed that a team of faculty members who had been previously assigned to prepare the test had provided ambiguous questions and several incorrect answers. I was embarrassed when several of the brighter students pointed out the errors to me. Of course, the test results had to be discarded. I saw the humor of it, but I was also disheartened.

My teaching schedule consisted of a one-hour lecture, twice a week, to all of my 180 students, and then one-hour sessions three times a week to six classes of 30 each, making for a total of 20 class hours—a teaching load that would be denounced as intolerable in any college.

Although English Composition is generally one of the dullest courses in a college curriculum, and my students were far more interested in learning about computers and engineering skills, I managed to survive the semester by working creatively to persuade them of the importance of written communication for their future careers. I can still remember my 20-minute lecture on the *comma,* using slides that illustrated the humorous and tragic consequences of a misuse or omission of that slight punctuation mark.

I liked the Old Westbury campus. I enjoyed strolling on the grounds and breathing air that was not poisoned by gas fumes. But I had never learned to drive a car, which would be a necessity if I were to continue to teach there. I decided to take driving lessons and buy a car as soon as I received my license. In the meantime, I got to the college by using the Long Island railroad and then taking a taxi. From time to time I would rely on students to take me to and from the railroad station, promising them, jokingly, an "automatic *A*" for the semester.

Although I was a horrible driver, as my AAA instructor repeatedly informed me, I amazed him and myself by passing the licensing test on my first attempt. However, on the day I received my license through the mail, I was also told I was being transferred to the Institute's Manhattan campus on West 70th Street to head the Humanities Department at an annual increase in salary of $1,000. I decided that living and working in New York City, I would not need a car. Instead, I used my driver's license as a credit reference until I let it lapse nine years later.

The Humanities "Department" actually consisted of one faculty member besides myself. I now taught Western Civilization, and I could rely on the copious notes I had taken during my undergraduate days. I taught a class in Homer's *Iliad* and *Odyssey,* indulging my desire to reread them and to stimulate class excitement in the two works. Similarly, I revived my interest in Coleridge, Wordsworth, Keats and Shelley by giving a course on the Romantic Poets, during which my undergraduate notes came in handy. Since I had complete liberty to decide on what courses to teach, I could favor my personal literary preferences. I did, however, teach two courses in technical writing, the only ones the dean was interested in.

* * * * *

There were some imaginative engineering professors on the college faculty who occasionally came up with mind-blowing concepts about which they asked our opinions. At one meeting, we were introduced to an "innovative technology" that would "revolutionize" college education. Take the subject of economics, they said. Suppose New York Tech hired a handful of the nation's best economists—men like John Galbraith and Milton Friedman—to prepare lectures for Economics I and II, including anticipated questions and persuasive answers. Those lectures could be put on video disks and marketed to every college in the country. It would mean tremendous savings in faculty salaries and, at the same time, provide students with high-quality instruction. The same principle could be applied to other liberal arts subjects. Colleges could employ junior instructors rather than high-priced professors to supervise the classrooms. These assistants could be trained by means of video on how best to perform their functions.

The faculty was asked what we thought of this proposal for a New York Tech project. We did not know whether to treat it with amusement or disgust, but we were unanimous in condemning it. Only a technocrat with a contempt for learning and its complexities would dream up such an absurd, horrifying concept, a faculty member said. Computerized learning machines can never replace the human element, the person-to-person interaction in education, I believe. And yet I had to admit that video, used as a *supplementary* educational tool, could be very helpful in stimulating and encouraging students, and providing them with basic knowledge. I shall always have an ambivalent attitude toward technological advances.

At another time, we were brought to a special classroom where, on a raised platform at the front, there was a huge console, containing state-of-the-art computerized equipment with all sorts of buttons, switches and gadgets. Around the room were about twenty enclosed desks, each to be equipped with a powerful personal computer. The team of inventors explained how this as yet unnamed "master mentor" would work. The instructor, operating the wide panel board, could communicate with one, several or all students, supplying them with instructional material or receiving copies of their homework assignments. He could do all this, and more, by pressing the appropriate buttons and toggle switches.

Students could communicate with each other or with the instructor, with electronic speed. If they wanted research material, they could plug into the library whose data base of information would be enormous. Appropriate software programs would be available from the mainframe computer with the flick of a finger. The inventors proudly hailed it as the academic communications system of the future. And what did we think of it?

We thought it was a fanciful idea that raised a number of problems. Would it be wise to put such sophisticated, expensive computer equipment in the hands of undergraduate students? Even one disgruntled student could cause considerable damage to the console and the computers. The answer we got was that there would be armed security guards to maintain surveillance of the equipment at all times! We pointed out the various ways in which students could screw up the system, including outright sabotage, and confound the hapless instructor at the console. To the disappointment of the inventors, we made it clear that we would not welcome "Professor Frankenstein" to our faculty. After its initial debut, the monster machine disappeared and was never heard from again.

Despite my occasional disagreements with members of the engineering faculty, I got along very well with them. As far as I could learn, they had accumulated years of experience in their specialty in private industry, although very few had more than a Bachelor's degree. They had been willing to leave their higher-paying jobs for the less pressured academic life and prestige as college professors.

When they found out I was a radical, I received a mixed reaction. A few faculty members avoided me, while others were eager to hear my views. I was able to interest several of them to sign a petition protesting American involvement in the Vietnam war, but I made no headway in my effort to form a union.

* * * * *

In 1967, my book, *Union Printers and Controlled Automation,* was published by Free Press, based largely on my Ph.D. dissertation. My co-author was Carl Schlesinger, a fellow printer, who supplied valuable historical photos for a section about the development of printing technology. With an introduction by Theodore Kheel, a lawyer, mediator and then president of Automation House, the book traced the history of the technology and labor-management relations of the printing industry from the invention of the Mergenthaler linotype in the 1880s to the advent of computerized typesetting, with 24 pages of illustrative photographs. Favorable reviews of the book appeared in *The New York Times, Editor & Publisher, Printing News* and a number of other publications. The book served to boost my reputation at the college. I distributed autographed copies to important members of the administration and faculty.

A month after the publication of the book, I was called to Washington to testify before the Senate Anti-Trust and Monopoly Committee. With the support of the International Typographical Union and its Local 6, I presented testimony to refute the highly publicized charges of the American Newspaper Publishers Association that the printer's union was responsible for the demise of four New York City newspapers: the *New York Mirror, World Telegram, Journal and Herald Tribune.* I presented data to show two reasons why the four newspapers had failed: a lack of advertising revenue and a failure to modernize their plants and equipment. The *Mirror*, for example, was the second largest morning newspaper in the United States, next to the *Daily News,* which was No. 1 in the country. The *Mirror* could not command the advertising lineage of its arch-rival, even though its flat rate was less than half of the *News*. The *News* prospered and the *Mirror* shut down, both operating under the same city-wide labor contracts.

I responded to anti-union charges by the publishers in a letter to *The New York Times,* in which I cited evidence of the unwillingness of the publishers of the merged *World Journal Tribune* to invest in new printing presses and typesetting equipment, and the gross mismanagement that hastened the death of the paper.

* * * * *

In 1968, after I had been promoted to senior professor of social sciences, I decided to participate in the Vietnam "teach-in" movement that was spreading to college campuses across the nation. Worried about possible reprisals, I carefully structured my teach-ins to present both sides of the American debate. I announced the "non-partisan" discussion on college bulletin boards and to all my classes. I made a special pitch for the political science students. The teach-ins were held on

Wednesdays, from 4 p.m. to 6 p.m and attracted an average of fifty students. As a result of the teach ins, a New York Tech Anti-Vietnam War Committee was formed.

The following year, a citywide college anti-war committee called for a parade of students along Fifth Avenue and down Broadway to demand an end to the Vietnam war. About 700 New York Tech students joined in the parade the first student demonstration at the college. I feared that I and student leaders would be subjected to disciplinary action. To our relief, we suffered no penalties. I suspect the college administration silently approved our action.

Some time later, I received a complimentary letter from the college president and founder, Alexander Schure, informing me that the Board of Trustees had granted me tenure as of September 1, 1969. My salary would be $13,000, an increase of $5,000 in four years.

Although I now had tenure, I had no intention of limiting my career to New York Tech. I was soon to move on.

23. Creating a Cornell Program

Although I enjoyed teaching young college students, I really preferred classes of trade unionists, where I could stimulate a lively exchange on current problems facing working people. It was ironic that I was to develop a successful labor program for Cornell University, 37 years after I had left its Ithaca campus as a freshman, in tears. I was fortunate to meet Dr. Lois Gray, then the director of Cornell University's extension division in New York City. She needed an instructor to teach an eight-week course in contemporary labor problems to a group of union printers. Since I was both a printer and a teacher, she considered me an ideal person for the job. I guess I did fairly well because I was given two more classes consisting of members of Electrical Workers Local 3.

It was early in 1968 when I got the idea for a two-year program that would combine labor classes with introductory survey courses in the liberal arts. I prepared a twelve-course curriculum that not only included the usual labor subjects like collective bargaining, grievance procedure and labor law, but also such courses as "The U.S. in World Affairs," "Short Stories of Other Cultures," "Science for the Citizen," and "Introduction to the Arts," in which students, as a class, would go to an art museum, see an off-Broadway play, attend a symphony concert and a ballet, and hear lectures on the arts. The program was designed to stimulate the students' interest in learning by exposing them to a variety of educational experiences. Dr. Gray was sufficiently impressed with my proposal for a two-year labor/liberal arts program to present it to her faculty.

The faculty unanimously opposed its adoption on several grounds: They did not think that trade unionists would be willing to commit themselves to two years of study; the classes by the end of the first year would be decimated by dropouts. They thought that working people would not be interested in "frill" liberal arts courses as I outlined them; they would require at least a half-dozen new adjunct teachers, and where would the money come from to pay them? There was also criticism that the program was too regimented; students had no choice about electives. Their strongest argument was that working people would not be willing to spend $300 for a two-year program that would give them no college credits upon completion but only a certificate from Cornell.

In actuality, the faculty wanted to squash a program they had not initiated and might not control. It appointed a committee to make a study of my proposal and bring back recommendations for further discussion. I knew what that meant.

At the time, I was a Professor of Social Sciences at the New York Institute of Technology and had no financial connection with Cornell. I decided, as a last resort, to make an end run around the faculty. In early April, I persuaded Dr. Gray to permit me to produce and mail a brochure describing the two-year program. We agreed that if there were a minimum of twenty-five people who would sign up for the program by mailing in a $10 registration fee plus $50 for the first trimester, Cornell would start a class on an experimental basis in October, with the proviso that if, at any point, the enrollment fell below twenty-five, the program would be scrapped.

Within two weeks, I completed the brochure and had it printed and mailed. By mid-May, we had applications and tuition fees from forty individuals from twenty-five different unions. By the end of June, we had eighty registered students from over fifty unions. No one, including me, had expected such an extraordinary response. The mix of students was far more diverse than in any of Cornell's previous programs. It covered a cross-section of the New York labor movement, and represented virtually every major industry and occupation. It included bakers. longshoremen, construction workers, taxi drivers, machinists, flight attendants, teamsters, garment workers, printers, transit workers, nurses, waiters, government employees, seamen, telephone operators, furriers, policemen and one detective from the homicide squad. Thirty-seven students were full-time union officers and twenty-three others held part-time positions as shop stewards, committee chairpersons or executive board members. About twenty percent were women and twenty-five percent were black and Hispanic.

Amazed at the results, the faculty agreed to accept and advertise the program as part of the regular Cornell extension division offerings. I was accepted as coordinator of what came to be known as Cornell University's Two-Year Labor/ Liberal Arts Program.

I spent a good part of that summer working on the schedule and sequence of the twelve courses, and designing attractive sub-topics for each of the ten sessions of every course. Thus, the students were given an advance outline of the 120 topics that would be covered during their two years of study. I realized that what I was doing violated the norms of academic practice, but my intuition told me that the trade union students would prefer my *table d'hôte* academic menu than the optional *à la carte* offerings of educational programs. I was proven right. They were pleased at being told what they could expect to learn, and they were impressed by the 120 topics. Amazingly, I and the other instructors followed the topics in my overall outline almost to the letter.

I personally interviewed every student who entered the program. I needed to get some idea of what they expected to get out of the program and to learn something about their ability to express themselves. I told them that they'd have to spend at least six hours a week in fulfilling their homework assignments and that at some point in the two years, they'd want to drop out. It had happened to me when I was a college student. I made them promise that before they'd consider quitting, they'd discuss it with me. Over the next two years, I saved quite a few souls.

Prior to the start of classes in the first week of October, I gave the eighty students a twelfth-grade diagnostic test. I had to assure them that the test wasn't for the purpose of judging them, but that it would help me in the preparation of reading and writing assignments. If they wished, they needn't sign their names to the test. We also promised remedial reading and writing tutors for those students who felt they needed assistance.

To cut down on possible absences, we told them that if they had to miss school on their regular class night because of some emergency, they could come on another night during that week and receive the same lessons with their same instructors; however, we made it clear that we did not want them to abuse the privilege, and that it was important for them to stay in their regular class.

The two courses in the first trimester were Contemporary Labor Problems, which I taught, and Oral Communications, including Parliamentary Procedure, taught by Dr. Marie Wittek, a speech professor. Students were given course materials which we wrote or collected from other sources. Every week, there were reading and writing assignments that were carefully reviewed in class, and an occasional weekend field trip.

Because of the unusual composition of our student body, we were able to hire prominent instructors, including Theodore Kheel for Collective Bargaining; Herbert Bienstock, then regional director of the Bureau of Labor Statistics, for Labor Economics; Jack Sheinkman, a lawyer who was secretary-treasurer of the Amalgamated Clothing Workers, for Labor Law, and Leslie Slote, a psychologist, for the Principles of Human Behavior course.

The classes went exceptionally well, largely because of the diverse composition of the students. With a total of 300 or more years of union experience from diversified industries in each classroom, the discussion of any labor topic was unusually rich and many-sided. Our program provided a forum in which union leaders and rank-and-filers could exchange views in a congenial, non-threatening atmosphere and develop relationships that extended beyond the classroom.

We invited the spouses of our students to sit in on our classes so they could see what their mates were doing and judge whether it was time well spent. In one case, the wife of a carpenter's union official visited his class and liked what she saw enough to enroll; they ended up graduating together. We decided that, in the future, we would encourage husband-wife enrollment as one of the ways of stabilizing the attendance.

In my eagerness to have Cornell adopt the program, I had agreed, foolishly, that it would be self-sustaining. Thus, to save money, I had to handle all of the administrative functions, including the collection of tuition fees and record-keeping, with the help of a part-time secretary. As the enrollment increased, the work became overwhelming. I was able to get a one-year leave of absence from New York Institute of Technology and go on the Cornell payroll as program director at a $2,000 loss in salary.

Contrary to what my colleagues anticipated, the class in the "Introduction to the Arts" was the most popular of the twelve courses. In the one trimester, students went to the Metropolitan Museum of Art, where they had a guided lecture tour by an art history instructor; they saw Tennessee Williams' "Camino Real," starring Jessica Tandy at Lincoln Center, and had an opportunity to talk with her after the performance; they attended an American Symphony Orchestra concert and met several of the union musicians at the intermission; and they saw George Balanchine's New York City Ballet company perform "The Prodigal Son." Some of the students brought their spouses and children to these cultural events.

By June 1970, when the first class graduated, enrollment in the two-year program had nearly trebled to include 225 students from over eighty local unions, with a large waiting list for the fall term. A month before, Cornell's two-year program had won a "Creative Programming Award for 1970" from the National University Extension Association.

A survey of our students showed that nearly two out of three were in decision-making positions in unions and communities. For ethnic minorities, the Cornell Certificate in Labor Studies became an important credential for advancement within trade unions and for rewarding careers in labor-management relations.

Favorable stories about the Two-Year Labor/Liberal Arts Program appeared in *The New York Times* and a number of academic publications. It was the subject of a favorable in-depth study by the prestigious Wharton School of the University of Pennsylvania in 1975, by which time Cornell had established three similar models of our two-year program in Long Island, Buffalo and Rochester.

One of the prime effects of the program was to whet our students' interest in continuing their education. Most of the students had a high school diploma and some had earned college credits. Two possessed graduate degrees but had entered the program because they felt they could learn a great deal about the labor movement in classrooms with so many union officers. Twenty-two students had never completed high school, but were clearly knowledgeable, articulate and functioning successfully on the job and in their community.

In response to their demand, I established a high school equivalency program that met two evenings a week. I was permitted to hire a young black woman, Occie Sussman, a former teacher at P.S. 8, to prepare our students to take the tests for a high school equivalency diploma. I assisted Ms. Sussman by teaching the math component of the five tests. I arranged for all of them to take the tests simultaneously on a hot July day. Nineteen of the twenty-two passed; the other three, who scored favorably on some of the five tests, vowed to continue their study and retake the exam at a future date.

By the end of the first year, the students grew increasingly confident about their ability to master academic work. Even before the first class had graduated, they were asking questions that were logical, but I was in no position to answer satisfactorily:

Why did they have to settle for a Cornell certificate rather than a college degree in industrial and labor relations? Why did Cornell have a labor school in non-industrial Ithaca and not one in New York City, which provided a living laboratory for the study of labor and industrial relations?

Where, I asked myself, could anyone find two hundred adults, many of them former school dropouts, eager to enroll in a degree-granting college? Surely, I thought, Cornell would welcome them and accommodate their desires.

Thus began the frustrating, uphill struggle to establish the Labor College.

24. How a Labor College Was Born

The historic struggle of New York City trade unionists, graduates of Cornell's two-year certificate program, to create an accredited labor college is unique in many respects. I know of no college or university in the United States where students played such a primary role in establishing an institution of higher learning. What is equally remarkable is that their persistent efforts overcame the numerous obstacles put in their path by, of all people, educators.

Early in April 1970, in response to requests from many students, I circulated a petition in our eight classes in the Two-Year Labor/Liberal Arts Program that asked Cornell's ILR School to consider the feasibility of starting an associate degree program in labor and industrial relations in New York City. On April 20, the newsletter which I edited announced that all of the classes had unanimously and enthusiastically endorsed the petition.

On May 5, a meeting of all students voted to establish a student association to pursue the campaign for a two-year college degree. On June 16, they met again to form a permanent Labor-Liberal Arts Student Association, adopt a constitution and elect the following officers: chairman, Bernard Rosenberg, business representative of Electrical Workers Local 3; co-chairman, Thomas J. Walker, contract enforcement officer for the National Maritime Union, and secretary, Marie Calera, business agent for Local 22, International Ladies' Garment Workers Union. An executive board composed of class representatives was also elected. I was hired as counselor to the association at a salary of a dollar a year.

To mobilize support for its campaign, the student association sent letters to government officials, labor leaders and educators. It also initiated a petition which, within a month, was signed by more than thirteen thousand union members.

The students' most important ally was Harry Van Arsdale Jr., president of the New York City Central Labor Council and business manager of Electrical Workers Local 3, whom I knew to have a strong interest in labor education. At my invitation, Van Arsdale spent an evening at the school, visiting all of the classes and listening intently to what was going on. He came away convinced that these students provided a real basis for establishing the kind of labor college that he had long envisioned. Soon after, the New York City Central Labor Council endorsed the campaign for a Cornell degree-granting campus in New York City which, psychologically, began to assume the image and the name, Labor College

The activity of the student association sent shock waves through the Cornell faculty in Ithaca. ILR administrators felt that it would be too embarrassing to deny the students' request head on. They decided on a threefold strategy to squash the student effort: (1) to enmesh student leaders in a maze of entangling negotiations with various *ad hoc* committees that would go nowhere; (2) to persuade influential educational authorities that our students were not academically prepared to matriculate in a degree program, but they could take individual Cornell classes if they wished, and (3) that I, as the "instigator" of the student movement, should be harassed to the point that I would quit as director of the two-year program. The suggestion that I be fired outright was rejected because of anticipated strong protests, not only from students but also from Van Arsdale, a labor leader they couldn't afford to antagonize.

The harassment I was subjected to took many forms. Although I was running the two-year program single-handedly except for the help of a part-time secretary, I was denied additional staff and resources to accommodate the expanded enrollment, totaling more than two hundred students for the fall term. I began to receive almost daily memos from the dean of the metropolitan division and the authorities in Ithaca demanding all kinds of time-consuming reports and documents with impossible deadlines. Meetings of the New York City Cornell faculty were held to which I was not invited.

One of the nastiest abuses I suffered was when they held back my salary for several months and then refused to pay me for the summer work I had done for the program on the grounds that it had not been officially authorized. They also refused me a salary increase, although all other faculty members received a six per cent merit raise.

I deeply resented their behavior but I refused to quit; actually I increased my activity in behalf of the students' goal. I wrote a four-page brochure, "Ten Good Reasons for a Labor College in New York City," under the imprint of the Student Association. It presented a detailed case for why Cornell should establish a division of its ILR school in New York City. The statement was widely circulated within the labor movement and among public officials and college faculties in New York City and Albany. In October, a resolution supporting a labor college was passed unanimously at the convention of the New York State AFL CIO. Interestingly, more than forty of our students were convention delegates.

There were a number of ILR faculty members who were sympathetic to our cause, but the majority were opposed, and for what seemed to them valid reasons. The ILR School faculty refused to put at risk its national reputation as one of the high-ranking institutions in its field. If an associate degree program were established in New York City under its auspices, its curriculum would have to be watered down and its prestige would be damaged. The students in the Labor/Liberal Arts program, no matter how strongly motivated, were academically unprepared to handle the normal Cornell curriculum, they insisted. Equally troublesome was the fear that it would be virtually impossible to administer and control a degree program based in New York City. If ILR faculty members were to play any role in the new program, they would have to constantly commute between Ithaca and New York City. At the same time, some faculty members expressed concern that if Cornell refused to create a degree program in New York City, some other college might do so, creating a competitive situation that might threaten its enrollment and fund-raising.

What finally emerged from the deliberations of the Cornell faculty was a consensus that, even if a two-year degree in New York City was desirable, it would take several years, at best, before it could be established, if at all.

When our students finally realized the reason for the ILR School's delaying tactics, they reacted with anger. They knew that if they waited two or three years, the Student Association would disintegrate and the students would lose interest. At a membership meeting, they resolved that a labor college had to come into existence for the fall term, starting September 27, 1971. Given our situation, it seemed utterly absurd to select a target date less than a year away.

At the request of the Student Association I prepared a draft of a "Proposed Model for a Labor College in New York City," which I submitted to their executive board for discussion and amendments on December 3, 1970. The 15-page model discussed administrative structure, admission requirements, tuition, teaching staff, curriculum, individualized learning, work-study projects and a number of other academic matters. Under the proposed model, the Labor College would be affiliated with the ILR School, but would function as a largely autonomous institution. The amended draft was then submitted to the membership meeting of the Student Association on January 7, 1971, where it was discussed, item by item, and then adopted unanimously.

And now Harry Van Arsdale, who had been operating behind the scenes, moved into the picture. He persuaded then Governor Nelson Rockefeller, a Republican, to meet with a committee of the Student Association and me to discuss our ideas for a labor college. The governor was pleased with what he heard. He responded: "This is a great idea, I like it...and I'm for it." He announced that he was assigning his staff member, Steve Hopkins, who was at the meeting, to maintain contact with the Student Association and monitor the progress of its campaign.

My confidence rose. Without any tangible supporting evidence, I had a feeling that Rockefeller, who had expanded the State University of New York by several new colleges, would create a labor college to please Van Arsdale, his strong political ally and friend.

On the blackboard in my office, I chalked in large letters, "Do not lose sight of the objective!" Underneath it were the words "_____days left to September 27, 1971, the starting date for the Labor College." From early March on, each afternoon I scrupulously filled in the number of days left in the countdown.

In April, at the invitation of the ILR faculty, I and twenty-four members of the Student Association attended a seminar on contemporary labor problems in Ithaca with Cornell's undergraduates. Our participants strongly impressed the Cornell students, whose knowledge of unions was based almost exclusively on text books and faculty lectures. To the surprise of the ILR faculty, their students urged that they be alllowed to spend a year in New York, attending classes of the Labor/Liberal Arts program. The visit also helped bolster the confidence of our students that they could perform well in a college-degree program.

Throughout the spring and well into summer, there were a series of meetings and a great deal of maneuvering between the ILR faculty and the Student Association. However, the deadlock was finally broken by Dr. Ernest Boyer, Chancellor of the State University of New York. Boyer's proposal was that a labor college be established in New York City as part of Empire State College, a new, experimental institution which was being promoted as a "university without walls."

What made Empire State so attractive to our students was that it would provide college credit for work and life experience, and a mentor system that would permit individualized study for college credit. Moreover, it would be offering four-year as well as two-year degrees. As a concession to the ILR School, Boyer proposed that its faculty would be allowed to offer a 30-credit curriculum package to the students, but the diploma would be issued by Empire State College.

At this point, the ILR administration in Ithaca offered to renew my contract for the 1971-72 academic year on a nine-month basis as a lecturer—its lowest rank—and at the same salary as when I had started, three years ago. It informed me that "you must understand that it does not qualify you for consideration for a permanent position, and there is no assurance of reappointment beyond the nine-month term." To accept this contract, I would have to give up my tenured position as professor of social science at the New York Institute of Technology, where I was earning a salary $4,000 more than the Cornell offer. I tried unsuccessfully to get New York Tech to extend my leave of absence. Cornell would not grant me a meeting to discuss the contract, nor would it agree to arbitration. They told me it was a "take it or leave it" offer and set a deadline for my response. My first impulse was to reject their insulting contract, but after several sleepless nights, I decided to accept. I did not want to desert the Cornell students at this critical stage in the campaign for a labor college.

Meanwhile, Van Arsdale continued to make his moves, now fully determined that a labor college would be established in the city. In July, he asked me to appear before the Electrical Workers Benefit Society, which owned a seven-story building on the corner of Lexington Avenue and 25th Street in Manhattan. After I had explained the urgent need for a building to house the new labor college, the board members voted to lease the property to the school for two years at an annual rental of one dollar a year.

Later that month, Van Arsdale, Bernie Rosenberg, the chairman of the Student Association, and I met with Governor Rockefeller at his New York office. After reviewing the situation, we told the governor that we favored affiliation with Empire State College under the Chancellor Boyer plan as the best way to establish an accredited labor college in the city. We noted that there were only two months left before the start of the fall term, and we asked him to use his authority to help us achieve our goal.

Apparently, there were some behind-the-scene conversations, because on August 4, Van Arsdale, at a meeting of the Student Association, tossed a bomb-shell that put an end to the chorus of conflicting views and proposals. He announced that the Labor College would officially come into existence on September 8, 1971 at a ceremony in its new seven-story building on 25th Street. Governor Rockefeller, Chancellor Boyer, Empire State College president James Hall, ILR Dean Robert McKersie and a host of other public officials, labor leaders and educators would be invited to participate. I was given the happy responsibility of preparing the invitations and mailing them to a list of individuals who had been helpful in our campaign.

There was enormous excitement among the city's unions when they learned that the labor college would actually come into existence. An ad in the newspaper of the New York City Central Labor Council brought applications for admission from nearly four hundred union members. Construction crews from the painters, electrical workers, carpenters, laborers and other building crafts volunteered their labor for the enormous task of renovating the acquired seven-story building into a school with classsrooms and suitable administrative offices. This was a "labor of love" for *their* college! Frequently working two shifts and on weekends, they finished the project on time.

On September 8, 1971, several hundred guests, including the Governor and dignitaries from the world of government, labor and education, gathered in the labor college building to mark this important milestone in the history of the labor movement. A number of unions participated in making this a festive occasion. The Bartenders Union brought caseloads of liquor, beer and soft drinks, and a staff to serve them; the Bakers, in addition to sending dozens of loaves of bread and quantities of rolls, presented a huge "birthday" cake; the Provision Salesmen's Union brought in mounds of delicatessen meat, and the National Maritime Union's catering staff contributed enormous platters of hors d'oeuvres. The spacious hall was decorated by members of the Garment Workers Union and others.

The speeches, including mine, consisted mostly of platitudes, but the audience, enjoying the occasion, greeted them with cheers. My most emotional moment of the event was when a beaming Harry Van Arsdale came from across the hall, put his arm around me and shook my hand, as we thanked each other.

Less than three weeks later, on September 27,1971, our wild prediction of a ten-month deadline came true. The Labor College began classes with an enrollment of 350 students and a waiting list of nearly four hundred more. One hundred students were enrolled in professional-level ILR courses in Collective Bargaining and the Economics of Wages and Employment. One of the instructors,, significantly, was Professor Robert Mc Kersie, ILR's new dean.

We had come a long way since April 1970, when the students first announced their campaign for a Cornell degree program. There was much cause for self-congratulation. Amid the general euphoria, I guess I was one of the few who realized the serious problems that awaited us at the new labor college. The college was the product of a "shot gun" marriage between two different philosophies of education. We would have to struggle to achieve our original goals.

25. *Stormy Days at the College*

The hastily arranged marriage between the newly-formed Empire State College and the "Labor College" quickly developed serious strains. There was a fundamental conflict of structure and mission which took a few years to ease but was never fully resolved. Empire State College, established in 1971 by the State University of New York as an experimental "university without walls," was based on students earning a degree through individualized study with a mentor. The traditional classroom and the standardized curriculum were eliminated; students designed their own curriculum for a degree in whatever field they desired under their mentor's guidance. They read books, wrote papers and, in some instances, did field work, reporting at stated intervals to their mentor, either by phone or at a meeting. This mode of learning had a strong appeal for some mature adults, especially professional people, who, for one reason or another, had not earned a college degree and wanted to obtain one in the shortest possible time without attending classes.

As attractive as the mentor system was to particular individuals, it was entirely unsuitable for trade union students seeking a degree in industrial and labor relations. It was clearly impossible to teach such subjects as union administration, collective bargaining or shop steward systems on a one-to-one basis, even assuming that Empire State could find qualified mentors for these and other basic subjects. Moreover, our students wanted classes; it was there that they enriched their knowledge through an interchange of views and experiences with other students. And they needed a formal curriculum with electives that would provide them with a rounded-out education. In short, the mentor mode of learning was a prescription for disaster. Unless Empire State would accommodate the needs of our students, the labor college we had worked so hard to create would die in its infancy.

Indeed, *there was no Labor College* as such, although we insisted on calling our instiitution by that name. Officially, we were the Labor Division of the Metropolitan Learning Center of Empire State College, one of perhaps eight or ten such centers scattered throughout the state. Neither the president of Empire State, Dr. James Hall, nor the dean of the Metropolitan Center, Dr. Bernard Stern, or his two professorial assistants had ever had any connection with unions, and it soon became evident that they had no interest whatsoever in the labor movement.

Suddenly, I became an important actor in the unfolding drama. Empire State, recognizing my successful role as director of the Cornell two-year program, offered me a contract as director of the Labor Division with the title of associate dean at a salary of $20,000 a year. However, Cornell would not release me from my contract, claiming that its two-year program would fall apart without my direction. A compromise was reached under which I would continue to be the director of the Cornell program until April 1972, but that in the meantime, I would serve as a consultant at Empire State's Labor Division for one day a week at a salary of $100 per day. I would become full-time on the Empire State payroll on April 1. Even while acting as consultant, I decided to initiate a weekly *Labor College Newsletter* to keep students informed of what was happening and to bolster their morale in the face of disturbing rumors and uncertainties. Student confusion was rampant because there was not a single piece of literature explaining admissions policy, curriculum, degree requirements and other topics of student concern. Nor was there any provision for textbooks, course materials or audio-visual equipment, because under the Empire State methodology, these were unnecessary. Students complained that they could not find a mentor to talk to because they were all gone by five o'clock, just when our working students were beginning to come to class. The *Newsletter* offered them an opportunity to bring their grievances to the attention of Dean Stern.

I also encouraged the establishment of a Labor College Student Association as a successor to the student organization at Cornell, which had been such an important force in promoting the college. The association met and drew up a list of serious student grievances, with proposals to rectify them.

The students were incensed when I told them that Dean Stern had failed to respond to the nearly four hundred trade unionists who had applied for admission to what they thought was the Labor College. Under questioning from the students, Stern said the Learning Center didn't have enough mentors to handle new applicants; he promised to write to all of them, explaining the situation and informing them that their request for admission would be considered at some future date.

My activity infuriated Dean Stern and his staff of mentors. He ordered me to cancel the newsletter. I said I couldn't; it was the publication of the Labor College Student Association. They accused me of inciting the students to make all sorts of unwarranted demands upon them. I replied that the Student Association membership would welcome their appearance at a meeting where perhaps they could respond to the many questions that were troubling them.

Dr. Stern informed Empire State administrators in Saratoga Springs that I was obstructing the Manhattan Learning Center and creating student hostility toward the mentoring system. He said it was the unanimous opinion of the mentors that under no circumstances should I be allowed to occupy the position of associate dean of the Labor Division. On December 23, in a letter to Dr. Stern, marked confidential and personal, Empire State's president, James Hall, asked for "recommendations" as to whether I should be hired. I could imagine Dr. Stern's response.

A week later, I received a phone call from Hall, informing me that the Manhattan Learning Center faculty did not consider me a "team player" and therefore I would not be hired as associate dean. I responded by threatening to institute a legal suit against him and Empire State for breaking my contract. I also said I would inform the Student Association of his action, and I warned that the consequences might prove unpleasant.

I offered a compromise proposal: I would be retained, not as associate dean, but as a mentor with the title of Professor of Labor Studies at the $20,000 salary that I had previously been offered. He tried to lower my proposed rank and salary, but I held firm. On January 6, I received a formal contract from Hall, confirming our agreement. No mention was made about rescinding the publication of the newsletter or disbanding the Student Association.

When students at the college found out that I was going to be a mentor, they flocked to me with a request that I serve them. In short order, I had more than fifty students on my roster, while the average for the other mentors was twelve.

To accommodate this large group of students, I set up two twelve-week classes, both of which I taught: American Foreign Policy and Labor's Role in American Politics. In deference to the Empire State philosophy, I offered students the option of taking each or both of the courses in the form of self-study assignments, for which I provided a reading list and topics for a series of short papers. Nearly all of the students preferred the classroom format.

In compliance with Empire State procedures, I made out "learning contracts" for each of the students and, instead of giving them a letter grade, I described their strengths and weaknesses in their class performance and homework assignments.

My work as a mentor was sharply criticized by Arthur Chickering, Empire State's Vice President for Academic Affairs. His five-page, single-spaced typewritten memo was succinctly summarized in one sentence: "It is obvious that developing thirty identical contracts for thirty very diverse persons, violates the basic ideas Empire State was established to test." He ordered the dean to make sure that such violations would not happen again. At no point was Chickering interested in the content of my classes or my innovative teaching methods, nor could he understand that people with diverse backgrounds could benefit by their participation in the same classroom.

I found myself in a difficult bind. In self-defense, I wanted to avoid Chickering's opposition because it might lead to my dismissal. On the other hand, I had a responsibility to my students, whose number had grown to seventy-five and whom I could not possibly serve on a one-to-one basis involving individualized study.

I sought to solve the dilemma by providing students with a learning contract that would be rich in content, give them options in their reading assignments and inspire some degree of individual creativity. For example, I designed one learning contract that required students to read a dozen stories in "The Contemporary American Short Story" and a dozen essays in "The Contemporary Critical Essay," and to write short reviews of each. In addition, they had to write an original short story based on their personal experience and an essay entitled, "This I Believe." Finally, they had to complete a take-home examination based on the material they had read. Students had the entire summer to fulfill this learning contract. I was available at the college for individual conferences or for tutorial assistance. There would be two workshops (I purposely refrained from calling them classes) in September to review the reading and writing assignments.

I thought the content of this learning contract and the built-in flexibility for each student would win Chickering's approval. Quite the contrary. He sent the dean another long memo in which he questioned why so many students with such diverse backgrounds would all choose to study short stories and essays.

Fortunately, the new dean, Dr. Jane Dahlberg, agreed with me that most labor students insisted on classes and did poorly in self-study programs supervised by a mentor. She also realized that if I had not conducted these classes, the Center would have lost most of its students. Because there was only one other faculty member besides me who knew anything about unions, I had to continue to provide classes with new subject matter for my students.

In September 1972, I organized a 12-week "Seminar in the Sociology of Work," with original research material that I had prepared during the summer. The seminar included field trips to such workplaces as the Brooklyn waterfront, a garment factory, *The New York Times* printing plant, a large bakery and a Consolidated Edison sub-station. I guess Chickering got tired of rebuking me, but what counted in my favor was that I was handling more tuition-paying students than the three Labor Division mentors combined.

From then on, traditional classes became the predominant mode of instruction at the learning center, although they were called "workshops," "seminars" or "study groups." Meanwhile, we had resolved another question that had been disturbing our students: Empire State agreed to award twenty credits to graduates of Cornell's two-year program.

* * * * *

Empire State President Hall and his staff in Saratoga Springs had never been happy with my presence at the Manhattan Learning Center. They were convinced that I was a subversive influence there and that I was determined to transform the Labor Division into an independent, genuine Labor College. When I applied for tenure in late November 1972, I was turned down and told that I would not be eligible until 1975. They had refused to count my three years with Cornell, even though the ILR School was a State University affiliate.

I had a premonition they were planning to get rid of me, when I heard they were about to hire a new dean of the Labor Division, Bill Goode, the educational director of the United Auto Workers. They thought that Goode, as dean, would be able to undermine my influence with the labor students, paving the way for my dismissal before 1975, when my request for tenure would be considered.

I prepared for battle. In January, I informed all ninety students who had chosen me as their mentor that unless I was granted tenure by Empire State by April 1, 1973, I would leave the Learning Center.

There was considerable consternation at my announcement. The Student Association set up a committee in my behalf and appealed to Empire State officials to grant me tenure. They would not budge from their position, and neither would I. I began to arrange interviews with several city colleges that were interested in having me on their faculty.

Early in March, less than a month away from my scheduled departure, the dean of the Manhattan Learning Center, Dr. Dahlberg, requested that I turn over the records of each of my students so they could be assigned a new mentor. I complied quickly, even offering my estimate of the educational needs of each student. I truly wanted the transition to be made with a minimum of disruption; if I had to leave the school, I intended to do so calmly and without bitterness. I discouraged the students from making me a *cause celèbre*.

Dr. Dahlberg invited all of the students on my roster to meet with her fourteen mentors on a Saturday morning at the Learning Center. At this meeting, each mentor would describe his or her educational expertise and students could then select which one they wished to work with. The dean said it would be helpful if I attended the meeting, and I agreed to do so.

That Saturday morning about seventy students showed up, glad to see me there. Dr. Dahlberg opened the meeting by praising my contributions to the college. She said that students should respect my wish to leave the school because I was denied tenure. She was confident that I would find a satisfactory position at another college.

When she had finished, John McGrath, an officer of the Dining Car Employees, leaped to his feet and proposed a motion that I be named dean of the college. The motion was seconded by shouts throughout the hall, followed by a call for a vote. Dr. Dahlberg, startled, did not know how to respond. She glanced helplessly at me. I took the floor and said the motion was out of order and would do nothing to solve the purpose of the meeting. A substitute motion was offered to set up a student committee that would meet with Empire State officials to make known the strong feeling of the students that they wanted me to have tenure and be their dean. The motion was approved unanimously; a committee was appointed to confer with Dr. Hall in Saratoga.

Dr. Dahlberg was about to introduce the fourteen mentors, sitting glumly on the sidelines almost like a jury, when another student rose to say, "We don't want to listen to them and their bullshit. We have only one mentor, Dr. Kelber, and we don't need anyone else. Tell them to go home."

For the next hour, Dr. Dahlberg and her mentors sat silent and uncomfortable, while student after student praised me in terms that, I confess, delighted me. Finally, the dean adjourned the meeting. Nothing had been accomplished. In tears, Dr. Dahlberg phoned President Hall in Saratoga. She described what had happened and pleaded that I be given tenure. Hall indicated he was not ready to yield under student pressure; it would set a bad precedent.

On March 30, two days before I was to leave, I received a phone call from President Hall, just as I was finishing packing my books. I was told I would receive tenure but only if the new dean, Bill Goode, would approve it. It was a face-saving proposal that I quickly accepted.

The next day, I had a tunafish sandwich and a cup of coffee with Goode, who was more of a trade unionist than an academic. After an agreeable discussion about problems facing the labor movement, he said he would be glad to recommend me for tenure and would so inform the president of the college.

On April 20, I received a letter from Ernest L. Boyer, chancellor of the State University of New York, informing me that I had been appointed to "continuing status as Professor, at the Manhattan Learning Center of Empire State College, effective May 1, 1973, at an annual salary of $21,808." I now had job security until my compulsory retirement in 1984.

* * * * *

That very week, while I was conducting my class in American Foreign Policy, a student made an off-hand suggestion that instead of taking the word of our textbooks on what was happening in Japan, we ought to go there and see for ourselves. Out of curiosity, I asked the class how many would be willing to go as a group and at their own expense. Nine students raised their hands. From this brief verbal exchange, we developed a 23-day tour of Japan, Taiwan, Hong Kong and Thailand, from June 9 to July 1, as the "Labor College Asian Study Group." Our group of sixteen included a garment worker, printer, nurse, carpenter, crane operator, auto mechanic, railroad worker, high school teacher and a city clerical employee. With the assistance of the AFL-CIO International Affairs Department and the U.S. labor attachés of the countries we visited, our study group was able to hold discussions with government, labor and industry leaders wherever we went. We inspected factories in the auto, chemical, garment, electronic, optical and other industries, as well as a housing project, a school, a department store and a public health center.

The group taped most of the briefing and discussion sessions, and also took more than two thousand photographs and slides to document its observations. Each student gathered printed material about labor conditions in his or her industry and also made personal notes to be used for writing their special reports for their college course.

Wherever we went, we were treated cordially as honored guests, with gifts, banquets, and press interviews. At each event, we were required to make appropriate introductory and farewell speeches to our hosts. I saw to it that every member of our group made at least two speeches during the course of the tour. We handed out hundreds of large blue-and-white buttons of the Labor College Asian Study Group, which became a coveted souvenir in each of the countries.

We were able to accomplish a great deal because we divided our delegation into sub-groups. We conferred with officers of Domai, the Japanese Confederation of Labor, and with the secretary-general of the Nikkeiren, the Japan Federation of Employers Associations, regarding Japan's domestic and external economic policies. After a morning conference with officials of the Japanese Ministry of Labor, we witnessed, in front of its headquarters, a mass picketline and sitdown of retired workers, who were demanding an increase in pension benefits.

In Osaka, Japan's second largest industrial city, we were the guests of the municipal administration. After a two-hour discussion of city government, electoral politics and labor conditions, we were taken to lunch at one of Osaka's finest restaurants, where each member of our group was given a "key to the city" and a handsomely illustrated book about Osaka.

In Taiwan, we were the guests of the Chinese Federation of Labor. One of the factories we visited was the Far East Textile Corporation where shirts, swimwear and underwear are made for such U.S. companies as Jantzen, Manhattan and B.V.D. at wages that are a fraction of what American workers receive.

At Today's Department Store, one of the largest in Taipei, a large banner over the store's entrance read "Welcome to New York Labor College Asian Study Group." After an elaborate tea lunch, we were briefed about the store's operations and the working conditions of its employees. On the fourth floor of the store, we watched a live performance of a Chinese opera. The president of the Department Store Union presented me with a beautiful kimono.

One afternoon, we were invited to the beautiful campus of the College of Chinese Culture, situated high up in the mountains. There, our group held a stimulating meeting with students in the Department of Industrial Relations.

Toward the end of our visit, I was asked to a private dinner with the head of the Chinese (not called Taiwanese) Federation of Labor. After numerous elaborate courses interspersed with frequent ceremonial toasts with *mai tai,* he got down to the reason why he had invited me. The AFL-CIO, which had been sending him $10,000 a month, had stopped payments several months ago. Would I intercede with George Meany to get him to renew the grants? Diplomatically, I promised to do my best. I was amused by the thought that I could influence Meany, whom I had not talked to since the late1930s when he was still president of the New York State Federation of Labor.

When we were ready to leave for Hong Kong, a dozen officials of the labor federation were at the airport to say goodbye to our group. Photographers were on hand to snap pictures of our delegation for the local newspapers and I was interviewed by reporters before we boarded the plane.

In Thailand, we visited the Kadar Industrial Co., Ltd., the largest toy manufacturing company in Southeast Asia. We were given a floor by floor tour of the showrooms and manufacturing units where hundreds of young women were employed in assembly-line production. We learned that the company is a major contractor for a number of large U.S. toy wholesalers and retailers. (In the early 1990's, scores of employees were burned to death in a horrible fire at the Kadar plant we had visited, caused by company negligence.)

One of our sub-groups visited a construction site in Bangkok where they were surprised to see women operating heavy-duty cranes and doing pick and shovel work. Another sub-group toured a silk manufacturing plant and observed workers producing the internationally famous Thai silk. A third group spent a full day in meetings with public health officials and inspection of hospitals and clinics.

On one sightseeing tour, we were taken on a motor launch up the Chao Phya River for a closeup view of Thailand's famous Floating Market and its native life. Many thousands of families live along the river basin or on floating houseboats. Later, we toured the fabulous Grand Palace (seen in the film, "The King and I"), the impressive Temple of the Emerald Buddha, the Great Throne Hall of the Chakri kings and other extravagantly constructed and decorated historic sites. In the evening, we ate a Thai dinner in native style and watched a performance of Thai singing and dancing. Toward the end of the show, members of our group joined the performers in a native dance, to the delight of the other restaurant diners. On our final night, the luxurious Oriental Hotel where we were staying gave us a fabulous farewell dinner, smorgasbord style, served by candlelight on a spacious lawn at the edge of the river.

When we returned home, our study group presented a slide show and individual reports of their trip to an audience of teachers, students and invited guests. To receive six credits for the tour, students had to write a term paper that described what they had learned about working conditions in the countries they had visited, with particular reference to their own industries. It was an expensive trip (close to $1,500 per student). but they all agreed it was well worth it, an experience they would never forget. The Empire State staff in Saratoga Springs was impressed with our elaborate study plan. Even Dr. Chickering gave it his approval.

* * * * *

On Labor Day 1973, about one hundred students participated in the first graduating class of the Labor College. It was gratifying to see them marching so proudly in their ceremonial caps and gowns down the aisles to the stage to receive their two- and four-year Bachelor of Arts or Bachelor of Science diplomas. What the applauding audience clearly observed was the substantial number of women, black and Hispanic students in the graduating class, reflecting the integrated character of the Labor College.

A few days later, I received the following note from President Hall: "I can only guess how very pleased and proud you were of the students who received their certificates and degrees last Monday. It is so seldom in the teaching profession that one has the opportunity to see his efforts rewarded in a reasonably short time. . . . I want to congratulate you and thank you for your contributions. The recognition and warmth which the students accorded you was well deserved."

26. A Study Tour in Maoist China

It was purely by chance (a bare mention of it in a letter I received from my wife, then in London with our daughter Laura)) that I learned about a study tour to China that was being organized by the Union of Radical Political Economists (URPE) for August, 1972. China was then very much in the news: President Nixon had startled the American people by his surprise visit to China in May, not quite three months before.

I don't know why I became so determined to go on the China tour. I had plenty to do at the college, where I was developing instructional materials for two new courses for the fall semester. Besides, I was involved in efforts to interest unions in supporting the presidential campaign of George McGovern. Anyway, I checked with URPE and was told that the group had already been chosen: it consisted of eighteen political economists from Yale, Harvard, M.I.T., Stanford, and several other major universities. Among them was President Roosevelt's grandson. There was also a long waiting list; if I wished, my name could be added for future tours.

I was ready to give up until I thought of a long-shot possibility that was worth pursuing. I called the URPE tour leader the next day and asked him whether members of his group were experienced in labor-management relations and the practical aspects of trade unionism. It appeared that the group had little expertise in these fields. I then explained in some detail why it would be useful to have someone like me with them when they met with Chinese labor officials and workers in their visits to factories. I mentioned my academic credentials as well as my trade union background. The URPE people were impressed but said they could not enlarge the group to include me. They would have me in mind in planning future study tours.

I did not hear from the organization for two weeks and had almost forgotten about going to China when, about a week before the start of the tour, I received a telephone call from the URPE office informing me that one of the economists had dropped out of the tour because of illness, and would I be interested in replacing him. "Yes," I shouted over the phone, and immediately began frantic activity to get ready. I rushed to get the prescribed innoculations and fill out the necessary paperwork for the trip. My passport had been renewed two years ago for my brief visit to the Soviet Union. Somehow, I managed to comply with a long list of things that had to be done before my departure, including a wire to Mim that I would be somewhere in China when she and Laura returned home.

* * * * *

After an overnight stay in Hong Kong, our party was taken on a one-hour train ride to the Chinese border where, following a brief inspection of our visas and luggage, we were served a delicious lunch. Then we boarded another train for a two-hour ride to Kwangchow (formerly Canton), a city of two million people. We were quartered on the twelfth floor of the People's Hotel, where we had a panoramic view of the city south of the Pearl River. Kwangchow is a noisy city that awakens and begins to bustle at dawn. In the streets, parks and along the river, there were crowds of people, moving purposely about their business. Street traffic was heavy with bicycles but few cars. Near our hotel, there was a group of elderly men and women doing their morning *T'ai Chi* exercises.

As we left our hotel for a stroll, we were followed by scores of curious Chinese who had never seen an American. They followed us into the Friendship Department Store where they watched intently as several in our party bought postcards or tried on blue Mao jackets.

Since we were one of the first American groups to come to China after the Nixon visit, we were treated like VIPs. Undoubtedly, the authorities had singled out URPE for an early invitation because they knew that its members were sympathetic toward their socialist system and would spread favorable reports of their tour when they returned home.

Within our group, there were several who were "China watchers." Until then, they had been studying China from outposts in Taiwan and Hong Kong. Now, for the first time, they were being allowed to go to the mainland, and they were determined to make the most of it. They had worked up a list of institutions they asked to visit and important officials they wanted to interview that was, by any measure, extensive but stopped short of including Chairman Mao.

Our tour to China came at a time when the Cultural Revolution was in full bloom and when Mao still had the status of a deity. Virtually every political, economic and social activity was linked in some degree with Mao's thoughts and teachings. At no time did we hear any explicit or implied criticism of the "Geat Helmsman."

Wherever we went, whether it was to a major machine tool factory, an agricultural commune, a coal mine or a hospital, the interviews followed a standard pattern. First, we and a committee of our hosts, usually led by the "most responsible person" (MRP) of the Revolutionary Committtee (RC), sat down at a conference table where we were immediately served tea. One of our group introduced us as the First Friendship Delegation of American Radical Political Economists (I was included, although I was not an URPE member), offered our greetings to the

People's Republic of China, and then explained our mission. The MRP, after thanking us for visiting his enterprise, presented a mass of statistics on the progress that had been made since the Cultural Revolution, compared with the previous period. All of this was stated with a mixture of pride and humility and usually concluded by his asking "our American friends" for criticisms and suggestions.

Our group, hungry for information that could be used for articles and speeches, eagerly scribbled down the steady stream of facts and figures we were given, taking it all on face value. Whatever enterprise we visited and to whomever we spoke, the detailed list of accomplishments was interspersed with what seemed to us excessive homage to Mao-tse Tung and his teachings. Portraits and statues of Mao were everywhere: at the railroad station, hospitals, schools and factories. Framed photographs of the Chairman were standard icons in the dwellings of workers and peasants. On one train ride, I looked out of the window to see Mao's name printed in enormous white letters on the side of a mountain.

Faith in the Cultural Revolution appeared unbounded. A proper understanding of Mao's thoughts was almost a precondition for solving economic and social problems, as well as for personal advancement. One of the slogans repeated everywhere was Mao's dictum of "self reliance": by practicing this virtue, people could accomplish miracles.

I remember interviewing a young woman in a machine tool factory. She was working on a stamping machine, monotonously stepping on a pedal and pulling a lever that produced a small metal part. I found out that she was eighteen years old, lived with her parents and had been working on the job for about a year. When I asked why she had chosen this kind of work, she replied, without a hint of resentment, that she had been sent here by the State, and she was glad she could be helpful to the State. She said she was managing to save modest sums from her monthly wage. On what did she expect to spend her savings? The answer: a several volume set of Chairman Mao's works!

It had not taken me long to realize that anyone I interviewed would give a "politically correct" response, and that our interpreters, so friendly and cooperative, were there to report any improper activity on our part or any unfavorable comments from the Chinese to whom we talked.

* * * * *

We had the same disturbing reaction when we visited Beijing University and met with members of the economics department. We had naively expected to have a frank discussion on problems of socialist economic development, including questions about advances in technology, productivity, banking, trade and related matters. Instead, our hosts responded to our probing questions with polite generalities. Our distinct impression was that they were uncomfortable when we sought to discuss topics they considered sensitive. It was clear to us from their attitude and from what we subsequently learned that the Cultural Revolution had downgraded intellectuals, especially those from middle- and upper-class backgrounds who had no manual labor experience.

The professors told us, approvingly, that before the Cultural Revolution, scores on the entrance examination determined admission to the university, but now, workers, peasants and soldiers could get into the university, even though they did not score highly on exams. Two years of work experience and good health were among the major requirements. (I thought we at the Labor College were also relaxing admission standards for workers and minorities and that, on the whole, we were pleased with the results.)

Our hosts saw to it that we spent at least part of our visit in sight-seeing. We were taken to the famous Tien-An-men Square, so expansive that it could accommodate a demonstration of a million people, and we spent some time in the impressive museums and palaces that surround the square. We visited the Forbidden City and marveled at its priceless treasures. And of course, we went to the Ming Tombs and the Great Wall and had our pictures taken to prove we were there. Our evening entertainment included a performance of a Beijing opera, "The Red Lantern," attended by Mao's wife, Chiang Ching, in a 10,000-seat auditorium.

While we enjoyed at least some of the sight-seeing and entertainment, we preferred to spend our limited time interviewing factory managers, railroad workers, store clerks, peasants, teachers, bank officials, soldiers and anyone else who could add to the mountain of facts we were piling up on life in China.

* * * * *

We gained some important insights into the operating principles of the Cultural Revolution when we visited the May 7th East Is Red Cadre School, about an hour's bus ride south of Beijing. The school, which then had some 800 students, was established in 1968 in line with Chairman Mao's directives that intellectuals from the city should go to the countryside to learn about and engage in manual labor. The school, we were told, had three objectives:

(1) To transform the students' ideology through self-study and group discussions of the basic works of Marxism-Leninism and Mao's Thought. There were no professional teachers here. Through daily study and self-criticism, students were expected to get rid of bourgeois ideas and revisionist ideology.

(2) To change the students' work outlook. They were to learn to respect manual labor and appreciate the practical farming skills of the peasants.

(3) To train students in practical work, such as farming and in the operation of small factories. They grew rice, peanuts, vegetables and fruit, and raised poultry and pigs for their food requirements. They also were trained to repair farm implements, build houses and dye textiles.

Students stayed at the school for a minimum of six months and up to two years, in some cases longer. They could return to their homes to visit their families for two days every two weeks. They were paid the same salary they formerly earned from their regular employer. They paid no rent, but were charged for food. They lived in dormitories, ten to a large, well-kept room. I did not observe much in the way of personal items. While the students I talked to said they came to the school voluntarily, I strongly suspected they were given no choice but to enroll.

I could respond sympathetically to the idea of closing the gap between intellectuals and blue-collar workers, but I did not think it could, or should, be done coercively and certainly not by the edict of one man. I wondered how many students would have elected to attend the May 7th schools if they had truly been given a free choice. I guess I was hardly the only one who wondered what would happen to China after Mao's death.

One of the unforgettable activities of the tour was our visit into the bowels of a Chinese coal mine. Little did I realize when I volunteered, that this would be one of the most traumatic experiences of my life. At one point, I thought I might never come up from the mine alive.

The visit to the Kai-lan coal mine, an hour's ride from Tangshan, started out uneventfully. As expected, we were met by the mine committee whose director, after serving us tea, briefed us with a stream of statistics on production, employment, safety, wages and employee benefits, comparing conditions before and after the Cultural Revolution. He then suggested that those of us who wished could go down into the mine to see the operation at close hand. I was among ten of our group who volunteered.

We were taken to a large room near the entrance to the mine and told to take off all our clothes, so that we could don coal miners' uniforms. That consisted of white longjohns, thick stockings, blue overalls, high rubber boots, a helmet with a miner's lamp and a heavy white towel, which we were told to wrap around our necks. We were then escorted to an elevator for the descent into the mine. On the way down, I remembered I had left my wallet in my pants, which I had hung up in an open locker against the wall. I hoped it wouldn't be stolen. Anyhow, there was nothing I could do about it now.

The ride to the floor of the mine seemed a lot longer than I had expected. We finally stepped into a dimly-lit clearing where several shuttle cars were waiting for us. Each car could hold two members of our group and two miners. We had a bumpy ride on the railroad tracks for perhaps a quarter of a mile. During the trip, the miner who sat opposite me kept coughing in my face and muttering what sounded like curses. I was glad to get out of the car and stretch my legs.

But not for long. We were lined up in a column and told we could proceed to the area where the miners were cutting the coal. At the outset, I could move ahead by hunching my shoulders and bending slightly forward from the waist. After about fifty yards, I could make progress only by crawling on my knees along a path that was barely two feet wide. It was insufferably hot. I couldn't see through my steamed eyeglasses, and I had no handkerchief to wipe them clean. Another hundred yards or so, I was crawling on my belly, soaking up the water underfoot, while water dripped down on me from the wooden beams overhead. Every time I tried to raise my head, my helmet would hit the timber above me. A couple of times my helmet fell off, and once I nearly lost my eyeglasses in the dark. My clothes were drenched from the muddy water and body sweat. I couldn't remember ever being so miserable in my life. I felt as victimized and hopeless as the coal miners in Zola's *Germinal*. At one point, I was so tired, I would have given anything to stop and rest, but I couldn't clog up the narrow path for the people behind me, and how could anyone have helped me?

Just as I thought I would faint from heat exhaustion, I heard voices ahead. With a final burst of energy, I squirmed forward to reach a clearing where more than a dozen miners greeted me. They gave me some orange drink, and I lay down on the ground to rest, as other members of our group, equally exhausted, joined me. Suddenly, there was a thunderous crash to the right of us, as the rotary saws and jack-hammers began cutting into the seam of coal. The coal dust was like a cloud around us. I thought we would get instant silicosis. My only concern was how quickly we could get out of there. To the great dismay of our group, there was no available elevator shaft close by that would take us to the surface. We would have to return along the same path from which we came.

After a fifteen-minute rest, we started on our way back. Somehow, the return trip was not as bad, perhaps because we knew that our situation would get better, not worse as we proceeded. We were glad to reach the shuttle cars so we could sit down during the ride to the elevator shaft.

How thrilled we were when we finally were able to breathe fresh air and gaze up in the sunshine at the blue sky! Back to the dressing room we went, where we removed our drenched clothing and threw aside the coal-sooted towel from our necks. After a refreshing shower, we slowly dressed and then went upstairs for an hour's nap before the afternoon meal. I felt the wallet in my pocket, but did not check the contents. Somehow, I felt it would be an insult to our hosts.

The meal was delicious. A huge carp on an enormous platter was placed in the center of the table, surrounded by large mounds of rice and vegetables. The miners on each side of me, with friendly smiles, competed to fill my plate and teacup. There was much laughter from the diners that I could not understand because my interpreter was elsewhere.

Before we departed, there were once again the standard speeches about friendship, peace and international solidarity and much vigorous hand-shaking.

On the bus that took us back to the hotel, I thought about the life of those miners. I tried to imagine how I would feel if I had to work, as they did, eight hours a day, five days a week in the dark, heat and coal dust for a year, five years, ten or a lifetime. To the Chinese, I must be a softie intellectual who should be spending time at hard manual labor in a May 7th school. For the first time during our trip, I longed to be home.

* * * * *

There were other memorable experiences less strenuous and more satisfying than the one in the coal mine. I particularly remember when I was invited to give a lecture to the Shanghai dock workers on how U.S. longshoremen were adapting to the containerization of ship cargo, a subject I had become familiar with some time ago. I enjoyed watching a basketball game between Chinese and Canadian teams and exchanging comments about the play through my interpreter with the fans sitting nearby. I was flattered to be taken on a private excursion on the new Beijing subway—just me and the motorman— in the four-car, electric-driven train. As we passed each of nine stations, five uniformed subway attendants, equally spaced on the platform, saluted the two of us. The motorman responded with a train whistle and I returned their salute. At the end of the short trip, a delegation awaited my arrival to continue their lecture on the Beijing subway system, whose construction had begun nine years earlier.

* * * * *

One of the curious things about our stay in China was that at no time did we feel any danger that we might be beaten or robbed. In fact, our rooms generally remained unlocked when we left the hotel. Discreetly, the authorities made sure we would suffer no crime, either to our person or property. This punctiliousness about protecting our possessions could be carried to absurd lengths. One day, when I was attending an important meeting with officials of a rural commune, I was perplexed to hear the chairman call out my name from a piece of paper he held in his hand. It appeared that two officials from our hotel were coming to see me and ask me some questions. I was alarmed. Had I done something to provoke the authorities ? Was I going to be picked up and brought back to Beijing for further questioning and possibly jailed? I did not pay much attention to the discussion as I awaited my fate.

About an hour later, two men in civilian clothes alighted from an army truck and soon located me. Opening a parcel that contained two pairs of socks, a pair of shorts and an undershirt, they wanted to know if these were mine. I recognized the items and nodded. Was I sure? Yes, I was sure. Would I sign the statement they handed me? Yes, I would and did. We shook hands, they got into their truck and returned to Beijing. Apparently, these items had fallen out of my laundry bag and I had not missed them.

The same kind of thing happened to me as I was about to board the plane for the trip back to Hong Kong and then home. A young man ran breathlessly to the tarmac, located me and handed me a small bag. It contained about a fifth of a bottle of shampoo, a half-used tube of toothpaste and a ball-point pen that I had left at the hotel. I was overwhelmed. I wanted to tip him, but that would have been insulting—at least in that year.

I remember staring at a large sign as we were just about to reenter Hong Kong. It read: "Beware of Pickpockets!"

27. My Series of Labor Pamphlets

Back in 1958, I had the idea of writing a series of *Straight Talk* pamphlets which would deal with issues facing the working class and would be distributed to union members, I actually did write and publish the first pamphlet, *Recessions— And How to Prevent Them,* that same year. The opening paragraphs describe the recession as it was then and reads as if I were describing a similar economic collapse more than twenty five years later:

"Millions of workers are abruptly denied a livelihood, not because they are shiftless or incompetent, but because they have broken past production records.

"Hardship and distress spread throughout the land, not because our stores and warehouses are empty but because they are overstocked.

"We are the wealthiest nation on earth, and yet our government goes deeper and deeper into debt, with no end in sight. Our people mortgage more and more of their future to creditors to make the present livable.

"We have the prospect of unlimited expansion of the economy through the application of automation, computer technology and other scientific developments. We can produce, on an ever-increasing scale, enough material goods to abolish poverty and free our people from basic economic worries. Yet, we are uncertain and even fearful about the future. For the record is clear and unmistakable: we are bungling and mismanaging even our present industrial capacity. Our nation's political leaders have offered us no fundamental cure—or even the hope of a cure— for these man-made disasters."

I printed 2,000 copies and sold about 1,200 at an average price of 25 cents. The orders I received from several left-wing union leaders and the complimentary letters from socialist-minded people adequately compensated me for the $200 loss in my first publishing venture.

* * * * *

It took fourteen years before the second *Straight Talk* pamphlet, with the cataclysmic title, *Must We Perish?*, was written in 1972. I was actually a latecomer to the anti-nuclear campaign in which my wife, Mim, had been active for a decade. Some book I had read on the subject in 1972 made me acutely aware of the potential destruction of a nuclear war. After a month of research, I wrote the 24-page pamphlet, hoping to sell it to the mushrooming peace organizations. I did sell 7,000 copies, including an order for 1,000 from Women Strike for Peace. Later, I republished the pamphlet in an inexpensive newspaper format with an introduction by William Winpisinger, then president of the International Association of Machinists. Several thousand copies were distributed to I.A.M. locals across the country and other unions.

In 1973, I wrote and published a third pamphlet, *A Report to Working People*, which discussed "the squeeze on your paycheck, your job and your future—and what to do about it."

The pamphlet was enthusiastically received by New York City unions and used as an educational tool in preparation for a demonstration in Washington against inflation and unemployment. In the first week of its publication, I sold 4,750 copies of the 10,000 I had printed. On the long bus ride to Washington, union members held group discussions around the various topics covered by the 56-page pamphlet. I actually made about $200 in profit, even though I kept the price low.

My most ambitious pamphlet was issued in 1978 uunder the provocative title, *How Much Socialism in the U.S.A.?* By the late 1970s, there were hardly any union leaders or even rank-and-filers within the AFL-CIO who dared identify themselves with socialist principles; the formerly vigorous left-wing was now virtually non-existent. To provide me with some protection against possible attacks by red-baiters and to whet the interest of the curious, I asked the following questions about socialism on the cover page:

"Too much? None at all? Too little?"

"Should we get rid of it?"

"Should we want more of it?"

"Is it worth talking about?"

In my introduction, after reviewing the reasons for the widespread anti-socialist prejudice in the United States, I said:

"Millions of Americans have come to realize that the capitalist system under which they live breeds poverty, unemployment, racial hatred, environmental pollution, swollen military budgets and a host of other evils. However, they see no satsifactory alternative and are therefore reconciled to enduring its humiliations and injustices as best they can while seeking some relief through political reforms."

I told readers that "I have written this pamphlet because I have become convinced there is a strong case for the establishment of socialism in the United States, and that the subject merits widespread, honest public debate."

An unusual feature of my 78-page pamphlet on socialism is that it makes no reference to the writings of the great socialist and Marxist thinkers of the past. I said: "I have based my arguments in favor of a Socialist America on readily available evidence from the everyday world and recent history . . . Thus, readers can judge the validity of my observations and conclusions in terms of their own experience and common sense."

Sad to say, the pamphlet sold poorly. Some left-wing organizations and book stores bought multiple copies; so did radical groups in colleges, but sales in unions were disappointing. I might have increased the sales if I could have afforded the money for advertising and paid more attention to promotion, but as a college professor with a heavy teaching schedule, I could spare little time for marketing. I had printed 5,000 copies and sold slightly more than 1,000 at $1 apiece. Fortunately, my good friend, Nat Cohen, a businessman who shared my views, covered the substantial losses on the pamphlet. The remaining copies, except for about fifty which I still possess, were sold for the price of the raw paper.

Coincident with this pamphlet, I briefly attempted to organize a Socialist Caucus of American Labor, issuing a brochure that contained a ringing declaration of socialist principles coupled with a fierce denunciation of the evils of capitalism. My effort as an individual to inject socialist consciousness into the labor movement was a complete failure, despite an occasional expression of approval from old-time leftists. I soon realized that either the time was not ripe for a socialist awakening or that the fault lay in my lack of leadership qualities or a base of support. Whatever the reason, I set my sights on more immediate problems where I knew I could find much broader support.

If my socialist pamphlet had a poor reception, my next one, *Sexism in the Labor Movement*, was a gratifying success, both in sales and influence. It exposed the blatant sexism on the part of the AFL-CIO leadership, including the fact that there was not even one woman on the 35-member Executive Council. While the pamphlet aroused widespread support from feminist organizations, it also caused embarrassment and anger among council officers.

George Meany, then AFL-CIO President, was so enraged that he ordered his public relations director, Al Zack, to send me the following letter on AFL-CIO stationery on March 15, 1978:

"President Meany is too polite to answer unfounded charges by an ignorant and biased self-appointed critic—a critic too lazy and ill-informed to be treated seriously. But I am not that polite. So, sir, my comment: 'Your pamphlet—and you—are full of shit.'

Zack, without realizing it, had given me an opportunity for a perfect response. For in the upper left-hand corner of the AFL-CIO stationery were the names of all the members of the Executive Council—*and not a woman among them!* That letter became an effective promotion piece that boosted sales and added to Meany's embarrassment. Subsequent pressure from women's groups finally compelled the AFL-CIO in 1980 to make room on the Executive Council for one woman, Joyce Miller, president of the Coalition of Labor Union Women. (At this writing, 16 years later, there are seven women on the council.)

In 1986, I wrote a pamphlet that turned out to be a best-seller, with sales of more than 100,000, not including reprints by a number of unions. It was called *Why Unions Are Good for You and Your Family*. (I seem to have gone in for long titles.) The pamphlet contained facts, figures and anecdotal naterial to prove that trade unions are important for the well-being of working people. It also sought to refute the arguments used by anti-labor propagandists to attack unions.

Local unions across the country ordered batches of the low-priced pamphlet, which could be used for winning the support of non-union workers during organizing campaigns. They could also be given to newly-organized members and mailed to the homes of unionists where the entire family could be informed about labor's message.

Two years later, I wrote one of my more ambitious pamphlets, *Human Rights for Working People.* It consisted of a trade union commentary on the recently published Catholic Church statement, *"Pastoral Letter on Catholic Social Teaching and the Economy.* My pamphlet endorsed the bishops' basic position that our society, acting through its public and private institutions, had the moral responsibility to enhance human dignity and protect not only the political rights of all people but their economic rights as well.

The pamphlet discussed the present deficiencies in the political, social and economic rights of working people and suggested ways by which trade unions could achieve the goals set forth in the pastoral letter. I arranged to have an introductory message by a former student of mine, Edward J. Cleary, a Catholic, who was president of the New York State AFL-CIO, which helped sales among New York trade unionists.

The pamphlet sold more than12,000 copies and received critical praise from influential union leaders, public officials and a number of Catholic bishops. AFL-CIO Secretary-Treasurer Thomas Donahue called it "a first rate job [that] advances one more step the effort to convince the mass of America of the bona fides of this labor movement." Reverend Monsignor George G. Higgins, a prelate close to the AFL-CIO leadership, called the pamphlet "a timely and significant contribution," and recommended it "not only to union members but to Americans of good-will in all walks of life."

Until this point, all my pamphlets had found favor with union officials within the AFL-CIO, except for the one on sexism. However, in 1990, I wrote a pamphlet, *Why Unions Are in Trouble and What They Can Do About It,* which caused a sensation among union leaders from coast-to-coast. Why I decided to write this critical pamphlet and what the consequences were to my career will be discussed in an appropriate context in a later chapter.

28. Compulsory College Education

Harry Van Arsdale and I had envisioned that the Labor College would be staffed with professors who had outstanding academic and labor credentials. With that kind of faculty, the college could attract serious union leaders as students from all parts of the country. The college could eventually become the "West Point" of the labor movement, training a new breed of union leaders who would be equipped to deal with the problems of a changing society. Van Arsdale, as president of the New York City Central Labor Council, was confident he could get sufficient financial support from local unions to build a hotel adjacent to the college, where out-of-town students, including those from foreign countries, would live while they matriculated in the school's degree programs.

The dream was not to materialize. Empire State's administrators in Saratoga Springs treated the "Labor College" as no different from its other dozen or so learning centers, restricting its funds and resources. Even worse, it put a limit on student enrollment, claiming budget constraints, so that recruiting was at a virtual standstill. It controlled the hiring of faculty members and would not pay the salaries that well-known labor professors enjoyed at other institutions.

Thus, the college's labor faculty consisted almost entirely of individuals who had undistinguished academic and labor credentials, had not published anything of note in their discipline and were not particularly effective as teachers. They made no effort to become known to the city's union leaders or acquainted wth their problems, and were unwilling to accept responsibility for recruiting new students, since Empire State did not make such activity a requirement when it hired them. The enthusiasm with which the city's unions had greeted the establishment of *their* college was all but gone. Empire State and its president, James Hall, used the words "Labor College" only on ceremonial occasions. For all practical purposes, it no longer existed, except that a dwindling number of trade unionists were taking its courses.

My efforts to get Van Arsdale to remedy the situation by putting pressure on Dr. Hall was to no avail. Although he was very disappointed about what was happening at the college, he felt it unwise to intervene; he would be accused of using labor's muscle to dictate how the college should be run. It could rekindle problems with right-wing educators, who had resented the creation of a college catering to trade unionists.

Van Arsdale found an ingenious way to resurrect the almost moribund Labor College by proposing to have his union's fifteen hundred electrical apprentices enroll as a group in a special two-year college program. It was a bombshell of a proposal that startled Dr. Hall and his aides in Saratoga, but one that was to their distinct advantage to accept. What other college or university had ever been handed 1,500 tuition-paid students *en masse,* requiring their *mandatory* attendance!

A self-educated labor leader who had never completed high school, Van Arsdale was keenly interested in having an educated union membership that could adapt to the changing technologies and the social problems they would face in the years ahead. What he proposed was mind-blowing and unprecedented: *compulsory college education.* Every union electrical apprentice would have to attend the Labor College and earn at least a two-year degree before being accepted as a qualified journeyperson. When he discussed it with me, I thought it was a great idea but very difficult to institute and finance. I learned once again never to underestimate his ability to turn dreams into reality.

Van Arsdale decided to put his proposal into practice in Electrical Workers Local 3, where he had been business manager for more than two decades and still wielded considerable influence as union treasurer. In November1976, the union's Joint Apprentice Committee, under his initiative, unanimously endorsed his proposal and forwarded a copy to the the Educational and Cultural Trust Fund of the Electrical Industry, a labor-management partnership, with a request that the Fund's trustees consider providing the financial means to implement the college program for apprentices.

To subsidize the education of approximately fifteen hundred electrical apprentices would be an enormous, if not impossible, financial burden. Understandably, the proposal aroused strong opposition from many of the major electrical contractors who served on the board as trustees. Some suggested that the college degree requirement be made voluntary rather than compulsory, and that the apprentices pay at least half the tuition. Van Arsdale, who was also a trustee and a dominant influence on the board, remained firm: the college program would have to be compulsory and the Fund would have to bear the entire financial cost.

I don't know how he managed to persuade a majority of the employers to go along with the plan (the union's trustees, of course, were no problem). Attending one of the board meetings, I was able to see the enormous respect they had for him and the deference they paid to whatever he proposed. Also, it must have helped that the Fund's multi-million-dollar annual income had grown as a result of several profitable years for the electrical industry.

Angry opposition to the compulsory program came from the apprentices themselves. Many of them said they wanted to become electricians and were not interested in going to college. What really upset them was that they would have to spend three hours in a classroom twice a week after their day's work on the job. And to make matters worse, their classes were to be held not at the Labor

College but at a shabby high school on 18th Street in Manhattan's Chelsea area, a building that had no student recreation room, library or eating facilities. I must say I felt sorry for them; I guess that I, too, would have felt rebellious.

For a while there was some talk about a boycott of the college, but the noisy protests quieted when word came down from union headquarters that anyone who failed to attend classes would be thrown out of the apprenticeship program. Their anger turned to sullenness; they determined to adopt a non-cooperative attitude and make life miserable for their teachers in the hope that the program would be withdrawn. After two of our instructors had found it impossible to maintain order in their class of apprentices (one woman teacher was brought to tears by the taunts and foul language she had to endure), I was asked to take over one of the more disruptive groups. I did not relish the assignment.

When I walked into the classroom, I was greeted with jeers and catcalls. On the blackboard were the words "Bullshit" and "Fuck you."

I stood in front of them and said, as coolly as I could: "I have the authority to remove any of you from this class if you do not behave properly. And if I do, you will no longer be an apprentice in this union."

There was a sudden hush. I continued: "I'm opening this door and anyone who doesn't want to be here can leave now. I'll be back in two minutes. I expect the blackboard to be cleaned and those of you who intend to remain here to be in your seats." The threat worked. When I returned, no one had left the room. The blackboard was clean. They were in their seats, somewhat subdued.

"Good," I said. "Now we've got to decide how we're going to spend the next fifteen weeks together. We can be miserable with each other and have a boring, useless time, or we can learn a few things and have some fun doing it. So what'll it be?" They said nothing, but I could see I was beginning to gain their confidence. I had to figure out how I could make the course, Labor and Politics, interesting to this captive audience, who had been up since five or six that morning, had put in a day's work and would not get home until 10 p.m. or even later.

I started by asking them if they knew their representative in Congress. About one-third raised their hands. I said the homework for next week was to find out the name of their congressman or congresswoman They could check with people in their community for this information, or if they wished, they could get it from the League of Women Voters, whose telephone number I put on the blackboard. That was their homework—nothing more. I could see they were pleased that there was no reading or writing assignment.

In the next session, after I had made sure that every student knew his representative in Congress, I asked them to discuss and then vote on which political issue they wanted to focus on for the rest of the term. They finally agreed on unemployment. It was an issue that directly concerned them, because the construction industry was starting to decline and many electricians were being laid off. We spent the balance of the session discussing the reasons for unemployment in our society. The optional homework assignment was to bring to class any newspaper or magazine article dealing with any aspect of the unemployment problem. The word got around that Dr. Kelber's class was a snap, not much sweat to it.

The following week, the students were asked to write on the spot a petition on unemployment. After some discussion, agreement was reached on whose wording they considered the best.The class was then divided into four competing teams in a contest to see which one would get the most signatures on their petitions. Xeroxed copies of the petition were distributed to each team.

Our fourth week was devoted to "field trips." No classroom work. Each team was deployed in places where it thought it could get the maximum number of signatures: in front of Madison Square Garden, Grand Central Station, Macy's, Times Square or other populated areas. I cautioned the teams not to make up phony signatures. I wanted addresses as well as names, and I would spot-check their petitions. Any team that turned in illegal signatures would be disqualified and its members penalized. All in all, some 1,600 signatures were obtained, the winning team with approximately 700. The petitions were mailed to President Jimmy Carter.

I brought cheers from the students when I announced there would be no term paper; all they had to do to pass the course was to write a letter to their representative in Congress on the subject of unemployment and get a satisfactory response. It turned out to be a lot more difficult than they had imagined.

Their first problem was to write a proper, persuasive letter. We discussed the various ways to do that so they would get a respectful answer. I rejected most of the letters that were initially submitted to me for approval, offering suggestions for rewriting. It took almost three weeks before all of the students had typed or handwritten and mailed their letters to their respective representatives.

From then on to the end of the semester, the first fifteen minutes of every class was devoted to a progress report on letters from members of Congress. I rejected the usual form-letter responses and told the students to insist on knowing what the representative was actually doing or planning to do about unemployment.

As the weeks went by, almost a third of the class had not received a response that I considered acceptable. I had students calling their representative almost daily, pleading for an answer to their letter and, in a few cases, going to the representative's local headquarters to get the cooperation of staff members. Toward the end of the semester, a few desperate students sent telegrams to their representatives stating that unless they received a personal letter from them dealing with the unemployment issue by next week, their instructor, Dr. Harry Kelber, would fail them for the course. The appeal worked. One representative phoned a student from Washington to assure him that a letter was in the mail. At the end of the term, all but two students had completed the assignment. I treasured the batch of letters the students had turned over to me, and I kept them in my files for several years.

Although I had managed to include classroom lectures on labor legislation, lobbying techniques and electoral politics, my unorthodox methods were not appreciated by my colleagues, who preferred traditional patterns of instruction.

Gradually, opposition to the program subsided, particularly among the first-year apprentices, who were conditioned to accept it as a necessary step to becoming an electrician. Van Arsdale helped a great deal to quiet the discontent of the second- and third-year apprentices by spending a week at the school, sitting attentively in class after class. Somehow, his presence had a magical effect on the apprentices, almost all of whom adored him. Whatever grumbling had persisted ceased after Van Arsdale's visit.

After just one year, the compulsory college-degree program for apprentices—the first of its kind anywhere—had been institutionalized, with strong support from employers, union officials, educators and students.

The introduction of fifteen hundred electrical apprentices as students in the Labor College (about four times the previous enrollment) had some extraordinary side-effects, both good and bad. In the first place, it solved the problem and expense of student recruitment. Empire State would get a lump-sum payment each semester to cover tuition for every one of those apprentices, each of whom would receive a stipend for books and incidental expenses. There would be no problem about dropouts, since the apprentices had no choice but to remain at the college for at least two years.

The apprentice program soon began to function as a college in itself. It had its own administrative staff and hired a corps of part-time teachers, "adjuncts," to cover approximately sixty classes. Meanwhile, no attention at all was paid to the recruitment of students from the labor movement at large, even though enrollment of members from other unions continued to shrink. No one on the faculty, except myself, had participated in the struggle to establish the Labor College, and they were not particularly interested in its original purposes.

The curriculum in the apprentice program was a makeshift affair, but the faculty was not motivated nor subject to any pressure from the electrical union to improve it. Imperceptibly, an unwrittten understanding developed between many of the part-time teachers and their students to relax academic standards. Teachers, wanting to be rehired, perhaps as full-timers, sought to become popular with their students by overlooking absences and lateness and failure to do homework assignments. Hardly anyone received a failing grade, since no teacher wanted to jeopardize a student's apprenticeship status. Grades of "incomplete" were eventually rectified on the basis of teacher-student consultations that were almost never reviewed. Empire State used the tuition windfall from the apprentice program to improve its facilities at its other learning centers across the state, while short-changing the Labor College. Members of the faculty were either not interested or too scared to complain, lest it endanger their chances of getting tenure. And although Van Arsdale and his associates were aware of what was going on, they were reluctant to interfere because it would be construed as "meddling" and applying union pressure on an academic institution.

The steady decline of the Labor College continued until April 1980, when a new program was instituted that revitalized the college, increased its enrollment among union officers and restored its original purpose. The program was designed to enable labor leaders with busy schedules to earn a two-year or four-year degree by completing a professional-level cirriculum that was relevant to their needs. But more about that later.

29. *Inventing a New Poetic Form*

In the late 1970s, I began to feel burnt out as a teacher. I could no longer bring my old enthusiasm to the classroom. My life at the college was dull and repetitive, worsened by lots of faculty bickering over petty administrative matters. I desperately needed to get away. Fortunately, I was entitled to a half-year paid sabbatical. In the spring of 1978, Mim and I set out for a seven-week "honeymoon" that took us to Spain, France, Italy and Switzerland. Mim needed a rest, too. Since 1971, she had been working as a speechwriter and policy adviser for Congresswoman Bella Abzug, an old friend from their high school and college days, commuting back and forth to Washington. When Bella narrowly lost her try for the Democratic nomination for the U.S. Senate in1976, she was appointed by President Carter to head his national women's commission, and Mim joined the staff as a policy coordinator and writer.

The trip was a welcome diversion: visits to historic sites and famous museums; meeting labor leaders as well as friends whom we had known in the States, and eating delicious meals at highly-recommended restaurants. The one thing I still remember vividly was standing alone on a platform near the apex of the Jungfrau in the Swiss Alps, where I could look down on the white, puffy clouds and adjacent snow peaks. I had an overpowering religious feeling, the kind I had never before experienced. On the way down, I thought of a poem I had read during my high school days and still remembered:

> A man is what he dreams,
> And I have dreamt of worlds of beauty and glory.
> I stand upon the summit of time
> Where the winds of eternity blow.
> Infinity beats in my heart,
> And with hands scooping up dawns,
> I gesture with the universe.

* * * * *

When I returned to the college at the end of my sabbatical, I once again felt dispirited. The atmosphere was dreary. The number of trade unionists at the college had continued to shrink during my absence, but the faculty was not alarmed since fifteen hundred electrical apprentices were still enrolled.

I needed to find something else to do, perhaps a hobby, to stimulate my flagging spirits. I started to write a novel, but gave up after a few weeks because I realized I did not have the talent and perseverance to be a fiction writer. I took up chess, joined the Manhattan chess club, but quit shortly after because it was obvious I'd be a low-rated "potzer." I tried to learn to play the piano, but found the exercises tedious and progress slow. Unlike some of my friends, I loathed being a collector of *anything*, whether stamps, rocks or whiskey bottles. I had no aptitude for anything mechanical and besides, there was no room in our apartment for a workshop. I did not care for golf and was too old for tennis. So what to do?

Luckily, the answer came from a source that I could never have imagined. I had been reading an anthology of world poetry and became fascinated by the Japanese *haiku*, a miniature poem that can capture an image, emotion or thought in three lines totaling seventeen syllables, structured in a 5-7-5 pattern.

I really can't recall how it happened, but one day I suddenly developed my own miniature poetic form, obviously inspired by *haiku*. I named it *septad*, because it had a formal seven-line structure consisting of 28 syllables with the lines staggered in sequence from one syllable to seven. As I described it:

"The septad offers the poet the opportunity for a wide range of expression. It is ideal for poetic aphorism, verbal picture-painting and social commentary. Despite its short, rigidly-structured form, a septad can express irony, humor and the shock of recognition, employing rhyme, alliteration and other poetic devices. Unlike longer poems, its impact on the reader is whole and immediate."

I found the septad a congenial poetic form that enabled me to express emotions and ideas in very few words. Many of my septads came to me almost whole upon awakening, requiring only slight adjustments of syllables, words or lines.

Through septads, I found I could express some of my political ideas in images that seemed to have greater immediate impact on readers than my lectures and writings. A few examples:

On democratic capitalism:
 In
the land
of the free,
winners do well:
they feed on losers.
Losers complain freely.
Winners, free, keep on feeding.

On environmental pollution:
The sky over the White House
is dark with birds screeching;
the Potomac, choked
with fish gasping:
"Give us clean
water.
air!"

On war:
Scars
of war
shame losers
to fight again.
The scars of winners
are badges of honor.
War. Scars. War. Scars. War. Scars. War.

On poverty:
Through
research,
polls, studies,
conferences
(heavily funded)
the poor now know—in depth—
about poverty. How else?

Over a half year, I composed several dozen septads and began thinking about publishing them in a book. I sent a packet of my best ones to about two dozen publishers and received not one favorable reply. A small number praised my work but indicated their book list for poetry was complete for the forseeable future. I tried sending a few to magazines that published poetry. More rejection slips came.

Finally, I decided to publish the poems on my own. Early in 1981, I printed 500 copies of a small paperback containing 64 selected septads under the imprimatur of Picket Press. The book was not priced (should I say it was priceless?); I had decided to give copies away as gifts for Christmas or other occasions to my many students, relatives, friends and neighbors. As time went on, I built up a collection of more than 150 septads and a dozen or so longer poems which I hoped to publish some day.

* * * * *

My interest in poetry stimulated a desire to study music. With the encouragement of my good friend and music mentor, Judith Siegman, I enrolled in night courses at Juilliard, where I spent a year on sight-singing and a rigorous class in harmonic theory. I had to defer my plan to take courses in music composition because I could not spare the time to attend class and submit to the arduous work that the course would require.

I developed a curious, utterly naive notion of what it took to create a musical composition. I observed, quite correctly, that all the notes of every musical scale were available to me on the piano. All I had to do was to consult my musical intuition and acquired taste, writing down on music paper the progression of notes that sounded right to me and captured the mood and rhythm of what I was attempting to compose. In the meantime, I would continue to enrich my knowledge of harmony and counterpoint so that I could test my compositions against established theory. I told myself I did not have to know how to play any musical instrument in order to compose. I could find the appropriate notes and chords by fingering them on my piano. I sounded like the proverbial monkey who, if given time without end, could type all the works of Shakespeare.

My first efforts were to set poems I admired to music. I wrote songs based on John Donne's "Devotion XII," Byron's "Ozymandias," Yeats' "The Lake Isle of Innisfree" and some poems of Emily Dickinson. I was too unsure of their quality and of my talent to show them to anybody, even Mim.

I was now determined that when I retired from the Labor College in 1984, I would devote a good part of my remaining years to poetry and music.

30. A Degree Program for Leaders

By the end of 1979, the Labor College consisted of little more than the approximately 1500 electrical union apprentices. Without the lump-sum tuition payments for the entire group by the Joint Board of the Electrical Industry, the college would have had to go out of existence, for enrollment from other unions totaled not more than 100 to 150 students. The dean's recruiting effort for the fall term had been a disaster. More students had dropped out than were newly enrolled.

In January, I came up with a plan that I thought could resurrect the original idea of a labor college. Specifically, I proposed establishing a Union Leadership/College Degree Program which would enable eligible union officers to earn two-year and four-year degrees upon completion of an innovative, but rigorous series of courses. I felt it was important to provide leadership training for union officers who, unlike their counterparts of the 1930's, had to deal with a variety of complex issues, including pension management, new technologies, environmental hazards, runaway plants and the growing power of multinational corporations. I proposed to hire recognized experts in each of these fields as adjunct instructors, an additional inducement to draw qualified labor leaders into the program. I also believed that if I could involve union officers in a college degree program, I would eventually be able to recruit a steady supply of their members as students. If I succeeded, the college could survive as a viable institution, even if the Joint Industry Board decided to stop paying the full tuition bill for its electrical apprentices.

But there were enormous difficulties that I had to overcome. The heavy workload and erratic schedules of labor leaders would not permit most of them to attend classes more than one night a week. At that rate, it would take them forever to earn a degree in any of the traditional colleges. Also, union leaders were frequently faced with emergencies, conferences or out-of-town assignments that would prevent them from coming to class on a prescribed night or at the required hour. Since that could happen several times during a semester, they would eventually be compelled to drop out of the course or receive a failing grade.

A number of union officials who had attended college and then dropped out told me that they had found many of the required classes boring and irrelevant to their lives and work. They had also resented the inflexible bureaucracy and arbitrary regulations of the traditional colleges where faculty and administrators were generally indifferent to their unique problems and special needs. I developed a set of policies and procedures for my proposed Union Leadership/College Degree Program that I felt reasonably confident would interest a sufficient number of labor leaders to enroll:

Students would be required to attend classes only one evening a week under a flexible schedule, so that if they had to be absent on their regular class night, they could come to school on another night during that week and receive the same instruction from their regular teacher. All sessions of all classes would be videotaped, so that if students had to be absent from class for a week or more, for whatever reason, they could watch the "replay" of their class on a television screen and be able to catch up on their homework assignment. They could arrange to see the videotape at their convenience. Students would be permitted to record their class sessions on tape recorders to be used for review or to help classmates who had missed a particular session. Finally, there'd be a week of makeup and review sessions at the end of the trimester for students who needed tutorial support.

I designed a curriculum that included ten required courses for an associate degree and an additional ten courses for the four-year baccalaureate degree. The courses covered virtually every type of activity that union leaders might be engaged in or about which they needed to be well informed, from collective bargaining, organizing, arbitration and labor law to the American economy, national and local politics, international relations, psychology and social legislation. In each of the courses, emphasis was to be put on speaking and writing skills. The capstone course would be on the theory and practice of union leadership.

Students would be able to earn six credits by attending school one night a week for three hours during a 12-week trimester, which would consist of classroom work and supervised independent study with a mentor. Thus, with summer study, they could obtain a total of 24 credits per year toward the 64 credits required to earn an associate degree, even if they limited their attendance to one night a week. Union officers could also expect to receive a substantial number of college credits for their work and life experience, a factor which would significantly accelerate their progress toward graduation. The curriculum also contained a list of 20 electives from which students could choose to fulfill the credit requirements for a degree.

When I presented the college faculty with a detailed description of my proposal for a degree program for union leaders, questions were raised about its feasibility. Dean Richard Dwyer pointed out that there were no funds, personnel or other resources that could be committed to the proposed program. Without financial and staff support, the program would die on the vine and not be worthy of further disussion by the faculty, he said. I chose to interpret the faculty position in more positive terms: it would not oppose my efforts to create the degree program, but I would have to do it without their cooperation.

By contrast, I received a strongly encouraging reception from Van Arsdale and other influential labor leaders when I presented my plan at a dinner meeting.

Van Arsdale mentioned he had met that very morning with a newly-elected local union president who had appealed for his help. He had won the election by effectively criticizing the incumbent. "What do I do now, Harry?" the man had asked.

There was a clear consensus that the labor movement needed leaders who had the professional training to deal with a rapidly changing economy and corporate managers who were using sophisticated techniques to defeat union organizing campaigns. I was promised the solid endorsement of the degree program by the New York City Central Labor Council and was assured of their support in my recruitment efforts.

Thus encouraged, and with the tacit approval of the dean, I put out a flyer, widely distributed among the city's unions, announcing the program, describing its principal features and inviting union officers, including shop stewards and professional staffers, to apply for admission. In order to guarantee a high caliber of committed students, I insisted on interviewing every applicant personally.

By the start of the spring semester, the degree program had an enrollment of 60 full-time officials from 49 different local unions, representing a cross-section of the city's industries and occupations. Among the students were officers of the Central Labor Council, Printing Trades Council, Building and Construction Trades Council, Black Trade Union Committee, Hispanic Labor Committee and the Coalition of Labor Union Women.

On April 1, 1980, the first classes of the Union Leadership Program (U.L.P.) were held. It also happened to be the first day of a city-wide subway strike. However, almost all of the students, except those officially involved in the conduct of the strike, were able to attend. Entering their classes, each student received a briefcase and writing pad on which were embossed the blue and gold insignia of the Labor College, with two mottos: "Aspire to Excellence" and "Serve the People."

From the outset, I tried to create a warm, informal atmosphere in the classroom and to weld the students into an academic community. Coffee and cookies were available at the start of class and during the break. I published a two-page weekly newsletter, *Spotlight,* which contained news of student activities outside the classroom. Students were fascinated by video playbacks of their often heated debates. Labor leaders from different industries were able to become friendly and even find a basis for cooperation in their union work.

What made the leadership program so unusual was the rich background and diversity of the student body. The average student had been a union member for twenty years, so that in each classroom, the instructor could draw on a total of four hundred years of experience in the discussion of a labor topic. There was no problem about getting outstanding labor experts to teach such a group of students.

Our early success created difficulties. The faculty resented the "elitism" of the leadership program and the special treatment that U.L.P. students were receiving. They accused me, with justification I suppose, of attempting to create a college within a college. They objected to my hiring "outsiders," while they were available to teach in the program. I told them frankly that none of them had the specialized knowledge and experience to hold the attention of these labor leaders.

The dean greeted the success of the program with ambivalence. He was pleased with the growth in enrollment and the presence of so many important labor leaders at the school. On the other hand, he worried that I might be upstaging him and become a threat to his position. He knew that I had no desire to be dean and that I welcomed his cooperation.

By the fall semester, student enrollment in the Union Leadership Program had doubled to 120 from 75 local unions. The recruitment had been accomplished by word-of-mouth advertising and a full-page story about the program in the *Labor Chronicle.* the official newspaper of the Central Labor Council. Exactly one year later after its creation— on April 1, 1981—the program had an enrollment of 175 full-time and part-time union officers and staff specialists from 93 different labor organizations, representing virtually every industry and occupation in the New York metropolitan area.

* * * * *

Although the U.L.P. was prospering even beyond my original expectations, I realized that sooner or later, the Empire State College administration in Saratoga Springs would try to weaken the program or dismantle it entirely by getting rid of me by one pretext or another. In their view, the program, especially if it were to expand, represented a threat to their principled opposition to traditional classroom instruction. With so many union leaders concentrated in one program, they feared that I might be laying the basis for a truly independent labor college to replace the current Center for Labor Studies.

I had no illusions about the vulnerability of my position. I had no official authorization from either Empire State or the local faculty to start the program, develop a special curriculum, recruit students and hire instructors. I realized that their strategy was to let me build the program and then, at some point, find a reason to replace me. I had taken a calculated risk that the program would become so important to Van Arsdale and other influential labor leaders, that they would prevent any attempt to remove me.

Despite the fact that the leadership program had nearly tripled in one year, my repeated requests for an associate director and secretary to handle the immense amount of paper work went unanswered. I could not even get an office typewriter for my personal use, so that I had no choice but to type classroom materials, the weekly newsletter and administrative records, such as attendance rosters and student evaluations, at home and on weekends. It was exhausting to conduct the program single-handed, while carrying a full teaching load. Inevitably, there was a backlog in the maintenance of student records.

I finally realized I was being sucked into a trap that could result in discrediting my performance and having students turn against me. At some point in the near future, the dean could call a meeting of students and say that because I had neglected to maintain proper records, they would not receive credit for their course work until a thorough investigation of the U.L.P. was completed. He could also tell them I had not followed faculty guidelines on curriculum, so they might not get credit for some of the courses they had taken. He could add that because of my administrative sloppiness, many of the students faced the possibility that they would not receive their degrees as scheduled.

I reached the boiling point when the dean refused to let me use the xerox machine to send out notices about the start of the fall term. He said I had used up my xerox "quota," the same number he had assigned to other individual faculty members. On August 29, I sent a memo to the dean informing him that unless I was assigned an associate director, a secretary, an adequate office and a typewriter, I would resign as program director.

The dean refused to accept my offer of resignation, but did little to satisfy my demands. He said that an administrative staff member would be assigned temporarily to work on the records; I could share a secretary with three other faculty members; he would see what he could do about office space, although he reminded me that no faculty member had a private office. I could not have a typewriter, because three had recently been stolen and the college was short of machines. He said that if I wrote out my course materials, newsletter and correspondence in longhand, he would assign a secretary to type them! With the fall term just a week away, I guess neither of us wanted a confrontation.

* * * * *

The showdown came on the morning of December 10, 1981, when I arrived at the school to find that several cabinet files containing all my records and course materials had been removed. When I went to the dean's office and demanded an explanation, he said he had dismissed me as director and was "restructuring" the program's administrative procedures. He would not discuss it further. He had timed his action during the intersession period when no students were at the college. Two days later, he announced my dismissal at a faculty meeting. I asked for the right to appeal the dean's decision, but I could not get a single teacher to support my request for a hearing. I learned he had assigned a new faculty member, Elena Michelson, to run the program as his special assistant.

When the students learned of my dismissal, they reacted with a mixture of anger, dismay and confusion. At my suggestion, they agreed to call a meeting of all students to hear the dean's defense of his decision and my version of his behavior. The students could then decide on a course of action that would save the leadership program. The dean reluctantly agreed to appear. What he did not know was that I had arranged to have the proceedings videotaped, so there would be an accurate record of who said what.

Worried about the future of the U.L.P. and what might happen to their own quest for a college degree, about 80 students came to the meeting at the school during a snowstorm on the Friday night of January 18, Dr. Martin Luther King's birthday. The meeting began with a speech by Dean Richard Dwyer in which he explained that he had removed me as director because I had permitted the program's administrative records to fall into a chaotic condition. He said that if he had allowed the situation to deteriorate further, students would have had difficulty in getting credits for courses they had completed, and he implied that their prospect for a degree could have been endangered. He also added that the integrity and reputation of the U.L.P. could be jeopardized if it left itself open to criticism from official college accrediting associations.

I started my response by describing the manner in which I had been dismissed. I said the students deserved an explanation as to why I had not been consulted in advance and why my records, including personal files, had been removed without my knowledge or approval. Was this kind of undemocratic behavior acceptable in, of all places, a labor college, I asked. I then reviewed my record of the past 20 months, itemizing the functions I had undertaken for the program, in addition to teaching classes four nights a week. I recalled the many times I had asked the dean for administrative help for record keeping and been rebuffed. I noted that, except for the electrical apprentices, the U.L.P. represented nearly half of the college enrollment, but had only one employee, myself, while the dean had a staff of nineteen, including an associate dean, nine faculty members, two counselors and five secretaries. I concluded by saying that if the dean had found a better director to replace me, I would willingly resign.

For the next hour and a half, the students took over. More than thirty of them defended me and insisted that I continue as director. Several denounced the dean's action as a raw power play—one called it a *coup d'état*. They wanted to know why the leadership program had been short-changed in regard to administrative personnel and resources. A few threatened to resign from the program if I were removed. One student suggested I take the leadership program to another college that would appreciate its worth.

When the dean was asked whom he had in mind to replace me as director, he replied that there would be no director. Empire State did not have a budget line for program director and therefore the title did not exist. The students kept pressing. Would he allow Dr. Kelber to run the U.L.P. under some other title that would not require budget approval? The answer was a flat no. I was a tenured professor, not a program director, and there would be no change in titles, he said.

At this point, the dean unveiled his new administrative plan for the U.L.P.. It was to be run by a tripartite group, a "troika," consisting of representatives from the faculty, the students and his own administrative staff, with Professor Michelson acting as coordinator. Student after student ridiculed what one called a "multi-headed monster," that could not possibly provide the kind of leadership that the program had enjoyed and still needed. Under insistent prodding, the dean said bluntly that under no circumstances would he restore me as head of the U.L.P., although I could continue teaching in the program. Throughout the heated exchange between students and the dean, I remained silent, seeing no reason to intervene. (I have a videotape of that dramatic meeting, which displays the quality of the students in the Leadership Program.) Finally, a motion was approved unanimously to inform Dr. John Jacobson, acting president of Empire State College, that the students wanted me restored as director and to request a meeting with him in New York City to discuss the future of the U.L.P.

I had strong doubts that a meeting with Jacobson, even if it took place, would accomplish the students' objectives. It was obvious to me that the dean had acted on instructions from Jacobson, who calculated that by firing me as director, he could emasculate the leadership program. Only the week before I was removed, Jacobson had succeeded in stripping me of some of my authority to run the program after a bitter confrontation in which he showed his hostility toward me and the leadership program. Evidently, he felt that now was the time to move in for the kill. The immediate cause of my conflict with Jacobson was control over a $25,000 grant which I had successfully solicited from the Joseph A. Beirne Foundation, an agency of the Communications Workers of America, for the purpose of developing video-taped educational materials for use in the leadership program. The money was deposited in the Amalgamated Bank and a committee of trustees was set up to supervise the new project; it consisted of then CWA Vice President Morton Bahr and several local CWA officers, all of whom were U.L.P. students.

Another issue for dispute was the Book and Coffee Fund that the students had set up to buy textbooks wholesale without each student having to spend time shopping for them. This fund, too, was deposited at the Amalgamated.

On November 18, 1981, Jacobson had sent me a registered letter insisting that I turn over the two funds and all relevant documents to Empire State College Foundation by November 25, just one week later. I replied by saying that I had no authority to do this; he should negotiate the matter with the CWA trustees who were administering the grant. As to the Book and Coffee Fund, this was money contributed by the students; I saw no reason why the fund should be transferred to Empire State.

I questioned why I had been given a one-week ultimatum when information about the two funds had been known for months by the dean and other administrators without objection. I said that the questions he had raised were technical in nature and could be resolved amicably through negotiation without disrupting the video project or the student fund activities.

Jacobson turned down my request, which I repeated by letter and several telephone calls. Instead, he prevailed on the general counsel of the State University of New York to send me a letter, dated December 4, which ordered me to hand over the bank records and other data to Empire State and to come to Saratoga Springs to sign papers that would transfer control of the two funds to college administrators. I was warned that if I failed to comply with these directives on or before December 11, 1981, "it would result in the University's taking such further steps as may be required."

I knew what that meant. They would have grounds for dismissing me even though I was a tenured professor. It was a bitter pill to swallow, but I had no real choice except to make the trip to Saratoga Springs and comply.

As I had anticipated, Jacobson held off meeting with the students and when he did, the outcome was disappointing. He presented the same reasons as the dean for refusing to restore me as U.L.P. director. He was confident that, in time, the students would adjust to the new situation. Several students suggested a strike against Empire State and withholding of tuition payments. I firmly scotched the idea, saying that it would be a sure way to kill the program.

Meanwhile, Professor Michelson and other members of the dean's staff, who now controlled the academic records, began to exert strong pressure on students to accept the dean's actions. It soon became known that those who were reconciled to my dismissal would be treated charitably when their academic records were reviewed and updated, while those who still publicly supported me would encounter problems during their evaluation, I realized I had not the slightest chance of being restored as director.

After my anger and bitterness had subsided, I concluded that my position was not all that bad. I would still be spending full-time as a teacher in the leadership program, with very little additional responsibilities and no pressure from the dean or the faculty. I could also serve as *ombudsman* to students who felt they had grievances against the college administration or the faculty. It would be difficult, but I thought I could maintain my influence in the program and prevent its destruction.

Having fired me as director, the dean now moved to isolate me from any policy-making positions on the faculty. Of the 17 faculty committees, he appointed me to only *one*, an insignificant one. I was denied any input on curriculum, recruiting, class assignments, personnel evaluation, professional training and other functions. I saw no point in complaining; I would get no support from any faculty member.

In the following months, the enrollment in the leadership program steadily declined, eventually reaching a low point of about 50 students, less than one third of the number from the time the dean had seized control. Classes had to be consolidated or cancelled. Many of the required courses were abandoned. A total of 80 union officers had dropped out of the program because all of the innovative features that had made their attendance and participation possible had been discarded.

Equally shocking was the debasement of academic evaluation standards as an accommodation to poorly-qualified students. A total of 44 students had grades of "incomplete." The same was true for all 14 students attending the Senior Seminar, the final required course before graduation.

I finally broke my silence at a faculty meeting at the start of the February 1983 winter term when the registration report showed that recruiting was virtually at a standstill and the dropouts were continuing. I wanted to know why, and what was being done by the recruiting committee to improve the situation. I also criticized faculty members for permitting such a huge number of "incompletes," and asked what steps were being taken to eliminate them.

The faculty refused to discuss these issues. They accused me of acting in an "uncollegial" manner by directly criticizing faculty members; if the U.L.P. was suffering losses in student enrollment, it was largely due to my disruptive behavior, they said. On February 15, I was brought up on charges by the faculty and censured. Empire State's president was notified that "The faculty and staff of the Center for Labor Studies are deeply concerned about Dr. Kelber's actions and are determined that our institution and its students, faculty and staff will not suffer as the result of his behavior." There was no mention of any instance of my alleged misbehavior.

The faculty went further by attacking the very concept of a union leadership program. I was ordered to appear before a faculty committee where I was denounced for fostering "elitism." Why should rank-and-filers be denied the opportunity to get the benefits of leadership training, they asked. A week later, the faculty voted to accept anyone into the U.L.P. without regard to their union status. Students would be encouraged to transfer into the program to fill its classes, where attendance in a couple of them had shrunk to as few as six. The new policy, which one faculty member called "recruitment from within," would go into effect for the 1983 fall term.

With all the frustration I was enduring, I enjoyed one gratifying moment when I was permitted to hand out baccalaureate degrees to 42 students of the Union Leadership Program— officers from 29 unions—at the graduation ceremony on June 24, 1983 at Hunter College. It was my valedictory.

The fall term was a disaster. The remaining union officers in the U.L.P. complained that the level of instruction had been watered down because of the influx of rank-and-filers. They were upset that the videotaping of class sessions, and other innovative features which they had enjoyed in the first year of the program had been discontinued. They observed that there was now not much difference between the U.L.P. classes and the others at the labor center. Many of them dropped out in mid-semester. The small number who remained in the program were frankly unhappy but were resolved to get a college degree, come what may.

By the 1984 spring term, the Union Leadership Program had vanished in all but name.

* * * * *

In retrospect, I concede that I acted in a high-handed, arrogant, individualistic manner. However, I doubt whether the Union Leadership Program would have gotten off the ground if I had been more conciliatory and compromising with the faculty. I am also convinced that if I had not taken the initiative, no one else at the college would have attempted to develop the program, probably the most important one in the history of the college.

Anyhow, I have the satisfaction of knowing that because of my efforts, at least 50 New York City union leaders were able to earn baccalaureate degrees by completing a unique, professional-level curriculum in labor studies.

31. My Retirement With Honors

On June 2, 1983, I received a communication from Dr. Hall, president of Empire State College, which exhilarated me but left me somewhat puzzled. It informed me that the Empire State College Council had voted to set up an endowment in labor studies in my name. It contained the text of the Council's resolution, passed on October 22, 1982 (this was ten months after I had been forceably removed as director of the Union Leadership Program). The resolution "recognize(s) your many contributions to the field of Labor Education and to the founding and development of the Center for Labor Studies [The Labor College] of Empire State College, State University of New York." Further on, it complimented me for creating and developing the Union Leadership Degree Program. I was told that the Harry Kelber Endowment in Labor Studies "would provide support for labor education for future generations of students."

I quickly realized that the initiative for the endowment must have come from Harry Van Arsdale. He had been disappointed with what was happening to the leadership program and saw the endowment as providing another vehicle for the promotion of labor education. He had probably persuaded Dr. Hall to set up a Chair in Labor Studies, the first of its kind in the state university, with an argument that he was to repeat on numerous occasions: there were dozens of academic chairs for business management in the nation's colleges; it was high time to create at least one academic chair for labor. Without letting me know, Van Arsdale had recommended that the chair be created in my name and that it should be inaugurated in 1984, when I was scheduled to retire from the college at age 70. To raise funds for the endowment, the New York City Central Labor Council voted to sponsor a testimonial dinner on May 9, 1984 at the Sheraton Hotel and to publish a commemorative journal with paid ads from local unions and business firms friendly to labor.

On September 14, a Labor Advisory Assembly was established with Van Arsdale and Sandra Feldman, president of the Teachers Union, as co-chairpersons; several committees were appointed to promote the dinner. The endowment letterhead included, on the reverse side, the names of participating union officers from 110 labor organizations. A phone bank was set up at council headquarters, staffed by a group of electrical union apprentices, to solicit the city's unions for dinner tickets at $125 each and for ads to the journal.

In January, I came up with the idea of creating a half-hour videotape about the birth and development of the labor college, which would be completed in time to be shown at the Sheraton dinner. I discussed the feasibility of my proposal with Arthur Kent, then president of Local 11 of the National Association of Broadcast Employees and Technicians, who was also a student in the leadership program. After checking with his union members at NBC, he said that several cameramen and broadcasting editors had agreed to volunteer their services for the video project in their spare time. It would be difficult to complete it by May 9th, but it was worth a try. What was needed right away was a script they could work on, Kent said.

I spent a long weekend writing a script which a trio of NBC staffers revised to make it suitable for a TV format. We were able to get Frederick O'Neal, president of the Associated Actors and Artistes of America, as narrator. I wrote a song, "Our Labor College," which served as the musical theme and title of the video.

The opening shot showed AFL-CIO President Lane Kirkland offering a few complimentary remarks about the importance of the labor college to the trade union movement. Most of the footage consisted of comments from students, labor leaders and college educators that provided a running story of how the college was started and how it grew.

For a time, it seemed almost impossible to make the May 9th deadline. In coordinating the camera work with the "actors" at different locations, we encountered frustrating delays. I was relieved of all classroom assignments so I could spend full time on the video. The pace of production picked up in mid-April and the editing by the NBC staff was completed just two days before the dinner. (Kent told me later that the volunteer labor on the project by NBC staffers was worth a minimum of $50,000.)

Now the question was how to show the video to the people in the hotel's grand ballroom. It required special equipment not available at the hotel but which NBC possessed. Somehow, the equipment was delivered to the ballroom barely in time to show the video and returned to NBC immediately after the performance.

The dinner itself was a gratifying success. Among the approximately 800 labor people in the ballroom were a great many who had been my students in the thirteen years I had taught at the college. Two tables near the podium had been set aside for my family and close friends.

The speeches were not especially memorable. I was amused by the laudatory remarks about me by President Hall and Dean Dwyer, both of whom had used their authority over the years to undercut me. After the savage attacks on me by the faculty, I confess I enjoyed the shower of praise I received from speaker after speaker. I felt redeemed when Hall handed me a plaque that announced the establishment of the endowment in labor studies in my name.

The journal, entitled "Labor's Salute to Education," was a financial success, if not a literary one. Van Arsdale's name was the magic that brought in large advertisements from organizations and business firms that I had never heard of. A few ads simply listed the name of the company below the words "Greetings from" or

"Best Wishes." But there were also warm messages from union leaders with whom I had a long personal relationship. I was later told that the affair had netted close to $60,000 and that the money would be deposited in the name of the endowment with the Empire State College Foundation.

In my prepared speech to wind up the affair, I concluded:

"I have served the labor movement in various capacities for fifty years, but I do not regard this occasion as my last hurrah. I view this Academic Chair not as the end of my career, but a new beginning. In the days and years ahead, as long as my strength holds out, I shall continue to serve the labor movement and do my utmost to justify the honor that you have bestowed upon me."

Little did I realize that the next dozen years would be among the most fruitful of my career.

32. *Education Director at Seventy*

In late July, a month after my retirement, Van Arsdale invited me to spend a weekend at Bayberry Land, the 314-acre estate in Southampton, L.I., owned by the Educational and Cultural Trust Fund of the Electrical Industry. A Local 3 member picked me up at my home Friday afternoon and drove me there.

I was quartered in what was actually a modern, furnished studio apartment. In addition to a large bedroom with a picture window looking out on Peconic Bay, there was a well-equipped kitchen, a dining area, a bathroom and ample closet space. That evening, I joined about 50 union members in the dining room where we were served a full-course dinner, after which we adjourned to the recreation hall for a social program.

In the morning, Van Arsdale showed me around the grounds. The property, bought for $131,000 in 1949, included more than a mile of beach front, a 28-room manor house, a library, greenhouse, large outdoor swimming pool, picnic area, and beautifully groomed lawns and flowerbeds. Bayberry, I was told, had three functions: (1) as a rest home where pensioners and members recovering from illness could stay for two weeks with their spouses in one of the sixty housekeeping units; (2) as an educational center, where union members could take part in week-long study programs and listen to well-known guest speakers; and (3) as a vacation resort for the children of Local 3 members. Camp Integrity offered them two weeks away from home in a supervised program of sports, arts and crafts.

I found it hard to believe that a single local union, in a partnership with employers, had purchased and was operating so unique a facility in one of the wealthiest areas in the United States. The adjacent property was occupied by an exclusive country club, whose golf course was a regular site for international tournaments. What impressed me especially was that the lawns and walkways were spotless. I didn't see a piece of litter anywhere in my stroll around the grounds.

* * * * *

I had a feeling that Van Arsdale had something on his mind when he invited me there. After lunch, I found out what it was. We were sitting on a bench on a hill overlooking the bay when he turned to me and said, "How would you like to work as our educational director?"

I was startled. I had not considered the possibility of another job after my retirement. I was too surprised to respond immediately. He explained that the current educational director was being transferred to another responsible position in the union. I would be an ideal replacement because of my academic credentials and experience as a labor educator.

I was not at all sure that I wanted to work for one union or that I would be able to get along with Van Arsdale, who could be a tough, strong-willed taskmaster. I remained silent, uncertain how to respond to the offer. He interpreted my silence as acceptance. It did not occur to him that I might refuse the position. Finally, I said I was flattered by the offer but I wanted some time to think it over.

I spent the rest of the weekend trying to come to a decision that made sense for a man of 70. The job would enable me to remain active in the labor movement in an influential position. Moreover, with Van Arsdale as my patron, I would have an opportunity to play a role in developing educational programs for the New York City Central Labor Council. I would be earning a salary in addition to my Social Security income. Strangely, I had not asked what my salary would be nor had he volunteered the information.

But there were bothersome problems to consider. I had very little administrative experience. Could I handle the many activities of the Educational and Cultural Fund, whose annual budget, I had been told, amounted to several million dollars? I had only the vaguest idea of what my responsibilities would be, only Harry's faith that I could cope with them. What if I failed him? Would I want to risk ending my career with a failure?

Equally troublesome was the problem of transportation. It would take me almost an hour and a half by subway and bus to get to the union's headquarters in Flushing from my house. Did I want to spend three hours in daily traveling? In rain, snow and late at night? How long could I keep it up?

What finally made me decide to take the job was that *I didn't want to stop working.* I needed a full-time, salaried position for my self-esteem. I couldn't see myself living the life of a "retiree." The thought of it depressed me. And if I were looking for a job, where would I get a better offer than Van Arsdale's at my age?

I called Mim to tell her the news. She was pleased, but wondered if I could endure the daily three-hour travel. I said I would use the time on the subway and bus to read the newspapers and plan my work. We would have to make some adjustments in our family life because, for the first time in some thirty years, I would be working a daytime schedule.

At Sunday lunch, just before I was preparing to leave Bayberry, I told Van Arsdale that I was ready to take the job. He was pleased. We shook hands; the deal was closed. Apparently, I needed no one else's approval but his. He asked me to come to union headquarters the following Wednesday morning to see my office and meet my staff. He would also show me around the headquarters and introduce me to the union officers and staff people.

In my first week on the job, I met the education director whom I was replacing; he was sullen and uncooperative. He had held the job for 10 years and was understandably bitter at being pushed out by Van Arsdale over the objection of the union's officers. The story I heard was that he had infuriated Harry by remarking that he was becoming senile. Whether or not the story was true or the entire reason for Harry's behavior, I could well understand the resentment of union officers at having an outsider like me hired for this important job; in fact, I sympathized with their position. However I had made a commitment to take the job and I wasn't going to back down.

I soon began to feel their displeasure. I discovered that important records of several educational programs had disappeared from the files. I was treated coolly by officers and staff, not one of whom would volunteer a word of encouragement. I sensed they were all hoping that I would fail and be forced to resign—a clear rebuke to Van Arsdale and his faith in my competence. I chose not to complain to him, but I was disheartened. What had I gotten into?

What bothered me even more was that the job was far more difficult than I had expected and required skills that were beyond my experience. I had assumed that my major function would be as a teacher, and that I would be required to design and prepare materials for needed educational programs. I was made aware of my new responsibilities by George Schuck, the chairman of the Educational and Cultural Fund. In particular, there were three traditional, annual events that I had to stage: (1) the Scholarship Breakfast, in mid-April, at which 30 full-tuition college scholarships were distributed to outstanding sons and daughters of Local 3 members before an audience of about 800 guests in the union's spacious auditorium; (2) the Spring Arts Festival, in late May, at which Local 3 family members could exhibit their painting, sculpture, photography, handicrafts and other art forms, and (3) the Members' Musicale, a sort of amateur night following the art show, which would feature singing, dancing, instrument playing and other performing talents from among the union's 36,000 families.

I quickly realized the enormous amount of detail that went into creating each of these events. The nearly six months I had to arrange the scholarship breakfast was hardly enough, and on the Saturday morning of the breakfast, I was nervous about whether the scrambled eggs and ham would be hot enough when they were served to the guests and whether the bouquets of flowers I had ordered would arrive on time to be presented on cue to the wives of the two "honorees," and where were the union members who were assigned to this detail? Fortunately, I had an unusually competent secretary, Vincenza (Vinnie) Russo, who had been in charge of these activities for several years and knew what to do and the pitfalls to be avoided.

The easiest part was the selection of the 30 scholarship winners from among several hundred applicants. I worked with a committee of five respected union members for a week, assessing the academic records of each of the applicants and reaching a consensus about the eventual winners. As I anticipated, I was subjected to pressure from several union officials who asked that I give "consideration" to their sons and daughters. To insure that the selection was fair, I insisted that each applicant be known only by an assigned number and not by name. Only my secretary and I knew the names of the winners, when we compiled the list on the evening before the Saturday breakfast.

Since none of the applicants had been told in advance whether or not they had won a scholarship, we were able to maintain the suspense and surprise of an Academy Award affair, with screams of joy and much audience hand clapping after the name of each winner was announced and as they trooped up to the stage to receive their certificates and shake hands with the presiding officers.

It was the protocol that caused me the greatest anxiety: how to arrange the seating of dignitaries on the wide, three-tiered dais so that no union official, employer, politician or educator would feel slighted. There was the problem of making sure they would arrive on time and that they were properly lined up to march down the aisle and take their assigned seats. I also had to assume the position of welcoming host to the hundred or so special guests whom we had invited for a pre-breakfast of juice, coffee and danish before the main event.

The breakfast went quite smoothly. It was no small feat for the catering staff to serve some eight hundred individuals using the union kitchen facilities adjoining the auditorium. I was relieved that the speakers had not overstepped the time I had alloted them and that the affair had concluded only three minutes behind my carefully plotted schedule. Van Arsdale was clearly pleased. I had not let him down in my first major trial. The only criticism I received at the staff meeting was that I had forgotten to have pitchers of water on stage for the speakers and reported complaints by some of the guests that the coffee was cold.

* * * * *

I hadn't the faintest idea how to organize an art show, but I had to learn quickly. Fortunately, I had the services of Dr. René Shapshak, a noted sculptor, whose work included busts of President Truman, Charles deGaulle and Mahatma Gandhi. Dr. Shapshak had been director of the union's Spring Arts Festival since its inception in 1969; over the years, he had worked out a procedure and schedule for arranging the art work around the auditorium and in a large adjoining room. All we had to do was to provide him with a crew of volunteers and the required materials to hang the scores of paintings and position an array of sculptures and artifacts. Amazingly, the auditorium was turned into a museum in just three evenings. We had Shapshak select three prize winners in each of more than a dozen categories.

Initially, my major task was to solicit art works from Local 3 families. I sent out two mailings, wrote several promotion pieces in the union publication, *Electrical Union World,* and addressed as many of the union's 36 divisions as I could. The results were gratifying. A week before the opening, we counted more than one hundred exhibitors with a total of 315 art works. On the opening night, we held a catered gala reception to which we invited five hundred prominent individuals from the world of labor, business, government and education. Thereafter, there was a steady stream of union members and people from the community to marvel at the work of these amateur artists. A half-dozen public schools and two private schools brought busloads of children to witness the exhibits and to hear lectures by several of the artists about their work.

My responsibilities included the preparation of a full-color, illustrated catalogue of some forty of the best art works selected by Dr. Shapshak with appropriate commentary. There appeared to be general agreement that the 1985 Spring Arts Festival compared favorably with preceding ones. I was happy to have survived this hurdle.

* * * * *

Organizing the Members' Musicale was fun, mainly because I had a marvelous take-charge guy, Jerry Sommer, to act as impressario. Jerry, a veteran electrician who held supervisory jobs on construction sites, was also a talented actor who had played in starring roles on off-Broadway musicals and dramas. As a result of our advertising campaign for talent, we received more than enough applicants to attend Jerry's evening and weekend auditions.

In less than three months, Jerry put together a program of eighteen acts that included singers, dancers, instrumentalists, comedians and even a magician, all of them union members or close relatives. On the night of the show, the 800-seat auditorium and balcony were completely filled by an enthusiastic audience ready to applaud every performer, especially their own kinfolk. We had the good sense to put a rock band on as the final act rather than earlier in the program as the group had requested. When the quartet began with a heavy metal rock number, the sound was so deafening that many of the senior citizens felt blasted out of their seats and rushed out of the hall as if the place was on fire. The unsigned review of the show that I was asked to write for the union newspaper was understandably laudatory and accurately reflected audience sentiment.

Thus, toward the end of my first year on the job, I had solidified my credentials. I had become known and accepted by large numbers of union members. Even those union officials who had opposed my hiring could offer no complaint about my competence as an administrator.

During that summer, I was supposed to conduct a series of seminars at Bayberry on contemporary labor problems. But after one weekend, I was stricken with a prostate condition that required immediate surgery. I had to sweat out three days before I got the verdict that my prostate was not cancerous. The good news shortened my convalescence. By the end of the summer, I was back at work, fully recovered.

* * * * *

In the six years I worked for the Educational and Cultural Fund, I found ample opportunity to use my skills as a teacher and to create new programs that benefited members of the union's manufacturing division who had heretofore been largely neglected by the previous education director.

The union's prize educational program was its week-long Critical Thinking in Human Relations seminar, held at Bayberry. It had been in operation since 1957 and boasted of more than 5,000 "graduates," all of them construction workers. A unique feature of the program was that students received the week's basic wage they would have earned on the job; they paid nothing for room and board and the use of Bayberry's many facilities.

The program was designed to develop the student's ability to analyze contemporary economic, political and social events through the use of problem-solving techniques and exercises. Its director was John Goodale, a gifted instructor who had been conducting the program for several years and who used a variety of educational formats, including games and puzzles supplemented by a roster of stimulating guest speakers, to maintain the interest of each class of between 25 and 30 students.

When Goodale died suddenly of a heart attack, the Fund's trustees made no effort to replace him. Some of the employer trustees were quite willing to see the program die or be drastically curtailed because it was so enormously expensive. After many months, when it appeared that the program was permanently ended, I volunteered to revive it on a three-day basis that would include the weekend. This would save the Fund a substantial sum of money since students would be reimbursed just for one lost day of work instead of for an entire week. Having obtained the approval of the trustees, I began to conduct the Bayberry seminars, holding three-day classes at least once a month with my co-teacher, Judy Siegman.

We generally followed Goodale's materials and curriculum, compressed into a shorter time schedule. This, however, was not suitable for manufacturing division members, many of whom were illiterate in English. I remember our teaching a class of 36 women employed at Leviton, a manufacturer of electrical supplies, in which several Polish and Hispanic members knew hardly a word of English. We assigned a few of the more competent students who knew Polish and Spanish as interpreters, but it was not satisfactory. Fortunately, we were able to develop lively discussions by having the women draw on their personal experiences at work, at home and in their family relationships, topics about which they had many interesting things to say.

Recognizing the widespread illiteracy within Local 3's ten thousand-member manufacturing division, Judy and I decided it would be in the union's interest to establish English as a Second Language (ESL) courses in each of the city's boroughs and in large factories. In one year, we created 18 ESL classes with a student population of nearly 400 union members. Most of the arduous, time-consuming work of hiring teachers, organizing classes and keeping records was handled by Judy. At Leviton, employees were able to attend ESL classes and also train for the High School Equivalency Diploma immediately after work on the company's premises, with sandwiches, juice and coffee supplied by the management.

We also initiated courses in stress management (it helped electricians with chronic backaches), computer literacy, occupational safety and skills development. However, one of the most unusual programs was our Pre-Retirement Seminar to which we invited groups of 25 members who had formally signified their intention to retire from work to spend a weekend at Bayberry with their spouses. At this seminar, the couples heard experts discuss financial, social, psychological and health problems that face retirees as they adjust to their new life styles. Most valuable were the conversations among the couples themselves as they compared notes about their future plans.

In separate meetings organized by gender, the men voiced complaints about differences with their spouses in regard to sex, personal responsibilites, retirement preferences and other matters; the women drew up their list of grievances and fears about adjusting to retirement. Moderators provided an up-beat effort to harmonize the differing viewpoints. By the end of the weekend, many of the couples had become good friends and had arranged to see each other later on.

After three of these weekend seminars, we found ourselves with a waiting list of about 125 pre-retirement couples, the result of word-of-mouth advertising by those who had attended the sessions.

* * * * *

After nearly six years on the job, I was getting bored with the work, although I appreciated the handsome salary of roughly $75,000 a year. The programs I had started were now routinized. I was thinking seriously of resigning if I could find more challenging educational work. By coincidence, Local 3's business manager, Thomas Van Arsdale, Harry's son, had decided to put pressure on me to resign. I first got wind of his intentions when an electrician without a college degree or any cultural pretensions was appointed as associate education director without informing me in advance or asking my approval. His assignment, it soon became clear, was to monitor my comings and goings, whom I saw and what I did, and provide a daily report to George Schuck, the head of the Joint Industry Board. The man was a nuisance, but I chose not to make an issue of his appointment. I gave him assignments which had little to do with the education programs I was conducting.

The inevitable confrontation came under circumstances which they least expected and which aroused their anger against me to a fever pitch. It was I, not they, who finally dictated the terms of my resignation. But that story, with all its implications and consequences, will be told in a later chapter.

33. *The Trade Union Leadership Institute*

On May 16, 1985, the Executive Board of the New York City Central Labor Council had unanimously endorsed the establishment of a Trade Union Leadership Institute. The action was taken on a motion by then Council President Harry Van Arsdale Jr., who stated that the institute was needed to "assist new, and often inexperienced union officers to develop the skills and knowledge they needed to serve the members of their organization effectively." Van Arsdale had hoped that the Labor College would perform that function, but was keenly disappointed at its declining enrollment and poor performance.

Because the council was operating at a deficit, Van Arsdale, to avoid controversy, did not ask for financial assistance for the new institute. The assumption was that it would function out of council headquarters and would use whatever resources and staff were available there. I was named the institute's unpaid coordinator. At a meeting a month later, officers from 52 unions heartily endorsed the institute and agreed to serve on its advisory board. It was decided that the institute would be financially self-sustaining; its income would depend on the charges it would levy on affiliated unions for various educational services.

My first project was to organize a 16-week leadership course, "Labor Strategies for Today and Tomorrow," for full-time and part-time union officials, to start that September. I spent a good part of the summer months recruiting students and preparing course materials that would deal with major aspects of a union leader's responsibilities, including organizing, collective bargaining, labor legislation, arbitration, union administration, pension funds, political action, public relations, international affairs and the impact of technological advances on unions. All of the three-hour weekly sessions were videotaped and open to inspection by any union. Forty-five officers from 34 unions paid $190 to attend the 16-week course. I was the principal instructor, supported by guest experts in particular subjects.

* * * * *

On February 16, 1986, Harry Van Arsdale Jr. died of prostate cancer. It was a grievous loss to the entire labor movement and the many thousands who had been touched personally by one of the outstanding union leaders of the century.

I remember being at his hospital bedside the day before he died. He held my hand and beckoned me to lean close to him. His eyes half-closed, he whispered, "What's happening at the Labor College?" I was moved to tears as I tried to think of an answer that would please him. I promised him that I'd do my best with the leadership institute. He squeezed my hand. The nurse came into the room to usher me out. She told me that he wouldn't last more than a day.

St. Patrick's Cathedral was filled to capacity and many hundreds of people stood outside to pay their respect to Van Arsdale at the memorial services. Governor Mario Cuomo and a host of state and city officials, business executives and, of course, union leaders and Local 3 members attended the ceremony, presided over by Cardinal John O'Connor.

Personally, I had lost a good friend and the one leader I respected more than any of those I had met during my career as a labor educator. Harry was both a visionary and a pragmatist, an unusual combination, a man with an indomitable will, who was able to turn his dreams into reality. As business manager of Local 3, he built a close, powerful partnership with the city's wealthy electrical contractors, the Joint Industry Board of the Electrical Industry, in which he clearly was the dominating influence. To support his strong belief that the families of working people should have decent, affordable housing, he played a principle role in building the 2,600-apartment complex, Electchester, in Queens, where he and his wife, Madeline, lived modestly. Although he never graduated from Townsend Harris High School, a school for gifted adolescents, because he had to work to help his family, he was a self-educated man. Without his strong commitment to worker education, there might never have been a labor college in New York City or the unique educational programs he established within his own union. With the cooperation of the industry's employers, he bought the 314-acre estate on Southampton, Long Island and built it into an educational and vacation resort for union members and their children as well as for retirees and their spouses, The wages and benefits he won for his union electricians were among the highest in the country. And Local 3, under his leadership, was one of the most powerful in New York and in the International Brotherhood of Electrical Workers, of which he was treasurer.

He was a brilliant organizer and strategist. As president of the New York City Çentral Labor Council, he assembled a team that unionized the New York City taxi fleets after John L. Lewis, Mike Quill of the Transport Workers and leaders of the Teamsters Union had tried and failed. (In recent years, the taxi union has lost members and influence.) In the 1960s and 1970's, he was an influential figure in the city's political life and was always called upon for help by unions involved in difficult strikes. Through his influence, the number of minorities in the Local 3 apprentice program increased significantly.

I had first met Harry about 1937 when I was editor of the *Building Trades Union Press* and he was fairly new in his elected position as business manager. He impressed me as a tough, shrewd, somewhat cocky individual with conservative political views like his associates in the construction industry. What singled him out above other union leaders was his vigorous campaign for the six-hour day, thirty-hour week, an objective which he was able to achieve in his own union. I was later to learn that in the mid-1920's he had been on a trade union delegation that visited the Soviet Union and met with several politburo members, but he was a strong anti-communist.

Harry was a short, muscular man, with a large, tough face, crowned by thinning brown hair which he brushed straight back. He wore well-tailored conservative suits and had an obsession about neatness. He was a fastidious eater and usually started dinner with one whiskey sour. He was equally at ease talking to apprentices or the politicians in Washington and City Hall. He had built a series of ethnic and occupation-based clubs within the union that served as his "machine" and assured his regular reelection. He made a point of getting around to the meetings or socials of the union's 36 divisions, but he was particularly fond of tbe apprentices and rarely missed any of their monthly meetings where his presence aroused adoring chants of "Harry! Harry! Harry!"

He had a peculiar hobby: pigeons. He once took me to the roof of the union's seven-story building in Manhattan where he had dozens of pigeons which he sheltered and fed, and occasionally let loose for their circling skyward flights. He seemed to care little for music, theater and fine art, nor did he play golf, tennis or sail. His waking hours were almost totally occupied with his union activities and the variety of individuals he had to deal with. He could be generous and helpful to those with problems, but he could also be tough and vindictive to those who tried to cross him.

I guess his principal hobby, the source of his greatest pleasure, was talking. At meetings of the Joint Industry Board or the union membership or at the Bayberry seminars, he could ramble on endlessly, with irrelevant, yet sometimes sage comments and whatever anecdotes occurred to him at the moment, and no one dared to interrupt him, only to hope that he would finally stop. The feeling was that he had earned the right to be garrulous.

Although Van Arsdale accomplished wonders for Local 3 members, he did not run a truly democratic union. Many of his relatives were placed on jobs within the union; the most glaring example of his nepotism was his son, Tom, who could not have been elected business manager without Harry's active intervention. He also surrounded himself with yes men who feared to contradict him even when they felt he was wrong. While he encouraged rank-and-file participation in various union committees, there was not much tolerance for dissenting opinions, either in the union newspaper or at membership meetings.

He once told me that his single ambition was to transform Local 3 into the outstanding union in the labor movement, a model to inspire other unions. He never quite realized that objective, although he left a legacy of remarkable achievements during his 50-year career as a labor leader.

I had a strong feeling that with Harry no longer there as my patron and protector, I would encounter difficulties from those union leaders who disapproved of my influence and activities. My intuition proved correct.

My principal concern was not to give Thomas Van Arsdale, Harry's son, who had now assumed the presidency of the Central Labor Council, any excuse to remove me from my position in the leadership institute. Unlike his father, Tommy, who was also business manager of Local 3, had never shown any interest in labor education. In the six years I served the union as education director, we talked, man-to-man, maybe three or four times; he never indicated, either in praise or criticism, what he thought of my work.

Tommy Van had to contend with another member of the Kelber family, my youngest daughter, Laura. After receiving a degree in philosophy from Yale University, where she had been active in various progressive causes, including support for the school's striking dining room employees, she decided on her own, in 1981, to become a union electrician. and was accepted into Local 3's five-year apprenticeship program. Even after she had became a full-fledged journeywomen, she and the small number of other women electricians were subjected to discrimination in the choice of jobs and sexual harassment at the worksite. Laura helped organize the women's caucus within the union and became one of its leaders. Because she was the author of several letters to Tom Van Arsdale requesting meetings to deal with the grievances of women electricians (letters which annoyed him but he refused to answer), Laura was assigned some of the toughest union jobs at workplaces that were difficult to reach and that had no toilet facilities for women. After I became education director, several union business representatives asked me if I "could do something" to stop Laura's activities. I said I wouldn't dare try and besides, I agreed with what Laura was doing.

In 1991 when Laura was pregnant, she was sent to a job that required lifting of heavy materials in an unenclosed worksite with a lack of toilet facilities. While the union practice was to give ailing male electricians light duty assignments, she was denied that opportunity. She had a miscarriage and sued her employer and the Joint Industry Board. She lost the case in federal court, but won on appeal.

I took special pains not to antagonize T.V.A., as many of his associates called him. I kept him informed about any program I started, and made sure that all my activity was clearly in line with the council's policies. I didn't mind that he would not comment; I chose to interpret his silence as approval.

Over the next four years, the Central Labor Council's institute conducted a series of short courses that won high praise and wide attendance from union officers and members. Some examples:

"The Know-How of Collective Bargaining" and "The Union Side of Arbitration," which was offered two evenings a week and Saturday mornings, were attended by 135 officers from 52 unions.

"Managing Union Investments" and "Public Speaking," two four-week classes, had an enrollment of 56 labor leaders from 29 unions.

"Shop Steward Training," an eight-session course, attracted 46 students from 17 unions.

In addition, one-day workshops and special classes were conducted for several unions, including transport workers, printers, sheet metal workers, hotel employees, carpenters and postal workers.

Profits from the sales of two pamphlets, which I had written under the institute's imprimatur, also went into its coffers. I made a special point of submitting detailed statements and receipts of income and expenditures to a council staff member, Annie Johnson, who kept the institute's financial records. Since I was not paid either for my administrative work or teaching, our only expenses were printing and mailing, videotaping, honoraria for guest teachers and refreshment for students. By November 1987, the institute had a balance of $14,479.71.

Understandably, the institute aroused strong resentment from the Labor College faculty which had been compelled to abandon its union leadership program for lack of qualified students from the labor movement. Tommy Van Arsdale, in one of our rare conversations, told me that the institute was "undermining" the enrollment at the Labor College; he vetoed a new two-year program which I was hoping to conduct jointly with the New York faculty of Cornell's School of Industrial and Labor Relations. It was obvious to me that Tommy was determined to abolish the institute, and he could achieve that objective by firing me. I was equally determined not to give him that opportunity. For two years after that conversation, I continued my work for the institute warily, doing nothing that would offer him an opening to attack me.

Then, in January 1990, I published an institute pamphlet, "Why Unions Are in Trouble . . . and What They Can Do About It." I had no doubt that Van Arsdale would use the pamphlet as a reason to fire me. I was prepared to fight back.

34. I Dare to Criticize AFL-CIO Hierarchy

By the end of the 1980s, the AFL-CIO and its affiliated unions had suffered grievous losses and were facing an uncertain future. Union membership had dropped to a low of 16 percent of the work force and was expected to fall even further. Unions, even the strongest ones, felt compelled to make costly concessions in pay and benefits to employers who threatened to shut down or move their factories to low-wage countries. Labor's legislative record was dismal, even with a Democratic-controlled Congress. The real wages of American workers had shrunk 12 percent in the past decade.

Given the punishing losses of the AFL-CIO in membership, economic strength and political influence, one would have expected widespread criticism of the federation's officers and demands for recruiting new, more creative and dynamic leaders. At the very least, one would have anticipated some admission by AFL-CIO leaders of faulty strategy, policy mistakes, weak performance or failure to mobilize workers to oppose corporate attacks on their jobs and living standards.

Incredibly, not one word of criticism of its top officers had been uttered at any AFL-CIO convention in the preceding twenty years. The same officers regularly won reelection, unanimously, without even token opposition or debate about their performance. The delegates to these conventions or even the officers and staff representatives didn't have to be taught the self-serving virtue of "loyalty." The 33 vice presidents on the AFL-CIO Executive Council had an unwritten agreement to avoid public criticism of the organization and each other, and they had many ways of punishing critics within the labor movement. It was no secret why many subordinate union officers and staffers remained silent about the undemocratic, self-perpetuating practices of the AFL-CIO hierarchy, even though they privately disapproved of their behavior. The penalties for speaking out could be harsh: loss of a job, blacklisting, possible physical harm, ostracism, and the end of a union career.

* * * * *

It was in late November 1989, that I decided, after much soul-searching, to write a pamphlet exposing the undemocratic character of the AFL-CIO leadership and describing the extent of their responsibility for labor's decline and weakened condition. I also intended to suggest a series of constitutional reforms and policy revisions that I believed could revitalize the federation.

I had no illusions about the response the pamphlet would receive. I'd be denounced as a disrupter and traitor who was giving aid and comfort to the "enemy" at a time when it was imperative for unions to maintain "unity." I could lose my job as education director for the electrical workers union and my unpaid position as coordinator of the Council's Trade Union Leadership Institute. My career in the labor movement could end with my being ostracized as a pariah. Was it wise to take that risk? On the other hand, I felt an obligation—a test of my integrity—to write the pamphlet. It was becoming increasingly difficult to remain silent about the AFL-CIO leadership's indifference to the needs of the rank-and-file. Since no one with respected credentials within the labor movement was prepared to speak out, why not me? At age 76 and at the end of my career, I was probably in the best position to take the risk. If this was to be my last hurrah, it would be one that I could be proud of. It might encourage other trade unionists to speak out. And if I lost my job, I could still live comfortably on my pensions and savings. I finally convinced myself it was the right thing to do. But how?

After presenting a detailed criticism of AFL-CIO policies and practices, I concluded my pamphlet with this comment about union leadership:

"The labor movement needs leaders who are not afraid of change and are open to any suggestion that promises to benefit their organization and their membership, even if it comes from their critics. It needs leaders who know how to handle criticism, even when it is unjustified, by using their powers of persuasion rather than relying solely on the authority of their office. It needs leaders who are secure enough so that they will try to train and develop other potential union officers without fear that they may be creating challengers for their position. Such leaders have a far better chance of gaining the loyalty and respect of the rank-and-file than those who use intimidation to crush any dissenting opinion. The future of the labor movement depends on developing leadership with these attributes."

* * * * *

Under normal circumstances, I would have shown a draft of the pamphlet to Tom Van Arsdale and other central labor council leaders. I decided not to, because I realized they would never permit its publication and would denounce me for even thinking such heresies. I showed the draft to only two progressive union officials, who agreed that what I had written was not only accurate but "dynamite." However, they tried to dissuade me from going ahead with it: I'd get clobbered and not have much to show for my effort. The only person who saw the final draft was Mim, who edited the typescript and gave me her support.

I also decided, after some consideration, to publish it under my title as coordinator of the Trade Union Leadership Institute as I had done with earlier pamphlets and to have the institute pay for the initial printing and mailing of 5,000 copies, amounting to about $7,000. My rationale was that the institute's bank balance of nearly $15,000 was based entirely on the profits from my educational programs and the sales of my pamphlets. At no time, had the council or any of its affiliated unions contributed even one penny to the institute, nor had I drawn any salary for my five years of work as teacher and coordinator. In the past two years, I had published two successful pamphlets under the imprimatur of the leadership institute without any questions by council leaders. I was confident that the sales of my new, provocative pamphlet would more than make up for the original cost of printing and mailing.

I realized I would be pilloried by Tommy and his associates, but I was ready to take the consequences. If bending the rules was the only way to pierce the blackout of criticism within the labor movement, I'd dare it. Most important, I was confident that every statement and opinion in the pamphlet was valid, and I could successfully defend them.

* * * * *

When the pamphlet appeared in January 1990, it was greeted with shock and anger by leaders in the upper echelons of the AFL-CIO. One member of the Executive Council phoned me to say that I had damaged my reputation irreparably at a time when my talents could have been used constructively. Another important labor leader conceded that everything I had written was true, but why did I have to go public with it? A few local union leaders who dared to speak to me either praised me for my courage or denounced me as a "loose cannon" or a Don Quixote.

Significantly, not one word about the pamphlet appeared in any labor publication; apparently, even the mention of it could invite censure. At no time, did any union leader challenge the damaging accusations I had made about the AFL-CIO hierarchy. It was felt that the best tactic was to ignore the pamphlet, bury it in silence, rather than dignify it by a response that could open up an embarrassing debate.

In the meantime, I was receiving scores of letters and financial contributions from local union officers and rank-and-filers from virtually every state in the nation. Bulk orders for the pamphlet were coming in not only from local unions but also central labor councils. On the basis of the returns I was getting, I felt confident I would be able to sell a second edition of 5,000 copies, yielding enough income to more than pay for the pamphlet's original costs.

* * * * *

As expected, the frontal attack on me came from the New York City Central Labor Council and the educational and cultural fund of the electrical industry, whose officers were seething over the embarrassment I had caused them. How had they allowed me to publish such an outrageous tract? And what were they going to do about Kelber, short of boiling him in oil?

George Schuck, chairman of the Educational and Cultural Fund, my boss, swung into action. After demanding—and receiving—my mailing list, he sent out a long letter to each person on the list, attacking my credibility and dismissing my accusations with scorn. He complained that the author had "purposely avoided disclosing his actions to anyone in a position to dissuade or prevent his scurrilous actions." I could understand his complaint.

Schuck then got around to his main point: "The American labor movement certainly has enough enemies outside of our ranks attempting to undermine and divide our unions. Unfortunately, the cancer within is more insidious and deadly because it sows the seeds of doubt and division from a position of apparent stature within an organization."

After characterizing me as a "self proclaimed, egocentric messiah," Schuck concluded his letter to the men and women on the mailing list with this comment: "I salute each of you for your understanding that worthwhile changes are developed by persuasion and tolerance of dissenting opinion, not through insurrection and character assassination by insinuation."

A few days later, after denouncing me at a staff meeting, Schuck handed me a letter of resignation, which he asked me to sign then and there. I refused, saying that I wanted a day to think it over. The next morning I went to his office and said I had a better solution, one that would serve both our interests. I would retire four months later, at the end of June, 1990. This would allow time to pick a worthy successor and provide continuity for the programs I had initiated. If he wanted to fire me on the spot, he had the power to do that, but he would have to do a lot of explaining; he had no basis for dismissing me for incompetence. Furthermore, I would start a legal suit to retain my job. Did he want a nasty fight that would be reported in the media and be read by the union membership? Or did he want the issue settled with no breath of conflict? Schuck wisely chose the latter.

During my final four months, my colleagues within the union and the educational fund took pains to avoid me lest they offend Tommy Van Arsdale and Schuck. When I left, there was not even a mention of my retirement in the union newspaper.

* * * * *

The response to the pamphlet by the leadership of the New York labor council was to fire me. On February 28, Thomas Van Arsdale sent me a registered letter in which he said: "After consideration and discussion with the officers and Executive Board, it was agreed that it was time for a change and that you be relieved of your position as Coordinator of the Institute." I was informed that my dismissal had been approved unanimously by the board.

Van Arsdale offered no specific reason for my discharge except for this irrelevant statement: "For some time, I have been dissatisfied that we have not been able to recruit very many trade union leaders to attend the Harry Van Arsdale Jr. School of Labor Studies." As he well knew, I had been retired from the college for six years and had no responsibility for recruiting students.

In my response, I stated that Van Arsdale had not given me any advance notice of his intention to dismiss me. In fact, he had never questioned my competence or criticized any of the programs I had conducted. I charged that the reason he had given for firing me was absurd and a blatant subterfuge. I demanded the right to appear before the executive board so I could defend myself. I was soon told that the board had denied my request, I got in touch with several members of the board to ask them why they had voted to dismiss me and to deny me a fair hearing. A few responded sheepishly that although I had done an outstanding job for the institute, they could not afford to challenge Van Arsdale on this issue. Interestingly, almost a third of the board members were my former students.

The council's secretary, Ted Jacobsen, on orders from Van Arsdale, moved swiftly to stop further distribution of the pamphlet. He seized control of my post office box by telling the authorities that I was no longer connected with the leadership institute. To the people who sent in orders for copies, he returned their checks and money orders with a form letter that the pamphlet was out of print. He warned my printer to have no business with me lest he lose all of his union customers. And he took over the institute's funds at the Amalgamated Bank.

I decided to publish a second edition of the pamphlet in 5,000 copies at my own expense, using a printer who was not fazed by the threat of a council boycott. I sold all the copies except for fifty, which I retained for my personal use.

Needless to say, the council's Trade Union Leadership Institute disappeared, as Van Arsdale had wished, nor was any effort ever made to revive it.

35. *My Novel,* 'The Labor Leader'

During my years as a teacher, I remember searching far and wide for a novel that offered an honest, flesh-and-blood portrait of a contemporary union leader. I thought it would make a good choice to add to the reading list for the union leadership classes. I checked publisher directories but could find none that answered what I was looking for. Why, I wondered, were labor leaders not worthy of decent fictional treatment, while there were numerous novels about the lives of businessmen? The public had only a stereotypical view of the average union leader, gleaned largely from newspapers, television and movies. He was a white-skinned male. He was tough, prone to violence, uncouth and uneducated, a sinister figure with links to the underworld of racketeers and killers. They knew almost nothing about how he spent his days and the pressures he was subjected to or how his job affected his family life. He was rarely treated as a sympathetic character.

Over the years, I had entertained vague thoughts about writing that much-needed novel about the life of a union leader, a composite of the many whom I had known intimately. It was on New Year's Day 1987, as one of my annual resolutions, that I finally decided to write the book.

Full of enthusiasm, I wrote the first two pages on January 1, my mind bubbling with plots and sub-plots. Trying to think of an eye-catching title for the novel, I ended up with one suggested by Mim that was unexciting but unmistakably explicit: *The Labor Leader.* By working on the novel at least two hours a day and more on weekends, I managed to accumulate about 400 manuscript pages by the end of the year. I was now confident that I could finish the few remaining chapters in 1988.

The protagonist of the novel is Marty Somers, the shrewd president of a large New York local of supermarket and chain store employees, which he has headed for 20 years. The action takes place during the autumn of 1972 at the time of the outbreak of the Watergate scandal, the windup of the Nixon-McGovern presidential campaign, and the on-again, off again peace negotiations to end the Vietnam War. In the opening pages of the novel, Somers is faced with one of his severest challenges: a Chicago conglomerate has informed him that it is closing three of its nine New York supermarkets and that it will shut down the remaining six unless the union agrees to large wage cuts and other concessions. In one of several sub-plots, the reader gets an insider's view of the surprising twists and turns in the bargaining strategies of Marty and the Chicago lawyers, climaxed by a tense, emotion-filled, sixteen-hour negotiating session and a tumultuous ratification meeting of the union membership.

In a series of "oral history" flashbacks, Marty relives the various crises of his turbulent career, from the time he emerged as a strike leader during the Great Depression and then joined the Communist Party through the many struggles that finally won him the presidency of his union. However, competent as Marty is in solving union problems, he is constantly reminded he is a failure as father and husband. His son, Phil, a naive idealist who is active in the ultra-radical Liberation Party, despises him for limiting his opposition to the Vietnam War to face-saving, no-risk gestures. His daughter, Nancy, is unhappily married to a womanizer, and Marty faces the unsettling prospect of becoming a surrogate father to his two grandsons. His wife, Rhoda, resents their boring, restricted social life and the demands that are put on the spouse of a dedicated labor leader. To add to Marty's unhappiness, he compulsively smokes, drinks and eats far too much to relieve the tensions and pressures of his work, and he is morbidly afraid of dying of a heart attack.

Marty becomes increasingly bitter and depressed, as he wavers between his gut belief in militancy to fight injustice and his acquired habit of pragmatic compromise. Overwhelmed by the burdens of his public and private life, Marty walks out of his office one afternoon to spend four fateful days alone and in hiding, in a mid-Manhattan hotel where he tries to figure out what he can do to make his life meaningful in the "home stretch" of his remaining years. On the final day of his midtown retreat, he reaches major decisions about his future.

* * * * *

The big, distasteful problem I now faced was getting a reputable publisher for the novel. I sent two chapters and a summary of the book to about two dozen publishers and was turned down by all of them. Some friends put me in touch with a literary agent, but she too was unsuccessful. I finally decided to publish it at my own expense under the imprimatur of Picket Press, a title I had used for my booklet of septad poetry. I checked with a friendly printer and was told that it would cost at least $8,000 to print a paperback edition of 2,000 copies. Where would I get that kind of money? I rejected the idea of drawing on my limited savings or taking out a loan. I was discouraged. I believed the novel would remain unpublished, at least for the forseeable future and perhaps forever.

Morton Bahr, then a vice president of the Communications Workers of America, suggested that I apply for a publishing grant of $10,000 to the Joseph Anthony Beirne Memorial Foundation, a CWA subsidiary named after the union's first president. Despite our future disagreements, Bahr and I had become good friends after I had persuaded him to go back to school and get a baccalaureate degree at the Labor College when I was a professor there. He used his considerable influence with the foundation's board to get my grant proposal approved. On March 10, 1989, I received a $10,000 check from the foundation. with their best wishes that *The Labor Leader* would become a best seller, an expectation that exceeded mine.

I immediately got in touch with the printer, handing him a floppy disk of my computerized manuscript. I said I wanted him to have printed copies by mid-June in time for the celebration of my 75th birthday on June 20. I realized it was a difficult deadline to meet; time had to be allowed for proof-reading, corrections and revisions, not to mention the actual printing and binding of the copies. The printer did not sound optimistic; all he could promise was that he would do his best, with the understanding that I would not hold up the job by making too many demands.

Meanwhile, Mim had gone ahead to arrange a birthday and book party in my honor at The Barge, a stationary ship on the waterfront at the Fulton Street ferry pier in Brooklyn Heights, well known for its classical music concerts. It was sufficiently spacious to accommodate the 150 guests she had invited: family members, friends and the many people with whom I had worked over the years. On the evening before the party, 200 copies of the book arrived at the Barge, much to my relief.

The party was a joyous affair. I was delighted to have so many people who had been such an important part of my life gathered in one place to share in the celebration. What the invitation had promised was there in good measure: "buffet, drinks, nostalgia, friendly conversation and glorious views." Charlie King, the folk singer, entertained the guests; his most rapt listener was my one-year-old grandson, Alex, who did not take his eyes off King throughout his performance. I was kept busy autographing copies of the book, enjoying this moment of celebrity.

* * * * *

The day after the book party came the hangover: How was I going to sell the book? I could not afford to hire an agent to promote and sell it, nor did I have the time or experience to handle the task myself; I still had a full-time job as a union education director and was also teaching classes two evenings a week.

I did poorly in publicizing the book. I was disappointed that *The New York Times* would not run a review, but I was angered that I could not get as much as a mention from the liberal *Nation,* the progressive weekly *Guardian* and the socialist *Monthly Review.* They were, however, willing to accept paid ads.

I decided to sell the book by mail, focusing on unions and their members. I prepared a promotion piece and mailed it to a list of more than 1,500 unions from a labor directory. The book was priced at $9.50 per copy, with reductions for bulk orders. The early results were gratifying, especially the orders for multiple copies from various unions. The New York State AFL-CIO ordered 50 copies for its executive board members and staffers. One railroad union asked for 55 copies to be distributed to delegates at its convention. Orders came in on official union stationery from national and local affiliates of the AFL-CIO. My records show that the book was bought by labor groups and individual unionists from 46 States. By March 1994, I had sold or given to libraries and friends all but 25 copies. Perhaps some day, *The Labor Leader* will be reprinted.

36. The High Price of Dissent

Although U.S. union leaders praise and honor dissenters in foreign countries who speak out against the dictatorial behavior of their governments, they will not tolerate critics in their own ranks and use strong measures to silence them. I knew in advance that I would lose my job and suffer ostracism when I undertook to expose the undemocratic practices of the AFL-CIO leadership. What I did not anticipate was the lengths to which they would go to turn me into a non-person. I soon found out how crude and vindictive they could be at the celebration of the 20th anniversary of the Labor College in September 1991.

It is a matter of record that I played the principal role in organizing the campaign that led to the establishment of the college. There are numerous official documents to show that I was hired as the first dean, that I was its first professor, that I established the largest and most successful college degree program for union leaders and that I personally recruited a majority of the students who attended the college during the 13 years I taught there. Yet, I was not invited to the celebration that was held at the college. I learned about it two weeks before the event and decided that I would attend anyway.

At the ceremony, there was an array of speakers, most of whom had not been involved in creating the college and some of whom had actually opposed its establishment. All of them were full of praise for the late Harry Van Arsdale Jr., who, as I wholeheartedly agreed, played the decisive role in founding the college. The chairman of the meeting, Vincent McElroen, editor of Local 3's *Electrical Union World* and one of my former students, presented the audience with a 10-minute review of the college since its inception in which he did not once mention my name or any of the programs I had initiated. I had no doubt that McElroen was acting on orders of his boss, Tom Van Arsdale. The ceremony was also to serve as one of several occasions for expunging my name from the college's history.

Assured that no speaker would even touch on the serious problems facing the college, I had decided in advance that this was an opportune occasion to describe what had been really happening. I distributed to the startled audience of union leaders, labor educators and public officials a four-page newsletter, whose front page headline read: "Labor College in Crisis," with a subhead: "Dean Resigns; Union Enrollment Sinks to New Low." I described the steady decline in student enrollment among union officers and members and told how the faculty had destroyed the Union Leadership Program on the grounds that it was "elitist." For the first time, I reported in some detail how Tom Van Arsdale had wiped out the Trade Union Leadership Institute that his father had created five years before.

The newsletter, which I called *The Labor Educator,* served notice on the national and local union leadership that I would not be silenced despite their efforts to turn me into a pariah within the labor movement.

* * * * *

This is an appropriate place to tell the bizarre story of what happened to the Endowment in Labor Studies which Empire State College had established in my name. The endowment had been officially announced by Dr. James Hall, the college president, on May 9, 1984 at my retirement dinner, where about $60,000 was raised by the city's unions in contributions toward its support. Hall had told the audience of several hundred union leaders that "the Endowment in Dr. Kelber's name will support in perpetuity scholarship, teaching and services in the study of labor."

The idea for the fund-raising dinner in my honor had originated with Harry Van Arsdale Jr. who felt strongly that there ought to be at least one endowed academic chair in labor studies, since there were scores of such chairs dedicated to corporate management. Without discussing it with me beforehand, he decided that the chair should be in my name. In support of the endowment, Van Arsdale organized a Labor Advisory Assembly, consisting of officers from more than 100 unions. The money that had been raised was deposited with the Empire State College Foundation.

Frankly, I did not consider an Empire State College academic chair much of an honor. I felt that Dr. Hall and his colleagues had yielded reluctantly to Van Arsdale's wishes, since they needed his political influence in Albany to defend their budget requirements. They had shown their hostility toward me on many occasions over the years. What I foresaw happening was that they would assign some professor to the chair, without consulting me or any union officials on their choice and without allowing us any input to his or her activity.

I paid no further attention to the endowment until July 1987 when, inadvertently, I learned that the dean of the labor college, Frank Goldsmith, had drawn a $175 check from the endowment account to pay for tickets to a dinner-dance of the Local 3 apprentice committee. My further investigation revealed that Goldsmith had spent more than $2,500 for tickets to the social functions of various unions, using endowment money. His additional expenditures included paying for a college boat ride, faculty dinners and other activities that were totally unrelated to the purposes of the endowment.

Shocked, I wrote to Dr. Hall requesting a detailed accounting of the endowment's income and expenditures since its inception in May 1984. I also noted that in the past three years, nothing had been done to fulfill the purposes for which the endowment had been established. His response on August 17 was typically bureaucratic. He refused to comment on the proof that I submitted of Dean Goldsmith's misuse of endowment funds. Instead, he said that he had directed Treasurer William Ferraro to "review all expenditures against this account to determine whether they have been consistent with its purposes." As to my criticism of the endowment's dormant state, he replied that he had asked a committee, including Dean Goldsmith, to "examine progress to date and to make recommendations to me for the future."

I decided to write to members of the executive board of the New York Central Labor Council, whose unions had contributed substantially to the endowment, informing them of what was going on and asking their intervention.. The board set up a committee to investigate the status of the endowment.

Apparently, Dr. Hall began getting angry protests from union officials because in his letter to me of October 6, he conceded that $4,126.74 had been "inappropriately" charged to the endowment and that this amount would be "restored directly to the account principal." To my amazement, he said that since Dean Goldsmith had acted in "good faith" in making these expenditures, he had reappointed him as the endowment's account director.

Actually, there were additional expenditures of $4,609.26 that could hardly be justified as complying with endowment guidelines, but I had no stomach for getting into a prolonged debate with Dr. Hall and his aides.

After receiving no word about the endowment for four years after my skirmish with Dr. Hall, I decided to find out what had been happening to it. On June 10, 1991, I wrote to Jamie Sidgmore, executive director of the Empire State College Foundation, requesting information about the endowment's operation and financial condition. Specifically, I asked for a year-by-year account of income and expenditures, a list of the individuals who were making policy decisions for the endowment and xerox copies of any meetings or policy statements. A month later, Ms. Sidgmore informed me that as of 1990, endowment funds had grown to $87,616. She listed "some of the projects" which had been funded, without giving any cost figures. They included the purchase of documents from the Library of Congress and the U.S. Government Printing Office and the purchase of New York Times microfiche for the college library.

I wrote to Dr. Hall on August 22, saying: "It is now more than seven years since the Endowment was created. It is high time that the funds of the Endowment were used on some appropriate educational project related to its individual purpose." He never answered my letter. In April 1993, I tried once again to find out what had happened to the endowment, but was told by Ms. Sidgmore that this information is "not available to the general public." I was informed that if I had any further inquiries, I should direct them to the foundation's lawyer.

It was now clear that the Empire State College Foundation had seized control of endowment funds and added them to its assets. New York union leaders did not seem interested in trying to reclaim authority over the endowment, probably because it carried my name.

I rejected the idea of suing the college foundation, not only because it would be costly and time-consuming, but because it would have been dismissed by my adversaries as an exercise in egotism. I informed Deborah Bernhardt, director of the Robert Wagner Labor Archives, that I would be pleased if endowment funds could be turned over to her organization for its educational projects; I volunteered to have my name removed from the title of the endowment. When she discussed this suggestion with influential union leaders on her board of directors, they were cool to the idea.

As late as 1994, ten years after the creation of the endowment, Empire State College Foundation still was in control of its funds which, by now, must exceed $100,000. Neither I nor any of the unions that contributed to the endowment receive any reports about its activities or expenditures. I have decided not to pursue the matter any further, to treat it as just another sad and disillusioning experience, best forgotten in the self-serving world of academe. Incidentally, since 1985, I have never received an invitation to attend the graduating exercises of the Labor College. I have not had any communication from either Dr. Hall or the Labor College dean. Although enrollment has dropped to an all-time low, my offer to help recruit trade unionists has been ignored.

37. Conducting Seminars in Russia

It was purely by chance that I was privileged to establish a warm relationship with leaders of the General Confederation of Trade Unions (GCTU), then claiming 130 million members in the Soviet Union, at a time when the economic reforms were getting under way.

In April 1991, a good friend of mine, Henry Foner, a former president of the New York Fur and Leather Workers Union, asked whether I would like to meet some Russian labor leaders who were visiting the United States. He had been invited to meet them but could not make it because of other commitments. I was uncertain that I would have the time to attend, but I finally did, on a dismal, rainy morning.

The meeting was held in a small room at the Hotel Edison, with barely a dozen Americans present. The speaker was Vladimir Kuzmenok, vice president of the General Confederation, a serious, soft-spoken man in his early forties, whose remarks were interpreted by Alexei Zharkov, a bright, sophisticated young man who worked in the GCTU's international department. Also present was Alexander Remisov, first secretary of the Soviet Embassy in Washington.

Kuzmenok excited my interest by his report on a nationwide congress of 2,300 trade unionists held in Moscow in October 1990. After five days of debate by several hundred delegates, they had decided to create a new, independent labor federation to replace the discredited All Union Central Council of Trade Unions, which had been a "transmission belt" for the Communist Party and the Soviet government. The delegates had proclaimed that their key priority was to "defend the interests of workers in the context of the country's transition to a market economy." A new set of leaders of the GCTU had been elected by secret ballot. What amazed me was that not a word of this extraordinary development had appeared in the American press.

After Kuzmenok's report to us, someone asked, "What can we do to help you?" He replied, "We don't need your money. What we need is your knowledge and experience. We have a great deal to learn about how to conduct democratic unions and how a market economy functions."

At the end of the meeting, I introduced myself to Kuzmenok, briefly mentioned my credentials and said I would very much like to be helpful. He suggested that I discuss the matter with Remisov, who was standing beside him and who spoke English fluently. Remisov proposed I write to him at the Soviet embassy in Washington, enclosing my *vitae* and the kind of activities I would like to conduct in Russia. He seemed sufficiently impressed with my academic and trade union credentials to invite me to Washington to discuss the content and duration of my visit to Moscow as a guest of the GCTU. At first, he offered to include me in a trade union delegation of West Coast labor leaders who would be spending ten days touring the Soviet Union and meeting Russian union officials. I turned it down because I believed it would be largely ceremonial without much informational value. Instead, I brashly suggested a 24-day visit on my own and outlined how I would spend that time to their advantage. GCTU headquarters in Moscow agreed to my unusual proposal and began working out the details of my visit.

It took several months before I could get the formal invitation that would enable me to get a visa. Tumultuous events were taking place in the Soviet Union, so that my forthcoming visit was hardly a priority item at GCTU headquarters. My trip, originally scheduled to start in June, was postponed to October but it was not until January 1992 that I finally arrived in Moscow.

The program they planned for me turned out to be even more intensive than the one I had requested. It consisted of lectures, seminars and private meetings with a variety of labor groups and individuals in Moscow and St. Petersburg (then still called Leningrad) that included these specific activities:

• Two-hour meetings with the heads of each of four major GCTU departments: legal, economic affairs, social insurance, and occupational safety and health.

• A speech about developments in the American labor movement to leaders of the Moscow and St. Petersburg labor federations, including union officers from more than a dozen industries.

• A private meeting with the deputy editor-in-chief of *Trud,* the national labor daily, which then had a circulation of more than eight million.

• A three-day series of lectures and workshops with students and faculty of the two most important labor colleges in the country.

• A discussion about creating an independent enterprise, based on employee stock ownership, with the trade union council leaders of Svetlana, a St. Petersburg factory complex of 30,000 workers producing a variety of scientific, medical and military instruments.

• A luncheon meeting with trade union officers from large machine tool factories in Moscow, Kiev and St. Petersburg.

• A report on the American labor press to editors of the weekly official newspapers of the Moscow and St. Petersburg labor federations.

• A meeting with Siberian coal miners who were attending a week-long conference in St. Petersburg.

For my "free" time, my GCTU hosts had arranged attendance at a number of cultural events, including ballet and opera at the famous Bolshoi Theatre, and a visit to the impressive art collection at the Hermitage, as well as museums, cathedrals, parks and other institutions of historical interest.

Remarkably, every event and appointment that was on the detailed three-page schedule, printed in both English and Russian, actually took place, and almost always on time. A staff car with a chauffeur was put at my disposal and Alexei Zharkov, whom I had met in New York, was assigned as my interpreter, guide and factotum. I was overwhelmed at the extent of their hospitality, especially since they were undergoing tremendous economic difficulties. I vowed to do everything I could to make my visit useful to them.

* * * * *

When I arrived in Moscow on Saturday, January 4, 1992, a week after the dissolution of the Soviet Union. Alexei was at the airport to meet me. We drove to the Sputnik, a 17-story, union-owned hotel named after the first Soviet space ship to orbit the earth. Two hours after I was settled in my modestly-furnished room and had been served a lunch of soup, beefsteak, salad, ice cream and tea, I was taken to GCTU headquarters on Leninskaya Street where I was introduced to several high-ranking leaders. I then had a long, private talk with Kuzmenok, the official who was most responsible for my trip. He briefed me on recent developments in the now-dissolved Soviet Union and their impact on the economy, the unions and the living standards of workers. He was interested in my report on the AFL-CIO convention which I had attended two months earlier.

In my discussions with the separate heads of the four GCTU departments, I began to appreciate the enormous problems and responsibilities the labor confederation faced, now that it was an independent organization, no longer under the control of the Soviet government and Communist Party. Under the emerging market economy, unions, for the first time, had to develop wage structures in every industry, a function that had previously been monopolized by Soviet bureaucrats and the party apparatus. Union leaders had to become proficient in the art of negotiating collective bargaining contracts with independent employers. They had to develop a cadre of staff people who could prepare a legislative agenda on economic and social issues and lobby deputies in parliament.They had to learn about how to conduct a union under democratic principles and how to involve rank-and-file members in decision-making.

At virtually every lecture, I emphasized that I was there to describe, and not necessarily recommend, the American model of a free market economy; they would have to decide for themselves what they approved or disapproved of in that system, based on their needs and circumstances. I did point out that American workers did not get the long vacations, maternity benefits, free medical care, child care, subsidized housing and other benefits which Russian workers took for granted and which might be imperiled in a market economy as practiced in the United States.

In the months before my visit, I had prepared material on ten topics which I incorporated in my series of lectures. They were:

• The role of democratic unions in a free market economy.

• The American economy—its strengths and weaknesses.
• Employer-employee relations in a private enterprise system.
• Economic and social discrimination against working women.
• Lobbying techniques for protective labor and social legislation.
•The role of government in the U.S. economy.
• Poverty and unemployment.
• Reasons for the decline of the American labor movement.
• Technology and worker productivity.
• Labor education in U.S. colleges and universities.

At every lecture, I was deluged with questions. They wanted to know about wages and benefits in various industries; the amount the average worker family spent on food, housing, transportation, education and clothing. They asked how unions were structured, the salary of union officers and the cost of membership dues. They wanted to know how many labor leaders were in Congress and what kind of a person was the billionaire businessman, Ross Perot.

A few of the questions about the United States were difficult to answer: Why was there so much unemployment in the richest country in the world? Why did racism persist? Why was there such great inequality in incomes? What about the high crime rate? Why did we allow the mafia to control some unions? Why was such a small percentage of American workers in unions, even though they could get better wages and benefits in union enterprises? I explained that there were many differing answers to these questions and then gave my own views.

At the Academy of Labor and Social Relations in Moscow, I met with some 40 young labor leaders from various republics of the former Soviet Union who were spending a total of 180 days there as a requirement for earning a college degree. More than a third of the students were women; all of them had been sent to the academy by their respective labor organizations on scholarships after they'd had at least one year's experience as a worker and union officer. The school's professors attended my workshops on collective bargaining, political action and union organizing and they graded the students on their role-playing performances and the papers they had to submit the following day on topics that I had proposed. I spent a long afternoon with the faculty, at their request, offering suggestions for revising their curriculum to take into account the country's transition toward a market economy. I can't remember ever talking so much in my entire life. Every night, I returned to my room utterly exhausted, yet glad that I was there.

* * * * *

I had arrived in Moscow on January 4, 1992, two days after the so-called "liberalization of prices" by the Russian government. In anticipation of huge price increases on virtually all consumer items, the population had been on a buying spree. Long lines of people stood in front of the state-owned stores, stocking up on food and other commodities, quickly stripping the shelves bare.

It was the beginning of a wild, spiraling inflation which saw prices rise to astronomic levels, so that workers and especially pensioners on fixed salaries could not afford even necessities. Prices of eggs, butter, milk, meat and other basic foods doubled and tripled almost daily. GCTU economists estimated that 80 per cent of the population now lived below the poverty line, unable to afford even a minimum "consumer basket" of food and other essentials.

I had a personal experience with the crazy manner in which prices were raised in what was starting to become a "market economy." I had decided I wanted calling cards with my name and address in Russian as well as English. The clerk at the hotel kiosk said I could have 100 cards printed for 200 rubles (about $1.20 at the then current rate of exchange). I said, fine. The next morning, when I submitted copy for the cards, she told me the price had gone up to 1500 rubles—more than seven times the original price. I asked why the exorbitant increase in less than one day. She said she didn't know; she was just carrying out orders. Although it was cheap by American standards, I decided not to purchase the cards.

To survive, many people were selling off their belongings so they could have enough money for food. Informal "markets" sprang up along popular thoroughfares where pensioners stood for hours, even in freezing weather, trying to sell a sweater, books, a tablecloth, a chess set, even a can of fish or a jar of jam—anything that could command a price. I saw one old woman peddling a toilet seat.

The unions had only limited success in their campaign to get the government to raise the minimum wage for workers and the allotments for pensioners. Even when wages were lifted, they were far outpaced by the steep climb of prices.

* * * * *

I was skeptical about the Federation of Independent Unions of Russia's claim of 70 million members (including six million for the Moscow Trade Union Federation), but I was told why it was in the interest of all Russian workers to belong to unions. In the former USSR, the major role of unions was to dispense social welfare benefits rather than to negotiate wage rates. Workers received enormous benefits. I was astounded to learn that women workers got 126 days of paid maternity leave and that their jobs were guaranteed for three years while they cared for their children. Workers also received free medical care; if they fell sick, they were entitled to as much as four months of convalescence at full pay. Education, I was told, was free, from elementary school through university. Union members got six weeks' vacation and enjoyed large discounts at vacation resorts; their children could go to summer camps at greatly reduced rates. These and other benefits made it worthwhile for workers to pay one percent a month in union dues through a checkoff system.

Nevertheless, I sensed there was a falling off of union membership and the decrease would continue unless the union leadership undertook a major campaign to establish their credibility with the nation's workers. Interestingly, a poll of 1,062 workers conducted by the Moscow Trade Union Federation showed that as many as 8.3 percent had decided to leave the union; 13.2 percent were thinking about leaving; 33.7 percent definitely intended to stay in the union, and 42.4 percent had not thought about leaving. I warned the federation leaders that corporations from the United States and Western Europe would make strong efforts to undermine their unions. I pointed out that the big McDonald's restaurant in Moscow was setting a precedent by operating non-union and that the Yeltsin government would discourage any attempt to unionize Western-owned enterprises because it was eager to attract foreign investments.

* * * * *

Apparently, I had impressed GCTU officials sufficiently to have them invite me to conduct a week-long seminar they were planning to hold the following September on the theme: "Democratic Unions in a Market Economy". I eagerly agreed to do it. Back home, from June to the opening of the seminar on September 7, 1992, I was fully occupied in assembling a team of ten labor educators, preparing educational materials and working out the many organizational details with Igor Yourgens, GCTU's first vice president. It was easy to deal with Yourgens, an attractive man, not quite forty, who spoke English fluently and was a highly-skilled administrator who had worked for UNESCO in Paris for several years.

I was informed that the seminar would be held at a training center in Saltykovka, a picturesque area in a forest about an hour's drive from Moscow. I was awed when I learned that there would be 145 participants, consisting of top-ranking officials of labor federations of the independent republics and leaders of 37 international unions, representing virtually every industry in the former Soviet Union. I began to worry whether I was competent enough to make the seminar worthwhile for this high-level gathering.

The ten-member team I selected to bring to Saltykovka had the specialized skills, teaching experience and attractive personalities I needed to conduct an effective seminar. There were two Cornell professors, two labor lawyers, three union representatives, two officers of state labor agencies, and a video camera specialist who also spoke Russian. Three of the instructors were women and one was an African-American. All of us served without any fee and paid our own airfare.

Through July and August, Yourgens in Moscow and I in New York worked out the countless details of this ambitious seminar in a series of communications by fax and phone. We agreed to divide the 145 labor leaders into five groups, based on geographic, ethnic and organizational considerations, and there would be daily plenary meetings in addition to classroom sessions. We prepared a daily agenda and decided on educational materials that could be translated into Russian and given to the participants in advance of the seminar.

Our painstaking preparations paid off in a smoothly conducted, successful seminar. Every group spent one full day of instruction on each of five topics:

1. The role of labor leaders in building a democratic union.
2. Collective bargaining in the public and private sectors.

3. Grievance procedures and conflict resolution.
4. Administering a democratic union.
5. Labor legislation and political action.

Every morning, the plenary session, from 9 to 10:15, dealt with broad aspects of democracy and the market economy as practiced in the United States, during which participants asked questions and offered comments. Classes ran for two hours in the morning and two hours in the afternoon. There were also evening lectures on topics suggested by students at which attendance was optional. Our instrutors were available for private discussions with individual labor leaders on their particular problems. I met with representatives of the Kazakhstan coal miners, Tadjikistan chemical workers and officers of the Belarus labor federation.

Saltykovka was an ideal location for our seminar. Its main buildings were set in a forest enviroment that provided a relaxed atmosphere. We each had our own room, modestly but comfortably furnished. The meals were ample and nourishing; the diningroom staff went out of their way to accommodate us.What was especially pleasing to me was that there were no phones except in the administration offices and they could be used by the students only in emergencies. There were no distractions. Our seminar was the only show in town and attendance guaranteed.

We had an excellent corps of interpreters, skilled in handling simultaneous translation in Russian and English, and we had a sufficient number of TV monitors, movie cameras, slide projectors and other equipment. The classes went exceptionally well; our teachers established a warm rapport with the students despite the language barrier. These labor leaders were eager to exchange experiences on any topic raised by their instructors.

In every class, there were at least a couple of students who had a bag of appropiate jokes, proverbs and one-liners that evoked laughter and good humor. And we never had the problem of student inattention. At the end of each day of classes, instructors were given gifts and mementoes by the students. (We had brought bags of pins and buttons from various unions to give to them.) I received, among many gifts, a bottle of Armenian brandy; a handwoven scarf from Kazakhstan amd a richly illustrated book about Tula, site of a famed samovar industry.

At the final plenary session in the large auditorium, participants were given an opportunity to evaluate the seminar. About thirty of them spoke about what they had learned about American unions and the economy and profusely thanked the instructors. They suggested that the GCTU hold seminars of this type every three months, so that scores of other union leaders could attend and benefit from this knowledge. They looked pleased and proud when they came to the stage to receive their diplomas to the applause of the people in the auditorium.

The seminar attracted considerable attention from the media, far more than I could possibly have anticipated. I was interviewed on television four times and my comments about the American economy and the AFL-CIO were broadcast on the main TV and radio networks. Our joint press conferences with GCTU leaders received favorable coverage in Russia, especially in the labor press. But not a word in the American media.

There was one unpleasant incident that caused fear and anxiety to my team of instructors during the seminar. Each of them was approached by the labor attaché of the U.S. State Department, Matthew Boyce, who asked for their names and places of employment. He informed them that by teaching in a GCTU-sponsored conference, they were violating the AFL-CIO's policy of "no contact" with the "official" Russian unions. Boyce appeared even more threatening to our instructors when he sat in on their classes and took notes of their lectures.

When Boyce came into my classroom uninvited, I told the students that we had an important guest, an officer of the U.S. State Department, and asked him to "say a few words" to the class. In his short speech, he said the AFL-CIO was helping democratic-minded workers in Russia to set up "alternative" unions to replace those still under communist control, and he quoted Lenin's characterization of unions as "schools for communism." When he had finished, one student after another rose to denounce him and the U.S. State Department for meddling in the internal affairs of unions in Russia and its neighboring republics. They bitterly resented the AFL-CIO's sponsorship of provocative dual unions at a time when they desperately needed international labor assistance. Several of them saw the AFL-CIO's behavior as part of a CIA plot to undermine the economy of Russia and reduce it to the level of a third-world country. A Moscow labor leader pointed out that the AFL CIO was pouring money and supplies into opposition unions that, at best, represented less than one percent of the work force but were able to play a disruptive role despite their small numbers.

I had not anticipated this reaction, and I guess I visibly showed my approval. The students asked my views about the dual unions, and I responded frankly, with Boyce, quite subdued, sitting nearby. I explained why I strongly disagreed with the AFL-CIO position, as expressed by its president, Lane Kirkland, and said I would urge American labor organizations to support the GCTU and its affiliated unions when I returned to the United States.

The news of our encounter with Boyce quickly spread to students in the other classes, and they had a similar reaction. However, the instructors, while privately agreeing with my views, were angered that I had allowed the students to attack Boyce and had expressed my own opinions in his presence. They were sure he would give a detailed report of the seminar to AFL-CIO leaders in Washington who would undoubtedly inform their employers that they had knowingly participated in a week-long meeting sponsored by a labor confederation which the AFL-CIO had branded as "communist controlled," even though it was under new, elected leadership. Several of my colleagues reminded me they had responsible government and academic positions that required them to present an even-handed approach to labor and management. Their superiors would be embarrassed by the publicity and might penalize them; they could lose their jobs and damage their careers.

I was shocked by their response. I said that even if the AFL-CIO were to relay its red-baiting charges to their employers, they should be able to defend their behavior, especially after their first-hand encounter with the labor leaders of Russia and the Commonwealth States. They remained bitter toward me. Why had I not warned them of what might happen? One instructor tearfully reminded me that he had a wife and two young children and could not afford to lose his job.

I was disappointed and depressed. There was not much I could do about it, except to promise them I would come to their defense if there were reprisals. It turned out that only one of the ten instructors, a lawyer for the communications workers union, encountered any difficulty when he returned home. He had decided to speak at a Moscow union rally that had no direct connection with our seminar and to grant a personal interview with *The Wall Street Journal,* which apparently embarrassed the union. The CWA president wanted to fire him, but a mutually acceptable settlement was worked out.

I decided that henceforth I would avoid the role of team leader. I did not want to be responsible for the career problems of colleagues, especially in potentially stressful situations. If I were to continue my unpaid relationship with the GCTU and its affiliated unions, it would have to be on a personal basis.

In January 1993, I was invited back by the Moscow and St. Petersburg trade union federations to give a series of lectures on labor developments in the United States. My ten-day visit included several private conferences at which I could raise numerous questions about unemployment, production, privatization, and union relations with the Yeltsin government. Subsequently, I met with leaders of the General Confederation of Trade Unions when they visited the United States. And in August, 1993, I conducted a three-day seminar for 25 of their leaders in New York City.

* * * * *

At the request of the GCTU leaders, I had been sending them a monthly budget of news that consisted of five single-spaced pages containing ten stories and ten "News in Brief" items. My news service was not limited to activities of the American labor movement, but also reported on economic, political and social developments in the United States. It contained running stories on the 1992 presidential elections, the economic recession and congressional legislation among other subjects.

The first issue of what I called *American Labor News Service* was faxed on May 1, 1992 to GCTU headquarters from which it was distributed to a mailing list of union publications and 1,500 labor leaders throughout the former Soviet Union. After publishing 17 monthly issues of *ALNS,* I regretfully had to end it in October, 1993. I was now involved in what was to become a continuing campaign to challenge the undemocratic practices of the AFL-CIO and could not afford to spend the energy and time that the news service required. I had tried to get other people, individually or as a group, to continue *ALNS,* but they were not willing to take over, especially since it was arduous, time-consuming, unpaid labor.

In the late spring of 1992, while I was in Moscow, I met Vyacheslav Boikov, deputy editor-in-chief of *Trud,* the daily labor newspaper which then boasted the largest circulation in the world. He had seen the initial issue of *ALNS* and was interested in receiving it on a regular basis. He introduced me to Anatoly Repin, the editor handling U.S. news. Repin was a short, wiry, bald-headed, middle-aged man who impressed me with his quick intelligence and sense of humor, and, what also pleased me, he spoke perfect American English. After a cordial conversation at *Trud's* editorial offices, he invited me to do a monthly column for the newspaper on developments in the American labor movement, an offer I immediately accepted. He had one of his photographers take a snapshot of me to be used with the column. At my request, he gave me a list of topics that he believed would attract the interest of Russian readers.

My first column in May 1992 was on an elementary subject, "Why Workers Should Join Unions." It was a question that had been repeatedly asked of me during my lectures. Since it was no longer mandatory for Russian workers to belong to unions, labor leaders had to be reminded of the arguments that would persuade them to remain as members. Repin gave me an official *Trud* press card containing my photo and describing me as a contributing writer of the newspaper. He said I could represent the paper for special stories and interviews in the United States.

After I had done a series of 16 columns over a period of a year and a half, I learned that Repin had been transferred to Egypt. I could not establish a working relationship with the new editor and so I ceased writing the column. At no time had it occurred to me to seek payment for my labors. I felt this was my voluntary contribution to these new, hard-pressed unions, I sympathized with those union leaders who were struggling to create a new economy that was neither communist nor capitalist but would preserve the best features of both systems.

The leaders of the GCTU and the Moscow and St. Petersburg Trade Union Federations went to great lengths to show their appreciation of my work. I was given the V.I.P. treatment wherever I went. I was permitted to have private discussions with their top leaders during which I learned a great deal about their difficult problems. They gave me copies of several publications, including *Trud,* in which my articles appeared. At one meeting, the editors of *Trud* presented me with a wrist watch, especially designed to celebrate the newspapers 70th anniversary, and an envelope containing 1,000 rubles, worth about $4 at the then current rate of exchange. The unions were especially pleased with my articles in *The Labor Educator* in which I informed American trade unionists of the efforts by AFL-CIO President Lane Kirkland to set up dual unions in Moscow and elsewhere to disrupt their mainstream unions—none of which had been reported in either the commercial or labor press of the United States. In appreciation of my continuing activity in their behalf, I was appointed to the unpaid, honorary position of Educational Consultant of the General Confederation of Trade Unions and the Independent Trade Unions of Russia.

In December 1994, I conducted a week-long seminar for a delegation of 27 top-ranking officers of labor federations from Russia and the

Commonwealth States at the Florida International University in Miami, and as recently as April 1996, I had meetings with a similar group in New York City. I have been given a standing invitation to visit Russia or any of the Commonwealth countries as a guest of their respective labor federations.

38. *I Run for AFL-CIO Vice President*

While researching AFL-CIO history, I was somewhat shocked to learn that since 1965, the official slate of the federation's Executive Council had been elected unanimously by voice vote every two years without even a single opposing candidate for the presidency or any of the 33 council seats. In 1965, Patrick Gorman, president of the Amalgamated Meat Cutters and an avowed socialist, had the temerity to seek a vice presidency and had been crushingly defeated under the AFL-CIO's system of convention delegate voting. In the only time that a printed ballot was ever used at a federation convention, all candidates on the official slate, with one exception, received more than 12.6 million votes, while Gorman lost with 2.3 million votes.

Thereafter, at every convention, the slate of executive council vice presidents was routinely approved as a group without opposition or even the pretense of debate in a ritualized ceremony that took between three and five minutes. There was no organized challenge to this "politburo" procedure, even by labor activists, since it was assumed that only presidents of international unions could occupy seats on the council.

At one point in my research, I examined the AFL-CIO Constitution. It was an eye-opener. Under Article V Section 2 dealing with officers of the federation, it appeared that there was one, and only one, requirement for holding office as an AFL-CIO vice president: *"Each officer shall be a member of an affiliated organization."* That was plain enough. *Any* member, even a rank-and-filer, could run for a seat on the executive council!

Section 3 of the same article brought another surprise:*"The officers shall be elected by the convention by written ballot, with each affiliate having the number of votes to which it is entitled on a roll-call vote, as provided in Article IV."* In electing the 33-member council by voice vote, every convention for the past 28 years had violated the federation's constitution! Of course, AFL-CIO leaders could claim that, since there were no opposing candidates, a formal printed ballot was unnecessary; but voting by ballot would give delegates an opportunity to register their approval or disapproval of individual council members.

Reading further, I discovered a series of undemocratic features of the constitution that explained how a hierarchy of international union presidents were able to assure themselves of reelection so they could exercise stranglehold control over AFL-CIO policies and activities. Article IV Section 8 provides that an international union may have as many convention votes as its membership, based on its per capita payments to the national AFL-CIO. By contrast, the constitution limits state AFL-CIOs and city labor council affiliates to one vote apiece. Thus, on any important issue at the 1991 convention, which, incidentally, I had attended, the 50 state AFL-CIOs and the 614 city labor councils could cast a combined total of 664 votes, compared with, say, the Federation of Grain Millers, which was entitled to 27,383 votes. The New York State AFL CIO, with an affiliated membership of 2.3 million unionists, had a single convention vote, while the Federation of Professional Athletes had 483 votes and the International Union of Horseshoers, 250.

While admitting that the affiliated state and city labor bodies played a principal role in carrying out AFL-CIO policies and were on "the firing line" in conducting labor's economic and political campaigns, the executive council had steadfastly refused to include an officer of a state or city labor organization on its slate of candidates. Clearly, the council, determined to preserve its self-perpetuating character, did not want even the possibility of grass-roots involvement in its decision-making.

* * * * *

Eight months before the 1993 AFL-CIO convention, which was to be held in San Francisco on October 4-7, I tried to interest a number of progressive labor leaders from several international unions to campaign for a seat on the council. While conceding that changes were needed in the AFL-CIO's top leadership, all of them rejected my suggestion. They did not want to get involved in an expensive, time-consuming campaign in which they had not the ghost of a chance of being elected. They declined to play the role of Don Quixote when there were serious issues affecting their members that required their attention and effort. Such excuses had been used for 28 years to give the AFL-CIO hierarchy a blank check in its exercise of power.

I don't know exactly when—it was sometime in April—when a crazy, utterly improbable idea came to me: *I, yes I, would run for AFL-CIO vice president!* At that point, I was not even a member of a union! The first thing I did was to renew my membership in the New York Typographical Union Local 6, from which I had taken an honorary withdrawal in 1965 after a 12-year affiliation. The typographical union had merged with the Communications Workers of America, an AFL-CIO affiliate. I now was legally eligible to run for high office, but what chance did I have that the federation leadership would recognize my candidacy?

Just after Labor Day, I announced on the front page of a special issue of *The Labor Educator* that I had decided to become a candidate for AFL-CIO vice president. I explained why I was eligible to run for this office, listed my credentials and said that, in a letter to President Lane Kirkland, I was insisting on a printed ballot and other rights to which I was entitled as a candidate. I also spelled out the undemocratic features of the AFL-CIO that needed to be reformed.

In one of my biting attacks on the incumbent leadership, I reprinted the verbatim text from the official AFL-CIO report of the election of officers at the 1991 convention, which unmistakably exposed its "politburo style" character. In another article entitled "Is the AFL CIO a Monarchy?", I pointed out that in the past 107 years, the AFL-CIO and its predecessor, the AFL, had had only four presidents, and the fourth, Lane Kirkland, was still in office. During this time, there had been 20 U.S. Presidents, 23 British Prime Ministers and nine Catholic Popes. I mailed copies of the newsletter containing my announcement to 15,000 local unions across the country, about 30 percent of all AFL-CIO affiliates.

To my friends in the labor movement, the announcement of my candidacy seemed a rash, egotistical gesture that would be universally ridiculed, especially since I held no union office and was not a convention delegate, just an ordinary union member. They most certainly would not support my efforts. If I persisted in this adventurist escapade, I would have to do it on my own and bear the financial cost.

Apparently, my announced candidacy created a sensation within the labor movement, mainly for its bravado rather than for representing a serious challenge to the AFL-CIO's top echelon. I learned that within the council, there was a division of opinion on how to handle my candidacy: some wanted to ignore it; others thought it would be wiser to recognize it: I would get so few votes that no one would ever again dare to challenge their official slate. I scored an initial victory when President Kirkland accepted my right to run for vice president, even though I held no position in any union. In response to my letter requesting nominating procedures, he informed me by fax on September 16, as follows :

"If you will advise me of the delegate who will nominate you, following his accreditation as a delegate by the Credentials Committee, your name and that of your nominator will be put forward in the same way that the candidates of the incumbents are put forward. Alternatively, and that is up to you, you may prefer to have your name put forward by a delegate when the floor is opened to further nominations."

I had clearly succeeded in exploding the long-held myth that only presidents of international unions were eligible to become vice presidents and occupy seats on the executive council! I was also assured there would be a printed ballot if the number of candidates exceeded the current 33 council seats.

With only six working days before the start of the convention, I urgently requested several prerogatives that would enable me to conduct a proper campaign in behalf of my candidacy. On September 23, Kirkland gave me the following assurances:

• I would be permitted to distribute my campaign literature outside the convention hall. "There would be no problems of intimidation or harassment."

• I would be welcomed in the guest section of the convention hall so that I could observe the proceedings. My wife would also be allowed in the hall as a guest.

• Pursuant to my nomination, I would be given five minutes to address the convention delegates.

• A typed list of credentialed delegates would be made available to me as soon as the report of the Credentials Committee was approved.

One paragraph in Kirkland's fax puzzled me. It said: "If more than 33 individuals are nominated to be an AFL-CIO Vice President, I shall—in light of the fact that your correspondence stating an interest to seek that office is first in time and in keeping with Article V Section 3 of the AFL-CIO Constitution—prepare the written ballot so that your name is listed first."

Why would Kirkland want my name to be listed first on the ballot, rather than having the names of all candidates listed alphabetically, I wondered. I guessed it was to make it easy for the delegates to ignore me and bullet-vote the official slate of candidates.

I had asked for a convention forum at which candidates could present their views to the delegates prior to the election, but I was told that no such event would be scheduled. "We leave it to each candidate to determine his/her own campaign strategy and own approach to communicating with delegates," Kirkland said.

I was, of course, delighted with Kirkland's response, especially his giving me an opportunity to address the convention. In no time, I started to draft my speech, selecting all the points I could make in five minutes. However, there was one problem that caused me great anxiety. Kirkland had insisted that my nominator be an accredited convention delegate approved by the Credentials Committee, whose report would be available to me barely one day before the actual nomination. In my September 28 fax to Kirkland, I said "there is nothing in the AFL-CIO Constitution that states that a nominator must be a convention delegate. If a candidate is not required to be a delegate, why should a nominator?" I said that on the first day of the convention, October 4, I would submit "a notarized statement from my nominator who, although not a delegate, has been president of a substantial and respected local union for ten years, from 1982 to 1992." My nominator was John Glasel, former president of the 15,000-member American Federation of Musicians, Local 802, who enthusiastically supported my candidacy.

Kirkland's reply the following day reiterated his position that I could be nominated only by a convention delegate. He said: "From the first, and without deviation, the AFL-CIO Constitution's provision for a convention election has been interpreted as providing that *only* an accredited delegate may make a nomination."

I fired back a protest. I challenged his arbitrary, unprecedented and illogical ruling. Who, I asked, had made that "interpretation" and when and where had it been made? Why was there no written documentation of this interpretation? I said he was using an unjustified technicality to jeopardize my candidacy and to prevent the first AFL-CIO election contest in nearly 30 years.

I decided that I had to find a convention delegate—just one out of more than

700—who would have the courage to nominate me. There were at least two or three dozen union officials from New York who I knew would be delegates but I could count only five who might conceivably support me. When I met with each of the five, I explained that in nominating me, they could simply say they were supporting my candidacy solely for the purpose of having the convention conduct its first contested election in 28 years and to correct past violations of the AFL-CIO constitution. I also assured them that I would gladly withdraw if any convention delegate decided to challenge the official slate.

Each of the five found a reason to reject my request. One said that he would like to nominate me but he could not afford to antagonize his international union president who had been very helpful to him. Another admitted he was a delegate, but said he did not plan to attend the convention because of other important commitments. A third said this was her first convention and she wanted to maintain a low profile. The other two were blunt: my nomination was a ridiculous gesture and they would have nothing to do with it.

I was disheartened, but not ready to give up. It was still possible that I might find *one* rebellious soul among the delegates who was outraged at the high-handed behavior of the AFL-CIO leadership and was willing to nominate me. I decided that, at the very least, I would go to the convention and campaign like a serious candidate for the few days before the nominating session on Wednesday morning.

* * * * *

Mim and I arrived in San Francisco on Saturday, October 2 and I immediately went to the floor of the Hilton Hotel where convention delegates were registering. I arranged several pieces of my campaign literature on a nearby table, alongside of which I displayed a large poster announcing my candidacy.

I received a mixed reaction from the delegates I approached after they had registered. Many looked startled as they accepted my basic, four-page campaign piece. Others, stone-faced, walked past me without taking my handout. About a dozen or so stopped long enough to listen to me and agreed to read my literature. I noted their names and union affiliation. I spent the entire Sunday, collaring delegates near the registration section and distributing my literature. Before the weekend was over, word of my candidacy had become widespread and a topic of conversation among many delegates.

At the opening Monday morning session, I appeared at the door of the convention hall with a leaflet which almost all of the delegates, prompted by curiosity, accepted as they entered the auditorium. Under a headline, "An Appeal to Every Convention Delegate to Stand Up for Fair Play and Democracy," the leaflet reviewed Kirkland's arbitrary ruling to reject my nominator. It went on to say: "President Kirkland's objections can be satisfied if one delegate—just one of the many hundreds of delegates at this convention—agrees to nominate me, not necessarily because he or she believes in my candidacy but because it is the fair-minded and democratic thing to do."

By that evening, four delegates separately approached me to say they were sympathetic to my purpose in seeking election and would give "serious consideration" to act as my nominator. The following morning, three of them came to me and said regretfully that they had talked it over with other delegates and had concluded they would be subjected to reprisals if they nominated me. But one delegate, a young president of a small central labor council on the West Coast remained steadfast. He spent time with me, taking notes about my background and discussing the points he would make in his nominating speech the next day. I could hardly sleep, I was so elated. I kept rehearsing my acceptance speech to the delegates until I had it almost memorized.

The delegates did not know how to regard my activity in what they were certain would be a futile effort. The way I was campaigning, they were becoming convinced that I had found a nominator. At every morning and afternoon session, I distributed a new leaflet exposing still another example of the undemocratic behavior of the AFL-CIO's self-serving bureaucracy. Delegates grew accustomed to accepting the leaflets, curious about what new charges I was making. Quite a few greeted me with sympathetic smiles, even an occasional pat on the back and a "give 'em hell, Harry." My candidacy appeared to be the only interesting development in what most of them were sure would be the traditional, cut-and-dried convention.

Early Wednesday morning, about an hour before the start of the nominating session, I suffered a terrible shock that left me trembling with rage and disappointment. My nominator had backed out! Ashamed and embarrassed, he told me he had been subjected to severe pressure from several superiors who warned him to have nothing to do with my candidacy. He couldn't afford to disobey them; they could destroy him.

Just as I was resigning myself to defeat, I was greeted at the entrance of the convention hall by Joseph Pascarella, a former student of mine, who was president of Macy's department store local union in New York. Joe, whom I had known since he was a rank-and-filer, said he was a delegate and heartily agreed to nominate me when I quickly explained my situation.

Mim and I sat tensely in the first row of the convention's guest section as we listened to Kirkland reading the list of the 33 incumbent vice presidents who were running for reelection, including three who had been recently appointed. There was a moment of silence in the hall when Kirkland asked for additional nominations. Then up rose Pascarella to announce that he, a vice president of the Retail, Wholesale and Department Store Union, was placing my name in nomination for the position of AFL-CIO vice president.

In a speech that lasted several minutes and was listened to attentively by the delegates, Pascarella described what he called my outstanding contributions to the New York labor movement and explained why I would be an asset to the executive council. He said that not only he, but a great many union leaders, had benefitted from what they had learned in my classes and seminars over many years. He noted that more than a dozen convention delegates, including a member of the executive council, were among my former students.

When Pascarella sat down, there was intense consultation on the dais, after which Kirkland announced that my nominator was not on the list of accredited delegates, and therefore my nomination was invalid. Pascarella was stunned. He had been given a delegate's badge when he had registered. He had been attending all sessions of the convention as a delegate, without challenge until now. He could not understand why his name was not on the list of accredited delegates.

I leaped from my seat and attempted to challenge Kirkland's ruling, but he refused to recognize me and ordered the security guards to usher me off the floor. Having disqualified my nomination, and in the absence of other nominees, Kirkland announced that the only candidates were the 33 council incumbents seeking re-election. In proceeding immediately with the election, Kirkland once more violated the AFL-CIO constitution, which explicitly requires elections to be held one day after nominations. Then, in barely one minute, all council members were re-elected as a bloc by a single voice vote.

It is worth noting that a substantial number of delegates had never met many of the council members, did not know what they stood for and had not heard them speak during the convention, but nevertheless, they voted for them.

* * * * *

My lone fight at the convention had been a grueling, exhausting experience, but I was glad I had undertaken it. I had succeeded in destroying the myth that only presidents of international unions could qualify for seats on the executive council. I hoped that at the 1995 convention, there would be independent candidates far better qualified than I, who would run for council seats with the backing of convention delegates on a program of democratic reform.

Mim and I spent several relaxing days with friends in Bolinas, California. Upon my return to New York, I published my account of the convention in *The Labor Educator.* Although in a few months I would be 80 years old, I was not ready to retire from my life's work as a labor activist.

39. Riding the Information Highway

It was sometime in May 1994 that I decided to plunge into the expanding world of computer networking. I was intrigued by the possibility of posting an uncensored message, even an article or newsletter, on an electronic bulletin board that subscribers all over the world could read and respond to within seconds if they wished.

I subscribed to the network system of the Institute for Global Communications (IGC), which consisted of four related divisions, all of interest to me: PeaceNET, EcoNET, LaborNET and Conflict NET. IGC appeared to attract progressive organizations and individuals with whom I eventually was able to share a great deal of useful information. I was especially pleased that I could now communicate swiftly by e-mail with Russian labor leaders on topics of mutual interest.

It took several months of frustrating trial-and-error effort and endless telephone calls to IGC headquarters in San Francisco before I was able to acquire the proficiency to take full advantage of the service.

I learned that the AFL-CIO had initiated its own computerized network as a subdivision of CompuServe, and I immediately subscribed. I was delighted to find that AFL-CIO LaborNET had more than 300 subscribers (it now has more than 3,000), most of them either high-ranking labor leaders or influential union staffers. A captive audience! Here was an opportunity to involve them in a debate on the undemocratic practices of the AFL-CIO if I could provoke their interest.

My first effort, a brief message with the startling title, "Is the AFL-CIO a Monarchy?", created more responses than anything that had appeared on the network. (I had previously used it in my newsletter.) I don't know how many were shocked to learn that in 108 years, the AFL-CIO and its predecessor, the American Federation of Labor, had only four presidents and the fourth, Lane Kirkland, was still in office. (Actually, there was a fifth president, in 1895, who lasted only one year.) I was both praised and denounced for my historical tidbit, but I had succeeded in starting a heated debate as to whether or not the AFL-CIO was or was not a democratic organization.

I announced that I would be posting a weekly column, *LaborTalk*, which would discuss how the AFL-CIO was responding to problems facing the nation's working people. I believe that Kirkland and council members were chagrined that I had found another channel for my criticism of their policies, but there was nothing they could do about it except maintain a strict silence, since they had no desire to call attention to my accusations by engaging me in debate. Another of my columns raised questions as to why the executive council refused to make the minutes of its closed-door meetings available to union members until 30 years after the event. There was some joking speculation about the nature of the secrets the council was burying.

Every Monday morning, a new *LaborTalk* column appeared on the AFL-CIO and IGC networks dealing with a variety of economic, political and social problems that were of concern to union leaders and members. I enjoyed writing the column and had no doubt that I could continue to do it indefinitely.

Learning that the AFL-CIO's 1995 convention would be held in New York City in October, I decided to use my column in the preceding months to build a case for democratic reform within the federation. I hoped my columns would provide campaign material for any independent candidates willing to challenge incumbents for council seats.

* * * * *

On July 13, 1994 the AFL-CIO suffered a major defeat in its effort to get Congress to pass legislation (HR5 and S55) that would prevent employers from permanently replacing workers who went out on strike. The federation and its affiliated international unions had given top priority to this issue for the past four years, had poured a flood of money, enormous resources and the time and energy of a multitude of staff people into the campaign, only to see what it called the Workplace Fairness bill go down to defeat by a filibuster of Senate Republicans and southern Democrats.

Noting that the AFL-CIO leadership had no intention of publicly discussing the reasons for the defeat, I wrote and distributed a four-page Blue Paper in which I set forth my own critical analysis of the legislation, charging Kirkland and the council with ineptitude on four specific counts:

Initial Mistakes: HR5-S55 did not define a "permanent" replacement of a striker. Employers could continue to hire as many scabs as they wanted and for as long as the strike lasted. There was nothing in the bills that prohibited any of the unfair labor practices that employers had used to defeat union organizing campaigns. It is true that the bill would allow strikers to return to work after the strike was lost, but only *unconditionally,* and on the employer's terms, which could be as bad or worse than before the strike began.

Faulty Judgment: It was politically important for the AFL-CIO to select issues that appealed to as broad a section of the population as possible. Unfortunately, the Workplace Fairness bill, despite its appealing name, was perceived not only as a "special interest" legislation but further limited to the concerns of actual and potential strikers.

Gross Misrepresentation: In order to sell HR5-S55 to union members, advocates of the bills, including high-ranking union leaders as well as President Clinton and Labor Secretary Robert Reich, sought to portray the legislation as strengthening unions in collective bargaining and rectifying the imbalance in power between labor and management. The bill contained no such inducements for labor. It dealt exclusively with the *aftermath* of a strike, permitting workers, if they so desired, to return to their jobs under whatever terms their employers insisted on.

A Weak Finish: Although the AFL-CIO knew that the Republicans would organize a filibuster in the Senate to defeat the striker replacement bill (as they had successfully done in 1991), they were able to muster only 57 of the 60 Senate votes needed for cloture, which would have broken the filibuster. (The two Democratic Senators from Arkansas, the President's home state, supported the filibuster.) The unions could have turned to a militant strategy, holding a continuous vigil of union members at the Capitol until the filibuster was broken. For whatever reason, Kirkland and the executive council decided not to confront the filibuster, and the bill died.

I reprinted the Blue Paper in the September issue of *The Labor Educator,* adding several thousand union leaders to the mailing list.

* * * * *

For months, AFL-CIO leaders had maintained an unbroken silence on my critical comments in *The Labor Educator* and my *Labor Talk* columns about their undemocratic policies and ineffective practices. Finally, they figured out a way to attack me.

On November 14, 1994, Michael Byrne, editor of the *AFL-CIO News,* posted a letter to me on AFL CIO LaborNET aimed at discrediting me with network subscribers. His purpose in writing the letter, he said, was "because there are lots of folks up here in labor cyberspace who do not know you, who may think you are a knowledgeable journalist because you do your periodic *LaborTalk.* "

However, it was in the concluding paragraph that Byrne pulled his below-the-belt punch: "Of course, you have your own newsletter, the so-called *Labor Educator,* which is free to assault Lane Kirkland, Tom Donahue and the 33 AFL-CIO vice presidents. . . . I have often wondered who you represent, and your comments in this section, 'Unpaid Russian Labor,' may provide a glimpse of who those patrons are. Your fees from the official trade unions of Russia, awash in the resources of the old Soviet system when the workers are going hungry, may help underwrite your newsletter and your trips to San Francisco, Miami, Chicago and Washington, where you try to be a thorn in the side of the AFL leadership. Whose interests are you serving there, exactly."

I confess I was startled to be accused of being a Soviet agent and the totally false charge that my newsletter was being financed by "Moscow gold." I had assumed that this kind of slanderous redbaiting had gone out of fashion with the collapse of the Soviet Union and the removal of Communist Party control.

In another posted reply to a union staffer who objected to his redbaiting, Byrne said: "There is an important issue in this debate. Is Harry Kelber allied with the people who are trying to suppress the real workers' movement in Russia? And if so, why, Harry?"

When I asked Byrne for an apology and threatened to sue him for libel, here was his sly response: "My words seem very clear to me. I was talking about the fees paid to you by the apparatchiks who run the official trade unions of Russia in return for the seminars you conducted in St. Petersburg and Moscow, which you mentioned back on Nov. 11. If you tell me how much they paid you, then perhaps I can gauge if in fact that money may have helped to underwrite your newsletter and your travel around the United States to campaign against the AFL-CIO. Then I'll have a better idea whether or not I owe you an apology. Was it a one-time fee? How much exactly?"

This was raw McCarthyism. Although the plain truth was that I took not a cent or a kopeck from the Russians, I was not going to be drawn into his "when did you stop beating your wife?" game. He was not my Grand Inquisitor. I checked with a lawyer friend who advised me I had an excellent chance of winning a libel suit, but it could be very costly and drag on for several years. I decided against suing. I did not want to be a cause célèbre and spend time and energy defending my reputation. Besides, I correctly sensed that Byrne's accusations were so absurd that few labor activists would take them seriously.

However, I decided to write to Kirkland, Donahue and the members of the executive council in response to Byrne's unwarranted attacks against me. I explained I did not get a penny in fees for the seminars I conducted for the union leaders of Russia and the Commonwealth States; that, in fact, I paid for my own roundtrip air fare each time I visited Russia. I had my air fare receipts and bank records to prove it. I stated:

"I went to Russia at the invitation of the General Confederation of Labor and the Moscow and St. Petersburg labor federations. They believed they could learn a great deal from the American labor experience in the struggle to protect the interests of their workers. I felt honored that they had selected me to conduct their periodic, week-long seminars on the overall theme, 'Democratic Unions in a Market Economy'."

Responding to Byrne's insinuations about the purpose and financing of *The Labor Educator,* I informed AFL-CIO leaders that I had founded the bi-monthly newsletter in 1991 because I felt there was a need for a critical, yet constructive voice within the labor movement. "I publish it at my own expense, except for the contributions I receive from trade unionists around the country who believe in what I am saying and doing," I said. "I can prove that I have never received any financial support for the newsletter from any Russian source."

In concluding, I urged that there be an end to Byrne's libelous attacks against me; otherwise, I would have to take "whatever actions I deem necessary to protect my name and reputation."

A short time later, I received a brief note from Kirkland on AFL-CIO stationery: "In re your letter of December 2, it is my view that you have every right to do whatever you are doing."

The redbaiting attacks ceased. Once again, AFL-CIO officials met my critical comments with their accustomed silence. Privately, several council members said that some of my proposals for revitalizing the federation made sense, but not one of them would utter a word publicly, either for or against any of my suggestions.

By June 1996, I had posted more than 100 *Labor Talk* columns, all of them now appearing on the Internet. Many of the columns have been reprinted by labor publications across the country.

40. The 1995 AFL-CIO Upheaval

The first visible cracks in the monolithic structure of the AFL-CIO, imposed from without and within, came at the February 20-23, 1995 meeting of the executive council in Bal Harbour, Florida, its favorite meeting place. At this session, there appeared 70 red-shirted men and women Road Warriors who had traveled 1,300 miles from Decatur, Illinois to plead for the council's support for their three hard-pressed local unions—Paperworkers, Auto Workers and Rubber Workers—locked in an uneven, long battle with three multinational corporations: the British-owned A. E. Staley Mfg. Co., a corn-processing company; Caterpillar, the world's leading manufacturer of earth-moving equipment, and Bridgestone/Firestone, the Japanese-owned tire company.

The presidents of the three Decatur locals had been informed in advance that I would be present at the Bal Harbour meeting and available to assist them. When they arrived at the hotel I met with them and we drafted a letter to the council describing the situation in Decatur and explaining why financial and organizational assistance was urgently needed. Copies of the letter were distributed to each council member in advance of their meeting.

The presence of these uninvited rank-and-filers created a sensation, as they roamed the lobby of the Sheraton, distributing literature and buttonholing anyone who would listen to their story. Council members were startled and then annoyed at this unheralded invasion of their privacy. The practice was to meet behind closed doors. Particularly irked and embarrassed were the international presidents of the three unions, who angrily informed the Decatur local officers that they and they alone would present the case for financial aid to the council.

The Road Warriors were visibly upset but determined to present their side of the story to the council. The more militant ones suggested they storm the council meeting and raise hell to get the attention of its members. They also wanted each of the 33 AFL-CIO vice presidents to sign an "honor roll" that pledged them to visit the Decatur "war zone." (In the 20 months since the Staley workers had been locked out, not one council officer had come to Decatur to pledge the support of their union, not even the heads of the three international unions.)

Fortunately, I was able to come up with a way to satisfy the rank-and-file group, thus avoiding the possibility of a nasty confrontation. At the press conference on February 20, when I asked President Kirkland whether he would allow representatives of the striking and locked-out workers of Decatur to address the council, he answered: "We will invite them to come into the council room this afternoon and we will address their concerns. There will be a resolution of support and as ever, the AFL-CIO stands ready to respond to any request that is made of us by the general officers of those unions."

Kirkland's invitation was greeted with jubilation. It was agreed that the three local union presidents—Dave Watts of the Paperworkers, Larry Solomon of the Auto Workers and Roger Gates of the Rubber Workers—would attend the council session, with Watts acting as the principal spokesperson. We had assumed that Watts would be permitted to address the council; I had drafted a five-minute speech for him which the three officers had approved.

It turned out that while the three local presidents were allowed to sit in on the council meeting, they were not given an opportunity to speak. Instead, their appeal was presented to the council by their international presidents. Surprisingly, all of the 33 council members, probably out of a feeling of guilt, signed the honor role that pledged them to visit Decatur. A few of the Warriors were disgruntled that Watts had not been allowed to speak, but they were appeased by the strong resolution of financial and organizational support that emerged from the council. As they got into their buses and vans, they were only dimly aware of the deepening crisis within the AFL-CIO's top leadership.

* * * * *

On January 28, 1995, only a month before the council meeting, the *Washington Post* ran a front page lead story headlined "Key Union Leaders Want Kirkland to Leave." The article went on to report that if Kirkland refused to step down on his own, union leaders were prepared to try to force him out and replace him with 66-year-old Secretary-Treasurer Thomas Donahue as an interim president until they could agree on a long-term replacement. The story, which mentioned no union leader by name, had been leaked to the newspaper's labor reporter, Frank Swoboda. It appeared that a number of presidents of the largest international unions had been meeting secretly and had concluded that Kirkland had to be retired; they were waiting for an opportune time to inform him of their decision.

The issue of Kirkland's future came to a boil on the second day of the Bal Harbour meeting, only a few hours after the council's action on the Decatur situation. In a tense, five-hour meeting, a coalition of 11 international union presidents, claiming 6.2 million members of the federation's 13.3 million. strongly urged Kirkland to retire. Kirkland angrily accused them of disloyalty, noting that they had never expressed their discontent with him to his face or in public, and that he had always been ready to consider any changes in the federation's programs and policies. The meeting ended in a frigid standoff.

On May 8, at a press conference at AFL-CIO headquarters in Washington, Kirkland announced he would run for reelection. Immediately after he finished his remarks, Gerald McEntee, president of the 1.1 million-member American Federation of State, County and Municipal Employees (AFSCME), rushed to the microphone before the reporters could leave and read a statement that his committee of union presidents would oppose Kirkland with its own slate of candidates. To complicate matters, Donahue declared he would retire as secretary-treasurer at the October convention rather than oppose Kirkland, his co-partner for the past 16 years.

For the first time in 40 years, the executive council was deeply split, with two factions starting to berate each other in public. In addition to McEntee, acting as spokesperson, the 11 dissident union presidents were led by John Sweeney of the Service Employees International Union and Ron Carey of the International Brotherhood of Teamsters, each with more than one million members. The challengers also included the presidents of three other large unions, the Laborers, Operating Engineers and Carpenters, from the traditionally conservative building trades.

Opposed to the insurgents were 21 council vice presidents, representing food workers, electricians, teachers, communications workers and other large unions, who constituted a 2 to 1 majority on the council. This "loyalist" group, while not enthusiastic about Kirkland's leadership, bitterly accused the dissidents of disrupting labor unity and creating a rift in the council that could have serious consequences for the union movement. Back-door meetings were held between members of the two groups in the hope of patching up their differences, but to no avail.

A month later, Kirkland developed second thoughts about continuing his bid for reelection. It had become clear to him that the committee of insurgent leaders, now expanded to 26 union presidents, had more than enough votes to defeat him at the convention. A new twist in the changing scenario surfaced when Donahue cancelled his retirement plan and declared he was now a candidate for the AFL-CIO presidency. His announcement created a real possibility of resolving the conflict within the council, since the dissident faction had originally wanted Donahue as president.

However, Donahue's change of heart had come too late. Having sharply attacked Kirkland's policies, the dissidents could not now support Donahue, who defended those policies and had helped to implement them. They went ahead with their plan to elect Sweeney as AFL-CIO president, with Richard Trumka, the miners' president, as secretary-treasurer and Linda Chavez-Thompson, an AFSCME vice president, as executive vice president, a new post that would have to be created at the convention by a constitutional amendment.

The battle was on.

* * * * *

I was excited about the cleavage within the AFL-CIO's top leadership. The upcoming election contest could provide opportunities for challenging both presidential candidates on a range of issues, including proposals for democratic reform. For the first time in the federation's history, there would be a fighting chance to elect progressive union leaders to the executive council and have an open debate at the convention.

In early June, I decided to run for one of the 33 AFL-CIO vice president seats on the council as I had done at the 1993 convention. I had hoped that my initiative would inspire at least several influential union leaders to become independent candidates. Unfortunately, those I contacted were unwilling to take the risk, because they felt their effort would be foredoomed to failure.

I chose a national conference of labor activists in the Decatur "war zone" on June 24th as an appropriate site and occasion to announce my candidacy. After I had presented my program for revitalizing the AFL-CIO and distributed a series of ten model resolutions that would form the basis of my campaign at the convention, the 170 conference delegates from 22 states unanimously endorsed me as their candidate. I also gained the endorsement of the Decatur presidents of the paper, auto and rubber workers unions with whom I had worked closely since our meeting at Bal Harbour. I had formed a bond of friendship with a great many of their striking and locked-out members during the three-day seminar I had conducted there in April on "Problems of the Labor Movement." Before I left Decatur, the presidents of two midwest central labor councils assured me that, as convention delegates, they would be glad to nominate me.

I carried on my campaign through *The Labor Educator* and my weekly *LaborTalk* postings on the AFL-CIO LaborNET. I sent letters to both Donahue and Sweeney about what I thought they might include in their campaign platform. In response to my critique of his basic campaign document, "Rebuilding the American Labor Movement," Sweeney wrote me on July 17th:

"Thank you very much for taking the time to give me your reaction to our platform for the AFL-CIO as well as your numerous good ideas for additions to that platform.

"A number of your suggestions are very interesting and I have passed along your memo to my staff to assist them in their work.

"Again, thanks for taking the time to write me and I hope we have a chance to talk about some of these ideas more in the near future."

* * * * *

The Donahue campaign received an important boost when Kirkland announced he would retire at the August council meeting instead of at the AFL-CIO convention in late October. This paved the way for Donahue's election as interim president by a 2 to 1 vote of the council. For secretary-treasurer, the council chose Barbara Easterling, a CWA secretary-treasurer and now the first woman to hold the AFL-CIO's No. 2 post.

The overall strategy of the two rival candidates was clear. Donahue, in the two and a half months before the convention, had to exploit the power of incumbency to convince a majority of the 700-odd convention delegates that he had the ability, energy, vision and leadership qualities to reinvigorate the labor movement. In practical terms, he had to cut deeply into Sweeney's support while gaining the backing of some 30 unions that had not yet committed themselves publicly to either candidate. Sweeney had to persuade the nation's union members that he represented a new, dynamic movement which would fight aggressively for the needs of working people. He could point to the fact that since 1980, when he became SEIU president, his union membership had nearly doubled from 650,000 to 1.1 million, while in the same period, overall AFL-CIO membership had declined from 27 percent of the work force to 14 percent. He could also boast that his executive board consisted of one-third women and people of color and that his 450-member organizing staff had achieved extraordinary victories by using militant, unorthodox methods.

Both Donahue and Sweeney agreed on four issues that were given top priority in their respective campaigns: well-financed union organizing drives, more aggressive political activity, a greater diversity in leadership positions and an upgraded AFL-CIO communications system. Their differences were reflected in their styles of leadership. Donahue habitually relied on consensus, as Kirkland had done. He tended to be cautious about undertaking new initiatives. As the federation's secretary-treasurer for 16 years, he had been primarily an in-house leader who helped to develop the AFL-CIO Organizing Institute and other federation agencies. He was noted for promoting the concept of labor-management partnerships as a model for the workplace of the future.

Sweeney did not believe in waiting for consensus if an initiative made sense and was urgently needed. The "Jobs with Justice" campaign, in which his union and a few others had been actively involved, was never endorsed by the executive council, nor was his "Justice for Janitors" organizing drive, which brought 35,000 low-paid workers into his union.

What made this election difficult for both candidates was that they had been good friends and cooperative colleagues over a 35-year period. There was a remarkable similarity in their backgrounds. They were both Irish Catholics and New Yorkers; they were born into workingclass families and were now in their sixties. They each got their start to national labor prominence from the same union: Building Service Employees Local 32B-32J in New York City. Donahue went on to become an executive assistant to then AFL-CIO President George Meany in 1973. Six years later, he was named as the federation's secretary-treasurer. Sweeney, in 1976, became president of Local 32B-32J, the largest local in the Service Employees International Union, which became the springboard for his election as SEIU president in 1980. Since then, he had been reelected to three successive four-year terms.

Both candidates and their running mates campaigned vigorously, barnstorming across the country, speaking at strike rallies, union conventions and local meetings in a frantic, exhausting schedule. Nevertheless, on the eve of the convention, nothing much had changed in their relative delegate support. Donahue had been able to induce only the Carpenters to switch to his side, still leaving Sweeney with a majority of convention votes. At the same time, Sweeney failed to develop a bandwagon drive from among Donahue's supporters, who held firm.

Donahue's last chance of rallying a delegate majority depended on how well he would fare in his two-hour convention debate with Sweeney. While he appeared to have won the debate, it was hardly by a knockout. Sweeney made a dignified presentation of his views and committed no blunders that Donahue could capitalize on, More important, Sweeney's orange-shirted supporters, including the scores of delegates from central labor councils attending an AFL-CIO convention for the first time, raucously cheered their candidate at every opportunity. On the applause meter, they easily outclassed the Donahue rooters.

A test of voting strength between the two candidates was decided early in the convention on a procedural issue. It came on a motion by the Sweeney forces to postpone, until after the election on Wednesday, a vote on a crucial constitutional issue—the creation of a new position of executive vice president. It was a smart tactical move by Sweeney, because if he had lost the vote on this highly controversial issue, it would have given strong momentum to Donahue's candidacy.

The motion to delay the vote on the constitutional amendment was approved on a roll-call vote—7,245,000 from 33 unions in favor of postponement and 5,756,038 from 45 unions opposed. That initial showdown was a grievous blow to Donahue's chances of winning. It now seemed evident that Sweeney's voting strength would remain solid right through the election.

* * * * *

It sounds bizarre, but until about an hour or so before the start of the nominating session, I was the only declared candidate for AFL-CIO vice president. For the months during the hot race for the presidency, neither the Sweeney nor Donahue camps had breathed a word about the executive council elections. They were in a quandary about how to avoid an open contest in which incumbents from major international unions would be pitted against each other and also have to face the unusual prospect of challengers.

But I, too, had problems. From the outset, behind-the-scenes efforts were made to disqualify me to avoid an unprecedented council election. As I had anticipated, I had difficulty in finding a delegate to nominate me. The two midwest labor council presidents who had promised to do so begged off. They had been told that their cooperative relationship with the head of their state federation would be jeopardized if they nominated me. One of them told me,"I feel lousy about doing this to you, Harry, but I have to do right by my members." All of the progressive delegates I approached declined on the grounds that they couldn't afford to take that risk, especially since I had no chance of winning. If I couldn't find one delegate with the guts to nominate me, my campaign was embarrassingly finished.

Luckily, I learned that Tom Deary, an international representative for the Electronic Workers, planned to attend the convention as a delegate from the Nashua, New Hampshire Labor Council. Tom and I had become good friends during our joint activity in behalf of the Staley and Caterpillar workers in Decatur. He was glad to nominate me and so informed AFL-CIO headquarters. I knew I could count on Tom to honor his promise.

Finding a delegate to second my nomination proved more difficult. I finally met an Ohio delegate who said he would be happy to accept the assignment. (He told me how much he enjoyed reading *The Labor Educator.*) I felt relieved; my anxieties were over. So I thought.

* * * * *

On the first day of the convention, 16 international union presidents, all of them Donahue supporters, came up with a proposal for voiding the necessity of having an election for executive council: a constitutional amendment to expand the council to include the presidents of all 78 affiliated international unions.

In one of the campaign pieces I mailed out to all delegates, I warned against this "power grab" by the same group that had controlled the council during the Kirkland era. Among its many faults, I noted, it would create a self-perpetuating council whose members would not be accountable to the rank-and-file for their actions. It would also make a mockery of the pledges to provide more council seats to women and people of color.

The issue aroused a stormy debate on the convention floor with each side calling on its heavy hitters to argue its case. It quickly became evident that the Sweeney forces had decided to oppose the amendment, even though the idea was attractive to some supporters who saw it as a way to solve the problem of council elections. After two days of debate, the roll call showed that the amendment had been handily defeated: 7,315,888 votes against to 5,686,521 in favor,

By winning two roll-call votes in the first two days of the convention, Sweeney was virtually assured he would win the presidency on the third day, when elections were scheduled. But what about the balloting for executive council?

That question was answered shortly before the start of nominations when representatives of the Sweeney and Donahue factions informed the delegates that they had agreed on a "unity" slate that would expand the number of council vice presidents from 33 to 51. The proposed new council would include 15 women and people of color, compared with only six in the outgoing council. The power brokers who had designed the unity slate would have preferred to have the convention accept their selections by acclamation, but since I was an independent candidate, there was no way to avoid an actual election with a printed ballot.

A last-minute effort to quash my candidacy was made by a prominent leader of the Sweeney faction. Moments before the nominations were to begin, the delegate who had promised to be my seconder came running toward me and, in an anguished voice, said he coudn't go through with it; his international union president had warned him not to do so.

Angered as well as frustrated, I wrote a note and had a sergeant-at-arms deliver it to that union president, informing him I would take steps to expose his outrageous behavior on the convention floor unless he permitted his subordinate to second my nomination. The note had its desired effect. In a matter of seconds, he rushed toward me, put his arm around my shoulder and said, "All right, Harry, I'll see that he does it." Tom Deary's nominating speech in my behalf and a mumbled seconding statement by my erstwhile ally went off without a hitch.

The printed ballot which AFL-CIO staffers hurriedly designed was an outrageous, crude way to discourage delegates from voting for me. To vote for the entire Unity ticket, all that was needed was a check mark at the upper left-hand side of the ballot. Delegates were forbidden to vote for some, but not all, candidates on the Unity slate. If they did, their ballot was voided.

The ballot was patently ridiculous as well as undemocratic in the way my candidacy was presented. My name appeared on the upper right, under which were listed the 51 names on the Unity slate. Delegates were not permitted to vote for me alone. If they did, their ballot would be declared void. The only way they could vote for me was if they also placed check marks alongside 50 of the 51 names on the Unity ticket, whether or not they approved of these candidates. If they checkmarked fewer than 50, their ballots would be cast aside as invalid.

Denied the right to scrutinize the counting of the ballots, I managed to see a group of four ballots thst were voided, even though the delegates had voted for me, because they had checked off an incorrect number of the required 50 names or none at all. Undoubtedly, many more were declared invalid for the same reason.

Despite these mickey-mouse obstacles, delegates from 45 AFL-CIO central labor councils from 24 states (about 10 percent of the total) voted for me. My votes came not only from labor councils in populated states like California, New York, Texas and Pennsylvania, but also from Alaska, Iowa, North Dakota, Alabama, Kentucky and Georgia.

Although I had known in advance that, given the federation's rigged voting system, I had not a hoot-in-hell chance of being elected, I had finally forced the AFL-CIO to hold an election for executive council for the first time in 30 years. And even more important, my long-time campaign to have the executive council enlarged to include more women and minorities had finally been realized.

41. Ambitious Plans Face Obstacles

Clearly, even with John Sweeney's new, forward-looking, aggressive leadership of the AFL-CIO, there was still a need for critics like me. On some issues, his "New Voice for American Workers" had laryngitis. The tactical problem for me was how to give strong support to the federation's worthwhile initiatives while reserving the right to criticize what I considered its serious shortcomings. Just as it was during the Kirkland era, any expressed dissent from the policies and actions of the new federation leaders would be considered a disruptive attack on the labor movement itself. At the very least, it was felt, the team of Sweeney, Trumka and Chavez-Thompson was entitled to a proper "honeymoon," while they undertook the difficult task of moving organized labor in the "right direction."

Indeed, the trio deserved a great deal of credit for the various programs they initiated to breathe life into what had become a near-moribund labor movement. They spent a great part of their post-election schedule on the road, talking with local union officers and members about their problems and offering frequent assistance as well as advice. In their "America Needs a Raise!" campaign, they began a tour of 29 cities where, at "town meetings," they exchanged views with unionists on how to deal with the injustices that working people were enduring. For thousands of union members, it was the first time they had ever seen and heard a national AFL-CIO leader face to face.

It was in the political arena that the federation created a sensation when on March 25, 1996 at a special one-day convention in Washington, D.C., it launched its campaign to reelect the Clinton-Gore ticket and reclaim Congress by defeating its GOP right-wing, anti-labor legislators. National Republican leaders were both alarmed and angry at the size and vigor of labor's political effort. With an AFL-CIO war chest of $35 million, brigades of college student volunteers for a "union summer" and an army of angry union members, there would be no shortage of people to staff phone banks. ring doorbells and handle all the necessary chores to get out a big labor vote. The federation's political operatives also had an aggressive battle plan that targeted 75 congressional districts where Republican incumbents had won their seats in 1994 by slender margins. For the first time in a long while, organized labor was emerging as a potent political force that the candidates of both major parties had to reckon with.

I was pleased that the Sweeney leadership was finally putting into practice some of the structural changes I had been recommending for the past five years in *The Labor Educator* and other forums, as well as in my campaign for vice president at the1993 and 1995 conventions. I had noted that ever since 1886, when the American Federation of Labor was formed, the affiliated state federations and central labor councils had been treated like stepchildren. In all that time, they had never held even one seat on the executive council. At federation conventions, they were limited to one vote apiece, while even small international unions had thousands of votes. They were denied membership on important committees and were little more than spectators at conventions. The international unions had maintained a self-perpetuating monopoly on the decision-making council and they were determined to keep it that way.

To me and other activists, it was obvious that the AFL-CIO's undemocratic structure was a major reason for its continuing decline. The state and city affiliates were on the frontlines, supplying the troops for all of labor's economic and political battles, and yet they had no voice in determining AFL-CIO policies and actions. It was imperative that they and their leaders be given a significant role in decision-making, both at the council level and at conventions.

Shortly after their election, Sweeney and his colleagues made a special effort to court the state and city labor affiliates, whose support they would have to depend on for their ambitious organizing and political campaigns. A 20-member State and Central Labor Council Advisory Committee was formed to make policy recommendations to federation leaders. Four state federation officers, elected at regional conferences, were added to the AFL CIO's General Board, heretofore limited to international union presidents. An unprecedented national conference of local unions was scheduled for the summer of 1996, where four officers were to be elected to serve on the federation's advisory committee. Through these and other structural innovations, Sweeney hoped to reach out to the rank-and-file and involve them in labor's battles.

I was also gratified that AFL-CIO leaders had followed through on my suggestion about publishing a booklet containing photographs and a short biography of each of the 51 members of the executive council. Until then, very few unionists knew what council members looked like, what union they belonged to, what their background was and what they stood for. This was at least a modest beginning. I intended to press for an end to the executive council's absurd practice of withholding its minutes from the membership for 30 years after each of its quarterly meetings. Union members had a right to know what was going on at those closed-door meetings.

I had urged that council members become public personalities by giving press interviews and getting invited as guests on radio and TV talk shows and other forums where they could promote labor's policies. But while Sweeney, Trumka and Chavez-Thompson managed to attract substantial media attention, most council members, for whatever reasons, preferred to stay out of the limelight.

I also noted that the Sweeney team had taken two major steps to improve its communications system. Not long after taking office, it began publishing *Work in Progress,* a weekly roundup of labor news on the AFL-CIO LaborNET, which contained short items detailing the activities of the federation and its affiliated unions. Through the electronic media, the national leadership can now get in touch, in a matter of seconds, with any union group or labor activist who has a computer and a modem. Indeed, an increasing number of unions are using the Internet, with WEB pages of their own, to communicate with their members. I hope that at some point, the AFL-CIO will establish a special channel through which subordinate union officers and rank-and-filers can express their views to the leadership in Washington and receive appropriate responses.

For years, I have been criticizing the *AFL-CIO News,* the federation's bi-weekly official newspaper, for a variety of reasons; it was essentially a house organ for the Kirkland leadership. Its dull and usually overwritten stories were of interest primarily to union officials, who comprised its main readership of approximately 60,000, a large number of whom received free copies. It scrupulously avoided controversy or unfavorable news, never mentioning any subject, group or individual who might displease the top leaders. Its photos were predictably dull: obligatory shots of union officers gathered around a conference table or addressing a strike rally, or group pictures of demonstrations or picketlines. It was an utterly humorless publication, rarely using satirical or wise-cracking comments to make a point. Not only was there no letters column, but at no time that I can remember was there any mention of a rank-and-file group or individual who was critical of the national AFL-CIO or an international union.

I was especially gratified that the federation had decided to discontinue the *AFL-CIO News* and planned to publish a mass-circulation monthly magazine, whose first issue is scheduled for September 1996. If the magazine can avoid the heavy-handed control by top federation officials and turn out a lively, well-edited publication whose stories, features, photos and cartoons are of interest to the average union member, I have no doubt that it can attain a circulation of 250,000 and possibly more.

The new magazine can build reader loyalty by running in-depth analysis of problems that are troubling working people or where there is division or unclarity on such issues as labor-management cooperation, organizing and affirmative action. Workers want to know what's behind the economic, political and social developments they hear about on television or read in their daily newspapers. And it ought to allow space for letters from readers. A board of editors and union representatives should select those letters that would interest readers, whether or not they deal with controversial topics or are critical of AFL-CIO leaders and their policies.

The AFL-CIO should consider establishing its own cable TV channel or at least broadcast a weekly labor program that is both informative and entertaining, as I and other labor activists have been advocating.

While the AFL-CIO leadership conducted a full-scale publicity campaign about its domestic policies, it maintained a public silence about its international activities. During his election campaign, Sweeney had made almost no mention of the federation's international affairs department and its four regional institutes, which had been tightly controlled by Lane Kirkland during his 16-year tenure as AFL-CIO president. Sweeney emphasized the importance of becoming more involved internationally "because so many of our American employers are corporations that are controlled abroad." He recommended the creation of a Transnational Corporate Monitoring Project "which would cooordinate and assist the efforts of the national union affiliates, their trade secretariats, and other groups in their fight to protect American workers."

There was no indication what the relationship would be between Sweeney's proposed transnational agency and the international affairs department which, according to rumors, was to be reorganized and its four institutes combined into one.

Under Kirkland, the AFL CIO's institutes operated in some 85 countries around the world, with multi-million dollar grants from U.S. government agencies as well as with funds from the federation's treasury. They were guided by Cold War principles, combatting native radical unions in Europe, Latin America, Asia and Africa, even to the point of setting up and financing competitive unions, as they did in El Salvador and Nicaragua. The institutes were especially active in Eastern Europe and the Soviet Union, before and after Communism's collapse. Kirkland set up dual unions in Russia and some of the Commonwealth States and went so far as to forbid American union leaders to have any contact with their Russian counterparts.

It was not clear whether Sweeney intended to change AFL-CIO's attitude toward the Russian unions, although a hopeful sign was the closing of the federation's Moscow office from which it directed much of its attacks on the officially-recognized unions.

At the February 1996 meeting of the executive council in Bal Harbour, I approached secretary-treasurer Richard Trumka to suggest that if he, Sweeney and other national union officers were interested, an informal meeting could be arranged with top union leaders of Russia and the Commonwealth States, either in Moscow or Washington, with no preconditions or publicity. I picked Trumka because he, as president of the United Mine Workers, had been in contact with Russia's independent mine unions. His reaction was neither encouraging nor hostile. I had the impression he would consult with Sweeney and others about the advisability of such a meeting. Late in March, I invited him to meet 33 of the most influential union leaders of Russia and the labor federation presidents of 10 Commonwealth States in New York City, where they would be participating in a four-day seminar I was conducting on April 8-11. Unfortunately, Trumka failed to respond to the invitation.

With U.S. corporations looking for lucrative investments and sources of cheap labor in Russia and the former Soviet republics, it is in the interests of American workers for the AFL-CIO to establish cooperative ties with the struggling unions in those countries. I am hopeful there will be a breakthrough on this issue in the not too distant future.

* * * * *

One of the main reasons why Sweeney was elected as AFL-CIO president was the widely-held belief that, on the basis of his record and program, he could reverse the continuing decline in union membership. In his campaign literature, he had said:

"The most critical challenge facing unions today is organizing. There is much we can do to strengthen us for today's battles—but without a massive increase in union membership, we cannot prevail in the long run. And while we must also rebuild our political efforts, we cannot wait for a change in the political climate to provide us with the opportunities to grow. We must first organize despite the law if we are ever to organize with the law."

The task of rebuilding the AFL-CIO membership was, to say the least, a formidable one. Sweeney laid out the difficulties in starkest terms: "In order to simply stop the decline of the labor movement, we need to gain more than a quarter of a million members every year—yet until recently, the labor movement has been losing about 100,000 members every year. . . . If we are to regain our position of strength, representing one worker in three, then we must add a million members a year for the next two decades."

Tooling up for a massive organizing effort to achieve these awesome membership goals, the AFL-CIO budgeted $20 million—one-third of its annual income—for organizing; it added $2.5 million to the AFL-CIO Organizing Institute; it pledged to train 1,000 new, full-time organizers, with an emphasis on women, minorities and young workers; it sought to create a contingent of seasoned organizers from various unions who could be deployed into critical strategic campaigns; it began to shape up plans for a major organizing drive in the South and Sun Belt.

While these and other structural changes were important in focusing unions and their leaders on the imperative of organizing, there were a number of critical problems that had to be surmounted in order to achieve significant membership gains. For one, the labor federation had to come up with an electrifying message or action that would generate an enthusiastic response among the nation's working population, both union and non-union. It had been done before, nearly 60 years ago, when the Committee for Industrial Organizations (CIO) had inspired millions of semi-skilled and unskilled workers to join unions that would provide them with higher wages, guaranteed benefits and, not least of all, personal dignity. (It should be added that all of this was accomplished during the New Deal, when the government was friendly to organized labor.)

How could the AFL-CIO establish a convincing image as "champion of the people." when far too many workers, rightly or unfairly, had a low opinion of unions and their leaders? Unless this problem was solved, the organizing drive, no matter how well-financed, would make only minimal gains.

Back on January 3, 1994, I had sent a memorandum to then AFL-CIO President Kirkland and all 33 members of the executive council proposing an organizing campaign that I said would (1) expand grass-roots support for the federation; (2) increase its moral and political influence, and (3) improve the climate for union organizing.

My plan called for organizing the multi-million army of unemployed and underemployed in a national campaign for jobs. I pointed out that this was an enormous constituency of blue-collar and white-collar workers from virtually every industry and occupation and included huge numbers of women, minorities and young workers. It appeared self-evident that these politically powerless men and women would welcome the efforts of the AFL-CIO to speak out in their behalf. I offered reasons why a crusade to organize the unemployed "was far easier, less costly, requires fewer resources and can be far more successful than organizing a non-union establishment." Hundreds of thousands of jobless people could be readily reached at the unemplement insurance offices, to which they had to apply for their benefit checks. A national list of the addresses and phone numbers of these offices was readily available.

I noted that this would be a low-budget campaign: only a small staff was needed to cover each insurance office, accessible to organizers during the normal workday. Most important, unions would not have to contend with resourceful, labor-hating employers operating on their own turf. I said that even when managers of insurance offices appeared hostile, they could be persuaded that it was in their interest to deal with complaints in an orderly manner through an organization representing their jobless clients. (In a pilot project I had undertaken a couple of years before at a large Brooklyn, N.Y. unemployment insurance center, I had encountered little difficulty in establishing a representative committee of applicants with whom the office manager agreed to meet regularly on their grievances.)

I predicted that a successful grass-roots effort in behalf of the unemployed would create a better climate for union organizing. It would become easier for organizers to win recruits in non-union companies, especially among workers who had been formerly unemployed and remembered that unions had been their friends in time of need. And it would be more difficult for labor-hating employers to bad-mouth unions.

Not one of the council members bothered to reply, nor did they offer any of their own proposals to persuade the nation's workers that they were their champions. (It should be noted that Sweeney and the ten other dissident international union presidents who worked to unseat Kirkland for his uninspiring leadership were then also council members.)

* * * * *

While hundreds of thousands of workers were being "downsized"—one of the many euphemisms for being arbitrarily fired or prematurely "retired"—the

AFL-CIO did nothing to challenge the practice except to bemoan it. It could have tried to intervene in defense of these dismissed workers, whether or not they belonged to unions, by demanding that the companies justify these permanent job cuts, consider measures to reduce their number through attrition, work-sharing and early retirements, and provide ample severance pay and interim or portable medical coverage. The unions also could have demanded negotiations to protect a company's remaining employees against speedup and abusive treatment. Such bold actions would have made unions relevant, not only to downsized workers but also to those still employed who feared they might be next in line to lose their jobs.

I had singled out the merger of the Chase and Chemical banks as a suitable target to test labor's challenge to the corporate downsizing epidemic after the two banks had announced they planned to terminate 12,000 employees. The unions could exert tremendous leverage, I said, because they were in a position to transfer their accounts to other banks and urge their members to do the same if Chase-Chemical managers refused to negotiate with them. Unfortunately, although my suggestion received a favorable response from a cross-section of the labor movement, the AFL-CIO Organizing Department let the opportunity slip by, while the banks went through with their planned job cuts unchallenged.

* * * * *

So what was the born-again AFL-CIO going to do about its proclaimed focus on organizing? One thing was obvious: the traditional method of organizing shop by shop would not get the unions off the treadmill where they were losing more members than they were winning. A union could spend two years or more trying to organize a company of 500 to 1,000 workers, and even if it won a labor board election (unions had about a 50 percent win record), that victory, in half the cases, could become meaningless in terms of negotiating a first contract, becaue many employers found various ways to avoid bargaining in good faith.

What AFL-CIO brain-trusters were concentrating on was strategic organizing of a substantial sector or region of an industry, preferably one that was not the subject of global competition. The construction industry, where wages of skilled craft workers were well above those in service industries, was a readily identifiable organizing target. In the late 1940s, better than 85 percent of the industry's workers belonged to various craft unions. Over the years, the aggregate membership of construction unions continued to shrink, until by 1996 it accounted for little more than 20 percent of the industry's employed work force. Even when building contractors agreed to hire union members at one worksite, they often employed non-union people at another worksite, a process known in the trade's crude sexist lingo as "double breasting," which the unions had failed to eradicate.

The nation's hotel chains were another potential, multi-union organizing target. There were scores of them under non-union management. In many cities, it was difficult to find a unionized hotel to house delegates and provide facilities for a conference or convention. The health care field, with dramatic changes taking place in the nation's hospitals, nursing homes, pharmaceutical companies, physician and nursing services, provides a major battlefield. Unions are now trying to hold on to their gains while expanding their campaign for new members. By building community coalitions with consumer and other interest groups, unions could enhance their organizing and bargaining power in relation to customer-dependent employers. Such coalitions could add muscle to union organizing efforts among masses of workers in department stores, supermarkets, fast-food chains, banks, public utilities and other service industries.

* * * * *

One of the AFL-CIO's spectacular initiatives has been its 1996 "Union Summer" program to recruit and train 1,000 college students and young workers into an exuberant, if temporary, organizing force in support of various union campaigns. As explained by President Sweeney, the program had a two-fold mission: "to harness the energy of young Americans of conscience for the cause of working people and to build into the next generation an understanding that the labor movement is at the heart of the struggle for social justice."

The young trainees, primarily women and people of color, were to receive a weekly stipend of $210 for three weeks of activity, with affiliated unions and state and local central bodies asked to provide their lodging, food and transportation. The project would run from late May until Labor Day.

"Union Summer" was an excellent way to acquaint idealistic college students with a challenging labor activity which might provide them with an exciting, uplifting experience akin to the Freedom Summer voting rights campaign of the 1960s. There was general agreement that with a minimum amount of training, the "three-weekers" could perform useful roles in the election campaign by staffing phone banks, talking to voters, participating in rallies and handling other political chores. And they would also have an opportunity to walk picket lines, make organizing house-calls and meet union leaders and members. But with two or three days of training, they could not possibly gain the knowledge to deal with sophisticated, anti-union employers. Unfortunately, they'd be back on their college campuses or workplaces by Labor Day, just when the Presidential and Congressional election campaigns would begin to heat up.

But what about the 1,000 full-time union organizers who, Sweeney had promised, would be trained within two years as shock troops in future AFL-CIO campaigns? Where would they come from, what credentials would they need as applicants, and what kind of training would they receive to equip them to challenge the bastions of non-union corporate power? I found it nearly impossible to gain specific details about the training of these organizers. The only publicized information dealt with top-level structure: recruiting and training would be handled by the AFL-CIO Organizing Institute with overall responsibility vested in a newly-established Organizing Department. A committee representing the executive council would also be involved in a policy-making and oversight role.

Without legions of highly-trained organizers, the AFL-CIO could not conceivably come close to achieving a record of victories that would translate into impressive gains in membership. But who would train these wannabe organizers? And what would the training consist of? Would it be of sufficient quality to match the knowledge and skills of professional union-busters, many of whom boasted they had a near-perfect record in defeating organizing drives?

At national AFL-CIO headquarters, there was a prevailing reluctance to talk about training and evaluating organizers. For some, it appeared to be a minor problem that would be handled effectively with the existing staff and resources. For others, it was much too sensitive a subject to be aired lest it reveal important data to anti-union employers. Not surprisingly, requests for information about the training program received vague answers or none at all.

I believe AFL-CIO leaders grossly underestimated what it would take to provide rigorous, professional-level training to 1,000 applicants in accord with a system of quality control. (Poorly equipped organizers can screw up a major campaign through ignorance or miscalculation.) The choice of a staff of instructors can be critical. Good organizers are not necessarily good instructors. Ideally, an instructor should have a wealth of knowledge and experience about organizing and the ability to convey this information to students in a clear, stimulating manner. Where would the Organizing Institute get a supply of such teachers sufficient to train 1,000 recruits? Equally important, a training program of this scope required a systematic, regularly up-dated instruction manual. The 3-day "Training Guide for Teaching Fellows," developed by the Organizing Institute for training instructors who would teach trainees, was admittedly superficial. If there was a more advanced manual of instruction, it was not available to labor educators like me and other interested union activists.

On March 8, 1996, I wrote to Sweeney and the 51 members of the executive council, offering some suggestions that I thought would be helpful for training and evaluating union organizers. I explained that my suggestions were based on my long experience as a labor educator and involvement in union organizing campaigns. I wrote:

"As director of the Trade Union Leadership Institute of the New York City Central Labor Council (1985-90), I designed, wrote textual material and was the principal instructor for a 15-week course on 'The Role of the Union Organizer.' Among its innovative features was a series of some 40 problems that a newly-trained organizer might encounter, from the day he or she is assigned to a targeted compamy to the end of the organizing campaign, win or lose.

"All sessions were videotaped, so that each student had to perform before the camera on a particular problem (say, addressing a group of non-union workers), and the class would critique his/her performance in the instant replay. By the end of the course, it was fairly easy to rank the capability of each student. The several classes we held were attended by labor leaders and activists from some 40 unions."

I suggested my instruction manual could be updated to take current circumstances into account. I noted that my organizing experience dated back to the 1930s when as a young editor of two weekly New York labor papers *(Building Trades Union Press* and *Trade Union Record)* and an adviser to CIO Regional Director Allan Haywood (a vice president of the United Mine Workers), I was a front-line observer and active participant in the greatest and most successful organizing campaign in labor history. I offered to volunteer as an instructor to train and evaluate organizers, and I hoped the AFL-CIO would accept my services.

Several weeks later, on April 26, I received the following reply from Sweeney:

"Thank you for your kind words and your interest in the AFL-CIO's developing organizing and political programs.

"As they are to all of us who have been privileged to serve the trade union movement in New York, your distinguished credentials as a labor educator and dedicated trade unionist are well known to me. I sincerely appreciate your favorable view of what the AFL-CIO and its affiliates are determined to do to revitalize the labor movement.

"Any project of this magnitude requires many stages of planning that lead to implementation. At the present time, we have implemented several early phases of our long-term plans for organizing activities. We have established a new AFL-CIO Department of Organizing, and we are assigning new duties to the Organizing Institute. At the present time, we are discussing with our affiliates our future plans for expanding training for organizers. As we develop these plans, we will be assessing our future needs for staff and consultants for education and training.

"Again, I appreciate your willingness to offer your talents and services to the AFL-CIO."

While I was pleased by Sweeney's compliments, I was also troubled by the sluggish development of the training program. The information about the AFL-CIO's organizing institute was old hat; it had been announced at the federation's convention in October 1995. And now, six months later, the AFL-CIO was still in the discussion stage with its affiliates about expanding its training program! At that tempo, how could 1,000 organizers be trained in two years?

Although I had not been offered a role as an instructor or consultant, I remained hopeful that I and other veteran educators would, at some point, be given an opportunity to participate in the training program.

* * * * *

Hard-pressed union officials, fighting defensively on a wide range of fronts, have had neither the time nor the inclination to formulate a long-term agenda for the labor movement. They operated on a day-to-day basis, as they always had, with no realistic idea of how they could shape the future to enable working families to achieve the "American Dream." Indeed, there was the grim possibility that the economic and political problems that now plagued them might worsen as they entered the 21st century. When asked about labor's future goals, union leaders could resort to quoting Samuel Gompers, the first AFL president. In an 1893 speech in Chicago, Gompers said:

"What does labor want? It wants the earth and the fullness thereof. There is nothing too beautiful, too lofty, too ennobling unless it is within the scope and comprehension of labor's aspirations and wants.

"We want more schoolhouses and less jails; more books and less arsenals; more learning and less vice, more constant work and less crime, more leisure and less greed, more justice and less revenge, in fact, more of the opportunities to cultivate our better natures and make childhood more joyful, womanhood more beautiful and manhood more noble."

It was most unlikely that organized labor could mount an inspirational crusade that might come even close to achieving Gompers' old-fashioned rhetorical goals. With all the labor-saving advances in technology, people were working longer and harder and under greater stress than they used to. Women were now 40 percent of the labor force and a majority of low-paid, part-time and temporary workers, most of them without the benefits of union membership. Unions were not calling for a six-hour workday to provide job opportunities for the unemployed; in fact, some of them were accepting a 12-hour workday with mandatory overtime in their contracts.

* * * * *

One question did get the attention of those unionists who dared to envision what it would be like to have a job in the workplace of the future. In a report on "The New American Workplace," the AFL-CIO Committee on the Evolution of Work presented a model for labor-management partnerships in which jobs, work processes and decision-making would be restructured to provide higher levels of individual worker participation in the workplace. The 38-page report, issued in February, 1994, proposed dramatic changes in the workplace, where management traditionally exercised authoritarian control over its employees. Workers would be encouraged to use their skills, training and ingenuity on the job; the foreman would be replaced by a team leader whose role was to lead, not dictate; workers, through their unions, would be given a decision-making role at all levels of the enterprise, and the rewards from the new system would be shared equitably through negotiations. The report concluded that "the time had come for labor and management to surmount past enmities and to forge the kind of partnerships which can generate more productive, humane and democratic systems of work organization."

So enthusiastic were high-ranking union leaders with their model that they called on affiliated unions to "take the initiative in stimulating, sustaining and institutionalizing a new system of work organization based upon full and equal labor-management partnerships." The report proposed a series of conferences and seminars to enable unions to become "more and more active in pushing our vision of a new model of work organization."

The effort to popularize the "equal partnership" concept never got off the ground. Critics like me quickly attacked the report as wishful thinking. It obviously did not square with what was happening in the real world where the nation's giant corporations were aggressively working to create a "union-free environment." Why would they accept unions as partners to share in management decisions, especially now when organized labor was in a state of continuing decline? Observing the indifferent and even hostile reaction to its report, the AFL-CIO abandoned its plan to organize regional union meetings to build sentiment for the partnership model.

But the idea of labor-management cooperation could not easily be dismissed. For years, there had been an ongoing, unresolved debate within the labor movement about the attitude unions should take toward the nation's corporations. Some unions, like the United Auto Workers and the Communications Workers, favored the development of collaborative relations with employers in their industries. They participated in a variety of company-sponsored programs with names like "quality of worklife," "employee involvement," "labor-management workteams," and "quality circles," all of them designed to "empower" employees so they could use their creative skills to increase productivity, quality control and other company objectives.

The argument of union leaders who favored this approach was that if they helped their companies to prosper, union members would have a better chance to gain wage increases and improved benefits. Realistically, this was their only sensible option, they said, adding: "Since we can't lick 'em, we better join 'em." Confrontational tactics designed to disrupt a company's operations were self-defeating, they insisted: there was no point in trying to kill the goose that was laying the golden eggs. Unions could not possibly match the wealth, power and influence of the nation's employers; if they were to survive and grow, they had to find ways to develop a working relationship with management. Examples could be cited where labor and management were working harmoniously for their mutual benefit.

On the other hand, there was strong evidence that employers were exploiting labor-management programs to increase productivity, diminish the role of unions and actually tighten their control of the workplace. When I had visited Decatur, I saw first-hand the effect of the unstinting cooperation that corn processing, auto, and tire workers had given to their respective multinational companies. In each case, management used their worker-participation programs to boost production, discharge militant employees, train eventual scabs and eliminate some of the protective features of their union contracts. Ultimately, after long and bitter struggles, the workers at Staley, Caterpillar and Bridgestone/ Firestone had to go back to their jobs, now fewer in number, under harsh, humiliating conditions.

I had no principled objection to the idea of a labor-management partnership, provided it was based on equality and was carefully defined. I felt that the only way that unions could achieve the status of respected partners was if they made impressive gains in membership and demonstrated their economic and political strength—the very results that corporate managers were determined to prevent. In the meantime, unions had to be on the alert to see that their authority was not undermined through these labor-management programs, which might serve as a prelude for leaving their members vulnerable to company abuse.

* * * * *

The corporate world has its own agenda for the future and it does not include a desire for a partnership with unions. The motivating force driving multinational corporations is the ever-present pressure to compete successfully against rivals for a greater share of the global market, and one of the obvious ways they can do that is to lower their production and marketing costs and develop more job-displacing technologies

Corporate apologists find it easy to justify the "downsizing" frenzy of the past few years. They say that as painful as these massive job cuts have been to working people, the situation could have become considerably worse if American companies had lost their market share in countries around the world. And they have been warning the nation's workers that they've got to work harder and longer for less pay and fewer benefits, unless they want to price themselves out of the global job market. On the corporate agenda for the 21st century is an expanding use of a contingent labor force—temps and part-timers—to reduce the need for full-time workers who command higher pay and benefits. There will be greater reliance, even by unionized companies, on low-cost outside contractors to cut the size of their higher-paid work force.

We have been warned that in the world of tomorrow, the idea of job security will be passé. We shall all be independent contractors, developing various skills in the hope of selling ourselves to employers in the job market. We shall be hired and fired several times during our lifetime. In the competitive struggle for survival, the best-equipped individuals will do well; those who fail, for whatever reason, can expect only minimum assistance from a government whose prime concern will be to balance the budget by curtailing social spending.

This is the vision that Corporate America holds out for workers in the coming century, On the evidence, it is a vision that Republican and Democratic leaders either share or are unwilling to challenge.

And what about the leaders of organized labor? Do they agree with this corporate blueprint of the future? If not, what is their vision of how we and our children will be working and living in the years ahead?

42. *The Musings of an Octogenarian*

So here I am, an old man with a lively mind and a body still free of debilitating, terminal illnesses. I am sitting alone on the terrace of my 14th floor co-op apartment, looking out across the East River at a panoramic, picture-card view of the New York skyline. With a cup of tea in my hand, I am in a reflective mood.

I remind myself that I've lived through most of this century, one of the most turbulent, transforming periods in the history of humankind. Born in 1914 at the start of the first World War, I have experienced dramatic, and often traumatic, historic events that have shaped my life: the Great Depression, the New Deal, the CIO, World War II, Vietnam, the civil rights movement, the Cold War and the collapse of the Soviet Union.

I've adjusted to and learned to utilize such miracles of technology as television, xerox, fax machines, computers, VCR's and cellular phones, I can send e-mail messages and surf World Wide Web pages on the Internet. Have they made me smarter or happier? Maybe.

I was around at the birth of the Nuclear Age, and I'm still haunted by the horrors of Hiroshima, Nagasaki and Chernobyl. I have seen the growing proliferation of nuclear bombs and other weaponry and I dread that some country or terrorist group will use them to further their ambitions or punish their enemies. I can't see the United Nations or any other institution preventing it, though they're trying.

I guess that at my age I won't outlive the cruddy social and cultural environment that surrounds us: crime, violence, poverty, drugs, corporate greed, corruption in government, urban blight, homelessness, pornography, broken marriages, battered wives, child abuse, virulent racism, uncontrolled sexism, ethnic hatred, widespread illiteracy—and I could probably add to the list. I have an awful feeling that it's going to get worse, not better. How will future generations be able to cope with all this?

As for me, I'm grateful that I was never caught up in the rat race to be rich or famous, and I can honestly say that I have not had a shred of envy for those who achieved wealth and celebrity. At the same time, I was never in financial want. I don't ever remember being unemployed. Although Mim and I and our kids lived in middle-class comfort, I never wanted us to own our own home or a country place or to acquire real property. I never invested in the stock market in the hope of enriching myself with "unearned income." In fact, we never owned an auto. People who knew us couldn't believe that neither I nor anyone else in my immediate family could drive a car; they wondered how we got along without one. The city's subway and bus system served us fine, and on special occasions, we relied on taxis, car service and helpful friends. I'm convinced I would have been a terrible driver and would end up killing innocent pedestrians.

As a child of the Depression, I feared getting into debt. I boasted that in more than a quarter of a century of using credit cards, I had never paid a penny in interest. But we were not penny-pinchers. From time to time, we dined out with friends at good restaurants, went to the theater, ballet and opera and had dinner parties at our house. We also spent more than an average amount of money on books and periodicals. Many of the hundreds of books we bought I shall never read, and I feel guilty as I stare at them on the shelves that line the walls in our living room and bedrooms.

* * * * *

I find it remarkable that no matter what my occupation—grocery clerk, editor, printer, college teacher—I always felt a gravitational pull toward unions. Unlike most of my formerly radical friends who became disillusioned, cynical and bitter about unions, I never lost faith in the labor movement, as imperfect as it is. After the experience of my first strike at age 19, I became convinced that unions were the only institutions that workers could rely on to fight for their interests. I still feel that way.

Truth is, I enjoyed being a radical. I felt morally clean, uncorrupted. I found fighting against injustice exhilarating and regarded every defeat—and there were many—a valid reason to fight that much harder. As I saw it, working for a union was a "calling," not a job. It was a priesthood in which we voluntarily agreed to work long hours, often under intolerable conditions and for little pay—the kind of existence that is compulsory for millions of workers. and whom we were committed to liberating.

I have a blurred image of the countless union meetings and demonstrations I attended, the causes I promoted or defended, the pamphlets and leaflets I wrote, the views I preached in so many college classrooms and seminars, the campaigns I waged and the picketlines I walked, Why had I spent my adult life doing this? Had it been worthwhile? Did I have any regrets? And now after all these years, what did I really believe in? Overwhelming questions that I often thought about in quiet moments, and tried to answer honestly to myself.

Looking back on my life, I can truthfully say I have no regrets or complaints. I was lucky to have jobs in which I could use my creative abilities without being closely supervised by a bureaucratic boss, union official, committee, board or agency. It satisfied my temperament as a loner. It was both my strength and weakness that I did my best creative work without seeking the input of others, especially in the early stages of a project. I hated being bossed and I avoided bossing others. As an educator, I believed in persuasion, not compulsion.

I avoided as many conferences as I could because I considered most of them time-wasting. I could not stand long-winded, self-serving speeches and the petty power struggles that went on at these meetings. Thinking back, I'm surprised that I never held an elective or even appointive position in any organization; the only time I ran for office was at two AFL-CIO conventions where I was sure of not being elected.

I guess what was most important for me was my sense of personal dignity and self-esteem, I think that's true of most working people, who feel keenly when they are abused on the job or discriminated against. That's an important lesson union organizers have to learn if they want to be successful. If I've had frustrations and various complaints during my years within the labor movement, they have faded or been long forgotten. Nostalgia can work wonders.

* * * * *

I occasionally ponder over the changes that have taken place in the labor movement over the past 60 years. I can remember the fierce fight leading to a historic split over the issue of craft versus industrial unionism at the 1935 AFL convention. Today, we see the Auto Workers organizing college teachers, Teamsters organizing police officers and Laborers organizing poultry workers. The fierce battles over union jurisdiction have all but disappeared. Some of the current major organizing campaigns are necessarily multi-union because that is the only way the labor movement can match the enormous power of giant conglomerates controlling plants in many industries.

I still believe that the most damaging blow to the labor movement was the CIO's purge of its 11 left-wing unions in 1950. In the union-splitting and internecine warfare that followed, militant communists and other radicals were driven out of the unions they had helped to build. The CIO grew more conservative and no longer enjoyed the enthusiastic loyalty it once had among union members.

I can recall the hosannas in the labor press when the AFL and CIO merged at the 1955 "unity" convention. It was going to be a new day for labor. No more waste of time and resources on jurisdictional strikes. Now a united labor movement would have the strength to organize the industries in the South and some of the giant corporations that had successfuly resisted unions.

A few activists like myself had serious questions about the likely effects of the merger. We realized that now that the CIO had kicked out its militant unions, it was not much different from the AFL, which it had formerly opposed. Thus, there was a logical basis for the merger. And since the AFL and CIO were no longer competitors in a fight for new members, the leaders of both groups could share in their new-found monopoly of power. Union leaders, even the most progressive ones, grew more remote from the rank-and-file, felt themselves not accountable to anyone and clung to their high offices long after they should have retired. Thus, the labor movement went through a period of stagnation before it entered into a stage of continuing decline.

Can John Sweeney reverse the heavy losses that the AFL-CIO has suffered in membership, economic strength and political influence? Certainly, he and his leadership team deserve high marks for trying. They have set admirable goals for union organizing and taken unprecented initiatives to develop labor's political clout, not only in the 1996 election, but afterwards, in every congressional district and on a year-round basis. All of this is a refreshing change from the stodgy, stand-pat behavior of the Kirkland era. Sweeney, as they say, is definitely pointed in a "new direction," but how far he will take the labor movement remains to be seen.

* * * * *

One of the major weaknesses of the AFL CIO is that it has been sluggish in developing a large crop of articulate, knowledgeable and skilled union leaders. Equally serious, there are only limited opportunities for local union leaders who have demonstrated their competence to rise to positions where they can function on a regional or national level. This, in my view, accounts for the stagnation that has existed and still exists within the labor movement.

It is understandable, if not especially praiseworthy, that top leaders of international unions or state and city labor organizations would want to stay in office for as long as they are in good physical and mental health. Once they get used to the prestige and perquisites of power and a more affluent lifestyle, they are reluctant to give them up. Inevitably, they develop a proprietary attitude toward the organization. They rate loyalty to themselves, even more important than competence, as the prime qualification in selecting their staff. Their staffs, in turn, make sure that their bosses are not upstaged by any potential challengers, especially those who come forward with new ideas that might be welcomed by the membership.

Union leaders who have held office for ten, twenty or more years generally become set in their attitudes and behavior. They resent criticism and tend to resist any suggestions for change. They often surround themselves with yes men, and they are wary of developing fresh leadership from the ranks lest it might result in a future challenge to their incumbency. The only possible rationale for keeping union leaders in office for more than a dozen years is that, with their wealth of experience, they are indispensable, and the organization would suffer if they were no longer at the helm. I don't buy that argument. In any union, there are undoubtedly enough members who, if given a chance, could assume leadership roles.

So what's the answer? A term limit of, say, 12 years and an age limit of 70 years have been suggested. I don't think high-ranking officials should consider it the end of the world when they retire after a dozen years in office or upon reaching the age of 70—and with a good pension. There are so many ways in which their acquired skills and experience can be put to good use in other careers to their liking. They might enjoy new challenges, and it would add variety to their lives. I believe I'm a good example. I've had some of the most exciting and rewarding years since I retired from the labor college at age 70.

Over the years, I have known hundreds of union officers and enjoyed a good working relationship with many of them. But there are three leaders whom I especially admired and who have influenced my behavior as a labor activist: John L. Lewis, president of the United Mine Workers, who headed the CIO; James Matles, secretary-treasurer of the United Electrical and Radio Workers, and Harry Van Arsdale, Jr., president of the New York City Central Labor Council and also business manager of Local 3 of the International Brotherhood of Electrical Workers.

The labor movement has never had such a dominating national leader as Lewis and probably never will again. When John L. spoke, the media paid attention, the nation listened and so did working people everywhere. I don't think the incredible achievements of the CIO would have been possible without his tough, militant leadership. He was not afraid to hire communists as organizers because he knew they were dedicated unionists and, as he told his associates, if they proved incompetent or untrustworthy, he could always fire them. They turned out to be his most valuable staffers, many of them later occupying leadership positions in the unionized auto, steel, communications, meat packing and electrical industries.

I met Lewis at the founding convention of the United Furniture Workers, where I was serving as the union's publicity director. I was awed by his imposing presence: he was well over six feet tall, with a large, leonine head on a bulky body. I can still hear that grave, sonorous voice in a speech studded with allusions to the Bible and Shakespeare. Somehow, I believe the tragic split within the CIO in 1950 could have been averted if Lewis had remained its president. It was unfortunate that his pride and arrogance forced him to resign after his strong opposition to a third term for President Roosevelt was rejected by a majority of CIO unions and members in the 1940 elections.

* * * * *

I met James Matles in the late 1930s, after he had maneuvered 15,000 members of the machinists union into the newly-established United Electrical, Radio and Machine Workers. As the UE's first director of organization, he played a principal role in building the union to a membership of 600,000 and winning excellent contracts from General Electric, Westinghouse and other corporate giants. Even his enemies agreed that he was a brilliant organizer and a shrewd strategist. He had a razor-sharp mind that rarely overlooked any detail in dealing with a problem. He was personally frugal and was a vigilant watchdog over the expense accounts of his field organizers. When he traveled, he stayed at the cheapest hotels and dined on soup and a sandwich. The salaries of UE officers were among the lowest in the labor movement.

Jim was a tall, handsome man, with a lean, wiry body and an intense manner. He had come to the United States from Romania as a youth and found a job as a skilled machinist in a union shop. I suspected he was a communist, but he never publicly declared himself as one. He had no hobby or cultural interests; he lived and breathed for the union. I knew him and his wife Ethel socially; we occasion-

The Musings of an Octogenarian

ally met for dinner at the homes of mutual friends, where the talk was mainly about the labor movement and politics.

Upon reaching the age of 65, and although still vigorous, Matles had decided to retire and make way for one of the union's many new leaders. In his retirement speech at the UE's 1975 convention in San Francisco. he told the delegates that he would continue to serve the union, without pay, as a volunteer organizer and educational coordinator. The convention ended on Friday, September 12. The following Monday, Jim was in Santa Barbara, the scene of a UE organizing drive. He spent all day there, passing out leaflets, speaking at plant gates and meeting with small groups of workers. Shortly after returning to his modest motel room, Matles collapsed and died of a heart attack.

* * * * *

I have a special affection for Harry Van Arsdale, because he had an unusual combination of leadership qualities unmatched by any union official I've ever known. He was both a visionary and pragmatist; I have described some of his pioneering achievements elsewhere in this book. He created a labor-management partnership in the electrical industry and remained its dominant figure to the end of his life—a model that no union to this day has ever duplicated. He and his wife Madeleine lived in a modest three-room apartment in the 2,600-family housing project, known as Electchester, which he inspired. He never lost touch with the rank-and-file, finding time to attend various club and division meetings, especially those of the apprentice electricians. He could spend a half hour talking to a group of apprentices, and moments later get on the phone with New York Governor Nelson Rockefeller or some high-ranking politicians in Washington. We became good friends from 1970, when we worked together to establish the labor college, until the last day of his life in 1986, when I was still working at the job he had created for me in his union.

What I've learned is that it's not easy to be a great labor leader. Those I admire especially are the self-confident ones who make a strong effort to involve the rank-and-file in meaningful activity and to develop future leaders of their union. My kind of union leader is one who knows how to accept criticism gracefully, without vindictiveness, whether the criticism is justified or not and to engage the critic in a dialogue about their differences. That's how many a good idea is salvaged. This may sound quirky and contradictory, but I believe it takes strong leaders to build democratic unions.

Like many trade unionists, I wonder—and worry—about the future of the labor movement. I don't think anyone really knows what will happen. The crystal ball is murky, and there are too many ifs, buts and maybes. What I profoundly believe is that the economic future of the nation's working people depends on the one institution that has the possibility of defending them, the organized labor movement. For all the critical commentary that organized labor has lost its former clout and is no longer a relevant factor in the American economy, the AFL-CIO still represents a formidable force of 13 million men and women, whose number is at least doubled when one includes their families. Its 55,000 local unions are rooted in cities and towns across the country. Its members produce a large part of the goods and services which all of us depend on in our daily lives. The AFL-CIO has been a sleeping giant that is now beginning to stir. But when it wakes up, where will it go and what will it do?

I believe that the supreme task facing the labor movement is to challenge Corporate America head on, both on the economic battlefield and in the political arena. The AFL-CIO must go beyond its rhetorical blasts against multinational corporations and its defensive skirmishes against the more aggressive ones where, as with Caterpillar and Bridgestone/Firestone, it comes out a loser.

The nation's major corporations have had a field-day at the expense of the American people. Through their acquisitions, mergers and restructuring operations, they have turned the nation's economy into a giant Monopoly game. In the process of reaping record-breaking profits, they have robbed hundreds of thousands of working people of their livelihood. They have been given tens of billions of dollars in tax breaks, subsidies and special grants, while urgently-needed social programs are starved for funds. (And now there is a proposal that they be given additional billions out of the U.S. Treasury if only they promise to be nice to their workers!)

There is a good reason why Big Business wants a shrunken federal government, one that frees them from regulatory restraints, They want the 21st century to adopt the *laissez faire* features of the 19th century, when they were free to do whatever they wanted and the public be damned. They are offering the nation's workforce a grim future of lower wages, fewer social services and a reduced standard of living and with no guarantees that tomorrow or the next day, they will still be lucky to have a job.

The all-important task of the labor movement is to change the rules of the game, to make corporations accountable to the American people, from whom they derive a substantial part of their income and profits. They must be treated as public institutions, with legal restrictions on their unjustified behavior.

We must find our way into the corporate boardrooms and put the spotlight on the directors. these anonymous, well-paid executives who make decisions behind their closed doors that take away the jobs of people they have never met. Since the managers and directors of these corporations can exert as much, and possibly more, influence over our incomes and our future than members of Comgress, we ought to learn all we can about each of them. We've got to *humanize* our relations with corporate executives, so that at any time they make a decision that we consider unfair to workers and contrary to the public interest, we will confront them face to face to demand a reconsideration of their actions. And that goes especially for their job-killer, downsizing operations.

If this intensified, personalized corporate campaign is to be successful, it must have a political component. It is beyond reason to expect either the Republican or

Democratic party to challenge corporate power, since they are dependent on Big Business contributions for their election campaigns. In fact, it is rare for congressional lawmakers of both parties to oppose anything on the corporate legislative agenda. In 1976 under President Jimmy Carter and in 1992 under President Bill Clinton, we had the ideal political setup: a Democratic Congress and a Democrat in the White House. We couldn't improve OSHA or get basic labor law reform or a fair tax measure. Does anyone remember anything to brag about in those Democratic-controlled administrations?

So the AFL-CIO has to build its own political organization. It must no longer be in the hip-pocket of the Democratic Party, with no place to go if it is snubbed or short-changed. An independent party can be built on the basis of a coalition of labor, women, minorities, senior citizens and all other Americans who have felt the lash of a heartless economic system. Such a coalition will have substantial bargaining power as opposed to the Republican and Democratic parties.

It's time to change American capitalism and the global marketplace, as we know it. This is the most important challenge we face as we move into the 21st century. The outcome of this struggle may well determine the economic fate of our children, grandchildren and future generations.

* * * * *

I find satisfaction in living long enough to become a patriarch. Wherever I go, I am usually the oldest, if not the wisest, person at any labor or family gathering. I am proud of my three daughters who have retained the moral values they learned in their childhood: Kathy, 53, a lawyer in Houston, whose practice is devoted to defending poor people who have been victimized; Karli, 41, a teacher of English as a Second Language, who has taught immigrants from various countries to adjust to American life, and Laura, 39, an electrician, who has fought for women's rights in her union and who is now seeking a new career in public health. And I am blessed with six grandchildren who help keep me young.

I have decided to close this autobiography on June 20, 1996, my 82nd birthday. But this does not mark the end of my career in the labor movement. I shall continue to write and edit *The Labor Educator*, post my weekly *LaborTalk* columns on computer networks and the Internet and, as always, offer advice and assistance to any union that calls upon me.

And who knows, some day I may write a sequel.

INDEX

USE THIS FORM

A.G. PUBLISHING
75 VARICK STREET
NEW YORK, N.Y. 10013

I wish to order _____ copy(ies) of "My 60 Years as a Labor Activist" by Harry Kelber.

Enclosed is my check for $ _____,which includes the cost of sales tax and shipping.

NAME _____
     (print clearly)

ADDRESS _____
        (street/no.)   (city)   (state)   (zip)

UNION _____
       (local)   (international)

Position in Union _____

Single copy is $17.50 each   6 to 10 copies @ $15 each
2 to 5 copies @ $16 each   11 to 25 copies @ $14 each

Special rates for unions and college labor programs

Make checks payable to: A.G. Publishing